A Deep Map of Western Grand Canyon and Upper Lake Mead Country

History and Memories of the Land of Long Shadows

Mary Richardson McBee

Old Lands Publishing
Tama, Iowa

Copyright ©1996-2014 Mary Richardson McBee

All rights reserved. No portion of this book may be reproduced, stored, or used in any form by any electronic, mechanical, or other means, without prior written permission of the author or publisher.

Cover: Petroglyph located near western entrance of Grand Canyon, sketch by D. Suzanne Wanatee-Buffalo. All 'Area Maps' included were also hand-drawn by Suzanne.

Old Lands Publishing

1589 305th St.

Tama, IA 52339

Design and layout by Bright Angel Press, Flagstaff, Arizona

Library of Congress Cataloging-in-publication data:

McBee, Mary Richardson

A Deep Map of Western Grand Canyon and Upper Lake Mead Country: History and Memories of the Land of Long Shadows

Includes bibliographical references, index, historical photos, maps.

ISBN: 978-0-9890775-0-7

1. Grand Canyon 2. Lake Mead 3. Southwest history 4. Public lands 5. Hualapai 6. Paiute 7. Native American slavery 8. Migrations west 9. National Park Service 10. Meadview 11. Joshua Tree Forest 12. McBee, Mary 13. Title 14. Grapevine Mesa 15. Lake Mead National Recreation Area 16. Lower Granite Gorge 17. Land of Long Shadows

Printed in the United States of America

Second Edition, September 2014

Dedicated To the Soul of this Land

Contents

Acknowledgments..vii
Locator and Area Maps..ix
Introduction...xi
Prologue..xiii

Part I: The Ones Who Came Before
Chapter One: Remote Beginnings..1
Chapter Two: The Paiute...15
Chapter Three: The Hualapai..23
Chapter Four: Trade Routes and Inroads......................................35

Part II: Raging River
Chapter Five: Pearce Ferry..39
Chapter Six: Grigg's Ferry...51
Chapter Seven: Bonelli's Ferry..79
Chapter Eight: Lower Granite Gorge..89

Part III: North-of-the-River Country
Chapter Nine: Shivwits Plateau..109
Chapter Ten: Grand Wash..143
Chapter Eleven: Gold Butte..173

Part IV: South-of-the-River Country
Chapter Twelve: White Hills..185
Chapter Thirteen: Gold Basin..201
Chapter Fourteen: Lost Basin..213
Chapter Fifteen: Music Mountains...275

Part V: The Leviathan
Chapter Sixteen: Lake Mead...299

Part VI: Splendor on the Mesa
Chapter Seventeen: The Joshua Tree Forest.................................347
Chapter Eighteen: Public Lands...359

Epilogue 2014	363
Endnotes	367
Bibliography	377
Author	387
Index	389

Acknowledgments

The explorations, research, and writing of this work actually took place during the 1980's. It consumed a decade of my life, yet to have the privilege of coming to know this spectacular and very special land in such depth was priceless. I was most fortunate to have simply been in the right place at the right time in order to collect these important stories and information and bring them all together into one work. I finished a rough draft in the early 1990's and copyrighted that work in 1996. Then, due to local demand and especially persistence from Jim Kiefer who also loved this land, I gave permission to the Meadview Friends of the Library to copy and sell the working manuscript in notebook form for a decade with profits to benefit their library fund, this manuscript simply being titled, *The Land of Long Shadows*. However, I am now most pleased that this finished work will finally be published and made available to the general public. Note, however, that most descriptive references (lake levels, condition of historic sites, old roads, boundaries, etc.) were based upon 1980-1990 information, not 2014.

I would like to give special thanks to Don McBee, without whom this land I never would have explored, nor would this book have ever been researched and written. And, to my daughter, Dawn Suzanne Wanatee-Buffalo, who provided years of moral support and encouragement, along with assistance on many aspects of this work from writing to computerizing .... and not the least, her beautifully hand-drawn and detailed 'Area Maps' for this book, along with her interpretive sketch of the thought-provoking ancient petroglyph from this area for the cover design. Without her, again, this book never would have happened. And, to my son, Dave, for unceasing computer support.

To the Lake Mead National Recreation Area staff at LMNRA Headquarters in Boulder City, NV., for access to invaluable library and files, with Superintendent Alan O'Neill providing timely encouragement and Robin Hourie going the extra mile deciphering the original manuscript.

To Everett Harris, seasoned and contrary hunter, miner, and back-country guide, determined to drag me into the remote Arizona Strip Country north of Grand Canyon to receive a most precious gift – an intimate perspective of this Land of Intrigue few had been so fortunate to know. To Dave Gensley, Greg Montgomery, and other hiking, boating, four-wheeling friends who shared many of these exciting explorations and adventures.

To Don Simonis, BLM Archeologist in Kingman, always willing to shoulder a pack to check out newly discovered findings, and for critiques on local Native American history. To the staff at Mohave Museum of History in Kingman for access to their materials and allowing Sharon Stoltenow-Baur to copy historic photos from several valuable collections.

To Sharon Stoltenow-Baur and Ron Seeba for work on many historic photos, to friends too numerous to mention for computer assistance, transcriptions, cataloguing, and proofing of the original version, to Ron Ziniel for excellent reproduction of the photo pages, and Ray and Chris Selinsky of Meadview for community and library updates. To my daughter, Suzanne, and Janey Swartz and Darrel Wanatee for further proofing.

To the Meskwaki Tribe of Iowa, and in particular, the Wanatee's and Tribal Historian and my son-in-law, Johnathan Buffalo, for helping me to perceive, at least in part, the soul of the Native American.

To my brother, Ken, who accompanied me on several explorations into the Arizona Strip, my brother Deane who provided copy and support services when those were beyond my means, and Deane and Ed and their spouses who persevered on back country jaunts. To my parents, Ray and Ruth Richardson, for remaining supportive, for accompanying me on countless unconventional journeys, and for their gift of the 'explorer gene'... always needing to know what's over the next horizon.

To the Write Ones, a great little local group of fun writer friends who provided additional impetus needed. To Bruce Grubbs of Flagstaff, author and publisher, who patiently led me through the maze of final preparations and publishing.

Lastly, to dear animal companions, both domestic and wild, from whom I've learned better to see while looking, to hear while listening, and to understand deeply the connections of all life.

For any errors in content, I take sole responsibility. -Mary Richardson McBee

Locator and Area Maps

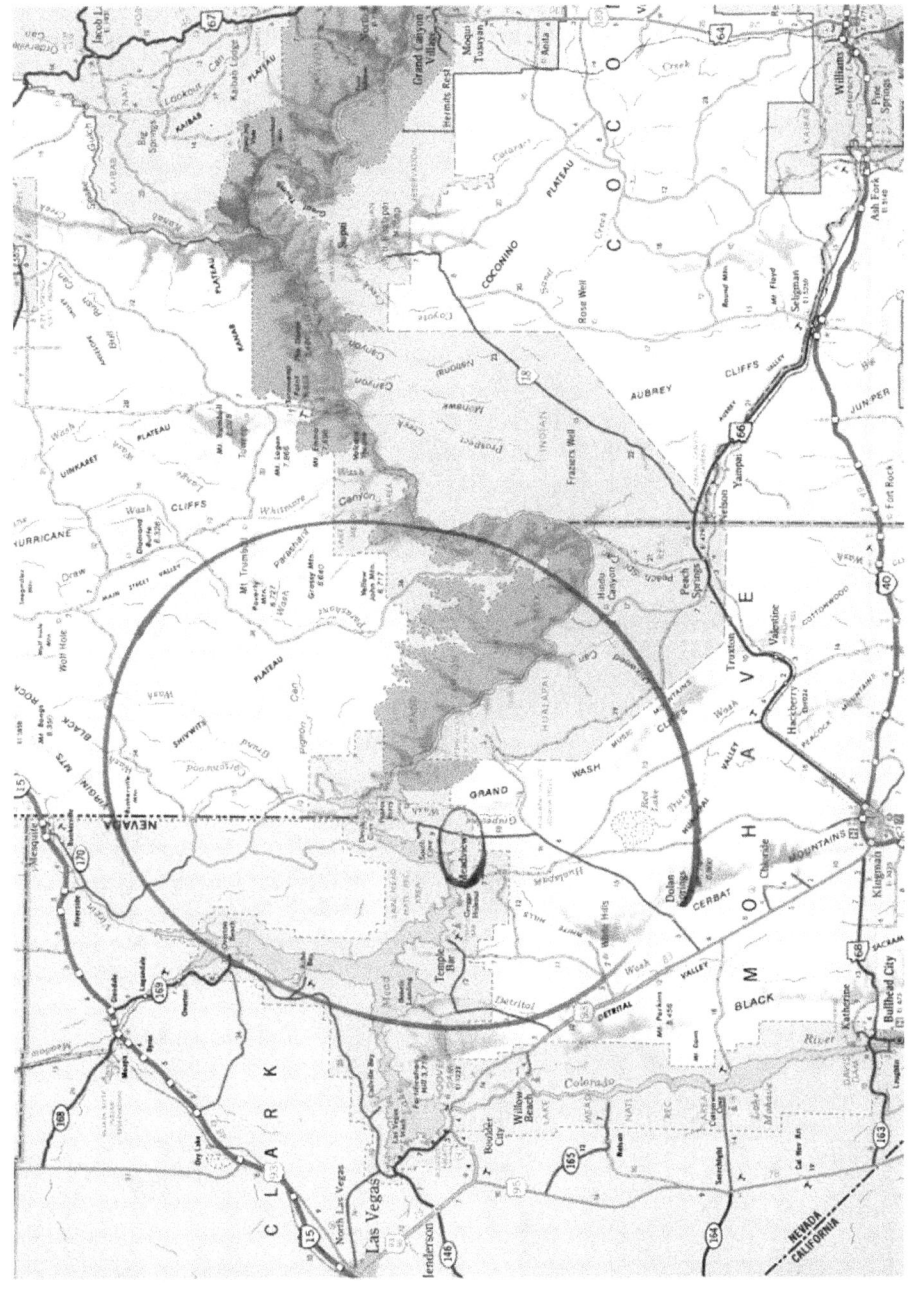

Excerpt from 1988 Arizona State Highway Map showing the general area of the book. Copyright ©1988 State of Arizona

Introduction

Many historical books are neatly sewn closed. Calculated from inception to be tightly woven, those are usually little more than verbose collections of manipulated information. While that precept does indeed allow easier marketing of contemporary manuscripts, its design neither encourages objectivity nor does it value intelligence gained by future audiences.

The Land of Long Shadows is an open book. Curiosity prompted its merit, curiosity dictated its words, and curiosity is the only validation required of its reader. *The Land of Long Shadows* is refreshingly like a soft-spoken mysterious story told near a fire rather than a stoic, sanitized lecture. The work defies the many academic standards usually required of homogenized history in order to be taken seriously. The first infraction committed by Mary McBee is that she does not adopt a posture presuming to know all aspects about everything that she recorded. The next demerit occurs when she freely indicates on numerous occasions that her information is greatly limited by her own understanding. *The Land of Long Shadows* reads more like a personal diary than a series of polite applauses. And that difference is why this book successfully embraces timelessness in a way that other contemporary historical endeavors fall short.

A great number of treks the author embarked upon during the course of writing this book, unintentionally – but predictably – resulted in cataloguing and collecting numerous intriguing stories and facts. Mary found undocumented petroglyphs, prehistoric caves, historic trails, made note of seasonal water characteristics, plant cycles, and animal movements and concentrations. Some readers won't be able to help but celebrate her exploration skills; hiking (often alone in very remote areas), rock-climbing and rappelling to access hidden spots, four-wheeling in remote canyons and on mesas where jeep trails often simply disappeared, and boating to explore canyons only accessible by water. But her explorations also included numerous visitations to multiple libraries and museums to uncover more information and to check resources, photographs, and references, as well as traveling many miles to interview former pioneer ranchers, miners, and Indians, in addition to authors, scholars, government personnel, and locals.

During Mary's treks, it became obvious to her that, especially in this remote and rugged area, the sheer power of the land is what ultimately dictated history, not vice versa. Considering the forceful antiquity of this land, encountering any pattern is not only natural but often unavoidable. Why does a petroglyph suddenly appear before a modern-day recreational hiker? Despite all other factors, the lay of the land commanded both the ancient hunter and today's hiker to occupy the same piece of Earth and to notice that same rock. In that one moment, Time evaporates. The land dictates history. With contours and resulting corridors, the land forever determines the movements, migrations, settlements and survival of all life forms. The land has its own special character, its own indomitable essence. And what has occurred there is actually only one continuing story, defined and shaped by that one particular piece of Earth.

The Land of Long Shadows is a reaffirmation. This work allows readers to remember things never known, and then graciously allows readers to write their own petroglyphs for some yet-unborn person to "discover" again.

I am privileged to have the opportunity to introduce this book, *The Land of Long Shadows,* written by Mary Richardson McBee. But the greatest honor I could possibly receive comes from being her daughter. -Dawn Suzanne Wanatee-Buffalo, March 1996

Prologue

One remote and relatively small piece of desert earth would not, at first, seem significant enough to warrant intense historical examination. During initial stages of collecting information, a six-month project and fifty-page booklet were envisioned. Well over a decade and thousands of on-foot, four-wheel, and highway miles later, the following tome resulted.

While studying history, we find it rather easy to relate to the joys, sorrows, tragedies and triumphs common to our human condition. Yet we can go farther, extend a wider view, and observe the larger patterns and meanings involved. Not just for those of humankind but for all life forms, and even for the land, itself.

The European culture from which so many of us descend has long viewed land from a narrow focus: what can we take from it, how can we conquer, control, and change it. We are only now beginning to sense our real place in the total scheme of things – to realize the land is much more than "yours, mine, or ours." It was here before we came, it has felt our immense impact, suffered our often destructive presence, and yet, if anything will survive after we're gone, the land is what will endure.

The focus of this book is an area of land covering a mere one hundred miles. A settlement called Meadview is nestled therein, resting atop Grapevine Mesa, with a view extending far north into the Virgin Mountains of Nevada and deep into Arizona Strip Country beyond the Grand Canyon – a spectacular panorama of great vast spaces and distant horizons.

Two thousand feet of sheer rock face, the picturesque Grand Wash Cliffs, form the eastern backdrop for this community, displaying constant changing patterns of deep earthen reds and golden yellow hues amidst the silence of magnificent glowing sunsets. These cliffs actually define the very westernmost edge of the immense Colorado Plateau country which covers four states and extends eastward to the Rockies. Visible from Meadview, one can make out an indistinct break in the Grand Wash Cliffs; therein lies the entrance to the seductive Lower Granite Gorge of Grand Canyon. The Colorado River lives there, flowing with deceptive gentleness from within and winding out into the long open expanse of Lake Mead.

An overlook just west of town brings one to the edge of a two thousand foot precipice, and far below stretches the eastern arm of Lake Mead. Two rugged and barren mountain ranges lie in the western distance. Farther still, the eye can see the snow-covered peaks of Mt. Charleston hovering over Las Vegas, Nevada.

Grapevine Mesa, upon which the settlement of Meadview rests, is located in northwestern Arizona, at the western end of Grand Canyon and easternmost section of Lake Mead. St. George, Utah, is eighty miles north and Las Vegas, Nevada, some sixty miles west – by way the black raven flies. By road, one can triple those distances since travel must go around either the Big Lake or the Great Canyon. These two extraordinary barriers have been of great historical import here for centuries.

Elevation on the mesa where Meadview is located is approximately three thousand feet above sea level. Extending for some thirty miles southerly on this mesa and beyond, is the most remarkable and lush Joshua Tree forest in the world. At higher elevations to the south and east are junipers and pinions. Lake levels below vary from 1000 to 1200 feet. Along lake shores are the more typical desert cacti, along with creosote bush, rabbit brush, and sage.

Grapevine Mesa was named for Grapevine Springs Canyon which intersects on its eastern edge. Within this side canyon, Grapevine Springs surges from beneath the canyon floor, rushes between sheer walls for nearly a quarter mile, then slows to form beautiful clear pools in descending terraces along the way, the upper ones abundant with grapevines and tall willowy horsetails. Eventually the water dwindles, once again disappearing into the earth just as the canyon opens into the larger main drainage of Grapevine Wash below.

This entire area is vast and gently rolling, yet sliced with rugged gorges and deep canyons. Jagged mountains and sheer cliffs have been torn, worn, and wrenched from the land. This was an immensely violent land in the past and it remains restless and changing today.

Desert Bighorn Sheep roam freely; mystical, like silent ghosts, always present but seldom seen. A few deer, coyotes, bobcats, occasional mountain lions.

The Paiutes called this, The Land of Long Shadows.

Part I: The Ones Who Came Before

Chapter One: Remote Beginnings

Although many questions exist regarding the pre-history and early history of this continent, it has previously been held by some authorities that early humans began arriving in North America approximately 20,000 years ago.[1] At that time in the southwest, the climate was cooler, there was more vegetation, and prehistoric animals still roamed – mammoths, huge buffalo, giant sloths, small horses, llama-like camels, and saber-toothed cats. It is believed by some that first humans arrived by migrating across a broad land bridge that intermittently connected Alaska to Siberia as ocean levels fluctuated, doing so in pursuit of large animals. These first people appeared to have been small bands of the Stone Age culture with only a few primitive tools and a very basic hunting, gathering, and nomadic life style. It is important to note, however, that a number of indigenous tribes on this continent have long disputed this theory, holding that they were here 'long before' this 20,000 year time frame.

By approximately 7,000 B.C., the climate had warmed and was similar to that of modern-day. Most of the large animals had vanished. Some say their disappearance was due to warmer temperatures and changing vegetation. Others point to evidence that earlier humans simply killed off these larger, more visible animals. Perhaps it was due to a combination of factors.

For whatever reason, by this time most humans in the southwest were finding it necessary to pursue the more elusive animals such as bighorn sheep and deer, and to rely more heavily on sustenance from rabbits, squirrels, rodents, reptiles and birds. They were also gathering many wild plant foods which meant having to establish seasonal movement patterns while in search of those plants. These people became known by archaeologists as the Desert Archaic Culture.

Several thousand years later, many of these groups had become somewhat more agricultural and stationary. This allowed for the invention of better weapons, pottery, clothing, and in certain areas, the development of larger social groups with more complex forms of architecture and religion.

In northwestern Arizona, three different cultural patterns developed by 200 A.D., these lasting well into what we now call "historic times," the 1500's, when Euro-Americans started arriving in great numbers and began recording their own version of history.

The first of these early cultures were the Basketmakers, later to become known as the Pueblo people. They were greatly influenced by the Anasazi culture to the east. Their main emphasis was on farming and they concentrated along regions here in the Overton Arm of Lake Mead and Moapa Valley in Nevada. They had a fairly settled lifestyle, raised crops in fertile valleys, built pit houses and other shelters in their large villages, and mined a natural salt dome in the earth nearby.

The Ones Who Came Before

However, by 1150 A.D., they abandoned everything and left. It's thought they may have headed eastward and joined their Anasazi cousins, although this theory is not conclusive. Postulation over their reasons for leaving include depletion of river valley resources from centuries of farming, but more likely, pressure from an influx of Paiute tribes from the north and west.

The second cultural pattern existing in this area was that of the aforementioned branch of Shoshonians, the Paiutes. They had a way of life especially suited to the harsh desert environment. They were mobile, hunted small game, gathered seasonal plants, and practiced only limited farming along the river valleys. Small Paiute bands ranged over long distances using natural rock shelters, caves, or temporary brush structures as protection from the elements. Paiute territory included present-day southern Nevada and adjoining parts of California and Utah, while in Arizona their boundaries extended from Cottonwood Valley to the south and beyond Lake Mead to the north. They were present in this area when frontiersmen began arriving in the early 1800's. These southern bands of Paiutes were eventually forced into small areas of reservation lands in southeast Nevada, southern Utah, and the Arizona Strip Country north of Grand Canyon, where they exist today.

The third cultural pattern here was the Hakataya, also known as the Yuman or Patayan (Patayan is Hualapai meaning "Old Ones"), people who lived in regions along the lower Colorado River and south of Grand Canyon. There were the upland Hakataya, the Cohonina, the Cerbat branch (pronounced; Ser-bat), ancestors of present-day Hualapai tribe (pronounced; wahl-a-pie), and the Amacavas (later known as the Mohave). Theirs was a hunting-gathering economy with some agriculture. The Hakataya, in general, seemed influenced by the more southerly Sinaguas and Hohokam in their customs and traits.

The fourth was the Fremont Culture, a more recently documented presence in this area. These people came from Utah and Nevada and were present along the north rim of Grand Canyon, within the inner Canyon, and may have ranged downriver as far as Grapevine Canyon on Lake Mohave, below present-day Boulder Dam.

The overlapping of Native American cultures in this region occurred naturally. Basketmakers (Pueblo-Anasazi) probably crossed the river here from the west and north as they traveled through these mesas and canyons, while Paiutes surely migrated from north of the river to south and back again. The Anasazi, and later, Paiutes and Hualapai, may have been responsible for many of the huge roasting pits still seen in this area today. It's likely the Cohonina came down the Grand Wash Cliffs (I've personally hiked down the face of the cliffs several routes) and the Cerbat branch of the Hakataya (later, the Hualapai), were present and through the area on many occasions. The Hualapai, Supai, and Mohave still occupy areas south of the river and Grand Canyon today.

An ancient and long-established Native American trade route called the Old Ute Trail came from the area in the Rocky Mountains now known as Grand Junction, Colorado, traveled southerly and came down through Grand Wash from the north, crossed the Colorado River at the west end of Grand Canyon near the base of the Grand Wash Cliffs (early explorers commonly called this the Old Ute Crossing), then proceeded south up Grapevine Wash to Grapevine Springs (Dinboah Springs), then to Tinaka (Grass Springs), this site eventually to become Grass Springs Ranch/Diamond Bar/Smith Ranch/then Grand Canyon Ranch. There the route split. One branch headed on south and then westerly toward the places down on the Colorado River now known as Willow Beach and Bullhead City, and there joined the Mohave Trail that went across southern California to the Pacific Ocean. The other branch turned east from Tinakah, went around the base of Grand Wash Cliffs, and on up to the top of the plateau (where the Hualapai Tribe now brings their tour buses up to the west entrance of their reservation), then east to Hopi and Navajo lands in northeastern Arizona. The Spanish also traded Native American slaves via this Old Ute Crossing, mainly Paiute slaves. When Mormons from Utah sought a good southbound river crossing around the western end of Grand Canyon in the 1850's and 60's, and when Lt. George Wheeler's mapping expedition crossed the river in 1871, all followed what was essentially the Old Ute Trail and Crossing, one well-used by indigenous peoples long before.

Finding sign of early Native American cultures here is difficult since recent indigenous peoples in this area were, out of necessity, mobile and versatile. Most did not build elaborate cliff dwellings as in some other places, nor were there highly developed agricultural villages of the type found near Overton. Chipping stations have been found (sites where rock tool-making occurred), as have broken pottery sherds, metates and manos (rock grinding slabs and stones), sleeping circles, and remnant signs of human occupation in low caves and rock overhangs. However, many often-used sites that existed along the river's edge were covered by water as Lake Mead filled in the late 1930's, resulting in most sites being inundated. Those that do remain are a valuable historic resource, warrant extensive study, and for this reason, any newly discovered sites should be treated with respect and reported to archaeologists trained to preserve and document such sites accurately. We simply cannot afford to lose more.

Sure evidence of ancient people, however, are the prehistoric rock symbol panels, and a number of fine examples exist in this area. Depending which authority one references, these are usually called petroglyphs (symbols chipped, pecked, or engraved into rock surfaces) and pictographs (symbols painted onto rock surfaces). Interpretation of these symbols is of great debate. Several authorities think they are nothing more than simple artistic doodles, others think these are religious in nature, still others are certain these symbols tell stories we simply have yet to understand.

Levan Martineau is a unique authority on rock symbols. His book, *The Rocks Begin To Speak*, an in-depth look at this topic, is most interesting reading. Martineau was raised by members of the Shivwits band of the Paiute tribe in Cedar City, Utah, after being orphaned at age twelve. He not only learned their language, but perhaps more important, adopted their conceptual thought patterns (ways of perceiving "reality" being quite distinct amongst different cultures).

The Ones Who Came Before

While maturing, he also became adept at universal sign language. He then went on to serve in the US Air Force in Korea and learned the science of cryptography, that of deciphering codes. Combining all these techniques learned during his life, Martineau devoted later years to the study and interpretation of rock symbols world-wide. His unique perspective on rock symbols, that these do, indeed, tell stories and/or give directions, deserves special thought and consideration despite much criticism from academia.

Other indications of primitive life found locally are the intriguing roasting pits mentioned earlier. One clear purpose of the pits was to dry and preserve mescal fruit. Randall Henderson wrote an article in *Desert Magazine*, August, 1951, describing the process he observed during a mescal roast amongst the Pai-Pai Indians in Baja, California. Although the roasting pits described here are much smaller than those in our area, the procedure is similar. Henderson told of how a man found an agave or mescal plant (also called Century plant), and, with a sharp stick, worked lose the center bud and stalk from the plant. The lower section of the bud was edible and looked something like a large pineapple. A roasting pit was dug (this only about two feet by three feet) and lined with rock. A wood fire was built in the pit and burned until the rocks were very hot. The bud was then thrown in on the coals, more rocks added, then a layer of dirt or sand. After about twelve hours, the pit was opened, the cracked rocks raked outward, and the charred bud taken out. The outer charred husks of the bud were removed and the heart of the bud split open and eaten. The author said the bud looked and tasted like southern cooked yams.

Claysprings Canyon, which cuts down through the Music Mountains and empties into Dry Red Lake in Hualapai Valley, was the scene of a mescal harvest using the huge roasting pits more typically found in our area. John Cureton Grounds, an early rancher here, describes one such roast in his book, *Trail Dust of the Southwest*:[2]

> During the spring of 1891, many Indians came out among the hills along Claysprings Canyon and gathered mescal. Mescal is a dagger plant growing a foot in height along rocky hills. Like all dagger plants similar to the Century plant, a certain time in the spring of the year, at flowering, they grow a tall shoot which bears the flowers and fruit or seed. These stalks grow ten inches or a foot during twenty-four hours. The Indians watch the mescal closely as they have to be ready for it when the mescal is ready to harvest. The plant puts out such a fast growth that one day late and it is lost. When the dagger cluster begins forming a head in the center, similar to an artichoke, it is ready to harvest. Prior to this harvest, the Indians will have a pit dug that will take care of the vicinity and plenty of cedar or pinon wood by the pit and a pile of rock to be heated with the wood. They use an oak stick three feet in length with a piece of sharp flint fastened to the end as a cutter. Each woman has one of these sticks and a long basket strapped to her back. The basket is large at the top and almost pointed at the bottom. They cut the mescal hearts and throw them over their shoulder into the basket. When loaded, they pile the

mescal by the hole that is already fired. The pit is filled with burning wood and rocks. At the end of the day when the fire is burned down and the rocks hot, they are taken from the hole by a simple set of green wooden tongs and laid around the edge of the pit. The mescal is now dumped into the pit on the hot rocks. As the pit is filled, the hot rocks that were pulled out are pushed back between the sides of the pit and the mescal. When the pit is filled, about four inches of cedar bark is laid over the top and covered with dirt. The pit is left to steam for three days, while the mescal crew works higher up the ridges to harvest the crops, as a few hundred feet on a north slope make a difference of a day in the growing season and allows more mescal to be harvested until they find nothing but bursted heads and sprouts, mescal season is over until the next year.

Grounds related that upon emptying the first pit, the mescal was devoured immediately and the heads had a doughy consistency with a taste of pure sugar and smoke. The women would unload the remaining pits, pile the mescal on the rocks alongside, and as the heads cooled, mash them flat over a pinion log, adding piece to piece until the mescal had the appearance of slabs of cardboard three feet by six feet in size. These sheets were laid in the sun to dry, then later rolled up, tied, and saved to be eaten another time. When the roll was opened after aging, sugar crystals were present on the inside.

The roasting pits in our region are unique because of their unusually large size, an average of twenty to thirty feet in diameter. Because agave doesn't always grow in the vicinity where some of these pits are found, one archaeologist surmised that Natives here might also have roasted buds from the great number of Joshua Trees and other Yucca-type plants.

South of the river, here on our Grapevine Mesa, some roasting pits have high, sloping sides of fire-cracked rock, with middle depressions nearly five feet deep. In contrast, others I found on top the Grand Wash Cliffs often have little or no depth at all, usually with only the outer ring of fire-cracked rocks visible on the soil surface. Some persons conjecture that the deeper more conspicuous pits are older and the shallow ones more recent. Others, including myself, think the shallow ones similar to those on top the cliffs, must be older, seemingly having taken centuries to fill in with soil and debris. To date, most of the large roasting pits south of the river have not yet been studied to any degree. Eilene Green, archeologist with the Bureau of Reclamation in Boulder City, Nevada, reported studies were done on similar large roasting pits just north of the river where radio-carbon dating revealed usage of nearly three thousand years.

Several historically important caves have been discovered in the larger vicinity. One is Gypsum Cave, located northwest of the lake and twenty miles east of Las Vegas, Nevada. This was a rare find and there is reason to mention it here. The cave is a series of chambers sloping downward from the entrance and into rooms, the largest being about three hundred feet in length and one hundred feet wide. Former water action in the limestone-bedded hills formed the cave and there are gypsum or selenite formations in the lower room. Excavations done in the early

The Ones Who Came Before

1930's revealed the cave had been occupied for many centuries. Upper layers contained numerous Native American materials of possible Paiute origin and layers below showed artifacts of Puebloid and earlier Basketmaker origins. At deeper levels of excavation, the hair, bones, and dung of the now-extinct Shasta Ground Sloths were found, along with evidence of other extinct animals such as miniature horses and small camels. Of particular interest was the fact that in one layer of sloth dung there was also found the remains of a torch and campfire. This led some archaeologists to conclude that humans had occupied this cave at the same time that ground sloths and other extinct animals were still in the area. Carbon 14 dating of sloth dung in the lower layers averaged about ten thousand years of age. Disagreement exists about the interpretation of these excavations, but if this conclusion is found to be true, it would lend credence to the theory that ancient humans did hunt prehistoric animals.

Rampart Cave (also known as the Sloth Cave) is an important cave located here in the lower or western end of Grand Canyon (also known as the Lower Granite Gorge), just west of Columbine Falls and about five hundred feet above river level. Due to this cave's extreme historical importance, the entrance to this cave has for some time been secured with a steel gate.

Rampart Cave was discovered in July of 1936 by a CCC (Civilian Conservation Corp) group and their foreman, Willis Evans, a Pitt River Indian from California. At that time, newly formed Lake Mead had backed water into the western end of Grand Canyon and vast amounts of debris from inundated shorelines cluttered the waters making navigation by boat extremely hazardous. A CCC crew was stationed in the Pearce Ferry area not far from the western entrance to Grand Canyon, and every day the crew would leave Pearce Ferry by boat, go up river into the canyon to collect drifting logs, then drag them to shore to be burned. One day as they worked their way into the lower gorge, Evans became intrigued with an opening he could see in the canyon wall high above. He and several workers disembarked on shore and made the long upward climb to the mouth of the cave. Upon entering, Evans was surprised to see huge dried dung balls covering the cave floor; dung nearly identical in appearance to sloth dung he'd helped excavate previously in Gypsum Cave, some sixty miles due west. He immediately recognized the importance of this site and contacted the National Park Service (NPS).

Park Service sent specialists to investigate and since the cave was located high in the canyon wall and the entrance provided such a remarkable view, the name Rampart was assigned. Crews were brought in to do test digs and as work progressed it became apparent that this was truly a unique scientific treasure. Several hundred fossils were uncovered, almost half belonging to the extinct Shasta Ground Sloth. Incredibly, even pieces of sloth hide were found still intact in this high and very dry desert cave. Other important finds were bones of a small prehistoric horse and mountain goat, now both extinct. The cave also contained remains of marmots, lizards and birds, ringtail cats, tortoise, and mountain sheep; species of animals still existing today. No sign of former human habitation was found in this cave.

Remote Beginnings

In the early 1940's, another major dig was initiated at Rampart Cave by the Smithsonian Institute and more fossils and dung were removed for study and testing. Radiocarbon dating of some fossils established an age of 40,000 years and sloth dung from various levels in the cave tested from 35,000 B.C. to 11,000 B.C.

During the late 1960's and early 1970's, Dr. Paul Martin from the University of Arizona led more research projects at Rampart Cave. He studied diets of the sloth as well as patterns of prehistoric plant growth. During one trip to Rampart Cave in 1975, Martin was accompanied by writer/historian James Michener. Michener was doing background study on why prehistoric animals had become extinct. In an article in *Readers Digest*, June, 1976, "Where Did the Animals Go?" Michener made the following comments:

> Recently, to learn first-hand what may have happened, I joined a field trip organized by America's most foremost authority on animal extinctions; Paul S. Martin, a lanky, sharp-eyed professor of geosciences at the University of Arizona. Some time ago he started to explore a remarkable cave hidden on an almost inaccessible mountain face high above the waters of a western river. He now proposed to revisit this cave.

Michener described difficulties accessing the cave, the spaciousness of the H-shaped cave which was nearly 150 feet in length, and his amazement at the grayish layers of dried dung that "smelled like dry cow chips." Michener went on to quote Martin:

> We can read the history of this cave like a book. The bottom dung was laid down over 40,000 years ago. Radio-carbon dating proves that. Sloths occupied the area until 32,000 years ago. Then see this line? For some reason, probably climatic, the sloths left and pack rats moved in. The rats stayed 13,000 years, as proved by this level. Then the sloths returned and lived here until their race died out, 11,000 years ago.

The giant sloths were described as large, awkward, and shaggy animals that moved around on their hind legs, using their front legs to pull down branches of trees for vegetation and grubbing. They were basically plant-eaters and not carnivorous. When Michener asked Martin why the sloths disappeared, Martin related a theory that has gained him wide notoriety, yet has also caused much debate. Martin surmised that at least 11,000 years ago a band of nomadic hunters arrived in North America, coming across the land bridge from Asia. By placing data into his computer, Martin calculated results showing that when these individuals reproduced normally, killed animals for their food, and gradually fanned out following their prey across the country, that 100 people would double their numbers every thirty years while moving southward in an ever-widening arc at a rate of up to twenty miles per year. Martin concluded that if only one person in four hunted actively and killed only one large animal per week, within ten years an entire tribe would be able to kill off huge numbers of large animals in any given area. In 293 years the original human population would have increased to

The Ones Who Came Before

almost 288,000 people, spread clear into Mexico, and could easily have killed off some 93 million large animals. Martin believes it was man, hunting and killing, who was the primary agent of exterminating the large animals.

I first saw Rampart Cave in 1974. My husband, Don McBee, was the first National Park Service Ranger assigned to reside on Grapevine Mesa and to cover the territory of upper Lake Mead, and, at that time, 40 miles on into the western part of Grand Canyon (then part of Lake Mead National Recreation Area). During a rare opportunity, my children, Dave and Suzanne, and I, accompanied Don and another Park Ranger by boat to the drop-off point to hike up to Rampart Cave. It was an incredible experience that whisked us back eons in time. Years later, Suzanne wrote the following letter to me:

> I remember scampering madly up the mountainside to the Sloth Cave as a child, intrigued because of the aloof manner in which it surveyed its world. I never saw it as something to be conquered or dissected, but rather as a gate to time-travel – simply stepping into its depths loosed a symphony of ancient echoes inside my mind. Restless last breaths still hung where the long-gone breather left them. I remember sitting in the half-light of the entrance with you, taking a pull from the water jug, looking down at the tiny boat way below, and thinking I was snug in the pupil of a great unblinking Cyclops, almost half-expecting it to stand up and stretch from its daydreams.

On July 14th of 1976, the worst fears of many were realized when Rampart Cave was discovered ablaze, apparently ignited by someone who had started a campfire at the entrance, a fire that quickly spread through the dry layers of dung. For seven months NPS personnel worked desperately trying to extinguish the fire that was slowly destroying this ancient and vast storehouse of information – a task made doubly difficult because sections of the cave ceiling were also collapsing. Eventually, their efforts proved successful, but in the meantime there had been irretrievable loss of prehistoric knowledge due to damage from this catastrophic fire.

The cave continues to have a steel-bar gate across the opening to protect what yet remains. And, to this day, individuals still occasionally destroy pieces of the gate in order to gain entrance and in so doing, again gravely endanger what might yet be learned from the priceless contents. NPS personnel have constantly repaired the gate over the years, however, as funding for Park Service has steadily decreased over recent decades, improvements in security have not been possible nor have further in-depth excavation projects ensued.

Muav Cave and additional important caves and overhangs in the western end of Grand Canyon were hurriedly examined in the 1930's while Lake Mead was filling. In some cases, workers had only a few days to excavate a site before water rose to within inches, and efforts had to be abandoned. Bits of knowledge were gained from these labors, but sadly, much was lost. More details on these belated salvage efforts will be included in the chapter on Lake Mead.

After the filling of Lake Mead, additional archaeological studies on important sites were completed. Several independent surveys were done from the 1930's to the 1960's but results were not carefully recorded. Some work was done in the 1960's and 1970's and information recorded, but many projects were not coordinated in a productive way. Over recent years, NPS has contracted with the Western Archaeological Center in Tucson to develop an organized program for research with long-term goals, but again, acquiring funding for this effort has been a major obstacle.

A great deal of work remains to be done and one cannot stress strongly enough how important it is that any remaining sites be left undisturbed. Archaeologists gain knowledge not only from artifacts found at a site, but also from an object's exact location in relation to other artifacts and layers. Anything with the appearance of a potential site should be left as is and reported to appropriate authorities as soon as possible.

For this reason, little information will be given in this book as to specific locations of known sites that have not yet been properly studied or excavated by trained personnel. Reference to actual locations will be made only if those sites are already well-known or have been officially designated by name on various maps of the area.

The Ones Who Came Before

Examples of rock art and artifacts found in the area

Remote Beginnings

Richard Montgomery in center of roasting pit located in Grapevine Wash

Dave Gensley beside roasting pit in Lower Granite Gorge

The Ones Who Came Before

Horace Emery thinks this is Willis Evans in front of Muav Caves. NPS photo, 1936

Entrance to Rampart Cave showing gate, NPS photo, 1936

Remote Beginnings

Preserved sloth dung lying exposed on floor of Rampart Cave. NPS photo, 1936

Paul Martin and James Michener in Rampart Cave, 1975

Chapter Two: The Paiute

One of two Native American tribes constantly present in our region when numbers of Euro-Americans first began arriving were the Paiute (pronounced "Pie-yoot"), a branch of the Shoshonean Cultural group related to the farther north Ute people. "Pai" means water, actually "standing water" – not in the context of stagnant or unmoving water, but in the sense that it's always there, a year around source. "Ute" originated from a Spanish/Mexican corruption of "Uta," while the Utes actually describe themselves as the "Nuche," meaning "The People."

The southern Paiute were widely dispersed from today's Las Vegas, Nevada, north into southern Utah and east up onto the plateaus. Their fluid southern boundary was the Colorado River and Grand Canyon. They were present in the Virgin Mountains, throughout the Grand Wash trough, and on the Shivwits Plateau – lands we look upon to the west, north, and northeast of our mesa. Hunting and gathering parties often times traveled through this, *The Land of Long Shadows*.

The Paiutes also called themselves the Nuwuvi.[1] They were a people of the land and a peaceful people. Their lives were intertwined with the cycles of nature; in order to survive in the barren desert lands, they knew they must live in harmony with those cycles. They lived mostly in small family groups and often seasonally located near a spring or other water source. They farmed around the water sources and, after planting, would leave for a time to gather wild food, then return to weed and tend the crops after those had sprouted. The women preferred various types of basketry over pottery as those were light-weight and mobile. They often placed crops that were gathered in large conical baskets carried on their backs.

Their life-style and historical stories are detailed well in *Nuwuvi: A Southern Paiute History*, published by the Paiute tribe in 1976. Written with the assistance of tribal elders, this book is one of few that does a fine job representing Paiute perspectives on their history, customs, and traditions, and I drew upon this source more than others.

Plants, seeds and roots were gathered throughout the summer months and into the fall. Seeds were hulled on a metate (grinding stone), then winnowed in large fan-shaped trays. After cleaning the hulls, seeds were parched with charcoal in basket trays, a step requiring skill because one had to toss both the seeds and charcoal to parch the seeds evenly and still keep the basket from burning. Some seeds were stored for winter use, often as flour to be mixed later with water to make a gruel.

Mesquite and screw beans were collected and prepared in this manner and were also used as a sort of candy, sucked on for their sweetness. Yucca was widely used, some varieties for soap, with leaves providing good fiber for the making of fine cordage for rope and sandals. As noted in the previous introduction, the heart at the base of the agave was roasted and baked. Some parts were also pounded into cakes and preserved, often used during travel. Mescal, a fermented drink, was made from the mountain agave, the yant.

The Ones Who Came Before

Pine nuts were also very important for the Paiute, either raw or roasted, and were often preserved in the form of flour and this was the basic element in food stores for the coming winter. The inner pine bark also served as food and the wood as fuel. The sap or "sunip" (in some sources, spelled "sanip") was chewed, with some of the more coarse sap used for mending, cementing, and waterproofing. It was also used for spiritual purposes. Juniper, currant, and raspberries were eaten fresh. Others such as the serviceberry were dried and made into a beverage.

The Paiutes, as all indigenous peoples, also used native plant life for medicinal purposes. They often drank tea made from yarrow and sage brush in order to relieve a variety of ailments. Sagebrush was used to assist in childbirth and as a remedy for headaches, colds, and worms. Another variety of sage was used to treat swellings and bruises. Yerba Santa was taken as a tea to remedy lung problems, and also used externally in treating rheumatism, partial paralysis, and colds. Various other plants were used as poultices for sprains and bruises and to constrict the blood vessels to stop bleeding.

The women were mostly responsible for gathering plants and working around the lodge. The men hunted, with deer being the chief large-game animal stalked and, when killed, the entire deer was utilized; some of it dried, some smoked, the hides used for clothing and moccasins and the brains in tanning processes. Desert big horn sheep and antelope were also hunted, but these were less plentiful. Bows of wood and horn were used, commonly backed by sinew. Arrows were constructed from arrow weed, the points made of stone or greasewood, and eagle or flicker feathers were used to insure straight flight. Small game such as rabbits and rodents were hunted throughout the year and there were also large-scale rabbit drives, these using large nets they had made, driving rabbits into them, then ensnaring and beating the rabbits with sticks.

Brush shelters were made for sleeping during warm summer months. During fall, the most important hunting season, they hunted deer and gathered the all-important pine nuts. More substantial homes called "kanees" were used during winter. Although there were a variety of kanees, the most common type was made by constructing domelike frames of supple but sturdy branches and covering these with layers of grass, brush, or bark stripped from junipers. Smoke holes were left in the tops. Various other types of shelters were used, even teepees in later years, a practice adopted from the more northern Utes.

Throughout the long winter months, the Paiute made various implements such as baskets, cordage, and clothing. Clothing was often made not only with hides, but also cliff rose bark, especially skirts for the women. Stiff sandals of yucca were worn as well as hide moccasins.

Rabbit skins were used to make blankets that were draped around the chest as a cape. Baskets were made in two ways, some being coiled and others twined. Willow was preferred for this purpose, although some considered squaw bush to be superior.

For many centuries the Paiute peoples survived with this hard but simple and sparse lifestyle -- one very well-adapted to this harsh landscape. However, this adaptation of living in small bands also made them more vulnerable to attacks and

The Paiute

raids from outsiders (both Native as well as incoming Euro-Americans) than those tribes having more complex social structures and who often formed larger groups.

In 1776, an exploration trip was commissioned by the Spanish government to find likely routes connecting Spanish settlements in New Mexico to those on the Pacific coast. It was led by Father Escalante, a Catholic Priest, and this group traveled from New Mexico to southern Utah, then into northern Arizona Strip country (north of Grand Canyon), and on toward the springs at present-day Las Vegas, Nevada. Father Escalante came into contact with Paiutes at a number of places and commented that these people had a thriving trade with the Havasupai, Hopi, and Mohave, south of Grand Canyon. His group, like most other explorer groups, often "conscripted" Native Americans (took individuals against their will, forcing them to guide the party to water sources, over mountain passes, and to various destinations). Father Escalante's exploration was a critical event for the Paiute as part of his route later became the well-traveled section of the Old Spanish Trail, which soon brought more and more invaders into and through Paiute lands.

After Escalante's expedition passed, Spanish fur traders and trappers soon followed. The Spanish may have introduced the commercial enterprise of slave trading to the northern Ute Indians, with many slaves being captured from the more dispersed and vulnerable Paiute bands who were located on lands through which the Old Trail passed. William Snow, in his article, *Utah Indians and the Spanish Slave Trade, 1929*,[2] stated, "almost continuously from Escalante's expedition until after the Mormons came, wandering Spaniards entered these valleys, not only for furs, but to traffic in Indian slaves."

The Old Spanish Trail that had become the major trade route between Spanish settlements in Mexico, New Mexico, and over to California, evolved with slave trading as a very important part of those trips. Spaniards often started from New Mexico with goods in-hand for trading purposes. When they reached the Navajo and Utes, they would trade for horses. As they proceeded on the trail, they would trade horses and goods for Native children (usually Paiute) who had been stolen or, if none were available, the Spanish themselves would raid Paiute camps for children. Upon reaching California, the Spanish would trade the children for more horses and goods – then return, picking up additional slave children on their way back. In the 1840's children were bringing about $50-75 each, but ten years later, prices had gone up; boys were bringing $100 or more and girls were sold for $150-200. Daniel Jones, in *Forty Years Among the Indians*, is quoted, "The Mexicans were as fully established and systematic in this trade as ever were the slavers on the seas and to them this was a very lucrative business."[3]

William Palmer, in *Indian Slavery on the Old Spanish Trail,* recorded some Paiute perspectives about slavery:[4]

> I asked how the Indian women felt about the slave traffic and the old man said they were scared to death. When a Spanish party was in the country, the women tried to take their children and run away and hide.... When their children were taken, some of the women would follow the caravans for days

seeking an opportunity to steal their children back. When one succeeded, she was hunted ruthlessly and if caught, was taken into slavery with her child. Still, this danger did not deter them from making the attempt. There are stories among the Indians about these women hunts which seem to be authenticated.

Near Cedar City there is a narrow box canyon known as Squaw Cave. Its sheer walls are fifty to sixty feet high. Some Spaniards were chasing an escaped [woman] around through those hills. Seeing that she could not escape, the woman ran with her pursuers close behind, to the edge of the cliff, and dived off head first, dashing herself to death on the rocky floor.

Down on the Virgin River, near the town of Virgin, there was a high rocky point that jutted out into the river which was called Thompsons Point. One spring when high waters were coming down the rivers, a Paiute woman who had stolen her child back from a party of Spanish slavers, was tracked and hunted for days. The Spaniards finally came upon her and trapped her on Thompson's Point. Rather than let her child go into slavery, she threw it off into the swollen river to drown.

The Spanish, however, were not the only cause of devastation for the Paiutes. Neighboring Native American tribes as well as occasional fur trappers, now becoming more frequent in the area, also conducted raids and took Paiute children to sell on the slave market. Fairly quotes;

Some Spanish and Anglo traders also participated in slave raiding. According to Thomas Farnham, a trader in the 1830's, Paiutes were 'hunted in the spring of the year, when weak and helpless, by a certain class of men, and when taken, are fattened, carried to Santa Fe and sold as slaves'... Indian agent, Garland Hurt, commenting on the effects of the early nineteenth century slave trade, noted that 'scarcely one half of the Py-eed children are permitted to grow up in a band; and a large majority of those being males, this and other causes are tending to depopulate their bands very rapidly'.[5]

The northern Ute Chief, Walkara, was notorious for his slaving. He was known to have killed Paiute children he had taken as slaves if Mormons or other pioneers refused to buy them. When Walkara died in 1855, he had two Indian women killed and buried with him, two live Paiute children, fifteen horses, and requested that two Mormons also be placed in his grave – the latter being a wish apparently not granted. During Walkara's reign, much slave trading took place across the Old Ute Crossing here at the west end of Grand Canyon. Later, in 1866, when the Utes were assigned the vast Uintah Reservation in northeastern Utah, some of what had once been their original lands, they then no longer raided outside their territory.

The Old Spanish Trail also caused other major disruptions in the Paiute culture. Each caravan brought with it many animals; sometimes there were two hundred or more men on horseback and as many as two thousand horses and mules loaded down with goods. Needless to say, all grasses and plants along the route, especially at spring areas and river edges where camps were commonly made, were completely depleted for some time after their passing.

In 1844, John Fremont's military party came over the trail and by this time remaining Paiutes had finally begun to retaliate against intruders. A band of Native Americans attacked a white party that was waiting to join Fremont's caravan and stole some horses during the attack. Kit Carson was accompanying Fremont's party at the time. Kit had a notorious reputation for having a short fuse and he and two other men pursued the band for over one hundred miles. Upon finding the camp, they opened fire, hitting two men and taking a boy captive while other Natives fled to safety. They then scalped two Native men who were still alive. An examination of the camp showed that the stolen horses had been killed and stewed in order to feed the band. Fremont later praised the boldness and bravery of Kit's vengeful actions.

Joseph Walker, another trapper, also joined up with Fremont en route. Walker prided himself in claiming to have killed close to one hundred Paiutes over three different trips he'd made across Nevada.

By 1848, Spanish trader caravans on the trail dwindled to an end as Mexican control of California ceased. The taking of Paiute slaves decreased, but the practice still continued between the Utes and New Mexicans. One year later, however, the California gold rush migration began and Spanish trading caravans were simply replaced by migrant trains equally destructive of all animal and vegetation life in their path.

The Mormons began arriving one year later, opening yet another chapter of suffering for the Paiutes, these being the first Euro-American immigrants to actually come with the purpose of settling permanently on Ute and Paiute lands, with the first act being to claim sole access to and ownership of valuable water sources.

During initial contacts between the Paiutes and new Mormon settlers, slavery was not discouraged. According to Gustive Larsen's article, "Journal of the Iron County Mission," written in 1850 and quoted in Nuwuvi[6], George A. Smith was leading a Mormon expedition into southern Utah when an incident occurred where he accused an old Paiute of shooting and killing one of his oxen. He offered the old man a deal, taking a twelve year old boy who was with him in exchange for the old man's life. Some five days later, the Mormons sent out word to the Paiutes that should they wish to trade their children or other articles of clothing or provisions, to come to the encampment. In 1851, Smith also gave the Ute Chief, Walkara, a letter stating his desire to trade horses, buckskins, and Paiute children, then went on to wish Walkara and his Utes good bargains, success, and prosperity. Chief Walkara was known as one of the notorious Native slave traders amongst tribes, some think because of previous Spanish influence. Other times, cases were documented where Paiute mothers with starving children would actually approach Mormon families asking them to buy one child so she could then have some way to feed her remaining youngsters – such was the state of destitution amongst the Paiutes at that time, with their lands, waters, and resources so totally usurped by alien immigrants.

The Ones Who Came Before

Brigham Young, Mormon Church President, wanted to make the conversion and "civilizing" of Native Americans a matter of prime import for Mormon settlements and advised his people to "settle peacefully" amongst them.

In 1852, a state law was passed outlawing slavery in Utah, however the law was worded very poorly, possibly intentionally, that "indenturing" Native Americans was still permissible. Terminology such as apprentices, adoptees, and servants, were soon commonly used to describe situations of Native American children who were with Mormon families. Mormon leaders encouraged members of their churches to adopt such children – as Brigham Young is quoted in *Nuwuvi*[7] "to buy up the Lamanite [Indian] children as fast as they could, and educate them and teach them the gospel so that many generations would not pass ere they should become a white and delightsome people."

In *Nuwuvi*, we also find a quote from Jacob Hamblin, one of the top Mormon leaders in southern Utah and a man comparably good to the Paiutes, who was additionally involved in the slave trade. In 1854, he wrote, "I bought an Indian boy about six years old. I gave, for him, a gun, a blanket, and some ammunition. Brother A.P. Hardy took him to Parowan and let Brother Judd have him. Brother Hardy was offered a horse for him by a gentile [non-Mormon].... I bought him that I might let a good man have him that would make him useful."[8] Eventually Hamblin also purchased two Paiute girls, purportedly so each of his wives would have a personal maid.

Other quotes from *Nuwuvi*:

> A few Indians seemed to have been treated humanely in most instances.... However, the Indians were simply unpaid servants or farmhands for the whites. They were often passed around like property. Many of the children, despite being adopted, died at an early age. Thomas D. Brown told how he purchased five children, only two of whom lived until the end of the year. Zadok Judd purchased at least three children, only one of whom survived until maturity... many of the white-held Paiutes eventually ran away to return to Indian life.

> The Mormon willingness to accept this kind of slave trade seems based on two things. First, was an ethnocentric attitude which made them unwilling to accept any worth of the careful balance the Paiutes had worked out with nature, an attitude that existed everywhere on the frontier. A second reason to purchase Indians was the belief that it was the Mormon mission to restore Christianity to the Indians, whom they believed had been former "lost" Christians. The most convenient way to accomplish the conversion was to raise children in their homes .... the settlers, however, in their relentless expansion into the fertile southern valleys of Utah that had served as the Paiutes livelihood, very rarely realized [or conveniently refused to acknowledge] the extent to which they, themselves, were directly responsible for the very impoverishment of the people they were trying to save.[9]

By 1858, many Mormons had become frustrated with efforts to try to convert and "civilize" the Paiutes and word came down from Hamblin, that, due to lack of success, the missionaries were to redirect their conversion efforts toward the Hopi and Navajo to the south and east. This essentially led to a total abandonment of the Paiutes. They became an ignored people in their own land – yet with no way to survive. Farmlands had crept in everywhere, prime hunting areas were grazed by huge herds of cattle and sheep, and ranchers demanded that the few remaining springs and seeps not be disturbed so their cattle could come to water. Messersmith, in *The History of Mohave County to 1912*, wrote that Euro-Americans were not remorseful in treating them like animals and even stooped to using poisons to kill them.

As a last means of survival, Paiute men, women, and children, worked as unskilled labor on farms, ranches, and in mines, usually for only a small pittance of pay and often just for food. Having been stripped of their lands, their native way of life and any remaining pride, many became beggers, prostitutes, and thieves. Some Mormons tried to convince newly baptized Paiutes that they should "begin farming," even though the Paiutes had farmed on a smaller scale long before Mormons arrived and now there were no fertile and productive farm lands available to them. The Paiute lifestyle had become so totally decimated that most suffered abject destitution; culturally, physically, and psychologically.

In 1869, partially due to well-intended persuasions from the great American explorer of the Colorado River region and Grand Canyon, Major John Wesley Powell, the government decided it should do something. Then followed a series of tragic attempts to set up reservations for the various bands of remaining Paiutes. However, once these were set up, during the following thirty years, most designated reservations were so badly used and abused by their assigned Euro-American agents (many of whom were simply nearby ranchers or farmers who obtained leases to use the reservation lands at very little cost) that Paiutes rarely were able to survive on those reservations.

By the 1940's, several Paiute bands, under the new Indian Reorganization Act, established their own constitutions and by-laws and set up their own governments. In 1954, President Eisenhower, in yet more renewed attempts to encourage Native Americans to become "self reliant" and just like other Americans, signed bills that terminated the federal government's trust relationship with most of the bands, which ultimately resulted once again in simply total abandonment. Still destitute Paiutes then had to sell off pieces of what remaining property existed as theirs in order to survive. However, by the 1960's and 70's, lawsuits presented to the Indian Claims Commission brought some financial judgments to a number of bands, and they are, to this day, attempting to survive and rebuild.

In 1975, Roman Malach, a retired educator who was an amateur historian then living in Kingman, Arizona, received financial assistance from the Arizona Bicentennial Commission to publish his book, *The Arizona Strip*. In this, Malach quotes the following statement written by Jenny Brown about Moccasin Springs, located in the Arizona Strip Country, and Malach classifies her comments as "fine history of the Moccasin Springs area."

The Ones Who Came Before

> An Indian wandering his way over the hills, down the canyon and through the valleys, stopped at a bubbling spring, was refreshed by its clear water, and left his moccasined footprints in the soft earth .... Later, a white man, finding the spring with Indian moccasin footprints and a lone moccasin left by other Indians, called it Moccasin Springs.

Stoffle and Evans illustrate all too clearly how the "pioneer spirit mythology" has been perpetuated even into recent times. They assert, "This statement perpetuates the myth of the free-living, wandering Indian with no ties to anywhere. The fact of the matter is that there were [at the time when settlers began arriving] perhaps 1175 people [Native Americans] living in this spring region and using this spring constantly to irrigate their farms."[10]

In the 1980's, the Kaibab Tribal Council, on lands near Fredonia, Arizona, north of Grand Canyon, voted to allow building of a huge toxic waste incinerator on their lands (despite much dissension from within the tribe) in hopes that more employment would lift their people out of poverty. Only time will tell if this development, born of self-preservation, will simply be yet another step in a vicious circle of destruction that had begun decades ago.

As of 1990, there are approximately one thousand Paiute people on their own lands, consisting of four tribal groups. About seventy-five Paiutes occupy a small reservation in Las Vegas, just over two hundred live on the Kaibab Reservation north of Grand Canyon, and another two hundred-fifty reside on the Moapa Reservation between Las Vegas and St. George, Utah. The Utah Paiute, the fourth group, actually has five bands totaling nearly five hundred people who live at Indian Peaks, Kanosh, Cedar City, Koosharem, and the Shivwits.

Chapter Three: The Hualapai

The other Native Americans predominant in this area are the Hualapai. Many spellings of their name exist: Xawalapaiy, Walapai, Hualpai, Walpi. "Hualapai" has been the most preferred by the people themselves, the name meaning Pine Tree Folk.

When Euro-Americans arrived on the scene, the Hualapai were dispersed throughout a large area from the Black Mountains near the Colorado River on the west and Bill Williams River just south of present-day Lake Havasu City, and east into the Juniper Mountains below present-day Seligman. Their northern boundary of sorts was the Colorado River and Grand Canyon. They were living on Grapevine Mesa and on top the Grand Wash Cliffs. They were present throughout our area of the *Land of Long Shadows*. This land was theirs.

Hualapai origin stories vary to some degree. One prominent version relates that Hualapai people originated in the Newberry Mountains on the California side of the Colorado River and then migrated to a cave called Waha'vo ("house for many people going in") in Matawidita Canyon (spelled Meriwhitica Canyon on many modern-day maps), one that empties into western Grand Canyon. The full name of this canyon was actually "Mata wai a' witi' ca si yava" and in Hualapai this referred to "pot holes in the hard surface of travertine on the long bench extending to a fall." In the sacred cave there, a divine human called Thata'kanava designated occupants to be in various tribes and the people then dispersed from this cave. Sometime later members of the other tribes were sent away and Thata'kanava told the Hualapai that only they would be able to keep Meriwhitica Canyon as the focus of their home lands.[1]

Meriwhitica Canyon cuts northeasterly from high plateau country of the Music Mountains and then north toward the Grand Canyon. An old horse trail leads from on top the plateau and down several miles into the canyon to a place where large trees surround springs that at one time flowed 700 gallons of water per minute. Lush vegetation is present on a sloping terrace there. Beyond the spring, the canyon ends abruptly in a sheer drop of craggy, pot hole-filled "flowing" earthen material called travertine. A narrow path winds down through this massive travertine deposit, eventually meeting Spencer Canyon, below. Spencer Canyon has a year-round flowing stream that meanders on down to enter Grand Canyon, still some five miles farther.

Even though various bands of Hualapai lived some distance from Meriwhitica, most kept this Canyon as a focal point and returned to raise important staple crops such as corn and squash, and to participate in important tribal ceremonies. Each band had designated garden areas in Meriwhitica: The Grass Springs [Tinaka Springs] band from the west (later the location of Grass Springs Ranch/Diamond Bar/Smith Ranch), the Clay Springs band to the south (from Clay Springs Canyon on the north side of Dry Red Lake), the Red Rock band from the east, and the Cerbat Mountain band, to name a few. Irrigation ditches were dug from the spring

The Ones Who Came Before

into the fields and travertine deposits hardened these ditches, many of which are readily visible today.

To this day, the sacred cave in Meriwhitica Canyon has ruins of stone masonry walls in its entrance, a puzzling aspect for archeologists since stone masonry was not an identified trait of historical Hualapai cultures. Archeological investigations during the 1930's and 1950's led one authority to conclude that from 700 A.D. until 1150 A.D., Cohonino peoples (from Flagstaff area) must have occupied this site, then were displaced by the Hualapai.

As early as 1776, the Spanish came through Hualapai homelands. Father Garces, another Catholic Priest, led an exploratory party near Hakoome, the Hualapai Indian village now called Beale Springs and that lies within the city limits of Kingman, Arizona. He reported the Hualapai met his party and that they and a Mohave guide were quite friendly and shared meat with them. Fortunately for the Hualapai, the Spanish chose to use this route very little in years that followed, at least sparing these people the terrible tragedies of Spanish slavery.

By 1850, however, Euro-Americans had begun to arrive. Captain Sitgreaves came through in 1851 and both Aubry and Lieutenant Whipple in 1854. Lt. Edward Beale came in 1853 and the first wagon trains arrived over Beale's road through present-day Kingman in 1858.

The Hualapai tried to remain at peace with the intruders. In a report written by John Dunn in 1865, an Indian Agent in Prescott:

> A Captain Thompson, now in command at Fort Whipple, went out on a scout into the Hualapai country with George Cooler as a guide, and surprised a Rancheria [encampment], killing a number of men, women, and children. He stated that the Indians did not retaliate... until their war chief, Anasa, of the Hualapai was killed soon after by some wanton and intoxicated squatters on a ranch 75 miles west of this place.[2]

Lieutenant Colonel Roger Jones, in another report dated July 21, 1869, stated;

> Prior to 1866, the Hualapai had been at peace with the whites, but in that year, their head chief, Wauba Yuma, was killed by a freighter [shot in the back at Beale Springs] on the mere suspicion that some of his young men had assisted in the killing of a white man at the tollgate near Aztec Pass.[3]

The Hualapai then waged war, many fatalities resulted, and they were ultimately rounded up and brought to Beale Springs (Kingman, Az). From 1871 to 1874, the Indians were held captive at Camp Beale Springs and kept in near-starving conditions. Then they were rounded up again and marched down to the Colorado Indian Reservation at La Paz (near present-day Parker, Arizona) on the Colorado River. To these mountain people, a forced move down to the hot barren lands in that low valley was devastating. Almost half the population died, as did most of their horses; intense heat, disease, and starvation all combined to take this huge toll. One year from the date they had been placed on the La Paz Reservation, survivors simply picked up and left to eventually find their way back north to their original mountain homelands.

The Hualapai

Nearly seven years after the Hualapai left captivity at LaPaz, a local newspaper summarized the situation:

> Since they returned to their old haunts they have been peaceably inclined. They have, to a great extent, been used as cheap laborers and have taken the place of Chinamen. The only difference is the Indians were here when the citizens of the United States came, not imported. ... Many pressures affected the Hualapai. Mounted hunters with rifles had so diminished big game as to decrease opportunities for their fire-drives. Declining use of fire, combined with the grazing of thousands of cattle Anglo-Americans introduced to Mojave County destroyed the thick stands of sele and similar seed-bearing plants that preferred to grow in burned over areas. As the wild plant food resources disappeared, Walapai [Hualapai] access to water also diminished. Cattlemen pre-empted key springs for ranch headquarters and discouraged Walapais from using other springs because the Indians frightened livestock away from the water. With jobs in the mine-ranch economy too scarce to support more than one-fifth of the tribal population, some Walapai women inevitably became money-earners at occupations other than cutting grass for hay. Some became washerwomen; others turned to prostitution in settlements where few Anglo-American women lived, and those virtually all married.4

A compassionate Major Mason of the Third Cavalry at Whipple barracks, Arizona Territory, wrote the following on June 16, 1882:

> Ten years ago they were cared for at Beale Springs. This place was a home for them and although during food-gathering season they scattered over a large extent of the country, yet, when sick or inclined, they returned to this point where they were sure of a safe abiding place. From here they were moved to La Paz on the Colorado River, and set down on the dust miles away from wood and grass. They are mountain Indians, and this was a sore tax upon them. Failure to feed them, on the part of proper authorities, and the intolerableness of their condition, drove them to the mountains, where, as I understand, they have remained up to this time, gathering seeds, the fruit of the cacti, and getting a little game occasionally and receiving what food a generously disposed military administration has been able to get from the Indian Department.
>
> Now every stream, water-hole, and square foot of arable land are taken by the white men and the Indian has no place to call his own. He is a homeless wanderer in his own land.
>
> In view of the foregoing, I would respectfully recommend, as a preliminary measure that a reservation be set aside for these Indians to include Peach Springs in Mohave County. There is ample water there for the whole tribe, plenty of good grazing in its vicinity, and within easy distance of the railroad, making minimum cost of furnishing them their supplies, and above all, giving them what all races of all nations crave and have a right to ... a home.[5]

The Ones Who Came Before

Charley Spencer, a former army scout who had come to know the Indians well and was living with a Hualapai woman (his story to come later) was asked to help set up boundaries for the new Hualapai Reservation. Since Charley lived on the reservation and ran cattle there, he, of course, pushed for generous boundaries. His recommendations were made and then a local man named Jim Smith was appointed to make a survey.

Morgan Jones wrote the following in the Walapai Papers:

> Jim Smith, better known as Pretty Jim, a prospector, cowboy and miner, was given the job of the first survey, which was made in the method of those days. A man or party of men or civilians or both, would start from some designated point, ride to some other point, and keep account of the time required to make the distance, then figure on a map the distance at so many miles for each hour it took to ride to that point.
>
> The Hualapai Reservation west line was started at a point near the mouth [west end] of the Grand Canyon. Jim Smith rode south to the highest point in the Music Mountain; from Music Mountain in a southeasterly direction to a high point or mountain southeast of Peach Springs; from there in a due east direction to another natural landmark; from there in a northeasterly direction to a point east of Peach Springs; then due north to the rim of Grand Canyon.[6]

In such a way the Hualapai Reservation was created in 1883. Yet, this in no way insured the Indians use of this land. Reservation lands continued to be grazed extensively by ranchers, just as businesses in Peach Springs were also run by non-Indians. Ranchers took over the water rights at Peach Springs, and in turn, sold those rights to the railroad. Indians were again discouraged from camping at outlying seeps and springs so as not to bother rancher's cattle.

Attempts were made by several Mohave County residents to petition the government to once again take the land from the Hualapai and return the reservation lands to public domain, but those efforts failed. Few jobs were available to Hualapai men in mining and ranching off the reservations. Many Hualapai women, as mentioned, had no options but to become washerwomen or maids for white families, or resort to prostitution.

In 1915, as an attempt to help the Hualapai develop some form of sustenance, the government issued ten head of cattle to every fifteen families under a plan where they would pay the government back. This, however, proved unsuccessful. By 1929, a Hualapai Chief, Paschilowhwa (called Jim Fielding by whites) and who had once served as an army scout, wrote the following letter to the Commissioner of Indian Affairs in Washington:

> Speaking for my tribe, the Hualapai Indians of Arizona, we understand that the agent here in Valentine wants to sell all our cattle, because he says there is no grass or water. We do not want to sell our cattle; but we want each of us to have our own cattle to work ourselves. We do not want the Government to work our cattle for us, as we are well able to do all this, and most of us have

worked cattle all our lives for different cattlemen in this section and we know how to do it.

This is what we want and what we think. We would be glad to have the office advise us; but let us do our own work and take care of our own property. We can and will work best for our interest, and each man in the tribe will look after his own cows better than the one or two men employed by the Government to do it for us.

The best part of our reservation is leased to white cattlemen, and they are making money on it. If our cattle had the run of this land, there would be no shortage of grass or water. We understand that a rental of $15,000 per year is collected for this land. We do not know what this money is used for, but it seems to us that if hay, salt, etc., have to be bought, that this money could go to pay for it and we would have to give 20% of our cattle money to pay for those things.

We do not want our young people to grow to depend on the Government to do things for them, but we want them to be independent and learn what it means to take care of their own property. We think that at least we can do as well as the average white man, as we do not see all of them successful or making any more of a living.[7]

Returning again to quote Morgan Jones from the Walapai Papers:

Bud Grounds moved his cattle from Quail Springs to Crozier in Truxton Canyon in the seventies. Late in 1886 or 1887, after Spencer was killed, he and Crozier bought the Spencer cattle and obtained a lease on the western part of the reservation. Their sons took the business after the old men were too old to ride and run the outfit. Later the Interior Department bought them out and started the Hualapai Indian Reservation as it is today.[8]

By the 1920's and 30's, more neighboring settlers were finally supporting the Hualapai in their efforts to keep their own land and become self-sufficient. However, the railroad issue greatly complicated things.

In those times, railroad corporations had been given, for free, alternating sections of land (640 acres each) throughout this part of the country. These alternating sections had been given outright to railroad corporations by the federal government to allow free access routes for the corporations on which to build rails, and also to provide good incentives and land investments so corporations would build tracks farther and farther west. As time passed, railroad corporations then sold many land sections for profits and continue doing so, and to this day, still own many sections of western lands far from the location of any existing railroad tracks. For nearly thirty years the railroad corporations also requested, and were allowed, to retain alternating sections through Indian lands, as is still the case on most Indian Reservations.

The Ones Who Came Before

In the 1920's, Mr. Fred Mahone read a petition to Senator Hayden asking that Congress repeal the railroad's possession of these lands on the Hualapai Reservation. In 1930, a petition from the American Legion Post in Kingman also asked that the Hualapai be allowed to keep their homeland within the reservation boundaries, in its entirety.[9]

Under the Indian Reorganization Act of 1934, strides forward were made in providing certain rights for Indians. Other governmental acts in years following allowed more freedom, self-government, and implemented various economic development programs.

In September of 1941, Frances Sanita, author of an article called "The Hualapai" in *Arizona Highways*, wrote the following:

> The primary material basis of Hualpai [Hualapai] life lies in their herds of range cattle supplemented by corn, beans, squash, melons and a few peaches. In former times meat was obtained by hunting and there was a great variety of game on their range. The few farm products are prepared in very much the same way as the wild food. Corn is parched and ground on the grinding slab (metate) and either eaten dry, made into a mush, or cooked as soup usually with meat. A bread is made by mixing corn meal with water and baking as a loaf on heated stones. Corn is also roasted in the green husks and eaten on the cob. Beans are boiled with or without meat. When meat is not used, a few spoonfuls of lard are added as seasoning for the beans. Squash and pumpkin are eaten fresh or sliced in long strips and dried in the sun.
>
> Formerly the Hualpai dwellings were dome-shaped or single-slant brush shelters built on a four post foundation, filled out with a framework of small poles and branches, and covered with cedar boughs, juniper bark, or other brush, according to locality. Most houses had the open shade common in the south and there called a ramada. The ramada is a framework supported by four posts, with a roof of small branches and earth. Only a few of these houses survive. The present-day dwellings are cabins of lumber, tin, cardboard, and canvas. The housing is poor both as to health and comfort, and a vital part of the new federal program is to make possible for the people to build from their own lumber. Some houses already have been built.

Ms. Sanita described beautiful Meriwitica Canyon as a spectacular gash into the earth possessing garden lands used from time immemorial, and told of how the Hualapai took refuge from the invading white man there and eventually had to be starved out of the canyon. She also mentioned the thirty thousand acres of tall yellow pine present on the highest lands on the reservation, stating, typically, that those resources demanded a "development beyond the powers of these primitive people."

During the 1970's, the Hualapai Council did, indeed show that it had adopted the consumptive attitude toward the land so long practiced by Euro-Americans who migrated here. The Council promoted development of many resources on tribal lands; sold timber from the yellow pine forest, sold permits to white hunters to pursue and kill game on their reservation, grazed thousands of cattle over the rangelands, and allowed mining ventures for uranium and other minerals – even though some factions within the tribe, those more traditional who maintained the Native "long view" of time, still did not believe such actions would be truly beneficial for their people over the centuries to come.

In 1987, the Tribe initiated additional plans to develop *Grand Canyon West* as a major tourist attraction on the remote far western end of the reservation, this on a high overlook on the south rim of western Grand Canyon. The Council, in partnership with non-Indians and Chinese, plans to bring in tour buses, planes, speed boats on the river, and helicopter rides down into Quartermaster Canyon, this part of the Grand Canyon long called "The Lower Granite Gorge." On the rim, they are also building a restaurant and ranch backdrop for tourists. [Authors comment, 2014: traveling by boat into the western end of Grand Canyon is now like entering a loud buzzing beehive of bustling activity, as is also the situation on the south rim above, not at all the quiet remoteness and beauty I experienced when hiking the area previously ... I no longer return.] As of 1990, approximately 1200 Hualapai Indians live on these Reservation lands.

Roy Purcell, artist and poet from Las Vegas, Nevada, graciously gave permission to be quoted from the introduction of his book, *Long Journey from Wikame:*[10]

> The year was 1956, I had wandered from the mountains of my youth for the first time into the desert of our great Southwest, awed by the immensity of time and space surrounding me in this alien land. My footprints led me one lonely day into a cluster of tumble down shacks on Highway 66, fifty miles east of Kingman, Arizona, the Walapai Reservation settlement of Peach Springs.
>
> An old man whose life had spanned more than a century sat in silence inside a dark door. More than a memory, he was a legend, having known in his span of years the passing of many worlds, many ways of life. His recollections, voiced in the shadow of his cluttered shack, carried me back thru time to make a journey from the creation of his people to his infancy and youth wandering among the hills....
>
> He had known the coming of the whites, the subjugation of his people, and had been pressed into service as a scout with General Crook in the Geronimo campaign. He had known the pain of change; the coming of the railroad, the auto and the airplane, and had watched in darkness as the culture that had conquered his people pressed the heavens to expand their power into space. His life had been a race with time, his torn frame tired, and his face as furrowed as the road that led me to his crude and unlatched door .... To these beautiful people this crude story is dedicated hoping their memories will make us wiser when we are left to wander our own paths born of darkness and a sense of shame.

The Ones Who Came Before

In the text of *Long Journey from Wikame*, Purcell goes on to tell the story related by the old Walapai. Only a few verses will be quoted here:

From among us had come men of dreams

Chosen on the holy mountain

To heal

Knowing our spirits

And knowing their cures.

Our way of life was our religion

We knew no cross

Each meal was a sacrament

For which we praised the earth

And the earth responded

Nourishing us

Year after year.

But with the coming of the whites

A dark shadow crossed the land

Bringing new and alien spirits

In the wind

Beyond healing powers

From the young god

On Wikame

And we were left struggling

Inside ourselves

Against a new and alien god.

With a lust for gold they came

Driving us from the springs

And our homes

And hunting us like deer

The Hualapai

Forcing upon us

A way of life

Outside our experience

Releasing powers

Which our healers

Could not cure.

We were isolated from our source

Of life

Our land

Left homeless

And herded without a country

And the old way

Was ripped from our souls

Like a tree

Uprooted from the earth.

We fought to keep ourselves intact

Frightened by values

We could not understand

Faced with a god of violence

Praising love

While living

In a cloak of envy

And of hate…

The Ones Who Came Before

Typical Pai Camp from Ghost Dance of 1889. George Wharton James, courtesy SW Museum, (it's likely this is the Grass Springs site on Grapevine Mesa)

Beryl Arnold looking into a "Kanee" at higher elevations on Hualapai Lands

The Hualapai

Ben Welch coming down Meriwhitica Canyon, 1987

Sacred Cave in Meriwhitica, 1987

The Ones Who Came Before

Don Simonis and author at cave entrance

Ben by Spencer Creek in Spencer Canyon, 1987

Chapter Four: Trade Routes and Inroads

By 1300-1400 A.D. two different trade routes from the north and around western Grand Canyon were being used extensively by ancient people. The first was the aforementioned Old Ute Trail that crossed at present-day Pearce Ferry, near the mouth of Grand Canyon. The other, a little farther west, came down along the Virgin River (now emptying into Overton Arm of Lake Mead), crossed at Detrital Valley (near Temple Bar), continued south and went down to Willow Beach on the Colorado River, crossing into California. The Virgin River route had developed largely because of river accessibility from both the north and south, and also the presence of a large salt mine. Salt was a major trade item for indigenous people and later, also for newcomers to the area.[1]

Down on the lower Colorado River, excavations done in 1951 showed that the Willow Beach site had been a major trade crossing for well over one thousand years.[2] Another lesser river crossing appeared to have been a bit farther south, near the present town of Bullhead City. One story is that the Natives crossed at "Bulls Head Rock" (now under the waters of Lake Mohave) because there they could avoid quicksand.

Another route had been established around the eastern end of Grand Canyon, this becoming known simply as the Ute Ford (where Lee's Ferry is now located). The Utes from Utah and Colorado used this old crossing, as well as the Hopi and Navajo... both for trading and raiding.

By 1600, before the pilgrims landed at Plymouth Rock, Spanish explorers had already made inroads along the lower Colorado River and from Santa Fe into eastern Arizona. In 1776, the year the Declaration of Independence was signed, Father Francisco Garces, another Spanish-assigned priest, led an expedition across the lower Colorado River and headed west into the Mohave Desert in California. In that same year, Father Escalante and Father Dominques, with soldiers and guides, explored parts of the Arizona Strip country north of Grand Canyon and traveled amongst surviving scattered bands of Paiutes, although their exact route through that area is in question.

By 1826, frontiersmen had begun making their own inroads into the southwest. Jedediah Smith and a trapping party came into southern Utah and were visiting at Corn Creek (now Santa Clara near St. George) when the Paiutes told Smith of the salt caves down on the Virgin River, so the party continued south on river, passed the confluence with the Muddy River and several miles farther, found the mountains and salt caves. There they observed a lone Paiute farmer in the valley and they traded for salt. The Smith party continued to the junction of the Colorado, crossed, and took a precarious route along the shore southward, nearly losing their lives in the process. Eventually they were led by Natives to the safety of a Mohave village in present-day Mohave Valley. (Historically, spellings of Mohave and Mojave have long been interchanged). There, the Mohave people helped ferry the supplies across the river on reed rafts. The party continued on into California, however, before long Mexican officials turned the party back since they were without visas or trapping permits. Smith and his party then headed north and east via central Nevada, across Utah, and into Wyoming. They felt at least consoled that they had found what they called a "new southern route" (one long known and used by Native Americans) to reach the lower Colorado River and travel on into California.

Gradually more trappers found their way west and south. Many fell victim to Native hostilities that sprang from competition for food, fur, water sources, and other necessities. As increasing numbers of groups headed west to trap and hunt, they also, in turn, would avenge their friends whose luck had run out at the hands of frustrated Natives.

In the spring of 1827, Ewing Young, Kit Carson, and James Ohio Pattie, with thirty other men, were on the Gila River in southwestern New Mexico and southeastern Arizona. From there they pushed westward hoping to trap along the Colorado River. After reaching the Colorado, Young's men built dugout canoes (reported as being just like the ones the Indians used) and trapped northward by water. They ran into hostile Mohave's who tried to claim the furs taken from their area but the trappers came out victors in this particular confrontation.

Just above present-day Mohave Valley, the group eventually split. The majority went back east toward Santa Fe, and thereupon viewed their travels as "opening a new route" across northern Arizona. James Ohio Pattie and Thomas L. Smith continued up the Colorado River along its south bank and eventually entered this area of the lower Grand Canyon. This then, is the first actual recorded instance I found of persons other than Native Americans traveling into the western end of Grand Canyon.

As the Pattie and Smith party traveled up into the canyon, they finally reached Spencer Creek, and there, for some unknown reason, three men left the main party. When they didn't return after two days a search team was sent out from the main camp and the mutilated bodies of the three men were found. The remaining trappers decided it would be wise to come back downstream. Upon doing so, they once again crossed the Colorado River at an undetermined point (probably the Old Ute Crossing at Pearce Ferry), then headed northeast (perhaps via Grand Wash), and on up through Utah.

As an interesting side note, in the fall of 1827, this same Thomas L. Smith, while trapping with partners in the Colorado Rockies, was attacked by Natives and his foot badly mangled. With help from companions, he cut off the foot, bandaged his leg, and somehow survived. He recuperated for a few years with Ute friends on the Green River in Utah and from then on became known as Pegleg Smith. By 1829, he and ninety Ute companions had trapped along many Utah Rivers and also traveled south near present-day Las Vegas, Nevada, while en route to California. Upon arriving in California, golden land of opportunity, they found more profit in stealing horses from Californians than in trapping, so this became their new vocation for the next ten years.[3]

By 1837, a few hardy, adventurous, and/or desperate settlers had begun following the trails of Natives, explorers, and trappers, west to California. Many followed the Old Spanish Trail.

Trade Routes and Inroads

The Mexican War of 1846 changed political control of California and three years later gold was struck there, which drew fortune hunters like bees to honey. Government survey crews were organized to establish several main travel routes to the west coast. Francis Aubrey, a French Canadian, spent two years planning a wagon road from Santa Fe to California via northern Arizona (Aubrey's names was eventually given to the Aubrey Cliffs northeast of Peach Springs). According to Melvin Smith's *The Colorado River: It's History in the Lower Canyon Area*, in 1853, when Aubrey and his party actually made the trip, they crossed the Colorado River just below Black Canyon, possibly in the Eldorado Canyon area. The group built rafts and spent five days getting animals and supplies across. One member of the party, a Mexican boy, discovered gold about one mile east of the crossing, and as word of the gold discovery spread, prospectors and settlers came to northwest Arizona in large numbers. Fort Mohave was quickly set up to help protect newcomers from Native uprisings that the government knew would inevitably result from increased pressure on these native people and their lands.

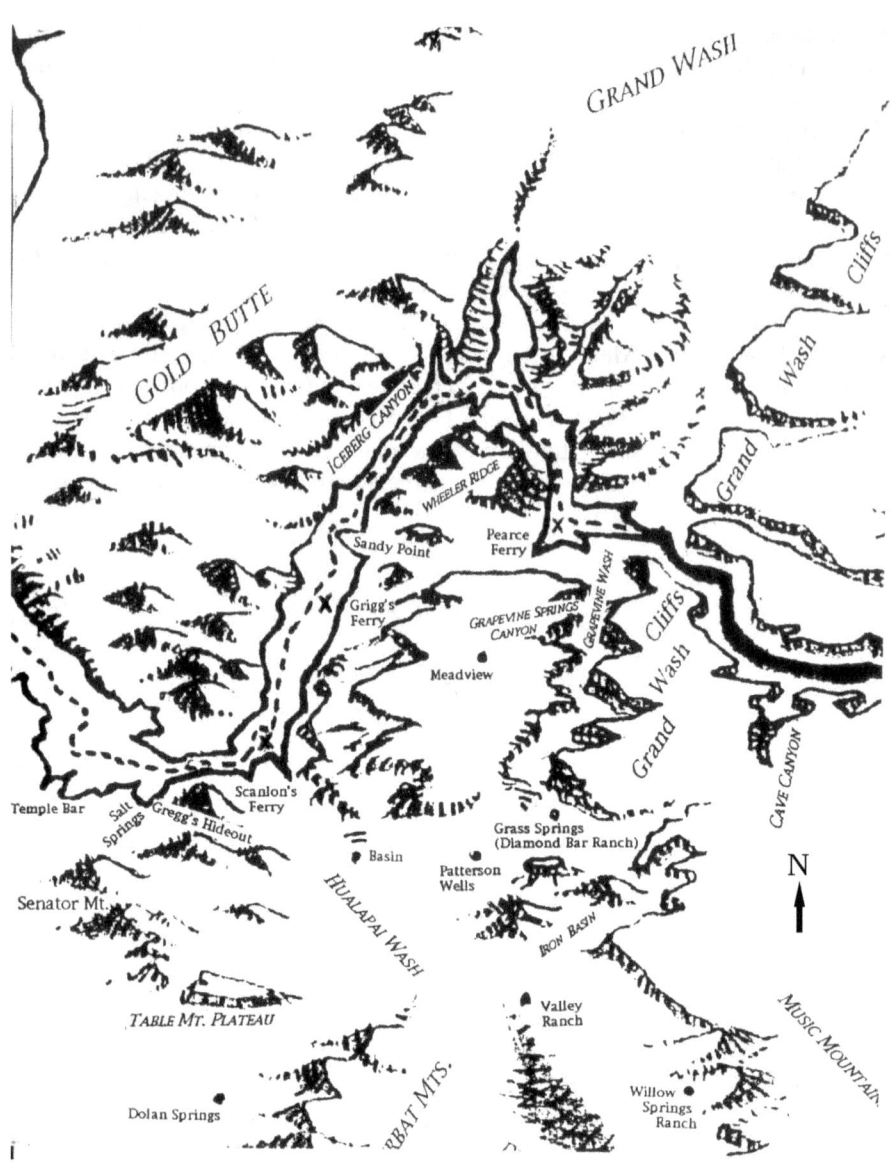

Excerpt from map showing detail of Pearce Ferry, Grigg's Ferry, and Scanlon's Ferry Crossings. Bonelli's Ferry was located farther northwest of Temple Bar and on the north shore. Map by D. Suzanne Wanatee-Buffalo

Part II: Raging River

Chapter Five: Pearce Ferry

Much of the following information about the historic western ferry crossings and lower canyon were made available in a remarkably researched PHD dissertation by Melvin T. Smith in 1972, for the University of Utah, with additional information drawn from a study done by Michael Belshaw and Ed Peplow Jr. for NPS in 1980.[1]

By 1860, Mormon leaders in Salt Lake City were seeking a southwest trade outlet to obtain a viable travel corridor for their members, one that would connect southern Utah to both central Arizona and to California and the Pacific Ocean. At St. George, Utah, in 1862, Jacob Hamblin and his men, who were preparing to start on their fourth trip to Oraibi in northeastern Arizona in attempts to convert Natives on the Hopi lands and secure settlements there, were instead, given instructions by Brigham Young, the Mormon leader in Salt Lake City, to search for a westerly route around Grand Canyon. Previously the men had traveled the eastern route, the Ute Ford crossing, near present-day Lee's Ferry.

Hamblin and his party headed south from St. George and into the Grand Wash trough, following the well-used Indian path, the Old Ute Trail. Just before reaching the Colorado River they came down Grand Wash Canyon (now Grand Wash Bay), following this to the river. They'd towed along a small skiff loaded onto wagon running gears, unloaded this, and used the skiff to cross the Colorado River at Grand Wash. The men had some difficulty taking out from the river on the south side due to the steep slope at Wheeler Ridge, but were finally able to continue traveling south and then on east to the Hopi village. They later returned to Utah via the eastern Ute Ford route once again.

It may have been this same trip that was described briefly in an article published in the *Meadview Monitor*, May, 1976. The article told how Mr. Ira Wakefield of Phoenix, Arizona, had given information to Pearl Glindmeier of Meadview that was taken "almost verbatim" from the diary of Mosiah Lyman Hancock. Hancock wrote of making a trip with Jacob Hamblin and nineteen other men in November of 1862, leaving from St. George, Utah, to search for a way over the desert to the San Francisco Mountains (near Flagstaff) and Moquis Indian villages (now called Hopi):

> ...We went from St. George to the mouth of the Grand Wash on the Colorado River. Isaac Riddle took a boat along that he had made. Andrew Gibbens stripped himself to the waist and helped swim the animals over the river. After the animals were over, we buried our boat and three days of provisions, hoping to meet here on our return home.

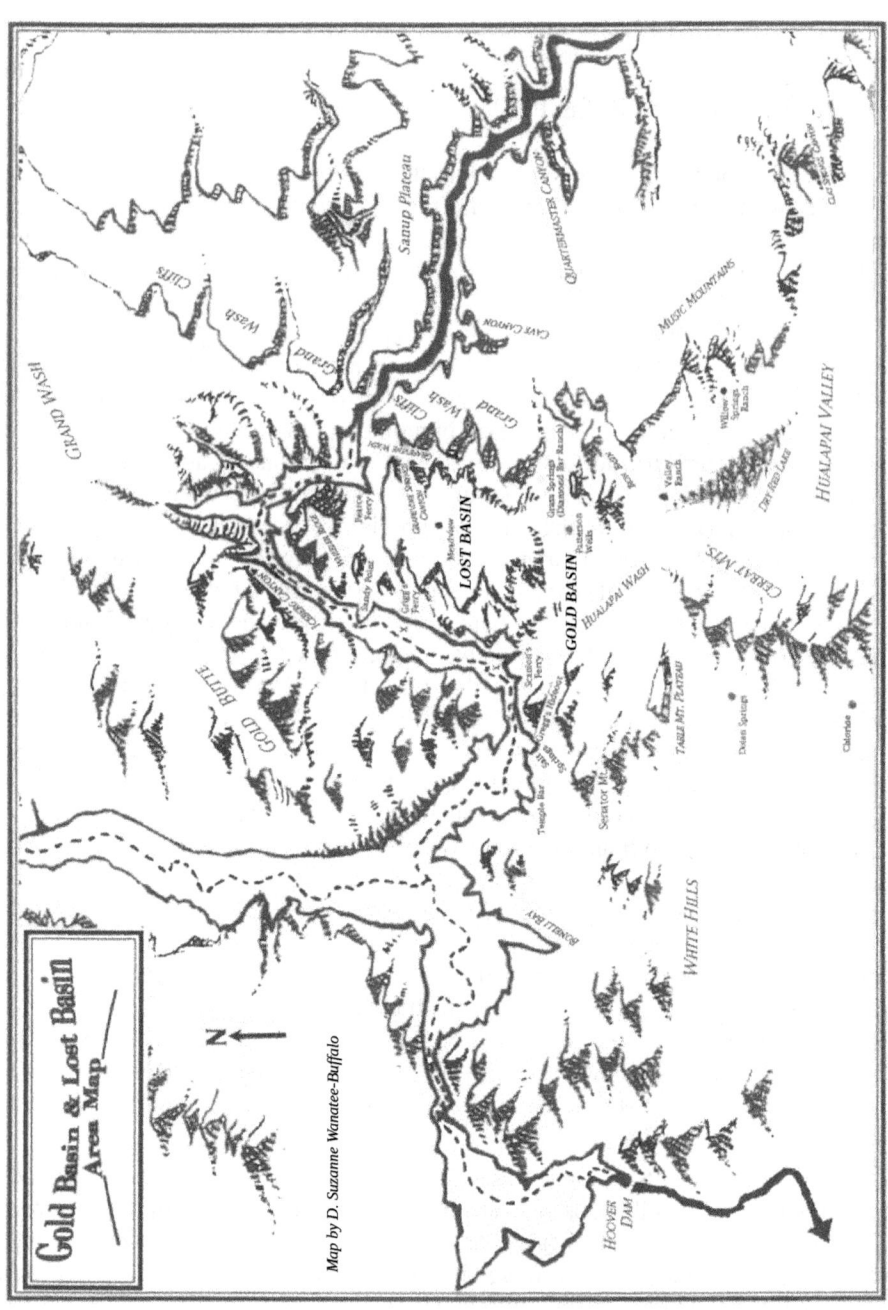

We went to Grass Springs where there was plenty of feed. The Indian guide had left us at the river and we obtained two more guides. Their heads were quite shaggy and they spoke a sort of Piute dialect. They were low in deportment and many of them were quite badly deformed. They were naked and when they first got sight of us, would run like wild deer until stopped by the guides. They would stop and look at us until by chance we might drop a cracker, then they would scramble for it. They were not farmers. All they seemed to comprehend was to keep out of our way and to eat cedar berries. I saw no other food among them. There were many of them not far from the river. When we went up the mountain country not far from the river, there were some deer.

When we came to the edge of the desert, our guides said they would never see us more. They left us soon after we left Peach Tree Springs, a spring with water fair, and which was surrounded by about 30 peach trees. We then steered for the San Francisco Mountains, to the east.

In March of 1863, Hamblin made another journey. The former trip and these following appear to be the first early recorded Euro-American large group crossings at what would later become known as Pearce Ferry.

This time, from the north shore, several of the men rigged a makeshift raft and crossed at Grand Wash, returning once more to the hidden boat remaining, but found the supplies spoiled. They took the boat back to the north shore. Some of the men who had remained on the north shore suggested there might be a better crossing farther upstream where they had heard of the "Old Ute Crossing." Several found an access route to that area by going north up Pigeon Wash to Snap Canyon, then down Snap for several miles, and east across the ridge into Pearce Wash, proceeding along the river to the crossing. Hamblin and his men then rowed the skiff upstream some distance above the rapids at Grand Wash and close to the area where Pearce's Ferry crossing was later to be located. There they crossed the river to the south side at Grapevine Wash and were surprised to find a white man waiting on the shore. It was Lewis Greely, nephew of Horace Greely of the New York Tribune, who had been sent to the river by another church leader, Erastus Snow, for the purpose of joining their party.

After crossing the river on this second trip, the men proceeded south up Grapevine Wash for eight miles to a spring and camped (no doubt at Grapevine Springs, known by Natives as Dinbah or Dinoah Springs), then moved on south to another spring known by Natives as Tinakah or Grass Springs (later, Grass Springs Ranch/Diamond Bar/Smith/Grand Canyon Ranch). From there they turned east and camped next at Milkweed Springs, which means they may have followed the same route going to the top of Grand Wash Cliffs as the present-day road that goes up through Grapevine Canyon and onto the plateau to the Hualapai Reservation, since there is a springs called Milkweed Springs at the head of Milkweed Canyon, this not far off the Buck and Doe road and about half-way to Peach Springs. Hamblin and his men eventually came to Cataract Canyon, visited briefly with some Havasupai Indians, then proceeded on east to the Little

Raging River

Colorado River and Hopi Villages. Upon returning home in May, they retraced their same route, again crossing near Pearce Ferry, and going on north to St. George.

In 1868, a group of St. George men under the guidance of Erastus Snow laid out a course for a regular wagon road leading from St. George to Pearce Ferry. According to Smith's dissertation, as well as the later report researched for NPS by Belshaw and Peplow, the route was located as follows:

> The road headed south from St. George and traveled to Black Rock Springs, went around the north and west side of Mustang Knolls, then down Black Canyon and Pocum Wash to the middle of Grand Wash. It continued down Grand Wash, then followed Pigeon Wash into Tasi Wash and to Tasi Springs. Here the road went up a side canyon to the east, crossed the wash and went up another side wash just above the mouth of Snap Canyon. Then it crossed another bench into Pearce Wash, and from there proceeded on to the Colorado River.

By this time Mormon Church authorities had become even more intent on finding reliable travel routes south from St. George and into Arizona. New outposts were being planned for the Mormon settlement of Mesa in south-central Arizona, and at Sunset near the Little Colorado River (close to present-day Holbrook on Interstate 40). It was still hoped a shorter and more reliable route could be established around the western end of Grand Canyon rather than the apparent longer one around the eastern end of Grand Canyon.

Interest had also increased over establishing this western river crossing since mining had taken hold in northern Arizona, southern Nevada, and southern Utah. With new finds in the Wallapai [Hualapai] District in northwest Arizona and also on the north side of Grand Canyon (to be discussed in "North of the River Country" section), two men, Al Huntington and Cy Hancock made plans to establish a possible "Hancocks Ferry" near the western end of Grand Canyon. Melvin Smith quoted excerpts from the Aug. 23, 1876, *Deseret News*, which in turn, acquired its data from the July 21 and July 28, 1876, *Wallapai Enterprise*. This told of how Huntington and Hancock had located some "rich placer mines with plenty of wood and water ... and decided to construct a ferry across the Colorado at the mouth of Grand Gulch." Their partner, a B.L. Duncan, expected to "soon run a line of buckboards between Mineral Park [in the Cerbats near Kingman] and Pioche [in Nevada]." Smith went on to state that this project was never completed even though the talked of road created new interest.

Two aspects of this report are puzzling. First, the quote "at the mouth of Grand Gulch." This may be in reference to a canyon coming down from the location of the Grand Gulch mine up on the Sanup Plateau, one eventually opening into the area of what is now known as Pearce Ferry. Secondly, I thought perhaps the partner mentioned, "B.L. Duncan," might have been related to the Tap Duncan's who settled later at Diamond Bar Ranch. There is a signature at Grapevine Springs (on the "Signature Wall" to be discussed later) of a B.T. Duncan from 1911, and while exploring near the Diamond Bar Ranch in the mid 1980's, I also found an inscribed name of Byron Duncan on a half-finished shack not far from the Diamond Bar Ranch. However, I have been unable to tie this family directly to the B. L. Duncan mentioned in the 1876 article. I did find several other passing references to the possible existence of a "Hancock's Ferry" but never could verify the actual creation or existence of any such ferry. Evidently plans for this ferry never actually materialized.

In 1876, a Mormon named Harrison Pearce did start operating a ferry boat to assist with crossings just west of the mouth of Grand Canyon. It's necessary to regress briefly in time to understand how he became involved, since his placement there was not voluntary.

A complicated series of events took place in southern Utah in the mid-1850's which will not be discussed in depth herein, but results of which led to the tragic massacre of nearly two hundred gentiles (non-Mormons), the Fancher party, who were crossing southern Utah in a wagon train in the fall of 1857. One version reported that Native Americans, encouraged by a group of Mormons and then joined by Mormon men dressed as Natives, initially attacked the wagon train while it was camped at Mountain Meadows, a pleasant high green valley located about thirty miles southwest of today's Cedar City, Utah. The Mormons involved helped kill everyone in the wagon train except children under the age of ten. One of the leading Mormons in southern Utah at that time, John D. Lee, actively participated in (some say, led) the massacre. Harrison Pearce, another active and devout Mormon who lived in the St. George area, also participated.

Much about the massacre remained cloaked in secrecy by members of the Mormon Church for years afterward, but finally, due to continued pressure from gentiles within the state of Utah as well as from those outside, it became apparent that someone would have to pay dues. Rightful or not, John D. Lee ended up getting the bulk of the blame. To escape pressure and investigations over those charges, he and several of his wives moved to the remote area at the east end of Grand Canyon on the Colorado River. Near the "Ute's Ford" crossing there, Lee established what he called the Lonely Dell Ranch and operated a ferry crossing to serve mainly Mormons, a crossing that then became known as Lee's Ferry. However, in 1875, Lee was captured when secretly trying to visit one of his other wives and family in Panguitch, Utah. He was tried and found guilty of murder, taken to the site of the Mountain Meadows Massacre, and, while sitting on the edge of his coffin, was shot dead by a firing squad and fell backward into his coffin.

Harrison Pearce was never officially charged with crimes associated with the massacre. He did, however, "receive a call" when church authorities ordered him to set up a ferry crossing service at the western end of Grand Canyon. He was, for all practical purposes, sentenced to provide ferry services, mainly for Mormon travelers, at this remote location.

Pearce, born in Georgia in 1818, had joined the Mormon religion and was baptized into the Church in 1845. He married, although a few years after bringing his wife and children to Salt Lake City, his wife passed away. By occupation

Raging River

Pearce was a teacher and musician. In 1857 Pearce was called to serve at the new Mormon settlement in southern Utah, at which time he brought with him a new wife, but this marriage did not last. Pearce and his older children then helped establish the town of Washington, Utah, near present-day St. George. Pearce served as the town's first postmaster, taught school, was elected sheriff of Washington County on one occasion, and also played in local bands and helped furnish music for theater presentations. In 1860, he took a third wife, a young Swiss convert, but no mention of her was made after that time. When Pearce was assigned to serve in the remote Pearce Ferry location, his two sons, James and Thomas, provided him with needed assistance.

Several more crossings at Pearce's Ferry were well documented. One began when several Mormon families assembled in St. George under the guidance of Bentley and Cunningham. They left early in March of 1877 to try the new route and ferry crossing west of Grand Canyon. There were ten wagons, thirty-five horses and mules, thirty cattle, and at least six families consisting of about twenty-six people. They came through Mokiac Springs, Wolf Hole, Hidden Springs, Pockum Pockets near Cane Springs, and into the Grand Wash drainage. From there, they proceeded on to Peep Pockets, Willow Springs and to Tasha Springs (Tassi Springs, near Tassi Ranch, about three miles north of 1980 water level at the north end of Grand Wash Bay). They reported there were two Natives living at Tasha Springs at that time. From Tassi, they ascended Pigeon Wash and had difficulty going down Snap Wash and over the ridge between Snap and Pearce Wash, having to use double and triple teams for some distance. The group camped on a ridge about two miles from the river where Pearce came over to meet them.

The next day they used Pearce's skiff to haul wagons and supplies across the river. They appeared to have had a pleasant crossing and toward evening Pearce treated the group to a moonlight boat ride. This, however, almost proved disastrous as Pearce became so totally enthralled with two of the girls as they sang a serenade that the group nearly drifted down over the rapids.

The following day was spent trying to swim the stock across. One man rode his mare into the river to lead the stock across but he was swept from her back in the swift current. He managed to grab onto her tail, but she swam back to the north bank and, again, all the stock followed. Some of the cattle were then hazed across, some pulled across behind the skiff, and some were brought across onboard. One man found he had a good "river horse" – she swam the crossing back and forth many times, driving stock and even helping to pull the skiff on one occasion.

The group left the river on March 21, traveled up Grapevine Wash to what they called Running Creek (Dinbah or Grapevine Springs) and the next day to Grass Springs (Tanaka). There they rested for one day, then continued south to a small springs east and above the Hualapai Valley (one of the springs in Iron Basin). From there, the group had great difficulty descending down a steep ridge into Hualapai Valley.

It's difficult to understand why they chose such a seemingly difficult route from Grass Springs at that point. Several friends and I hiked this route and were baffled. For a wagon to have descended down the ridge from the saddle in Iron

Basin and into Hualapai Valley would have taken great effort. The travelers would have had to unload wagons, lower them down a very steep incline, reload, and livestock would have had a very difficult time coming down this steep rocky terrain. There were two easier routes leading out from Grass Springs; the one turning west to detour only a few miles around Iron Basin, then descend gently past today's Patterson Corrals into Hualapai Valley – the other, to head east from Grass Springs, travel up through the pass to the top of Grand Wash Cliffs, then east, as several of Hamblin's parties previously had done.

A plausible explanation might be that tensions were apparently especially strained with Natives at that time. An interview in June of 1986 with Sadie Pearl Duncan, a Kingman resident who spent some time at the Diamond Bar Ranch in the 1930's, revealed Sadie remembering her Aunt telling about a group that had once come through and that they had been trying to avoid travel where they could be easily seen as the "Indians were on the warpath and that some were camped near Patterson Well."

Regardless, the group eventually did succeed in descending from Iron Basin down into Willow Springs, proceeded thirty-five miles across Hualapai Valley to the Stevens Ranch, then to Hackberry, beyond which they followed the Beale Road east to Flagstaff and the Little Colorado River, arriving around the 27th of April. After the conclusion of their two month trip, they wrote back to Brigham Young recommending that others not take this route.

A few other groups persisted over the next several years, however. David Kimball led a large group from St. George in the fall of 1879. Kimball sent instructions on this route to the Deseret News, March 24, 1880, after their trip was completed, giving estimated miles from one spring to the next. The information relevant to this area showed:

Black Willow Springs - 28 miles

Tahshari Springs (Tassi) - 10 miles

Colorado River (Pearce Ferry) - 12 miles

Running Creek (heavy grade & sand) - 8 miles

Grass Springs (heavy, carry water) - 14 miles

Iron Springs - 6 miles

Granite Springs (via Granite Pass) - 8 miles

Hackberry Springs (good road, carry water) - 35 miles

The next recorded trip took place in the fall of 1880. Another call had been placed by the Mormon Church for more families to settle in the Little Colorado River area. Several families, including those of N.R. Tuttle and John Tate responded. In St. George, the men were persuaded by Erastus Snow and James Bleak to haul lumber to the Pearce Ferry crossing when they went, in order to help build a new ferry boat. Their pay for hauling the lumber to the crossing was to be in tithing script and cotton factory credit.

On the way this group traveled through Price City and Bentleys Canyon (on top of the plateau), then to Wolf Hole, Pockum Pockets, and Cane Springs. While camped at Cane Springs their horses got loose and went all the way back to Wolf Hole and Tate had to retrieve them. From Cane Springs the group traveled to Grand Wash and Willow Springs (Black Willow Springs) where they found two Native women gathering squash, then proceeded on to Tassi Springs where there were five Native families living. They went on up Pigeon Wash and camped. The next day found them working their way down Snap Canyon, over a ridge, and to the Colorado River. On the north shore of the river was a small, flat, very weathered and cracked boat. The men used some pine gum traded from one of the Native women at Tassi Springs and caulked the boat enough so it could be used. No mention is made here of Harrison Pearce, so perhaps he was not at the crossing operating his ferry when this particular party came through.

A few days later they began work on a larger ferry boat, making two pontoon boats, three feet by ten feet and fourteen inches deep, then planked those together. The ferry was loaded with several wagons and, with ropes tied on the opposite bank, the ferry was pulled across. The men then tried to get the animals to swim across. After several attempts, two horses being led by men on the ferry did swim across. The third horse was a highly valued and fine horse. As they tried to lead him across, he balked in the deeper water, reared back and fought until someone let loose of the lead rope, then the horse simply sank into the river and disappeared.

The group decided they'd look a bit farther upstream for a better fording site (probably the Old Ute Crossing – location to be discussed shortly). Tate then tried swimming his horse across there several times but was swept downstream each time. Finally they decided to build a stall on the ferry so they could haul the stock over and this worked successfully. The whole process took them nearly a week.

In 1881, another Mormon party came to Pearce Ferry. The families of J.E. Stevens, Swenn Neilson, and Peter Nasstram traveled from St. George to the river. Again, no mention is made of Pearce being at the crossing. They managed the crossing quite well until loading two large oxen. The oxen became frightened and sat down, overloading the back of the ferry, which then began sinking. Two Paiutes tried to help by pulling on the boat, which proved fruitless. The boatman finally untied the oxen and let them swim back to the north shore again. The Paiutes also jumped into the current and swam for shore. The ferry, however, kept sinking. Naastram arrived in a skiff and rescued Nielson from the raft. Stevens soon found himself riding the partially sunken ferry through the rapids. Luckily he and the ferry made it through and landed on the shore below. The men pulled the ferry back upstream after which they finally did get the oxen across successfully.

During the summer of 1881, Harrison Pearce contacted several St. George merchants seeking funds to build a larger ferry boat. Woolley, Lund, and Judd, merchants and investors in St. George, decided to finance the ferry. Two loads of lumber were hauled to the crossing and another new ferry was built.

Take note of the name "Judd." Scratched on a unique rock wall at Grapevine Springs are many historic names (story to come later). One of the oldest on this, what I call "Signature Wall," is "J. Judd May 7, 1883." Recalling this and taking in this new discovery that one of the merchants who invested in the ferry was named Judd, my curiosity piqued once again. Then, one day in 1986, while passing through St. George with my mother and Ardee Buck, we took time to drive around and I noticed a quaint, old-fashioned candy store just across the street from an elementary school. The sign outside the candy store read, "owned by Thomas Judd." I soon found Mr. Judd inside, selling candy to a swarm of school children during their noon break. After the children left, Mr. Judd was kind enough to provide more information. He stated that his grandfather, Thomas Judd, was one of the merchants of Wooley, Lund, and Judd, who had often made business investments in St. George and surrounding areas. His grandfather also had a brother, Joseph, who was in and about this area during the 1880's and was the only J. Judd of whom he was aware. This Joseph may well be the "J. Judd" who left his name on the cliff wall at Grapevine Springs. Perhaps he and his brother, Thomas, had gone to Pearce Ferry in 1883 to check out their investment and had traveled on up to the springs during this visit, at which time Joseph had carved his name on to the wall.

In the 1950's, Mary Abigail Pearce Thomas, daughter of Harrison Pearce, wrote of her memories about Pearce Ferry when she visited her father there at age twelve:

> There were hundreds of quail [Gambel Quail, native to the area] everywhere. My father would call them and they would come like chickens. I used to go everywhere with him. He went out on a hill north of the ferry and got sand and washed out gold. The Indians had a farm on Grand Wash and raised vegetables. They would bring vegetables and take back fish. We also spent many hours exploring. Just back a little way there was a rock with a flat top and there was marked on top like three men lying down with their arms and legs stretched out. We used to go there and find all kinds of petrified things. We got rocks there to build a room.[2]

During the summer of 1882, another Mormon party from Milford and Frisco arrived at the river crossing, found the river in flood stage, and Pearce would not attempt to bring them across. The group retraced their route to above Tassi, turned west, went through St. Thomas Gap to the Virgin River, then came down the Virgin and crossed the Colorado at Stones Ferry (near Bonelli's) at Rioville. Needless to say, the report they sent back to Salt Lake City regarding Pearce's ferry crossing was not one of praise.

At this time, Daniel Bonelli, in Rioville, wrote letters to newspapers in Utah criticizing formerly published information that encouraged use of Pearce's Ferry as a main travel route. He stressed the hardships suffered during crossings there

Raging River

and pointed out that several groups had found it necessary to detour from Pearce's Ferry, backtrack, then travel overland to use his ferry at Rioville. This, plus the coming of railroads and other new wagon roads, brought less travel through this area and led to decreased use of Pearce's ferry as a crossing.

Sometime between late 1882 and early 1883, Harrison Pearce wrote to John Taylor of the Mormon Church and asked to be released from his call for serving at the ferry crossing, and requested the church pay off the $1200 debt to Wooley, Lund, and Judd. He estimated the worth of the ferry at approximately $3000. Pearce stated that he wanted to join his son, James, in Taylor, Arizona, to make his declining years more comfortable. Thus, he was released. Pearce passed away a few years later, at which time he was again back up in St. George, Utah.

In Smiths dissertation, there is a photograph of the Pearce Ferry area, looking upstream toward the entrance of Grand Canyon, one that was taken by E. C. LaRue in October of 1923, before Lake Mead had formed (this photo is also on file at Mohave Museum in Kingman, and appeared in the May, 1924, National Geographic Magazine). In the lower left corner of the photo are the remains of the rock walls of a structure. This is on the south shore where Pearce's rock house was said to have stood and could well be the ruins of his house. This site was later covered by the rising waters of Lake Mead in the 30's. Today one can still see remnants of the old road that came down from the north to the ferry crossing but this ends where the lake waters have shorn off the bench as the road turned toward the river. This old wagon road traveling north, however, is badly washed out at several spots as one follows it away from the shoreline until eventually becoming indiscernible. Maps from the early years (1880's on) often misspelled Pearce's name and the crossing became known as Pierce Ferry. In recent years, efforts have been made to correct this on publications.

A few miners and ranchers made crossings in years following, but for the most part, there was little additional activity regarding specific "crossings" at Pearce Ferry until after the turn of the century.

Little mention was made in these old historic reports regarding any pre-planning to deal with difficulties in crossing the river at this western end of the Canyon at different times of the year. Spring run-off from high mountains to the northeast as well as flash floods during summer rains in the Canyon, often made this part of the river extremely difficult to cross. Timing could be everything on this deceptively peaceful, yet very powerful, river.

Pearce Ferry

Harrison Pearce, NPS photo, undated

Original river course at Pearce Ferry, looking upstream into canyon (notice rock cabin remnants, lower center.) Photo by E. C. LaRue, Oct 1923

Upstream view showing west portal of the Grand Canyon. Grapevine Wash is on the right. The old Pearce Ferry road shows on the gravel slope to the left. Householder Collection, 1924

Chapter Six: Grigg's Ferry

Downstream from Pearce Ferry some fifteen miles or so, there existed another crossing on the Colorado River called Scanlons or Grigg's Ferry. Confusion exists regarding same, including the apparent misconceptions that these were two separate ferry crossings being operated simultaneously, and also that Grigg was spelled Gregg.

This ferry was located in the area now known as Greggs Basin on Lake Mead, between the present-day South Cove boat landing and Hualapai Wash, both on the east bank of what was the original river, and with Scanlon Wash located on the west bank. Thanks to information from Charles Grigg of Kingman, Arizona, grandson of William Grigg, and especially to Richard Smith of Chloride, step grandson of William Grigg, who spent many a lengthy hour relating family stories and providing valuable historic photos, much more accurate information is now available.[1]

Before Euro-Americans arrived, Native Americans used a crossing in the Greggs Basin area, although not to the extent of the Old Ute Crossing closer to the mouth of Grand Canyon. Hualapai Wash was a natural travel course to the river and very old faded petroglyphs still exist along this draw. There also was a good flowing spring not far from the river. Sand bars were present at the mouth of Hualapai Wash and extended out into the river. On the opposite western bank, a trail led northwesterly toward a wide sloping valley, later called Scanlons Wash, this leading up into the peninsular Gold Butte area of Nevada.

Michael Scanlon was a miner who first arrived in Mohave County in the 1880's. Dan Messersmith, in his *The History of Mohave County to 1912*, (1991) recorded little about the man except that his name was spelled Scanlan rather than Scanlon, however, abundant information exists supporting that the spelling of Scanlon was correct. Michael Scanlon prospected into Gold Basin and Lost Basin and worked a number of mines here. He eventually built Scanlon's Mill at Scanlon Springs in Hualapai Wash (these springs later went under the rising waters of Lake Mead). By 1885, Scanlon had a camp built at that spring and also a ferry boat down on the river to take himself and other miners across to the far side. It's recorded that Mike Scanlon established a post office in Lost Basin on July 11, 1882, and discontinued it in 1891. He also had a post office in Gold Basin at the old Burnt Mill Ranch site in September 20, 1890, and discontinued that in 1894. He patented the Scanlon-Childers mine, now known as the Empire-Manhattan, located just over the west edge of Grapevine Mesa. Scanlon eventually served on the Mohave County Board of Supervisors and was, for a time, chairperson. His full obituary will appear in the chapter on Lost Basin.

Scanlon also built a road going up the opposite Nevada shore, into, appropriately named, Scanlon Wash. This road took a difficult route, proceeding up a rugged mountain-side and then into the high basins of Gold Butte. The steep portion of the road is commonly known as Scanlon Dugway. The road that ran on into the high basin eventually connected with another to the north that ran from St.

Raging River

George (via Grand Wash) to the town of St. Thomas, which was at that time an active center on the Virgin River (St. Thomas was later inundated by waters of the Overton Arm of Lake Mead). In 1891, Mike Scanlon sold his ferry operation at Hualapai Wash to William Grigg. He then lived in Mineral Park (near today's Kingman) and Chloride and passed away there in 1912.

Several early crossings in the Scanlon ferry area were reported by Smith. A small group with several wagons and ten horses crossed in about 1885. Scanlon took them from Hualapai Wash to Scanlon's Wash where the party then went north. After a few days the party camped at Pakoon Springs (in Grand Wash) and while there, their horses ran off with wild horses, leaving the party stranded. The owner walked all the way to Price City, south of St. George, where he got J. J. Sullivan to bring horses and equipment.

In the fall of 1890, Preston Nutter, well-known rancher and land baron from Utah (story to come later), purchased some 5000 head of cattle in Arizona and moved them across the river in this area. The Nutter party came down Hualapai Wash and after looking up and down the shore for several days, often pushing their horses off steep banks into the river trying to find places for cattle to cross, finally settled on a spot near the location of Scanlon's Ferry. They managed to get 2,200 head of cattle to swim the river (no mention of what happened to the other 2,800) and then drove them northwest toward the Virgin River. There was a bad heat spell as they traveled across Gold Butte and the men and horses suffered greatly and many more cattle died. Eventually the cattle drive headed across Grand Wash and up into the Strip area.

When Robert Stanton, the engineer who did a railroad survey through the Grand Canyon in spring of 1890, floated by, he spoke of Scanlon's Ferry being in an open and flat area and mentioned Scanlon had an irrigated garden.

William Grigg walked into what is now called Gregg Basin from Silver Reef, Utah, (near present-day St. George) in the early 1890's. After buying Scanlon's ferry operation, William made some changes. Rather than occupy the camp at Hualapai Wash Bay, he chose a nice spot several miles north and set back from the east shore of the river, and there, built his ranch beside several springs and cottonwoods. He made two large pleasant ponds and eventually planted many trees, including figs and palms. He also extended the access road that ran from Hualapai Wash to the river so the road forked near the river, veered northward along the east shore, then headed on to the Grigg Ranch. The ferry crossing, itself, he located just below the ranch on the river shoreline, directly across from Scanlon's Wash.

After getting settled at his new site, William sent for his wife, Bessie, who was still in Silver Reef, Utah. Bessie, who had been previously married and had two sons, Tom and Bill Smith, had married William at Silver Reef and their first child, Edith, was born there. Upon hearing from William, Bessie, then very much pregnant with their second child, took her three children and joined a group of Mormons who were coming through, in order to join William at the ranch where this party planned to cross the river and travel southeasterly. They reached Griggs Ferry barely before her next child was born.

Grigg's Ferry

William Grigg eventually developed a very pleasant oasis down at this ranch. The ponds were beautiful and the fig and palm trees grew tall. He had fields of alfalfa and wheat, livestock of all kinds, and cattle grazed both sides of the river. William also built another access road to his ranch and ferry, this one a bit more challenging than the one along the river. The upper part of this road starts from on top Grapevine Mesa, the beginnings still visible right near the historic marker at the overlook on top the mesa, near the turn-off to Meadview. The old road works its way down the steep ridge and then swings north following the large flat valley. An even better view of this old road can be obtained by turning west off Pearce Ferry Road at the Meadview sign (four-wheel required) and following the old rim road out onto an unnamed point jutting west toward the lake (an outcropping overlook I called Christopher's Point, after my small grandson with whom I often visited this high promontory during the early 1980's).

After Griggs road reaches the valley floor, it soon becomes almost indiscernible, but follows the long valley north for several miles before coming to a low narrow place along a rock ledge. Located in those narrows are a number of very faint petroglyphs of ancient Native American origin, along with some black outlines of what appears to be a drawing of a miner, and also two names etched into the rock wall, "Fay-Tom" (story later, this is Tom, Williams stepson, and his wife, Fay). From there, the road angles west about one-quarter mile following the deepening wash, then veers up onto the left bank, at which point the land has been cut off abruptly by water action from the lake. From a boat, one can observe the end of this road as it comes out along the south shore of aptly named Wagon Trail Bay. Imagine, if you will, the road continuing downward to where the river once ran and you'll be looking at the location of the old Grigg's Ranch and Grigg's Ferry. On some navigational charts this underwater location is marked as the "Smith Ranch site." However, according to Richard Smith, it was always called the Griggs Ranch, never the Smith Ranch. Here, too, is the source of the name for today's Gregg Basin, although the correct spelling should be Grigg.

And what of the story behind "Gregg's Hideout," the current-day landing located south of Gregg's Basin? This road and boat landing were built much later, in the 1940's, under the direction of the Mohave County Board of Supervisors, simply to serve as an access point to Lake Mead for fishermen. According to Charles (Chuck) Grigg (John Griggs son and William Griggs grandson), his father, John, did help point out the area where he thought a good access road might be made to the lake, but the name Gregg's Hideout was tagged on by Johnny Mullin, a friend of Griggs, then serving as County Supervisor, as an afterthought and to give recognition to the Grigg family who had lived just upstream during a previous time. Alas, no exotic tales of a bandit's lair therein.

When William and Bessie Grigg were first ranching in Grigg Basin, another government survey took place just below the location of their ranch and this will be described before following the Grigg story further.

By 1902, the government and various utility companies began looking more seriously at possible dam sites on the lower Colorado River below Grand Canyon. Before the monumental dam project later to become Hoover or Boulder Dam was

Raging River

envisioned, two engineers, Lippincott and D. J. McPherson, were contracted to make a preliminary study by Edison Electric Company of a dam site in this area, right near the upper entrance to Virgin Canyon where Hualapai Wash drains into Greggs Basin. Dave Huntsinger, former Chief Naturalist for Lake Mead National Recreation Area, who retired in Chloride, Arizona, mentioned to me that he had in his possession a copy of both Lippincott's interesting pre-report as well as his diary notes when his group went on the river to study this area. Huntsinger said Sylvia Young had sent it to him and she had received same from Hugh McPherson Elliot, grandson of D. J. McPherson, the engineer who worked with Lippincott on the project.

Excerpts from this report will be quoted extensively here as they provide interesting details about this area at the start of the century and because information from this report is not generally accessible elsewhere.

> I received instructions from Mr. H.H. Sinclair, General Manager of your company, to proceed to certain points in the canyon of the Colorado River, names below, and make a preliminary report based upon the reconnaissance, both as to the physical feasibility of generating electric power by the water of the Colorado River and of selling said power to the mining districts bordering the river, mostly in Mojave County, Arizona.

> I left Los Angeles on this trip on October 6, last [1902], meeting with Mr. D. J. McPherson, a civil engineer whom I believe is presenting this proposition to your company, at Cloride,[Chloride] Arizona. At Cloride, Mr. S. W. Alger[?]nes employed the boatman to assist us on our trip down the River, which extended from a point called Greggs Ferry to The Needles, from which point I entrained to Los Angeles, reaching this latter place on October 16th.

> ...Both in connection with the expense of constructing a power plant and the present expense of doing business under existing conditions, the cost of a few of the stable supplies of this district will be of interest. Alfalfa hay at Cloride end of railroad costs $22.00 a ton, and delivered at the Colorado River costs from $25.00 to $30.00. California crude oil ranges from $1.62 a barrel to $2.10 at Cloride. Distillate at the same point costs 22 cents per gallon, and railroad freight from Los Angeles to Cloride to the river may be taken at $20.00 a ton, or at a rate of 1 cent per pound. Driftwood for fuel may be obtained along the river in small and uncertain quantities at a cost of $5.00 a cord. It is pine and cottonwood. The prevailing wages of miners in this district are $3.50 a day, day laborers from $2.00 to $2.50 a day. There is a good deal of Indian labor along the river which might possibly by obtained for $1.50 a day, but these men are only competent to do the lower grades of work.

> ...The town of Cloride seems to be the center of the mining district in Mojave County, Arizona. It is the typical mushroom mining town, consisting largely of unpainted shanties strung along either side of one long street which is

ungraded and little cared for. There are two stores, perhaps half a dozen saloons, two 'hotels,' no blacksmith shop and no harness shop. The town has the appearance of being built hurriedly and in such a manner that it can be abandoned without serious loss. The present population of Cloride is about five hundred people. The mines around Cloride and vicinity are largely galena, carrying silver, lead and gold.

The town of Whitehills, which is twenty-eight miles northerly of Cloride, from 1888 to about 1894 was the center of a greater mining activity than at present exists at Cloride. There were perhaps one hundred houses in Whitehills, all at present vacant with the possible exception of a dozen. They have two saloons left, but no store. The 'hotel' is unique, but the meals are sold at seventy-five cents each. Whitehills was a vigorous silver camp and produced a great deal of very high grade ore. The town at present is said to be suffering because of the low price of silver and also the fact that the mines are worked out, although shafts have not been sunk to depths greater than 500 or 600 feet.

There are numerous groups of prospects or claims scattered throughout the region around Cloride, but Cloride and Whitehills are the only 'towns' that were seen on the trip through this district. Kingman is a place of considerable importance, but I believe there are no mines closer than ten to fifteen miles from Kingman. Generally speaking the district extending from Kingman northerly to the Colorado River, and down the Colorado River to The Needles, seems to be extensively 'mineralized.' Freight rates and smelter charges, however, are so high that it is practically prohibitory to ship rock of value less than $50.00 or $75.00 a ton from points twenty miles from the railroad. At Cloride, rock of less value than $35.00 a ton is not shipped but is held, often in dumps, for some future date when it may possibly be more economically reduced. The ores are gold, silver, and copper in varying proportions and relations.

Geologically the country is largely of a porphyritic or volcanic formation and certainly has the appearance of being badly broken and faulted throughout the entire area. I am informed that this is one of the serious difficulties encountered in the mines, that is, the ledges frequently fault and are lost. There are few, if any, shafts driven to depths of over 600 feet, and the miners claim that this is not deep enough to demonstrate the reliability and value of their properties.

The high price of power is certainly a very great detriment to the general development of the country, as is also the universal lack of water throughout the region, except along the river.

…While this country may in the future develop some very great mining properties which would consume a large amount of power, this certainly is not yet in sight. Satisfactory evidence was not present of the development, either in the mines themselves or in the towns that supply them, of a market for the output of five thousand or ten thousand horsepower from the Colorado River.

...The Walapai dam site is situated at the point where the Walapai Wash discharges into the Colorado River. The canyon at this point boxes up for a distance of some seven hundred feet and has a prevailing width of from 275 to 500 feet. I believe the bedrock to be extensively covered with detritus at this point. The dam would necessarily have to be an overflow structure as no spillway opportunity offers at this or any other point observed on the river. The walls of the canyon are porphery and are badly shattered. Ledges of quartz and harder material run throughout the mass in varying directions. High water marks at the upper end of the dam site were noted twenty-five feet above the present low water stage of the river, and at the lower end of the gorge nineteen feet above the present stage. I do not see how it would be practical to put in a masonry overflow dam founded on bedrock at this point. I think that probably a loose rock dam with very flat slopes and low height might be made to stay in one place, but it certainly would be a difficult and experimental piece of work. Probably a cribwork structure would be the most feasible. The river has quite a flat grade and its volume will vary from a minimum of 4000 feet per second to a maximum of over 100,000 feet per second in flood stage. A wagon road comes to the dam site. There would be twenty miles of the pole line on rocky lands.

I have not prepared estimates on the cost of constructing a dam here; first, because there are better sites at lower points on the river in equally advantageous positions, and secondly, because I desire further instructions before proceeding to the task of preparing plans and computations of the cost. Sufficient, however, to say that it would certainly be accomplished with a very considerable expense, although I believe it is possible to put a structure in this canyon that would stand.

More interesting are the notes following that Lippincott wrote about the actual survey he and his group did on the river on October 9, 1902.

Diary of a River Journey

October 9, 1902. The Gregg (Scanlon) Ferry is run by William Gregg, P.O. Hackberry. There is a small farm here with vegetables, etc. This is about three miles above the dam site. The road from White Hills and Hackberry goes to Greggs Ferry and the dam site. Distance from Cloride to ferry is sixty miles; approximately the same from Hackberry. Store and blacksmith shop at Hackberry. Stores at Cloride.

The boat is 14 feet long and three feet beam, and flat bottom and square ends. It is made of rough Arizona pine. It was built at White Hills. The sides are sixteen inches high and it draws six inches of water. The boat is too small and should have a pointed bow for rowing purposes, as it is desirable to row almost continually in going downstream in order to gain headway for steering. It is very important to have air tight compartments at the two ends of the boat in which some supplies can be stored, so that if the boat should be upset in the rapids all provisions would not be lost, and the boat would not sink.

The start was made from the river at the Walapai dam site. At this point there is a long rapids with waves running from two to three feet high at this present low stage of the river. The boat fouled on a rock in the first one hundred yards and had to be unloaded and caulked. We made a second start at 3 p.m. and had a very interesting ride through this first rapid which was by far the most vigorous encountered this day. We passed through about eight miles of box canyon. Rock porphery, the canyon ranging from 300 to 500 feet wide at water line. Reached Senator Mill about 5:30 p.m. Distance traveled eight miles. This is a ten stamp mill and is in operation. [Senator Mill was in Salt Springs Wash].

October 10th. Started at 7 a.m. from Senator Mill. The valley through which the river ran this day's trip was open and the side walls were of soft sandstone and volcanic conglomerate. It is six miles from Senator Mill to the Temple Bar Mill. Just before reaching the mill there is a very prominent sandstone butte on the right bank which is quite beautiful. The Temple Bar mill is a large pumping plant to lift water for hydraulic gravel sluicing. The plant was built about 1898 and is now abandoned except that a watchman is kept there. It is a matter of common belief that the French company building this mill expended $250,000 on the plant. There is a telephone line to Kingman from Temple Bar. It was thought the mill could be run with driftwood, but this was found to be not true. Coal was then tried but its cost ranging from $25.00 to $30.00 a ton made it prohibitory as a fuel. From Temple Bar to Rioville [near Bonelli's Ferry on north shore] is about twelve miles. At this latter point the stage line from Cloride, Arizona, to St. Thomas and St. George, Nevada, crosses the river by ferry. Mr. Daniel Boenilla lives here and has a farm raising hay, etc. He maintains a weather bureau station and says that the rainfall the past year was .22 inch. The distance from Cloride to Rioville is sixty-five miles. Freight from Cloride is $20.00 per ton. The trip was continued to the head of Boulder rapids about three miles below. A series of small rapids passed this day, not dangerous, but some of them shallow. Mr. Boenilla says that there are no operating mines in his vicinity, but that there is a great deal of mineral which is not worked because of high smelting charges and of high cost of power. One great trouble is that the absence of water in the mountains as well as fuel prevents the generation of steam power, so that shafts cannot be sunk to depths over 150 feet which can be done by hand. Camped at mouth of Saco Valley Wash [Sacramento Wash].

Raging River

October 11th. Traveled over a series of small riffles to the entrance of a narrow box canyon which is Boulder Canyon [between present-day Temple Bar and Boulder Beach]. ... Near the upper end the canyon is 215 feet wide and a sounding showed fourteen feet of water. The rock of the canyon is granite and in large true ledges. The sides of the canyon are very steep on the right bank, say 60 degrees from horizontal and on the left 75 degrees. The rock sides are just about as steep as they can stand. This box canyon is about half a mile long with widths varying from 240 feet to 300 feet, and cliffs as described above. Depths of water vary from 14 feet to 40 feet. At the lower end of the box, two side drainage lines enter one on each side offering possible opportunities for the construction of power houses, etc. This is the best dam site that was observed during the trip down the river, both as to the narrowness of the river or availability of large quantities of rock for use in the dam. A dam twenty or twenty-five feet high would overflow the farmlands of Mr. Boenilla which, however, are not of great value. A crib-work structure would probably be the most feasible form of construction for this point. A wagon road comes within ten or twelve miles of the dam site.

Below the box [canyon] about half a mile there is a long rapid that is quite rough and numerous rocks are in the channel, making it bad for a boat in low water. As many as six boulders were struck by the boat in running this rapid. Passed through the remaining part of Boulder Canyon to Old Fort Callville without event of interest. The Canyon widens after passing the first box and offers no opportunity for dam sites...

In conclusion it may be stated, First, that an excellent dam site, as far as width of canyon and side walls is concerned, exists near Rioville at the head of Boulder Canyon, and Mr. McPherson filed notice appropriating water rights to his use of power at this point on October 11th. No surveys, however, have been made to claim public lands within the reservoir site that would be flooded. Second, that a dam site at the mouth of Walapai Wash is of indifferent value. Third, that there are other possible dam sites on this river, notably Black Canyon [where Boulder/Hoover Dam was later built downriver], that are not filed upon and it would be difficult for one person or corporation to control them all. Fourth, that while the district in question is very generally mineralized, it is exceedingly remote from ordinary transportation facilities and there are very few actually producing mining properties on an established basis, and as far as power consumption is concerned, no towns. Fifth, a power company to be successful would have to very liberally assist in the general development of the country before it could obtain substantial returns for its investment. An effort was made to get someone to go to work at the Walapai dam site (first visited) but Mr. William Gregg, Post Office, Hackberry, Arizona, was not at home. If desirable, arrangements can be made with Mr. Daniel Boenilla, Rioville, Lincoln County, Nevada, to begin work on the Boulder Canyon Dam site.

Grigg's Ferry

Awaiting further instructions, I am,

Very truly yours,

(signed) Lippincott

Perhaps the misspelling of "Gregg" originated from this report, as well as the assumption that Scanlons and Grigg's were the same ferry site. And, of course, Boulder Canyon was not the site eventually chosen as the dam site, but instead, Black Canyon, on downstream where the monumental Hoover Dam now sits.

In 1912, when Emery Kolb and his brother made their trip down the length of the Colorado River, they reported Grigg's Ferry being "in charge of a Cornish man, who also had as pretty a little ranch as one could expect to find in such an unlikely place." Kolb said the ranch had lots of livestock, date and fig trees, honey, and that the owner sold them food supplies he had produced.[2]

With that, we return back to the Griggs Ranch and the information provided by Richard Smith of Chloride, grandson of William Grigg. The Grigg family grew in number and over the years four more children were born to William and Bessie; John, Lottie, Janey, and Nettie. William's mother, Mary, came to live with them but passed away in the late 1890's. She was buried near the ranch and later, when the waters of Lake Mead began to rise, her grave was moved to the cemetery in town. William Grigg, himself, passed away in about 1913. William's two stepsons, Tom and Bill Smith (Tom was Richard Smiths father), grew up on the ranch and helped their mother, Bessie, with ranching operations and the ferry boat crossing during following years.

Richard said that his father, Tom, talked about the Indians who still occasionally came down to the river near the ranch, usually to gather mesquite beans as there were a number of mesquite and willow trees along the water's edge. Richard also remembered his grandmother mentioning how she wished she'd picked up some of the metates, cast-off necklaces, and other Indian relics that had been lying along the river.

Some of the persons interviewed remembered the two boys at the Griggs ranch and called them "Tom and Willy Grigg," however, according to Richard, Tom and William always retained their last name of Smith. After the boys matured, a day came when an old man introduced them to two young women, the Kittrell sisters, Fay and Irene. The two brothers eventually married the sisters and both couples then lived at the ranch, intermittently, working the cattle, operating the ferry, tending the fields, and mining at various camps in the area. Here then, we discover the origin of the "Fay-Tom" inscription still clearly legible on the rock wall along the cut down the old wagon trail road. This was Tom and Fay Smith, and Richard estimated the inscription must have been chipped into the wall sometime around 1920.

In 1922, Bessie Grigg recorded her brand in both Nevada and Arizona, this being the "Flying Cross." Tom Smith recorded his brand as the "Lazy SV," and William Smith, the "Triangle A Triangle."

Raging River

Slim Waring, a rancher from the Arizona Strip country north of the Grand Canyon, crossed a herd of cattle at Grigg's Ferry in 1916. George Harman also crossed with a herd. Sharlot Hall, in her book, *Sharlot Hall on the Arizona Strip*, 1911, mentioned stopping at Gold Butte on the Nevada side, which had "passed its prime," then went down to Grigg's Ferry, crossing there into Arizona. She described the ferry boat as rather rickety and said the ride was very exciting. Her party then went up Hualapai Wash, though the Yucca forest (Joshua Trees) to Dolan Springs, into Chloride, and on into Kingman.

As years passed, Tom and Fay Smith had three children: Thomas, Richard (our source for much information) and Howard. Richard Smith was born at Grigg's Ranch in 1925 and lived there until the waters of Lake Mead inundated the area in 1935-36. Bill (Tom's brother) and his wife, Irene, had two children, James and Betty.

Tom Smith had a 1928 Model A Ford Sedan and when they came out from the ranch, they usually drove south along the valley and river, then traveled up through Hualapai Wash. It took all day just to get into town, they'd spend the second day there, and the third day they would come home again. On the way home, they'd oftentimes return to the ranch via the steeper new road William had previously built down off the mesa.

On rare occasions, they'd also come out this steep route, but it was a real challenge. Tom would bring his pair of small mules along (he called them "Jeanettes," saying they were not "Jennys") and when they got to the steep "s" turns coming up the side of the mesa, he'd hook the mules up to the front of the Model A and they would pull the car to the top where the overlook and historic marker are now located. He'd unhook the mules and ride them back down to the ranch, mount his horse, ride it back up to the top, turn it loose, whereupon the horse would return to the ranch by itself. The family would then proceed to drive into town. Richard said his father related that the first car he ever saw make it all the way to the top of that steep road by itself was a 1929 Buick.

Richard had memories from the ranch of watching his Uncle Bill get his gun, saddle, and gear together in the morning, then Bill and Richard's father, Tom, would tie Bill's horse behind their rowboat and they'd row across the river with the horse swimming behind. Bill would saddle his horse, work cattle across the other side all day, and come evening, he'd "give a holler" from the other side and Tom would row back to pick him up again.

They had all kinds of animals at the ranch; pigs, turkeys, chickens, mules, horses, dogs, cats, and even bees. There was one pet pig that followed family members relentlessly and often tagged along after Tom during his daily routine. On days when Tom would swim his horse across the river to work the cattle on the other side, the pig would swim right along behind. She'd root around over there all day while he worked the cattle, then when he swam his horse back at the end of the day, she'd swim back home behind him. For some reason, the thought of a pig swimming leisurely back and forth across the mighty Colorado seems oddly incongruous.

Grigg's Ferry

Richard also related how the family coped with ants, an unpleasant phenomenon common in desert country. The family would simply set coffee cans half-filled with water under the legs of tables, chairs, and beds, and this would keep the ants down. Bob Watkins, from Meadview, recalled Chuck Grigg telling him the family used bamboo reeds to run water from the springs into the house. They would put plugs in the ends of the reeds when water was not needed, then simply unplug the reeds when they wanted water.

During river crossings, the men maneuvered the ferry boat competently, pulling it upstream some distance, then using a long oar to steer it across the river as they worked downward and to the opposite shore. Richard Smith had in his possession an old journal showing some of the fees charged for various services and crossings there from 1917-1924. Selected items taken from the notes are copied as written (question marks designate words neither he nor I could decipher):

June 17, 1917 Ferrying over river

1 man 2 Jacks $3.00

2 wagons 10.00

1 man 1 horse 1.00

meals 2.00

horse feed 1.00

1 man 3 horse, horse feed 4.50

1 man 5 horses, horse feed 7.00

(Lea [?] Anderson not paid)

2 ways, 2 men, 2 horses, 2 jacks, feed 8.00

1 borow [sic] wagon 5.00

Brooks o wagon cross

3 horses 1 wagon

2 horses 1 wagon, hay (.25) 5.25

4 horses 1 wagon 7.00

1 man on foot, eggs 1.20

1 man on foot, 1 meal 1.50

2 teams over river 10.00

1 chicken (.75)

Raging River

3 ¾ lbs. dates (.75) 1.50

1 man 2 mules 3.00

1 single reg job on ranch 4.50

Joney [John?] Nelson and automobeal [sic] 5.00

28 lbs. dates 5.60

1 single pig nothing

1 team 2 ways 10.00

2 men 4 jacks honey (.45) 6.45

automobeal [sic] 2 ways, help on [?] 5.00

Government outfit 10 mules, 5 wagons, from the 1st of Jan. 1918 30.00

1 man 2 horses, 2 nights feed 5.00

2 men 3 jacks 2 ways 5.00

2 men 7 horses, feed 14.50

on ferrying and loaned out

Heady [?] Brinkman

twenty dollars [sic] in cash 20.00

2 trips over riv 10.00

helping up mountain 5.00

25 received 25.00

10 dollars credit yet 10.00

corn, onions, carot [sic], melons, pumpkins (seed) 14.00

1 man 4 jacks, feed 6.50

32 head cattle, 75 cts. Per head 24.00

helping cattle on mountain 2.00

Jim Rivers [?] bill ferrying hay 6.00

cash on yearling stear [sic] 35.00

1919 ferrying over river 9/5

2 men, 6 horses, feed 10.50

6 meals, 3 super [sic], 3 breakfast 3.00

48 horses pastur [sic], 10 cts. head 4.80

helping swimming horses 4.00

by cash $20.00

ferrying and hay 3/18, 1918

W. T. Grounds and Co.

3/18 7 horses 2 men 9.00

5 horses feed 2.50

30 horses pasture 3.00

4/2 2 men, 6 horses 8.00

6 horses feed 3.00

4/20 4 horses feed 2.00

1919

Clay Springs Cattle Co.

8/30 3 horses feed, 2 meals 6.00

8/31 3 horses feed, 6 meals 8.00

9/1 9 horses feed, 8 meals 5.50

9/1 river Crossing 20.00

9/12 G. T. Duncan 1919

bill of ferrying and working

2 men, 5 horses over riv. 7.00

3 days harrowing 15.00

1 day work on fence at Patterson wells 3.00

W. S. [?] Brooks bill

6/14 2 boxes matches .20

6/14 3 lbs. honey .45

Raging River

7/19 15 lbs. honey 2.25

7/22 1 plug tobacco .60

7/29 75 lbs. what [wheat?] 2.25

32 lbs. wheat .96

9 lbs. beans 16 cts. Lb. 1.45

7 ½ lbs. sugar .75

Chas. Cox bill

15 lbs. honey 2.25

hay .25

shoeing horse and shoes 1.25

25 coal .50

1 black hen .75

2 days plowing .10

Oct. 5 1919

40 chickens 46.25

10/16 1 pig dressed (120 x 25 lbs.) 30.00

2 live pigs 60.00

11/24 13 turkeys [?] 119 lbs. (.40 cts) 52.80

1/1 1920 from county clerk 55.00

1 bull of John Nelson 50.00

Bigs

Trip to Ceneter mill [Senator Mill in Salt Springs Wash] 8.00

and back to basin 1 day 8.00

and back to river 1 day 8.00

and back to basin 1 day 8.00

and back to river 1 day 8.00

crosing [sic] sittleboat crosing [sic] auto 5.60 [?]

14 lbs. port Burchard $3.50

Various notes, sketches, and words to an old song were also handwritten in the journal. And on the last page, the brands were once again penciled in, but with one additional noted: "H+", "H Cross."

Richard has clear memories of the untamed Colorado River being very changeable; sometimes it was calm and smooth and moved along so quietly, other times it was wild and turbulent, making such a roar it sounded like a freight train thundering through the valley.

By 1928, Tom was working more at the mines in both Lost Basin and Gold Basin. At one time he owned half interest, along with Mrs. Henry Selde from Bend, Oregon, in the Mockingbird and Bluebird Mines. While mining at the Cyclopic in Gold Basin or at the old Scanlon Mill, Tom often took his family along and they'd stay in cabins or tents.

Just before the 1930's, the United States Bureau of Reclamation purchased all the ranches and homes located within a certain distance from the Colorado River and the boundaries of where new Lake Mead would form. Griggs Ranch was one of these. Richard recalled his father received somewhere in the amount of $3000 for their ranch.

In the early 1930's when Bessie and her sons and their families were notified that they must move out, they had a big round-up of all the cattle and took as much equipment and goods as possible. As they were leaving, Tom turned loose his favorite horse and two mules so the animals could live out the remainder of their lives wild and free.

One time, as the waters of Lake Mead were rising, Richard remembered his father bringing him back out to the area by car and traveling the old road down Hualapai Wash. At the end of the wash, they turned north and started on the road toward the ranch, but by then the water had reached back into coves and was over parts of the road, already making it impassable. They turned back, never to see the old home site again.

Raging River

Richard Smith in Chloride, AZ, 1987, source of valuable information and many historic photos for this chapter

Grigg's Ranch, upper pond, before 1920

Grigg's Ferry

Grigg's Ranch

Tom Smith on ferry

Raging River

Bill and Irene fishing

Bill Smith holding rope (Richard thought the woman was Grandmother Grigg)

Grigg's Ferry

Tom and Fay, Bill and Irene at ranch, about 1924

Haying time at Grigg's Ranch

Raging River

Tom, Irene, and Bill and swarm of bees at ranch

Prince, bred at Griggs's Ferry. Tom Smith, owner, 20 years of age

Grigg's Ferry

Fay in dug-out boat

At top, after being pulled up by little mules. Bessie, Tom and Bill, 1923 or 1924 (this is at the present historic overlook at Meadview, AZ)

Raging River

Fay, Richard, and Tommy at Cyclopic Mine, around 1929

Tommy (4) and Richard (2 ½) at Cyclopic Mine

Grigg's Ferry

Mill Crusher at Scanlon Springs

Scanlon Springs Camp in Hualapai Wash, looking northerly, 1929-30

Raging River

Feb 1930, Colorado River at camp by mill. Tom, Tommy, Richard. X in background is mountains in Nevada. River is below dots. Tom built this cabin.

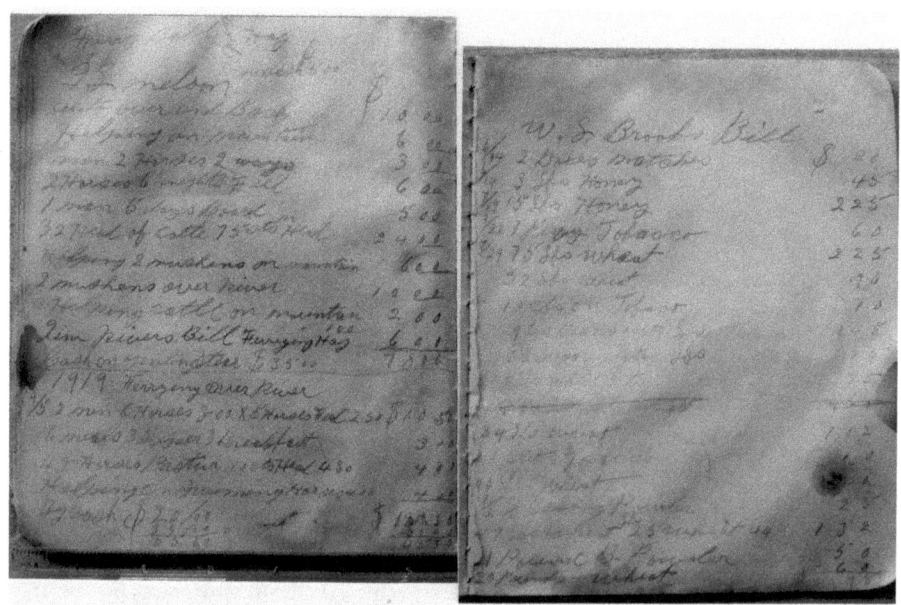

Several pages from old Grigg journal

Grigg's Ferry

Lake at Scanlon Springs where Griggs used to have the mill, June 4, 1936

Fay-Tom inscription and petroglyphs along old Griggs Road, Susan Pettijohn inspecting, 1989

Looking down old Grigg Road from overlook at Meadview, 1987

Grigg's Ferry

W-3 Party with the Smiths, 1923, Best Wishes, R. W. Burchard

Upstream view of valley at Griggs Ferry from a point just below Hualapai damsite, 9-27-24. Householder Collection at Mohave Museum in Kingman, AZ

Raging River

Camp on gravel bar at lower end of Hualapai Rapids, 1924. Householder Collection

Chapter Seven: Bonelli's Ferry

Downstream from Griggs Ferry in what is called Virgin Basin near present-day Temple Bar, there were two more ferry crossings. The oldest was called Stone's Ferry. This existed by 1870 and was located west of Detrital Wash. Several sources say this ferry may have been named after a man named Stone.[1,2] Other sources suggest the name was derived from the crossing, itself – "in low water, rocks were visible in the river and Indians were reported to have crossed on them," and an early 1880 Eckhoff map also designates this spot simply as "stones."[3,4] In 1871, the ferry was run by Jim Thompson who was later a pioneer at Oak Creek Canyon near Sedona, Arizona.[5] In the spring of 1876, Thompson sold the ferry to Daniel Bonelli. By 1877, Bonelli had moved the ferry operation upstream several miles and across to the north side, allowing easier crossing from Detrital Wash on the south shore and then to the mouth of the Virgin River on the north side.[6]

Daniel Bonelli was born in Switzerland in 1836. He had become a convert to Mormonism in his home country and was banished from there for converting several hundred of his countrymen to the Mormon faith. While onboard ship to America in 1859, he met Ann Haigh, and they were soon married. They traveled to St. Louis and went by ox-team from there to Salt Lake City. They stayed in Salt Lake City for a time until Brigham Young asked Bonelli to help establish the new Mormon settlement in southern Utah.

Bonelli helped lead a wagon train of Mormons to southern Utah, arriving in Santa Clara (near present-day St. George) in 1861. The new settlers lived in dugouts with brush roofs but those were quickly swept away by storms. They then put up buildings in the shape of a fort which was also swept away in floods, along with their crops. The party decided to move farther down along the Virgin River to Beaver Dam (near present-day Littlefield, Arizona). The new settlement grew and prospered at Beaver Dam until 1868 when another flood hit, this one sending a seven-foot wall of water through the area destroying all homes and crops once again. Bonelli, not one to give up, decided to move his family still farther downriver to the newly forming town of St. Thomas, located at the confluence of the Muddy and Virgin Rivers.

St. Thomas had originally been part of Arizona Territories, but in 1866 Congress ceded the area to Nevada. Mormons resisted this move and continued to pay taxes to Arizona for several years. In 1870 a new land survey supported Nevada's claim to the area. Then trouble brewed for the Mormons once again as Nevada demanded payment of several years back taxes which few residents could afford. Most chose to return to northern Utah, however, Daniel Bonelli and his wife and family opted to stay.

Bonelli kept his farm and croplands at St. Thomas but decided that with mining increasing in northern Arizona and southern Nevada and more people needing transportation across the Colorado, having a ferry located right at the junction of the Colorado and Virgin Rivers would be ideal. Hence his purchase of Stone's

Raging River

Ferry and the subsequent move of the ferry location. Near the new location, using driftwood that had come all the way down the rivers (including tree trunks, fallen railroad ties from bridges, etc.), he built a home on the east shore of the Virgin River. Next he built a large natural stone home on a mesa above. New lumber he needed was hauled in on a trail from Mt. Trumbull up on the Shivwits Plateau over 150 miles away, at a cost of $150 per thousand feet. A huge cellar was dug into the hillside behind the house. Walls and foundations of the house were made of natural stone and heavy painted canvas was used for ceilings and inside walls. Five of the rooms even had fireplaces. It was an impressive home for such a remote and obscure place.

By 1881, Bonelli had a herd of cattle on the Arizona side of the river, some fields of crops and vegetables near his river home, a post office and small store and the ferry crossing, and employed a number of Natives and several Euro-Americans as laborers. Bonelli called the place Rioville. He sold beef, hay, vegetables, and salt obtained from the salt mines on the Virgin, to Mormons, miners and travelers. According to Messersmith's *History of Mohave County to 1912*, Bonelli's daughter, Elizabeth, eventually became the third wife of Mormon leader Jacob Hamblin.

Minor traffic came to Bonelli's via the lower Colorado River. After ringbolts were finally installed along the cliff walls at Roaring Rapids downriver in Black Canyon, it was possible for boats to be winched through that rapids and paddle-wheel river boats sometimes reached as far as Bonelli's where they took on food and other supplies to be delivered to mining communities back down along the river.

Heading south from St. Thomas, the road to Bonelli's crossing descended to the river just east of his rock house. Accessing the ferry was not difficult from this direction, in contrast to a steep and difficult exit on the south bank. Native workers often pulled the boat upriver on the north shore for several hundred yards so they could row across the river to hit the south side just above the steep banks in Detrital Wash.

The post office at Bonelli's Rioville served as a way station for pony express mail riders as well as wagon mail deliveries and for occasional stage coaches traveling from Kingman and heading north to mining centers in Pioche, Nevada. Lippincott had stated:

> …From Temple Bar to Rioville the distance is about twelve miles. At this latter point the stage line from Chloride, Arizona, to St. Thomas and St. George, Nevada, crosses the river by a ferry. Mr. Daniel Boenilla lives here and has a farm raising hay…

The famed cross-country pony express of which many have heard, appears to have actually operated for little more than one year, from April 1860 to October 1861, over a route from St. Joseph, Missouri, to the west coast, nearly 2000 miles. The route did cross Nevada, however, where many shorter pony express routes had been running prior to the famous one and continued for quite some time afterward. Interesting stories exist about these pony express riders. Many of them

Bonelli's Ferry

were young boys since contractors wanted light-weight riders who would not tire the horses quickly.

The following information comes from an article written by Georgia Lewis, published in the *Nevadan*, August 30, 1970, called "Star Pony Express and Its Boy Riders."

> The riders filled a great need in the remote and sparsely settled areas of Southern Nevada, from Pioche to St. Thomas and Rioville. Northern Nevada mail routes had been well established by the 1860's. But it was only Las Vegas, in the south, that had a good postal service. Leonard Conger had carried the U.S. mail from Salt Lake to San Bernardino, passing through Las Vegas, from 1851 to 1854. He traveled alone during those three years as he rode along the Old Spanish Trail. Major Chorpenning took over the route in 1854.
>
> The settlement now known as Las Vegas established a post office called Bringhurst in 1855. This area was then in New Mexico territory which already had a [town named] Las Vegas. Chorpenning sub-contracted the route to a Mr. Leach, and Conger continued to ride the mail for him through to Salt Lake. Helping him were John Hunt, Jim Hunter, and David Savage. Conger's son was later to become a Star Pony Express rider.

New settlements and communities would often give mail to people passing through in hopes they would take it on to existing mail routes. Sometimes men and boys would gather enough subscriptions to run their own express route that joined up with U.S. Postal routes. They usually charged fifty cents to one dollar a letter. Communities would petition the government for a mail route and when contracts finally came through, contractors would often sub-contract these out to settlers who lived along the route, each one's area covering from twenty to forty miles.

The Star Pony Express ran from Pioche, Nevada, to St. Thomas (130 miles), then to Rioville (Bonelli's) where it crossed the Colorado River. From the river crossing, riders headed on down to the El Dorado mining camp (about ten miles below present-day Willow Beach on the Colorado River, some twenty miles due south of Bonelli's) then back to Mineral Park (between today's Kingman and Chloride). This route of 229 very rugged miles was covered three times weekly. A minimum age of sixteen was set for riders but it's said few were ever that old.

Lewis quoted some memoirs from Ute V. Perkins, who at the age of 12, in 1882, rode the route from St. Thomas to Mineral Park:

> Leaving St. Thomas at 7 a.m., going south to Rioville. Eating lunch there, changing to a fresh horse, being ferried across the Colorado, then heading southwest to Eldorado; arriving there from about 11 p.m. to 1 a.m. .... At Eldorado, changing mail, getting breakfast, changing horses...

According to Perkins, he then rode to Mountain Springs in the White Hills (between present-day communities of White Hills and Dolan Springs), a distance

Raging River

of about fifteen miles from Eldorado. He changed horses again and rode another twenty miles to Mineral Park, arriving there at 7 p.m. Keep in mind, according to his recollections, Ute Perkins was only twelve years old at that time, and his brother, Joe, who was only ten, also rode part of this route at other times.

By 1900 populations had grown and loads were becoming too heavy for the boys to carry on horseback. Wagons and regular mail carriers took over most of the delivery, and eventually, when the railroads came through, those took most of the postal contracts.

Belshaw and Peplow found in their research that for a short time, Harry Gentry of St. Thomas also ran a stage line through Rioville while on his route from Pioche, Nevada, to Hackberry, Arizona, which means this stage line probably traveled across the Hackberry or Antares Road in Hualapai Valley.

Associated with Bonelli's ferry, too, is the story of "Mouse," a Paiute who could not adjust to the lifestyle being imposed upon him. One version of the story is told by George E. Perkins in an article entitled "Trail of a Renegade Pahute," in the *Desert Magazine,* November, 1939. Perkins was a member of the posse that eventually pursued Mouse.

> My first acquaintance with the Pahute outlaw, Mouse, was during the winter of 1898 when I was working for Daniel Bonelli who operated a ferry on the Colorado River near the junction of the Virgin. Bonelli also had an alfalfa ranch in the river bottom and supplied hay to the mining camps of White Hills, Arizona, and Eldorado Canyon, Nevada, and to travelers who followed this old trail across the desert.
>
> He employed a crew of men to operate the ferry and ranch and among them were several Indians, mostly Pahutes. The Indians were good hands for both the ferry and ranch as they were acclimated to the 120 degree summer temperatures. Mouse was an industrious worker but was feared and hated by the other Indians. It was characteristic of the Pahutes to become sullen and brood for days over a fancied wrong. In this frame of mind they sometimes became killers and had been known to vent their wrath on white and friendly members of their own tribe. On such occasions a posse would immediately take the trail and when the murderer was captured, would be dealt with according to the custom of the country, and buried on the spot. Mouse was an Indian of this type.

Perkins goes on to tell that one evening several Paiutes from their nearby camps came to the Bonelli ranch house and reported that Mouse had gone crazy and was shooting everything up with his six-shooter. They admitted to have been drinking liquor in their camp that night. Perkins and several other armed white men went to the camp and convinced Mouse to give up his gun, although Mouse showed obvious resentment over their intrusion.

The next day Bonelli fired Mouse and took him across to the Arizona side of the river. From there Mouse went to the White Hills mining camp and worked several months as chore boy and handy man at the company store. Then one

Bonelli's Ferry

evening he stole a 30-30 rifle and cartridges from the store, took a horse owned by a freighter, and headed back toward Nevada.

He rode through the mountains toward Las Vegas ranch (where the city of Las Vegas now stands). Upon reaching the Colorado River, about five miles upstream from present-day Hoover Dam, his horse became mired in quicksand and Mouse left the horse there to die, going on up the river toward Bonelli's some twenty miles distant. He came to a camp of prospectors consisting of two men named Stearns and Davis, and an eighty year old man, Major Greenowat. He joined them in camp and they fed him. During the evening Mouse told the men of a rich gold ledge about ten miles farther up the river and said he would lead them to it the next day. The next morning Stearns and Davis left, following Mouse. The Major stayed in camp.

Several days later a horse was found missing from Bonelli's ferry and Mouse was suspected of the theft. Native workers picked up the trail and followed it to the Virgin River, across, and then upstream. Joe Perkins, the ranch foreman, along with one of the Paiutes, saddled up and continued following the trail. After going some twelve miles along the Virgin, the trail took off up Bitter Springs Wash for another twenty, then went into such rough rocky country that they lost the trail. Having few supplies, they returned to Bonelli's. Shortly thereafter, George Perkins left with a Paiute who was familiar with the Las Vegas ranch country and they spent several days in that area talking to ranchers and miners. Finding out Mouse had come there on foot, they tried to pick up Mouse's trail again, but to no avail. They started back for Bonelli's and upon reaching the river opposite the campsite of Stearns, Davis, and Major Greenowat, Perkins fired several shots to get the Major's attention, who then came over in his boat and picked them up. That evening in camp, the Major told Perkins that Stearns and Davis had left with an Indian named Mouse some five days previous. This concerned Perkins but he made no comment.

The next day when they arrived at the ferry landing, the men told Bonelli and others of their concerns for Stearns and Davis. There were two other men camped at the ferry that night, also, Richmond and Galloway. These men had started from far up north on the Green River in Wyoming and come all the way down river, reportedly through the Grand Canyon, in two small boats decked with canvas, en route to Needles, California. Galloway and Richmond decided to stay a few days and join the forming search party consisting of Perkins, two white hands, and a Native tracker.

The men went back to Major Greenowats camp on the river where they picked up the trail of his two partners and Mouse. They followed the trail high into the Boulder Canyon range and after a strenuous day of crossing canyons and climbing ledges, found the mutilated bodies of Stearns and Davis at the base of a cliff. Davis's gun was gone as were Stearns high top boots. It took the men two more days to get the bodies back to the Major's camp, and from there, Richmond and Galloway transported the bodies and Major Greenowat by boat down the river to Needles.

Raging River

For nearly two years thereafter, Mouse stayed in hiding near Indian Springs at the north end of Mount Charleston (west of Las Vegas) and in the Sheep Mountain range, to the north. Several times he was glimpsed briefly by prospectors or he would loot a camp or kill a range steer for jerky to live on. A few times he was thought to be in the Muddy Mountains and Valley of Fire areas east of Las Vegas. He had become an outcast from his own people and in Mohave County, Arizona, and Lincoln County, Nevada (later to be Clark County) and there were rewards for him, dead or alive.

A July Fourth celebration was held in Overton, Nevada, in 1901, one well-attended by settlers and prospectors from all around, along with many Paiutes. After the celebration was over an elderly Native woman returned to her camp and discovered a head of cabbage missing from her small garden. The Paiutes saw the tracks and figured Mouse was in the area.

Another posse was formed consisting of both Euro-Americans and Native Americans and Perkins was one who joined the group. They followed the tracks through the Valley of Fire and to some natural tanks (natural pocket areas in large boulders where rainwater remains trapped). From there the trail led out across rocky mesas and down to St. Thomas, then doubled back once more to the Valley of Fire. The trail then struck out heading thirty miles to the north end of Moapa Valley, Meadow Valley Wash, and to Cane Spring.

After eight days of tracking during the intense desert heat of July the bare feet of the Native American trackers were terribly blistered, but still, no one wanted to give up. When the trail doubled back toward Warm Springs, they sensed there were closing in on Mouse.

Continuing the Perkins story:

> When we caught sight of him, he was crossing a smooth clay flat four miles north of Warm Springs. Instantly guns were brought into play. The pursuing Indians fired the first shots and Mouse returned the fire. He would empty his gun and then turn and run while he was reloading. The battle ended when the renegade dropped in his tracks. When we caught up with him, he was dead with three bullets through his body. The Indians wanted to make sure of their job and fired several shots into his body after we came to him.

> He still had the rifle stolen from White Hills store and the six-shooter taken from the body of Davis. The boots he had taken from Stearns had been made into moccasins. The heavy mustache he had formerly worn had been plucked out, evidently in an effort to disguise himself.

> The hunt for Mouse was over and we were now confronted with the problem of getting him back to one of the ranches where he could be identified. The Pahutes, superstitious about such things, refused to touch the body. After much persuasion and the promise of a generous share of the reward money, they finally helped lash the body on a pack animal. We took him nine miles to a ranch owned by two squaw men. Several ranchers gathered here and held an inquest and made the affidavits necessary to collect the reward. After paying

the expenses of the posse, the money was divided equally among the Indian trailers who had done such excellent work in following him.

The body was buried in a shallow grave in an arroyo a short distance away ... and that was the end of the trail for Mouse.

Today, Valley of Fire is an oft-visited State Park just east of Las Vegas, a beautiful place of vivid red rock outcroppings with intriguing shapes and numerous displays of ancient Native American petroglyphs. One natural tank is a deep clear water hole at the end of a red-earthed path with towering smooth rocks on each side. This is designated as "Mouse's Tank" as it was considered to be one of the campsites Mouse had occupied and is a special place many visitors choose to see.

Bonelli expanded more into cattle ranching as years passed. R. G. Patterson had been cattle ranching and mining in the area south of Bonelli's Ferry for some time prior to Bonelli's arrival, on two ranches, the Mountain Springs Ranch (combined with a way station of the same name), and the Doling's Springs Ranch. Around the 1880's, Bonelli extended his grazing area and must have bought out Patterson, for by 1900, Bonelli's rangelands extended through what is now the Dolan Springs and Hualapai Valley areas.

Bonelli's ferry crossing and Rioville began declining in importance after 1900. More Mormon residents had moved into the towns of St. Thomas, Mesquite, and Bunkerville, and so much water was being diverted from upriver on the Virgin that Bonelli's own fields suffered immensely. There was also litigation involved in rights over the salt mine, and the railroads coming across southern Nevada had begun diverting traffic and delivery of goods away from his river crossing.

In 1903, as Bonelli was returning from a trip to Pioche, he suffered a stroke. He died the next year and was buried on the mesa overlooking the Colorado River. The remaining family members left the Bonelli home, and the ferry and ranch site eventually began the slow return to desert land once again. The post office there closed in 1906.

In an interview in 1988 with Chic Perkins of Overton, Nevada, Perkins recalled a trip made with his father and another man down to the old Bonelli house in about 1930. He said they found two bales of letters in an old building there -- old army postcards and lots of other mail—and they just left them. He wished now they had brought those out as he figured the letters were most likely still in the house when it was inundated with water shortly thereafter.

In 1934 when the waters of Lake Mead began to rise, Bonelli's grave was moved to Kingman where a son lived. The big stone Bonelli home soon disappeared under the waters of the newly forming lake. Daniel Bonelli had given names to several landmarks in the Temple Bar area, including the majestic red butte across from Temple Bar that he called "The Mormon Temple" (now known as simply "The Temple"), and also, I was told, the name of "Temple Bar" and "Napoleons Tomb."

George Bonelli, Daniel's son, built a fine wood home for his wife, Effie, in Kingman in 1894, but this house was destroyed by fire in 1915. He then had another home built out of stone, using tufa rock quarried from a canyon just

Raging River

outside of Kingman. This was similar in basic plan to the first home, yet had the thick rock composition reminiscent of his father's old home at Bonelli's Landing on the Colorado River. This home is now owned by the city of Kingman and has been placed on the National Register of Historic Places where it is accessible for public tours.

Bonelli home at Bonelli Landing and Ferry Crossing. Courtesy Mohave Museum in Kingman, AZ

Raging River

Mining near Temple Bar, Bonelli's Ferry in background. Courtesy Mohave Museum

Boat Harbor at Temple Bar, Jan. 16, 1948, Courtesy Bureau of Reclamation

Chapter Eight: Lower Granite Gorge

Having covered much information about the three historic ferry crossings at the west end of Grand Canyon, we now go to the Colorado River, itself, to what would eventually become the uppermost part of Lake Mead, especially extending into the intriguing Lower Granite Gorge (western-most part of Grand Canyon).

Almost fifty miles of the Colorado River in the Lower Granite Gorge was originally designated as being within Lake Mead National Recreation Area boundaries, which meant my husband, Don, a Lake Mead NPS Ranger, routinely patrolled much of the lower canyon by boat, as well as most of upper Lake Mead. During such patrols, since I also served as a volunteer for LMNRA, Don would often drop me off at various side canyons in western Grand Canyon for solo hiking explorations, after which I would report any significant findings to staff at Headquarters. This was a rare privilege, to say the least, and being able to experience the Lower Granite Gorge in such a way prompted more queries for me about the history of the Canyon, itself.

Brief mention will be made here of the mystery of "D. Julien," a trapper and fur trader who may or may not have made an earlier unrecorded entrance into the Grand Canyon on the Colorado River from the north, sometime in 1836. Some details about Julien were provided by Charles Kelly.[1]

First records of Denis Julien, apparently one of the early French-Canadian settlers, appear in St. Louis, Missouri, where he and his Native American wife had their children baptized from 1793-1804. In 1807 and 1810, he received licenses to trade with the Sioux and Ioway tribes to the north. Julien was also one who witnessed the signing of the 1815 Iowa Treaty.

Of particular interest to me, a native Iowan, was learning that one of the most valuable trade items in this country at that time was "bar lead sourced from lead mines north of St. Louis," these long worked by Native Americans, which, reportedly by the early 1800's, furnished bullets for all hunting and trapping activities between the Mississippi River and Pacific Ocean. I had known of an extensive lead mine long worked by Natives in Dubuque, Iowa, lastly by the Fox (Meskwaki) tribe, an area along the west side of the Mississippi River north of St. Louis. Julien Dubuque, another Frenchman associated with the then French enclave in St. Louis, Missouri, was involved with this mine. Julien Dubuque eventually married a Meskwaki(Fox) woman and, of course, helped mine the riches from this lead mine. The city of Dubuque, IA., eventually took its name from this man.

Denis Julien, the other Frenchman, migrated the rivers westward in 1831 and ultimately worked with Antoine Robidoux on a trapping expedition in Uintah Basin in northeast Utah. More than five different rock inscriptions have been found by "D. Julien 1836" on the Green River and also farther south on the Colorado River, the last of which is just above a treacherous rapids in Cataract Canyon, upstream of Lee's Ferry. Whether Julien lost his life in the rapids at

Raging River

Cataract Canyon, or if he ventured on down into Grand Canyon to never resurface again, is unknown.

In 1864, another boat trip was attempted going up into this western end of Grand Canyon, one not as successful as the previous 1827 attempt by trappers James Ohio Pattie and Pegleg Smith. Prospectors by the name of Gass, Ferry, and Butterfield, accompanied by an unnamed Native guide, started out from Eldorado Canyon in the lower Colorado River, came up river, entered the lower end of Grand Canyon and pushed and pulled their boat some nineteen miles into the lower gorge. Discouraged by the rapids, they gave up, built a rock cairn on each bank, and returned downriver.

Then there is the fascinating saga of James White who may or may not have floated through the entire canyon in 1867, perhaps the first Euro-American to actually do so. White was born in New York in 1837 and raised in Kenosha, Wisconsin. At age 23, he followed the gold rush to Colorado and soon relocated to Virginia City, Nevada. During the Civil War in 1861, White went into the army and was located at Fort Yuma, California, and according to the story, while there, gold was discovered just upriver at La Paz and Eldorado Canyon. White then went to Texas with the Army and eventually was arrested by the military for stealing supplies in order to buy whiskey. He was sentenced to hard labor but released when the war ended in 1865. At that time White wandered into Kansas and got work as a stagecoach driver on the Santa Fe Trail. Shortly thereafter he joined several other men to go prospecting back in Colorado once more, their venture financed with funds received from the sale of fourteen horses they'd stolen from Natives in the area. They prospected along the Mancos River and then down the San Juan to the Colorado River. In a letter to his brother in Kenosha, Wisconsin, dated September 26, 1867, White purportedly wrote and sent the following letter:

Dear Brother,

It has been some time since I heard from you. I got no answer from the last letter I wrote you, for soon after I wrote I went prospecting with Captain Baker and George Strohl in the San Juan Mountains. We found very good prospects but nothing would pay. Then we started down the San Juan River. We traveled down about 200 miles, then we crossed over on the Colorado and camped. We laid over one day. We found we could not travel down the river and the horses had sore feet. We had made up our minds to turn back when we were attacked by fifteen or twenty Ute Indians. They killed Baker, and George Strohl and myself took four ropes off our horses, an axe, ten pounds of flour and our guns. We had fifteen miles to walk to the Colorado. We got to the river just at night. We built a raft that night. We got finished about ten o'clock. We had good sailing for three days, the fourth day George Strohl was washed off the raft and drowned, and that left me alone. I thought it would be my turn next. I then pulled off my pants and boots. I then tied a rope to my waist. I went over falls up to fifteen feet high. My raft would tip over three or four times a day. The third we had lost our flour, and for seven days I had nothing to eat but a rawhide knife sheath. The eighth day I got some mesquite beans. The thirteenth day I met a party of friendly Indians. They would not give me anything to eat so I gave them my pistol for the hind parts of a dog. I had one of them for supper and the other for breakfast. The sixteenth day I arrived in Callville, where I was taken care of by James Ferry. I was ten days without pants or boots or hat. I was so sunburned I could hardly walk. The Indians took seven head of horses from us. I wish I could write you half of what I underwent. I saw the hardest time that any man ever did in this world, but thank God I got through it safe. I am well again. Direct your letter to Callville, Ariz.

James White[2]

When White's raft approached Callville (downstream of present-day Temple Bar, Arizona, on Lake Mead) Native Americans who were working loading rock salt onto barges to be towed downstream to mines, spotted his raft and dragged him ashore. White was described as in terrible shape; badly sunburned, battered and bruised, and very weak and emaciated. He, only thirty at the time, was said to have the appearance of a seventy year old man.

Various authorities (foremost of whom was Robert Brewster Stanton, his story following), strongly questioned whether White actually did travel the entire 700 miles distance in sixteen days or whether he may have actually started at Diamond Creek or some other lower access point. However, most of those who talked with White, including some prominent people who interviewed the man shortly after his arrival at Callville, found his story very credible.

On May 24, 1869, the famed Major John Wesley Powell led his exploratory expedition through the reportedly unexplored (by Euro-Americans) depths of Grand Canyon. Their experiences were eloquently recorded by Powell in his book, *The Exploration of the Colorado River.* Omitting information on the majority of their journey, we will pick up on the story just before they emerged from Grand Canyon and entered our area.

On the 28th of August when supplies were nearly gone and the group was on the last part of the trip, the men reached a place where the rapids looked worse than any previous so decided to camp overnight. After much troubled debate, the Howland brothers and William Dunn elected to leave the group, feeling it was outright suicide to stay on the river any longer. This location became called, appropriately, Separation Rapids, at the mouth of Separation Canyon. Powell was greatly distraught over their leaving but he and the remaining men continued on through the wild rapids and lower part of the gorge, then exited the great canyon only one day later.

Here are a few excerpts from Powell's book describing their exit from the Canyon near today's Pearce Ferry:

> August 29. We start very early this morning. The river still continues swift, but we have no serious difficulty, and at twelve o'clock emerge from the Grand Canyon of the Colorado. We are in a valley now, and low mountains

are seen in the distance, coming to the river below. We recognize this as Grand Wash ..... Tonight we camp on the left bank, in a mesquite thicket.

...Ever before us has been an unknown danger, heavier than immediate peril. Every waking hour passed in the Grand Canyon has been one of toil. We have watched with deep solicitude the steady disappearance of our scant supply of rations, and from time to time have seen the river snatch a portion of the little left, while we were a-hungered. And danger and toil were endured in those gloomy depths, where ofttimes clouds hid the sky by day and but a narrow zone of stars could be seen at night. Only during the few hours of deep sleep, consequent on hard labor, has the roar of the waters hushed. Now the danger is over, now the toil ceased, now the gloom had disappeared, now the firmament is bounded only by the horizon, and what a vast expanse of constellations can be seen! ... The river rolls by us in silent majesty; the quiet of the camp is sweet; our joy is almost ecstasy. We sit till long after midnight talking of the Grand Canyon...[3]

Powell's party proceeded downriver, going through two or three low canyons, where they discovered a band of Natives in a valley (probably near present-day South Cove or Hualapai Wash), although those people scampered away and hid when the men landed and called to them. A few miles further, around a short bend in the river, the party met up with another camp of Natives (perhaps below Salt Springs, just west of Gregg's Hideout on Lake Mead). This camp was without lodges but had small shelters of boughs in the sand. Powell's men landed and tried to talk with them also, but all went into hiding except one man dressed in a hat, a woman wearing only a string of beads, and two children. Powell tried talking with them in what he thought was their own language (probably thinking they were Paiutes, however, were more likely Hualapai), but was unable to secure any information about local Natives or white people, so once again the party pushed off. Later that day they sighted two whites and a Native on the north shore hauling in a fishing seine and upon speaking with them, Powell was delighted and relieved to learn they had finally arrived at the long-sought mouth of the Rio Virgen (the Virgin River that then entered the Colorado River, but now empties into Overton Arm of Lake Mead).

It was later determined that the Howland brothers and William Dunn from the Powell party had worked their way north up through Separation Canyon to the north rim, and there were killed by Natives. Some evidence leads to the belief that they were killed by several Paiutes led by Toab, who were, in turn, retaliating for a rumored attack by miners upon a Native woman in the same vicinity. The bodies of the three men were never found, however, a watch that Sumner had given to Howland was traded in by a Native at a later date (this covered more in next chapter). A plaque has been placed on the north shore of Separation Canyon commemorating the lost lives of the three men. North Howland and South Howland Coves near Iceberg Canyon on Lake Mead, as well as Bradley Bay, were all named after men from the Powell expedition.

Lower Granite Gorge

In September of 1869, Lt. George M. Wheeler arrived on the scene. Wheeler Ridge, located between today's South Cove and Pearce Ferry roads, was named after this man. Wheeler had previously done some reconnaissance of this lower part of the river, however, it was in 1871 that he did a prolonged series of topographical surveys of the lower regions of the Colorado River. His survey group consisted of thirty-four men, including fourteen Mohave Indians who provided most of the manpower for pulling the boats and skiffs upstream. They started from Fort Mohave with three boats and a barge and also sent two expeditions overland. All planned to meet at the mouth of Grand Canyon around October 5 and from there, hoped to push up river into the Canyon and to Diamond Creek.

The river crew traveled through Boulder Canyon, passed the confluence of the Virgin River and continued upstream into Virgin Canyon. Wheeler mentions naming the deep cut "Virgin Canyon" because it was new territory to them (the Virgin River, on the other hand, which does not go through Virgin Canyon, appears to have gotten its name from either a member of Jedediah Smith's group in 1827, or from Thomas Virgin, an associate of the explorer John Fremont, depending which source one wants to believe). The men then passed through rough rapids in Iceberg Canyon and proceeded on to Grand Wash where, on Oct. 4th, they met up on the north shore with one of the two overland survey crews headed by Lieutenant Lockwood. Lockwood and his men had covered a large land area, traveling through where Las Vegas is today, then northeast through present-day Santa Clara and St. George in Utah, back down along the Muddy River, then by Pakoon Springs in the Grand Wash trough, and returning to the Colorado River.

Upon accomplishing the rendezvous they continued on and some of the men were left with the barge near the Pearce Ferry area. Lt. Lockwood took several of his men south up Grapevine Wash, to Tanaka Springs (Grass Springs), and to Truxton Springs (near today's Valentine, AZ) and from there via Peach Springs Canyon back to the river at Diamond Creek. The main part of the expedition at Pearce Ferry was directed to continue upstream with three boats. These men struggled through rapid after rapid, all of which increased in difficulty as days passed. One boat was lost in the effort, along with many supplies and valuable records. By October 19, the river crew was becoming destitute and discouraged so a decision was made to send two men up a side canyon on the south side to see if they could reach Diamond Creek by land. The two arrived at Diamond Creek in only one day and then sent a message in a bottle downriver to Wheeler's group, advising them how close they actually were to Diamond Creek. With renewed energies and enthusiasm the crew pushed on and arrived at Diamond Creek that evening. After feasting and resting, some of the men returned downriver to the barge near Pearce Ferry and then back down to Fort Mohave, taking only five days to travel what had required thirty-three days to do going upriver to Diamond Creek. Lt. Wheeler and the remainder of the crew traveled back overland. During those expeditions, topographical drawings made by Lt. Wheeler and Lt. Lockwood provided excellent mapping information for this previously little known area.

Raging River

It is of interest to try to identify the exact location of the oft-mentioned "Old Ute Crossing" near Pearce Ferry. Early Mormon explorers who visited the area in the mid-1800's always referred to this spot as the Old Ute Crossing. Lt. Wheeler sometimes called it by this name, and other times called it the Santa Fe Crossing, and even the Spanish Crossing.

This is somewhat confusing, especially reference to a so-called "Spanish Crossing." James McClintock, in *Mormon Settlement in Arizona* stated, "The Spanish Trail is outlined on a fur-trade map in the Bancroft library, covering a period from 1807 to 1843. The Spanish Trail seems to have been considered a western extension of the Santa Fe Trail."[4]

One Mormon report mentioned Natives using the Old Ute Crossing above Pearce's Ferry, just east of Grand Wash. Another report states:

> ...about a mile and a half below the mouth of the canyon were small rapids and the Old Ute Crossing, and three miles downstream the outwash of Grapevine Wash produced a major rapids above which Pearce's Ferry was located, and four miles below that, the debris of Grand Wash formed another major rapid above which crossing had been made, however, the steep banks on Wheeler Ridge made ascent on the south side extremely difficult.[5]

Lt. Wheeler had also mentioned that one and one-half to two miles downstream from the Grand Wash Cliffs, a dike cut across the river which was called the Old Ute Crossing. On another occasion after Wheeler and his party left the Pearce Ferry area by boat and were headed upstream, they spoke of passing the Old Ute Crossing a few miles upriver. Another time, he said:

> ...near the foot of Grand Canyon the river widens and the rapids are more shallow ... that this was the best point yet for fording, still, in the lowest waters, swimming would be necessary and at high water, doubtless the swift current would prohibit this method again.[6]

In 1880-81, a United States Geological Survey (USGS) was conducted through the entire canyon and this was led by Clarence Edward Dutton. Dutton named many landforms in the main part of Grand Canyon after deities and wrote the first official geological book about the canyon, one that also contained illustrations by artists William Henry Holmes and the exquisite works of Thomas Moran.

In 1889, Frank Mason Brown, a Denver real estate man, became inspired by an idea from S. S. Harper, a prospector. He decided to have a survey done for a possible railroad line that would follow the Colorado River from Grand Junction, Colorado, go through the entire length of the Grand Canyon, and then to Yuma, Arizona. His main incentive for this was to haul coal from Colorado to California, as, at that time, most of the coal in San Diego was coming from Australia, England, and Canada.

He chose as his chief engineer, Robert Brewster Stanton. Brown, Stanton, and fourteen other men left Green River, Utah, by boat on May 25, 1889. The group split up when approaching the eastern entrance to the Grand Canyon; some stayed to do a field instrument survey at Lee's Ferry while the rest proceeded into the Canyon.

On July 10, Brown's boat capsized in a rapids just twelve miles below Lee's Ferry. He drowned and his body was never found. Stanton took command of the expedition at that point. On July 15 at Mile 25.2, another boat capsized in the rapids and two more men drowned, Hansbrough and Richards. Hansbrough's remains were found the next year but Richard's body was never recovered. After this incident Stanton decided to temporarily abandon the survey so they cached their supplies and equipment and left the river.

In early December, Stanton and eleven other men resumed the survey with newer, heavier boats and also life preservers. Several men left the survey party at various points along the river, but Stanton and six remaining men completed the survey, successfully navigating the entire Canyon. In March of 1890, they passed through the Pearce Ferry area and Stanton commented that it was abandoned at that time but mentioned that the old road and rock house were still plainly visible.

In August of 1896, George Flavell and Ramon Montas, two boatsmen and trappers, put in at Green River, Wyoming, and successfully passed through the Grand Canyon in late October, arriving in Needles, California, in early November.

Then trapper and prospector Nathanial Galloway, from Utah, who had extensive boating experience on the Green and Colorado Rivers, developed a lightweight boat and became the first to use the stern-first method of going through rapids (turning the boat around so the front, or bow, was pointed upstream). Galloway and another man came through the Grand Canyon in 1897. In 1909, an Ohio Industrialist, Julius F. Stone, employed Galloway to take him on a pleasure trip, starting from Green River, Wyoming, down through the Grand Canyon and to Needles, California. Galloway was one of the few to make more than one river trip through the Grand Canyon in those very early years (Galloway, recall, was also in the story about the Indian, Mouse, in the previous chapter).

Elias "Hum" Woolley and two other companions from Los Angeles made a prospecting trip through the Canyon during September of 1901. Two more prospectors, Edwin Monett and Charles Russell, made a difficult winter trip through the Canyon in 1907.

The famed Kolb brothers, Ellsworth and Emery, made their historic photographic river voyage from Green River, Wyoming, to Needles, California in 1911. Soon after, Ellsworth wrote *Through the Grand Canyon from Wyoming to Mexico*, a classic work published in 1914 and containing many of their photos. The Kolb brothers then established a photographic studio on the South Rim of Grand Canyon that soon became legend.

In 1923, Emery Kolb served as head boatman for a mapping expedition led by Claude Birdseye that resulted in the first accurate topographic map of the Canyon. This may have been the same trip referenced by another source where it was reported that Emery Kolb was head boatman for engineer Roland Burchard's survey crew that completed topographical surveys from Lee's Ferry through the Canyon during the same year, and upon arriving at Griggs Basin, the group

Raging River

documented their visit with the Smiths at Grigg's Ferry (near present day South Cove) with photos, some of which are shown herein from Richard Smiths collection.

At this point, some interesting more recent "crossings" and events that took place in the Pearce Ferry area, itself, at the mouth of Grand Canyon, after 1900, will be recounted.

Around 1916, William F. Grounds Jr. (known as Billy), an early Mohave County rancher, sent a crew to the old Pearce Ferry landing to build a new ferry and set up a cable in order to assist with livestock crossings. The following incident is related in John Cureton Grounds book, *Trail Dust of the Southwest*:

> Walter Brown was in charge of the crew. They pulled the cable across the river and stretched it to the proper tension, and a large new ferry was built to cross cattle to the Hurricane Valley Ranch [in Arizona Strip country north of Grand Canyon]. The crew had worked for months on this project and everything appeared in good condition. They started the ferry across the river and the cable slackened. In the mix up, Walter Brown had his glove caught in the rollers and cut two fingers off his right hand. They found the trouble after it was too late. They had tightened the cable over a large cottonwood log and anchored it. The weight of the ferry caused the cable to cut through the log and gain slack. Walter Brown was hurried to a doctor and his hand was taken care of. The ferry was a total loss of twenty thousand dollars plus Walters hand being disfigured.[7]

In the fall of 1986, Shannon Peters, a volunteer for the National Park Service who spent a number of winters helping in the Pearce Ferry area, discovered an old rusted pulley with heavy cable still attached, half imbedded on the north shore of the lake where the old ferry road entered the water. This was placed in the display case at the South Cove Ranger Station. It is not known if this pulley and cable were from the above-mentioned incident or from another time.

Nellie Iverson Cox, in her book, *Footprints on the Arizona Strip*, told of another tragic incident that occurred at the Pearce Ferry crossing.[8]

> It was the spring of 1921, early and still quite cold, when Billy Brink and quite a few others rode to Pearce Ferry to receive the large herd of cattle being brought to the Walking X Ranch [in Arizona Strip country]. The river was high and the cattle refused to enter the stream which was swollen with spring run-off. With Billy on the north side of the river were Henry Ferguson, Luther Swanner, Walter Pymm, Jack Welch, and others. On the south side, with the herd, were Harold and Archie McCain and probably a number of men whose names we have not been able to determine [Leonard Neal, from the Neal Ranch later stated to me that he was in the group on the south shore.] All were riding good horses, although they were weak since the grass had not yet come. Billy, determined, finally, to ride across the river and force the cattle to swim the current. The men had already spent a number of fruitless days at the spot. Billy asked Walter Pymm to change horses with him. Old

June, the mare he was riding, not being as strong as Dixie, the one Walter was on. He then took off his gun and other articles and told Pymm he could have them in case he, Billy, did not make it.

The horses were no more anxious to venture into the dangerous flood than were the cattle across the river. According to some reports, Billy made several attempts to get Dixie into the water and finally rode back a ways and then went at a run toward the water, plunging immediately into its murky depths.

Dixie was a good horse and tried his best to swim across, but in the middle of the stream an undertow caught him and pulled him under ... No one is sure what it was that Billy Brink called out in those last desperate seconds before he went under for the last time ... no lasso rope could possibly be thrown far enough or accurately enough to reach him. And a log ridden into the stream by Jack Welch did not reach him either, the horse and rider disappearing into a rapid some distance below.

A net was placed across Black Canyon far below near the location of present-day Hoover Dam, where Billy's body was later recovered. Edna Brink, Billy's wife and a schoolteacher in the Arizona Strip, positively identified her husband's body by the collar and piece of the shirt he was still wearing.

"Billy drowned one morning" remembers Luther Swanner, "and it was a day and a night later when we found Dixie. Henry Ferguson and I had both gone back to Tassi since we were working for Nutter at the time, and then returned to the river later. The horse was about fifteen feet from the bank, with one foot sticking out of the water and muck. I managed to put my rope on the foot and pulled it out to where we were able to cut the cinch and recover the saddle."[9]

Another study took place on prospective dam sites from the lower Grand Canyon area and down to Needles, California, in the fall of 1924. E. C. LaRue was commissioned to lead this expedition. Notes from his project, *Colorado River Dam Site Investigation, Lower Grand Canyon to Needles, September-October 1924,* along with excellent photographs, were found on file at the Mohave Museum in Kingman, Arizona. Due to exceptionally interesting and entertaining detail as well as informative descriptions of places and events, the study will be quoted here in some length.

Sept. 10, 1924. Arrived in Kingman, Arizona, 5:30 a.m. All members of the party assembled at Kingman during the day, the personnel of the party being: H. W. Dennis, Engineer, Southern Cal. Edison Co., I. C. Cockroft, Engineer, Southern Cal. Edison Co., L. T. Eliel, expert in photographic mapping, George F. Holbrook, Hydraulic Engineer, USGS., Samuel Levine, cook, and myself.

We wished to launch our boats on the Colorado River at Pierce's Ferry. This ferry has been abandoned for 20 years or more. We learned in advance that it would be very difficult for a truck or touring car to negotiate the sand in Grapevine Wash especially on the return trip. I was unable to hire a truck at Kingman equipped with pneumatic tires. It therefore seemed best to use one of the Edison Company trucks equipped with seven gears and built especially to carry heavy loads over soft sand. Inasmuch as it seemed necessary to have this truck on the job, the truck was used to transport one of the boats from Los Angeles to Kingman. The other boat was shipped from Topock to Kingman by rail. With two boats and a canoe, 1200 lbs. of supplies, and with the truck driver and assistant making 8 men in all, it was apparent that it would be necessary to use two trucks. We located a pneumatic tire truck at Oatman which at one time was a Packard touring car. We loaded the second boat on the Oatman truck, divided up the supplies between the two trucks and before dark had everything loaded and ready to go.

Sept. 11, 1924. Left Kingman at 5:30 a.m. and arrived Pierce's Ferry at 4:45 p.m.; the distance from Kingman to Pierce's Ferry being 84 miles by auto road. Both trucks reached the river. However it was necessary for the Edison Co. truck to break trail by using its low gear which moved the truck forward at a rate of 2 miles per hour. Having a trail broken, the Packard truck was able to follow. The road was good for a distance of about 70 miles; the last 14 miles leading down Grapevine Wash to the river was dry sand and in many places boulders made driving rather difficult.

Sept. 12 ... Made camp at Pierce's Ferry, overhauled the boats, and tuned up the 3 ½ H. P. Evinrude motor. The Oatman truck returned to Kingman. However, it was necessary for the Edison Co. truck to follow until the old Packard was well out of Grapevine Wash. The Edison Co. truck then returned to Pierce's Ferry. A little flood came down the river about dark and caused some alarm for we were camped on a bar about 4 feet above the river. The river came up 2 feet in 3 hours.

Sept. 13 ... Started up river with motor boat and canoe at 10 a.m. We finally used flashlight batteries to get the motor started. About one mile above Pierce's Ferry, the canoe upset with Eliel aboard. He swam to the bank holding fast to the canoe. No damage was done except the soaking of Mr. Dennis' briefcase which contained his maps, notes, etc. Camped at 4 p.m. at a point 5 miles above Pierce's Ferry.

Sept. 14 ... Broke camp at 7:30 a.m. Passed a bad riffle just above camp where it was necessary to unload and portage our supplies about 400 feet. The boat was skidded over the rocks in a shallow part of the rapid. This was accomplished by two men lifting on the boat and four pulling on a 100-foot rope. Passed about 6 such riffles during the day. The motor was used for short stretches between riffles. Camped about 4 p.m. at the foot of a bad riffle 9 ¼ miles above Pierce's Ferry. Saw two mountain sheep this morning. When we landed to camp this evening, I saw a fox, which was small, gray, and had a large tail tinged with red. Everybody was tired tonight. In the water all day, either pulling on the rope or lifting on the boat.

Sept. 15 ... Out at daylight and immediately after breakfast all our beds and supplies were loaded on the canoe and floated to the head of a backwater channel. From this point the supplies were carried across a boulder bar to a point on the river above a bad riffle. The empty boat was pulled over the riffle by means of a rope. Used the motor for about half a mile when we had to land and pull the boat over a small rapid. About half a mile above Travertine Wall at elevation 940 feet above sea level, we met an accident which ended our boating. We tried to pull the loaded boat over a short rapid. Five men on the rope was not enough. The boat filled with water and turned over and most of its cargo floated away. Cockroft, who was in the boat, swam ashore and made a run for the canoe which was parked on the beach 100 feet downstream. By using the canoe he was able to save everything that remained afloat. My panorama camera was picked up a half mile down the river. It was filled with the muddy water of the Colorado, even in the space between the lenses. All six beds were saved readily as they did not sink. After the boat was turned over and bailed out, we put a rope on Eliel and later on Cockroft, so that they might explore the bottom of the river for the purpose of recovering some of our food supplies. Our destination was 3 miles further upstream and it was my intention to reach this point on foot if we could save enough food to keep us alive for two days. Cockroft and Eliel did good work. Of course we had a rope tied around their chests so that if anything went wrong, we could pull them out, but they succeeded in recovering sufficient food to enable us to remain on the job. They would wade around in the water where the boat upset and on locating something with their feet which did not feel like a rock, they would dive for it. The most valuable find was a sack containing 12 cans of meat, beans, peas, corn, etc. The dutch oven was recovered without the lid; also the frying pan and some of the cooking utensils. Although it was a rather serious matter, we could not help but laugh when Cockroft dove down in the muddy waters of the Colorado and came up with a handful of prunes. We lost the ham, bacon, potatoes, sugar, salt, first-aid medicine chest, Mr. Dennis' vanity bag, containing his toilet articles and extra clothing; we also lost 5 buckets, coffee pot, pliers, dishes, knives and forks, etc. The most serious loss was the alidade and my 3-A special camera. After about an hour of work we got our wet goods spread out on the rocks to dry. The cook was trying to fix up a lunch out of what was left. It was about 2 p.m. when a flood came on and in a few minutes put out the cooks fire. He built another fire about 3 feet higher and by the time he finished cooking, the river caught this one and put it out. In the meantime, we were all busy moving our belongings that had been saved from the wreck. We had to move several times that afternoon to keep out of the way of the flood. By dark the river had risen about 10 feet. We pulled the boat up high and dry, also the canoe, and moved all provisions to a point 30 feet above the river and we parked for the night on top of the Tapeats sandstone, 40 feet above the river. Here we spent a peaceful night out of range of any reasonable flood. My bed was not dried out so I borrowed a blanket from Holbrook.

Sept. 16 ... Having saved two loaves of bread and some eggs, we had French toast for breakfast. The bread had been in the river but we dried it in the sun, cut the mud off the outside, and all was well. Having lost the coffee pot, the cook made coffee in the dutch oven. It was awful ... black as tar, and the worst I have ever tasted.

Having finished breakfast, 5 of us walked 3 miles up the river to a possible damsite where we found granite in the river channel and the Tapeats sandstone standing up 40 or 50 feet in the wall [location of potential Bridge Canyon Dam site?]. We returned to camp about 3 p.m. where we remained during the night as the river was too high to travel safely in the heavily loaded boats.

Sept. 17 ... Up at 4:30 a.m. and found the river still pretty high. Mountain sheep on the canyon wall opposite our camp seem to be satisfied that we had no business in the canyon. We loaded our boat and started our downstream trip. After the upset the motor would not start so we had to use the oars. The rapid ¼ mile below camp was too rough to run with the loaded boat so we carried the supplies to the lower end of the rapid, a distance of about 300 feet. Cockroft decided he could run the rapid with the canoe. He did run it, but the canoe was upside down. He had some ride and finally got out about ¼ mile below the rapid. He ran the motor boat through safely after it had been unloaded. We had no further trouble and reached our camp at Pierce's Ferry at 1:15 p.m.

Mr. Dennis and I left Pierce's Ferry by motor truck at 3 p.m. arriving at Kingman at 10:20 p.m. Mr. Dennis telegraphed to Los Angeles for another Alidade and extra parts for the Evinrude motor.

The diary goes on covering the purchase of new equipment and supplies, then continues:

September 23 ... Broke camp at Pierce's Ferry at 9 a.m. Ran Grapevine Wash rapid with boats unloaded. Eliel ran the canoe through without trouble. Cockroft ran the motor boat which we had named 'Redwall' and I ran the other boat which we have given the name 'Tapeats.' When Mr. Dennis went to Kingman the last trip he ordered another Evinrude motor. This 2 H. P. Evinrude was installed on the 'Tapeats.' However, we decided not to use the motors until we had reached quieter water below Grand Wash. It became very apparent that heavily loaded open boats would not stand very rough water. The waves in Grapevine Wash rapid were probably 2 and 3 feet high. If the boat should turn sideways, these waves would cause serious trouble. We all got through the Grapevine Wash rapid without serious trouble. I shipped about a bucketful of water. About 3 miles below Pierce's Ferry we came to another rapid which was rather rough for open boats. It was a very hard pull to keep the boats out of the big waves. Eliel slipped by with the canoe without trouble and I was able to keep the 'Tapeats' out of the big waves. Cockcroft got over too far and it was necessary for him to land below the rapid and bail out.

We had lunch just above the entrance to Grand Wash Canyon. We had landed and tied our boats to the roots of a willow tree. A lunch was being spread out on the bank when I saw a rattlesnake coiled and resting comfortably about 18 inches from the root to which we had just tied the boat. I suggested that we let him alone until we finished our lunch for I wanted Mr. Eliel to see a real rattlesnake in his native haunts. This was the first one he had ever seen. After lunch I went up on the hills to take pictures leaving about 5 men in camp to kill the rattlesnake. We then moved down the river about half a mile when I decided to land to inspect a possible damsite. Mr. Holbrook jumped out to tie the boat to a rock but we selected the wrong rock for it was being guarded by another rattlesnake. This snake had 12 rattles.

The walls in Grand Wash Canyon are composed of the Redwall and Muav limestone. The conditions appeared favorable for a damsite so it was decided that a survey would be necessary. We moved down the river and established our camp at Grand Wash where we could obtain clear water from the springs.

Due to the low stage of the river, the rapids just below Grand Wash is rather rough. However, this rapid causes quiet water in Grand Wash Canyon [now Grand Wash Bay?]. We could easily move upstream with the motor boat or the canoe for the purpose of making the damsite survey.

During the evening a hot wind came up from the south which made life miserable for us until about midnight.

Sept. 24 ... Up at 5 a.m. The entire day was spent on the survey of a damsite in Grand Wash Canyon. The motor boat and canoe was used to good advantage. Saw 2 mountain sheep today. Strong wind downstream. Not very hot in the shade, but in the sun, I will say so! Survey finished late in the afternoon.

Sept. 25 ... Broke camp at Grand Wash and carried nearly all of the load to the lower end of Grand Wash rapid. This was a long portage, being about 2000 feet. I ran the 'Tapeats' through first and Cockcroft followed with the 'Redwall.' Had hard pull to keep out of bad water but we both landed safely below. All our supplies were loaded on the boats and moved down ¼ mile where we came to another bad one. This one might really be called a rapid for it was on the right side of the island where the channel was narrow and full of big rocks. It did not seem possible to run our open boats through this rapid either loaded or empty. I therefore ordered that all supplies be portaged and that the boats be let down with a rope. Eliel decided that he could run the rapid with the canoe, avoiding the rocks and keeping out of rough water. He had two cases of gasoline in the canoe for ballast. He was a good swimmer so I decided to let him try it. He ran this rapid the same as Cockroft ran the other further up the river, that is, upside down. When his canoe turned over he was in pretty rough water and Cockroft ran to the lower end of the rapid and jumped in to help Eliel to shore. The two of them in the water were unable to hold on to the canoe and had to let it go. The canoe went down the river about ½ mile where it drifted into an eddy. Before I could get down there, Cockroft had stripped and jumped into the river and was swimming to the other side. I would have stopped this if I had not been so far away for the river was full of boils and whirls and appeared a dangerous place for even a good swimmer. However, he reached the right bank safely. He swam out to the canoe, which was about 150 feet from shore, and had a hard struggle to swim and tow the canoe to the bank. He would swim for awhile and then go back to the canoe to rest. He finally landed and on turning the canoe over, found that the two cases of gasoline had not disappeared. It was, of course, unnecessary for Mr. Cockroft to swim the river for we could have easily rescued the canoe after we had portaged our boats over the rapid.

In trying to land his boat above this rapid, Cockroft struck a submerged rock which caused our cook to pitch head first into the river. He got his first bath since he left Kingman. He cannot swim and was pretty badly scared when Cockroft grabbed him by the neck and pulled him back into the boat.

We reached the head of Iceberg Canyon by noon, having made very slow progress on account of the low stage of the river. When we passed through this part of the canyon last year, there was hardly a ripple on the surface, the river being at a much higher stage. The rapid which I have just described would have deserved study before plunging into it with the Grand Canyon boats which were decked over. In Iceberg Canyon we encountered a strong upstream wind which caused waves 3 feet high. We could make no progress whatever with the oars. If we had not had a motor, it would have been necessary to pull up to the bank and camp. However, the 3 ½ H. P. motor towing the 'Tapeats' and the canoe was able to make 2 to 3 miles an hour against the wind. We camped at the lower end of Iceberg Canyon, having made only 10 ½ miles after a hard days work.

Sept. 26 ... Passed through Grigg's Ferry Valley, reaching the head of Virgin Canyon by 9 a. m. There is no ferry at this point, just a row boat to cross passengers and supplies. I decided that the conditions at Hualapai Rapid at the head of the Virgin Canyon were favorable for a dam site. A survey was therefore ordered. We let our boats over Hualapai Rapid with a rope, after portaging our supplies. Camp was made on a boulder bar at the lower end of the rapid. The remainder of the day was spent in surveying the damsite. Eliel spent the day mapping the site by means of the photographic method while

Lower Granite Gorge

Holbrook, with Mr. Dennis acting as recorder, proceeded with the plane table survey. Cooler tonight and, thank goodness, there is no wind.

Sept. 27 ... The entire day was spent in mapping the Hualapai Dam site.

Sept. 28 ... Finished the survey of Hualapai Rapid Dam site at 11 a.m. Broke camp after lunch and moved down the river 3 miles, or to mile 304.7, where a short strip of topography was taken at another possible damsite. Camp was made at the lower end of Virgin Canyon.

Sept. 29 ... Broke camp at Mile 306 at 8 a. m. Using the motor boat towing the 'Tapeats' and the canoe. Had our lunch at the mouth of Virgin River. Reached the Calville dam site at 5 p.m., having traveled 36 miles.

Thus ended the adventure in this area of yet another group of river explorers. It's uncertain if LaRue was aware of the former viability of dam sites survey done by Lippincott in 1902, some 22 years earlier (described in previous Grigg's Ferry chapter), wherein Lippincott had concluded that the Hualapai Rapid/Virgin Canyon would not be a good site.

In 1928, a mystery occurred in the Lower Grand Canyon that involved a honeymoon couple, Glen and Bessie Hyde. Even though never actually completing their trip through the Canyon and reaching their destination of Pearce Ferry, the story is of such interest that a summary of it will be included in this work.[10,11]

While visiting in San Francisco, a spirited young art student from back east, Bessie, met an adventurous 28 year-old part-time Idaho rancher, Glen Hyde. Glen loved running rivers and had been down several Canadian Rivers and the Salmon River in Idaho, and had recently built a crude twenty-foot long craft carrying sweep oars at each end that he wanted to try on the Colorado River. He and Bessie were soon married and Glen convinced Bessie they should take a thrilling honeymoon journey down the Colorado.

They started at Green River, Wyoming, on October of 1928. The first half of the trip progressed well with Bessie counting the days by cutting notches in the gunwale of the boat and noting Sundays with a cross. They carried a diary, camera, and a copy of Ellsworth Kolb's book, *Through the Grand Canyon from Wyoming to Mexico,* yet they took no life jackets along.

Glen hoped to set two records. One, to actually run all the rapids rather than get out, walk around and line the boat through the most dangerous ones as was commonly done, and two, for Bessie to be the first woman to make such a trip.

After passing Lee's Ferry in early November, they entered Marble Canyon where Glen was thrown from the boat in a rapids. Bessie was able to hang on to the sweep oars and still throw Glen a rope, no doubt saving both the boat and Glen's life. Upon arriving at Bright Angel Creek en route, the Hyde's hiked up to the south rim and visited Emery Kolb at the brothers studio. Kolb noticed Bessie seemed reluctant to return to the river. He tried to convince Glen to take life

Raging River

jackets along, but to no avail, and the two hiked back down to the river and continued their journey.

On December 21, the *Kingman Miner* reported the Hydes to be two weeks overdue. Glen's father came from Idaho and offered a large reward for information about the couple. Finally an army plane flying low in the canyon spotted a boat hung up in mid-stream just below Diamond Creek, so Mr. Hyde asked Emery Kolb to board the plane in order to view the boat. After several low passes, Kolb readily identified the boat as the one having belonged to the Hydes.

A party including Mr. Hyde, Kolb, and several others, made their way down Peach Springs Canyon to Diamond Creek with the intention of launching there. While the men worked to repair an old boat located at Diamond Creek, Mr. Hyde walked seven miles above Diamond Creek and reported finding footprints he thought to be that of Glen and Bessie. Mr. Hyde and a deputy then returned to Peach Springs.

The Kolb brothers and NPS Ranger Jim Brooks floated downriver to the still upright Hyde boat, and from it collected a gun, the diary, and camera. They then continued down to Spencer Canyon where they met another party coming in by land.

It was thought, from the marks Bessie had left on the gunwale and notes in her diary, that she and Glen had lost their lives near mile 232 on the river, just five miles upstream from where the boat was found. Kolb surmised that Bessie, standing ashore, may have been holding the boat with a line while Glen checked a rapids, since they had mentioned this was the method they used before running rapids. He thought Bessie may have been pulled into the river and Glen might then also have been swept away while trying to save her.

If this had been the case, however, it seemed strange that neither body was ever found downstream, as was usually the case with drownings in the canyon. Others thought perhaps the boat had broken loose while tied and left the two stranded in a location where they could not hike out. However, no search parties ever found sign of their bodies in side canyons. Over the years, the disappearance of Glen and Bessie Hyde continued to be mystifying. Then, two more happenings eventually took place which raised even more questions.

After the death of the last Kolb brother in the mid-1970's, human bones were discovered in a canvas boat located in a garage beside the Kolb studio on the south rim of Grand Canyon. The skull was marked with a bullet hole and a small silver buckle was beside the bones – a buckle very much resembling one worn by Glen in one of the last photos taken of he and Bessie. The Coconino Sheriff's Department had the bones studied by a forensic and physical anthropologist at the University of Arizona who concluded these were not those of Glen Hyde. Which left another unanswered question; then whose bones were these?

Perhaps even more mystifying, during a river trip in the 1970's, river runners leading a trip down through the Grand Canyon reported another strange happening. One evening while crew and passengers were spinning tales around a campfire along the river, an elderly woman passenger told a story of her own. She said her name was Bessie and that while she and her husband, Glen, were running the Colorado in 1928, he became increasingly belligerent and difficult. She told how he began beating her, so later, while he slept, she stabbed him, rolled his body into the river, released the boat into the current, then hiked out of the canyon and began a new life under a new name.

Whether this is a true tale remains unknown and the Hyde mystery still haunts those who travel the depths of the canyon.

Another drowning occurred in the Canyon in about 1931, that of Iven Bundy, and in this story still another bit of information surfaces about the Hydes.

Iven was a Mormon in his early twenties who lived in Bundyville in the Arizona Strip country, south of St. George, Utah. One day he and his cousin, Floyd Iverson, were down near the Colorado River herding their father's sheep. It was April and the weather was warm so the boys decided to go for a swim and see if they could make it across the current. Floyd was successful but Iven became caught in a whirlpool and went under.

In her book, *Footprints on the Arizona Strip,* Nellie Iverson Cox tells about the search for the body of Iven, as told by Chester Bundy, Iven's Uncle. Chester had been herding sheep down in Mule Canyon when he got word that Iven had drowned in the Colorado. (It would appear Iven's death had occurred in the area of Whitmore Wash, just west of Toroweap Overlook). Chester and a few others went down to the river to see if they could find anything. It was raining when they arrived and they built a fire in a cave in hopes of keeping warm for the night. As soon as the fire warmed the cave, centipedes, scorpions and all sorts of other varmints came crawling in, so none of the men slept much that night. The next morning they went back up to Mt. Trumbull.

Quoting Bundy from Cox's book:[12]

> Roy [Iven's father who was crippled from arthritis] wanted Floyd, Pat, and me to take a galvanized boat which weighed one hundred and eighty pounds and had an air chamber in each end, and go down the river. Aunt Rettie fixed us some grub ... cookies, beans, and jerky, and we started. South of Parashaunt we had the bad luck to upset the boat and since things weren't properly tied in, we lost a lot of our food and a box of dynamite we had brought to blow up fish for eating. We had made an agreement with Albert Snyder that we would build a signal fire if we were going on down the river. We did, and he gave us a signal in return.

They reached Diamond Creek on Sunday where they tried to get some trout, but to no avail. The story continued:

When we got back down to the first landing at Diamond Creek, we saw this big wooden boat with something written on the side. A young honeymooning couple had vanished two months before while going down the river and believed to have drowned up above Diamond Creek, their boat coming on over the rapids afterward. The boy's father had sent a party to search for them, thinking they might have gone up a canyon and choked to death, but no trace of them had been found.

> A Government survey camp had been at this point at one time and had built a blacksmith shop. A big two-foot-wide plank had served as a place to put tools. I lay down to rest on an old bed springs which lay partly under this bench. Of course, I looked up, and there I saw written the name of the young couple! [Apparently proving that they had reached this point alive instead of drowning farther up river]. Later on I notified "Doc" Marsden, the first man to run a power boat through the Grand Canyon, of what I had found.

They left Diamond Creek and reached Separation two days later, although by then, really didn't know where they were. The men tried to find a safe way through Separation Rapids but finally gave up, then headed north up Separation Canyon on foot. After a number of unsuccessful detours into box canyons, they finally found a way through a third branch canyon and made it out to the top of the north rim, and from there, managed to locate a settlement.

Bundy continued:

> Later on we read a description of a body which had been found by two prospectors down at Greggs Ferry. But it didn't sound like Iven's body. The men had buried the remains and reported it at Kingman but nothing was done about it. Then, a year later, my brother, Omer, was on jury duty at Kingman and one of the jurors was one of the men who had helped bury the body. He told Omer that the newspaper account had not given a correct description at all, and told Omer the true facts. We felt it was Iven, but of course, were not sure. They then got to working on Boulder Dam and the Government offered to move any of the graves in the area to any place the families desired. Iven's sister, Barbara, went down, looked at the teeth, and judging by the way they were worn off, she figured it was Iven.

Today (1990) the Colorado River enters eastern Grand Canyon at about 3100 feet above sea level. By the time the river reaches the west end of the Canyon and the backwaters of Lake Mead, water levels range from 1100-1200 feet elevation. The river averages a depth of fifty feet within the Canyon, with the deepest location having been measured at 110 feet at mile 114.3.[13]

Glen and Bessie Hyde. Courtesy Mohave Museum, Kingman, AZ

Part III: North-of-the-River Country

Chapter Nine: Shivwits Plateau

Looking northeast from my front porch, a singular dark-capped point stands out above the long line of cliff walls marching north from the mouth of Grand Canyon. The cliffs themselves reach some 5000 feet in height; the distant dark point, 6700 feet. It's known locally and on current topographical maps as "Snap Point" and the dark cap consists of thick stands of pine and juniper. During long hot summer months on this high desert on Grapevine Mesa, the early morning sun rises there over Snap Point, then climbs high in the sky to bear down upon us with relentless intensity.

Snap Point arises from a long narrow bench called the Sanup Plateau, just above the Grand Wash Cliffs on the north side of the river. Snap is situated below the Shivwits Plateau farther east, this, the first of five plateaus extending from the Grand Canyon and northward toward Utah. These plateaus form stair-steps climbing upward as one goes east. The Sanup Plateau, this first layer above the Grand Wash Cliffs north of the river, is also called the "Esplanade" on some maps, a Spanish word meaning level bench or open space of land.

The origin of the name Snap Point was long baffling to me. No known explorer or pioneer of that name seemed to have passed through this area. No living rancher or miner seemed to know why it was called "Snap." However, in maps and reports of the early 1900s, I found several references to a Sanup Point in that same location, and even older maps from 1865-1880 have it marked "Sanup Peak." It appears, as so often happens with map versions over time, what originally had been called Sanup Peak, then Sanup Point, must later have been erringly designated as the present Snap Point.

What then, might be the origin of "Sanup"? There is a Paiute word, sanip, that refers to the sap of the pinyon tree. Paiutes often traveled to the higher mesas and plateaus during summer to gather this sap and were known to walk from Grand Wash on up to the Sanup Plateau for this reason. I assume sanup may simply be a varied spelling of sanip.

The next step up easterly, the Shivwits Plateau, is some twenty-five miles wide and nearly eighty miles in length. The Shivwits name means "People of the Springs" and was adopted from the name of the Shivwits band of southern Paiutes who frequented these areas and the lower Grand Wash trough for a good thousand years before the arrival of Euro-Americans. The Uinkaret Plateau forms the next step, this meaning "People of the Pines," the name of another Southern Paiute band. Another step farther east is the Kanab Plateau, followed by the Kaibab Plateau, and lastly the Paria Plateau. All these vast plateau areas located north of Grand Canyon to Utah's border, and across the Grand Wash drainage and west to

North-of-the-River Country

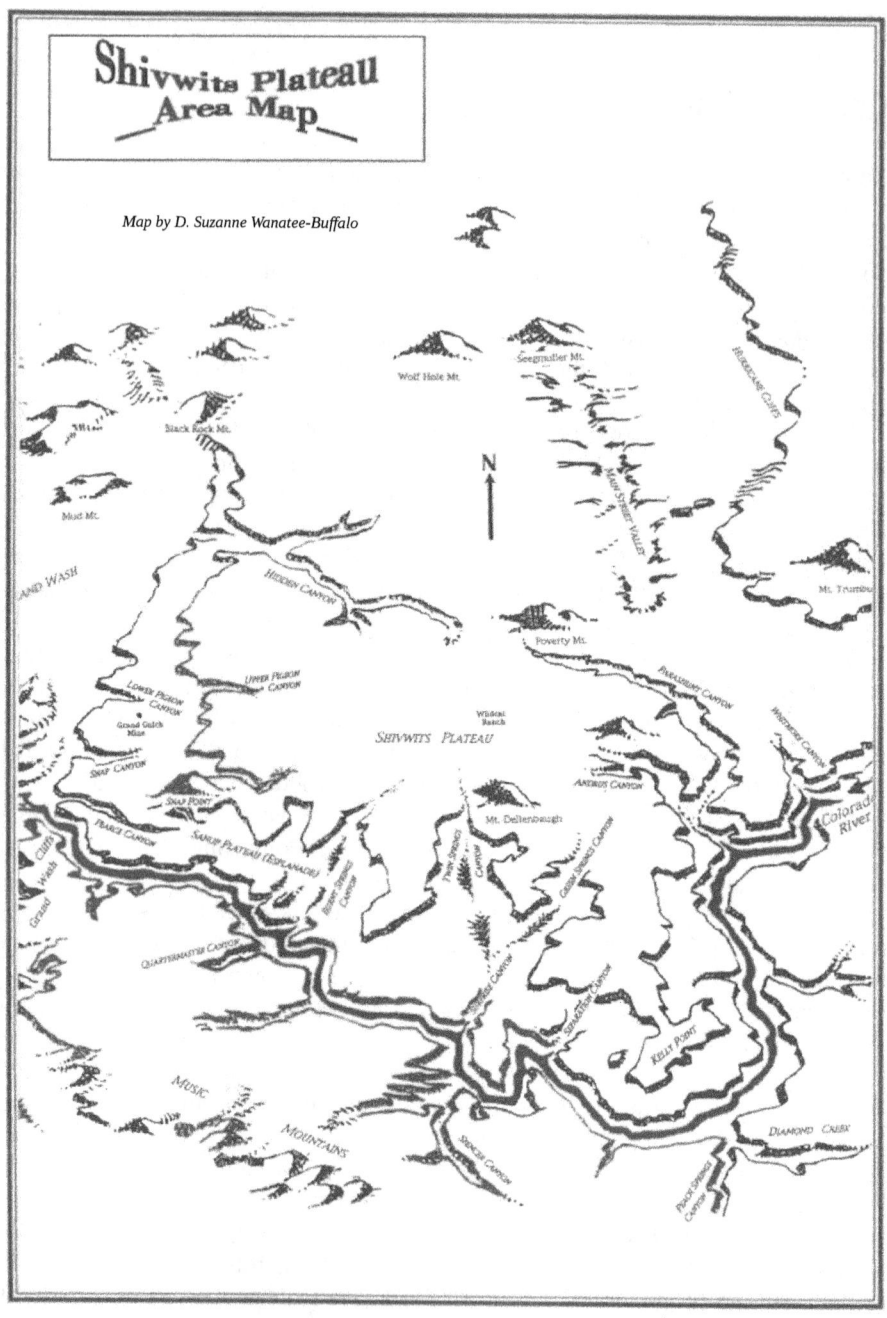

Map by D. Suzanne Wanatee-Buffalo

the Virgin Mountain range in Nevada, make up the incredibly wild and beautiful lands known locally as the "Arizona Strip Country."

The tallest point of the Shivwits Plateau is Mt. Dellenbaugh, a high pine-covered volcanic cone almost 7000 feet in elevation. The mountain was named after Frederick Dellenbaugh (by either Major Powell or Dellenbaugh, himself), an artist who traveled with one of Powell's expeditions up into this plateau region and later wrote an account of the journey. Dellenbaugh mentioned in early 1900 writings that on the summit of this mountain was located a circular ruin about twenty feet in diameter with what remained of walls by then only two feet high. I question, however, whether these were actually remnants from a taller wall or if they may have been the edges of a rock hunting blind, as Natives in this area often built short-walled enclosures on high points to serve as blinds for hiding, while companions below drove mountain sheep up toward the peaks and into their arrows and spears.

Thick blue-grey stands of sagebrush cover many of the open meadows on lower parts of the Shivwits Plateau, with pine forests flourishing in the higher portions. The southern portion of the plateau, known as the Parashunt, a Paiute word meaning "lots of water," consists of extensive remnants of basalt lava. On the southern edge, the land drops off into sheer and deep canyons, disappearing into the vast Great Canyon below.

The northern part of the Shivwits slopes gently down to 5000-6000 foot elevation, with more open terrain of junipers, sagebrush, grasses, and upland cactus. Here and in adjoining lower elevations we find the unique and striking "pockets," natural formations that have long held fascination for humankind. There are the Red Pockets, Whitney Pockets, White Pockets, Pa's Pockets, etc. These are stark outcrops of bare rock protruding suddenly from the ground; large masses of colorful, curious, and exotic sandstone slickrock forms with spires, ledges, and swirls. The pocket areas have long been spiritual connecting places for ancient people of the past and remain so today. The Euro-American name, "pockets," came from a more practical function; rainwater collected in these depressions and potholes often retained valuable moisture throughout drought seasons in this land of such little rain.

Access to the Shivwits Plateau area of the Arizona Strip country is most easily attained by heading south from St. George, Utah, and proceeding down a long lonely gravel road through what is somewhat paradoxically called Mainstreet Valley, and on which one passes a location called Wolf Hole. Wolf Hole was named by Major Powell because the Paiutes called this Shinabitze-spitz Springs; Shinuav being the word for canine predator, either wolf or coyote. At the end of Mainstreet Road is the former community of Mt. Trumbull (not to be confused with the mountain, Mt. Trumbull, farther east), also formerly known as Bundyville, where there is presently just one old empty one-room schoolhouse on the corner. Turn right and head into vast Shivwits Plateau country. Have good detailed maps, and fuel, food, and water for a minimum of two-three days. It's also advisable to go with more than one rugged four-wheel drive vehicle. Many map references to "roads" in this part of the country refer to everything from one lane gravel roads across flats to rugged jeep trails through steep canyons and into sandy washes (often washed out), or just merely wagon trails.

Jonreed Luaritzen, who grew up in Strip country, expressed the following poetic insight in *Arizona Highways*, June of 1951:

> Perhaps the chief value of the Lonesome Country is that in between its flashes of gaiety and enriching experience are wide mesas of stillness where the mind may rest and renew itself in the search for lost meanings and new paths. On its sheer rims or in its dreaming depths you may find a treasure, if it is treasure you seek, but it will be the riches that were hidden in yourself.

James Ohio Pattie may have been the first Euro-American to cross up the Grand Wash Cliffs and proceed onto the Shivwits Plateau as early as 1827, but insufficient details of his party's route leaves this uncertain.

Mormon expansion into southern Utah during the early 1850's resulted in a number of families settling farther south and into remote areas of Arizona Strip. By 1863, Dr. James Whitmore and Robert McIntyre started ranch headquarters at Pipe Springs, an excellent year-around water source just south of the Utah border and west of present-day Fredonia, Arizona. Another Mormon, William Maxwell, settled at Moccasin Springs, and a settlement was also established at Millersburg (now Beaver Dams near Littlefield). In 1866, both Whitmore and McIntyre were killed by Native Americans. Paiutes were blamed for the deaths and punished but it's since been thought by some historians that raiding Navajos from east of the Colorado River, who often made excursions into that high country, were more likely responsible.

Recall Major John Wesley Powell's first river expedition through Grand Canyon in 1869 and the three men, Dunn and the Howland brothers, who left the party at Separation Canyon to hike out northerly and ultimately arrive on the Shivwits Plateau only to be killed by Natives. Various accounts and suppositions have surfaced as to why the men were killed, by whom, and where. Probably one of the most reliable was given by Old Simon, the Paiute who lived for many years at Tassi Springs down in Grand Wash and at Snap Springs up on the plateau.[1] Old Simon told how, when he was a boy, three white men had climbed to the top of the plateau and come upon a camp of his people where they were well received. Then after the men left, news circulated amongst the Paiutes that some miners had attacked a Native woman to the south. Toab, a Paiute with a history of violence (including the rumor that he, himself, had once killed a Native woman at Wolf Hole) was in the camp. According to Old Simon, Toab and several friends decided these were probably the same men and that they should pursue and kill them in retribution.

Controversy exists over the exact route taken by Powell's men via Separation Canyon and up onto the plateau, as well as where the ambush took place. On top of Mt. Dellenbaugh an inscription on a rock reads "W Dunn 1869 - Water" along with an arrow pointing northerly. This deteriorating inscription was barely visible when my brother, Ken, and I located and viewed it in the fall of 1989. Of the various studies that have ensued regarding questions over which route of travel was taken and location of the ambush, re-enactment of the route as done by National Park Service personnel and Michael Belshaw in 1978 seem to lend the most viable conclusions. The place of ambush was probably not Ambush Pockets (also known as Penns Pockets) as Dellenbaugh had designated in his original 1904 account, but instead, at Log Spring, just north of Mt. Dellenbaugh. Belshaw stated that local folklore also gave credence to this conclusion.[2,3,4,5]

Famed Canyon hiker, Dr. Harvey Butchart, who covered over 12,000 miles on foot during forty years of hiking incredibly rugged Grand Canyon backcountry terrain and who is known as the true "Mountain Goat of Grand Canyon," has been up and down Separation Canyon a number of times. Butchart expressed some thoughts in his book, *Grand Canyon Treks II*, on possible routes he thought the men may have taken up to the plateau.[6]

The Sanup and Shivwits Plateau countries contained sought-after minerals and were soon designated the "Bentley Mining District" named after Richard Bentley who was an early miner in the area. Richard Bentley and Samuel Cunningham, recall, had helped the first caravan of Mormons cross at Pearce's ferry in 1877.

The Grand Gulch Mine was the largest and most historically significant mine in this district and is located on the Sanup Plateau just below and northwest of Snap Point. Unusually high grade copper ore was found there, dispersed through a thick layer of sandstone. However, with the location being high on an intermediate cliff bench as well as extremely remote (some 85 miles south of St. George and over 50 miles east of St. Thomas, Nevada) there have been great physical obstacles to development of this mine throughout its history.

Disagreement exists over when and how the mine was discovered. Rowland Callaway, foreman at the mine in the early 1900's, stated the deposit was reported by a Native to Richard Bentley and Samuel Adams in 1851, and that Mr. Adams, who was employed by Bishop Snow in St. George, bought the prospect from the Native for a horse and some flour. Some historians discount this story since St. George did not exist until 1861 and Bishop Snow did not settle there until then. There is, of course, the possibility that Adams was employed by Snow when Snow still lived in Salt Lake City and the reference to Snow as being from St. George was made years later when Snow actually did live there.

W. P. Jennings, a former owner and manager of the mine during it's early days, stated the Grand Gulch Mine was made known to several white men by some Natives in 1871. Samuel Adams then filed on the claim and it became known as the Adams Lode.

Another source, Othel Milne, who worked at the mine off and on from 1902-1918, told that in 1885 a Native informed Sam Adams and Joe Cunningham about green rock west of Pigeon Springs, so Adams and Cunningham, who were in the Parashunt area at the time, headed on over with pack horses. On their way, Toab and several other Paiutes surprised them in camp and wanted to take their supplies and horses. Cunningham told Toab that the government would arrest those responsible and Toab and his men would then not get any supplies being handed out in St. George. The Paiutes left.

North-of-the-River Country

Two interviews with Othel Milne of Washington, Utah, regarding the Grand Gulch Mine, are available for recount. One was done by Owen Wright in 1969 in a Bureau of Land Management manuscript entitled, *Background History of the Arizona Strip District*. The other was obtained when I spoke with Lola Esplin (Buster Esplin's wife at Wildcat Ranch) in 1988, who was most gracious to allow use of excerpts from her 1974 interview with Milne here.

Milne related that when the richest copper ores were first taken out of the Grand Gulch Mine, they were hauled clear to Milford, Utah, quite some distance north of St. George. One carload assayed 55% copper with small amounts of silver but most were about 15% copper. The ore ran from the surface to nearly 250 feet underground, with the shaft having been excavated to a depth of 500 feet. Water was brought in daily by wagon from Pigeon Springs seven miles distant, to supply the crew and camp needs. At one time the crew numbered eighty but normally ran about forty-five. Plenty of food was available as several men would go out on the range, shoot and dress a cow, then save the hide for the rancher who'd be reimbursed later for the beef.

If any of the crew became injured or ill while in this remote location, results were often devastating. Milne said Will Baxter, who'd been running the hoist that brought men up from the shaft, was injured badly after falling about fifteen feet and had to be taken all the way to St. George by buckboard over the rough trails to find treatment. Milne, himself, was then brought up from working in the mine to take over running the hoist, a move which made him very happy since he then received double the ordinary miner's pay which was about $2 a day and board.

According to Milne, the heat of summer at this higher elevation desert mine site wasn't a big problem since the men were working underground most of the time. Likewise, the three bedroom bunkhouse made of heavy rock stayed relatively cool as did the other rock house which contained three large rooms; one for eating, one for an office, and the other for women's quarters.

For a time a Fairbanks-Morse truck with solid tires was used to haul ore. Milne said this worked fine when going over rocks but would sink whenever trying to cross sand. The main engine was an old gasoline Fairbanks-Morse; a one-cylinder, four cycle, very strong and reliable engine. The road they sometimes used for traveling to St. George, after traveling over the rough sections and up onto the plateau, then went by D. M. Parker's store at Wolf Hole. Parker always stocked supplies for surrounding cattlemen and sheepmen at his store until he got appendicitis and had to go into St. George for surgery. Upon Parker's return home from the hospital all his good friends came by and they had a big supper with lots of whisky for everyone, and Milne said all of it together finished Parker off.

Milne recalled:

> Rowland Calloway was the boss out there. He was born out around Pioche, Nv., and he was a wonderful good man around the mine. He was foreman at the Apex Mine for six years during which time he married Ida Keates from St. George. Then he took his wife and children and moved somewhere else. Later when he was working at the Grand Gulch Mine, his wife was living in Provo

and she came out to the mine just once and he shipped her right back to Provo. The way I figured it out, the imported cook from Los Angeles was better looking. Anyway, he didn't want his wife there. Rowland [Calloway] worked at the Grand Gulch Mine for 14 or 15 years. He was still a young man when the mine shut down in 1918 ... Calloway never married again as far as I knew, and I don't know whether the cook from Los Angeles was married or not. I heard they took a trip together to Florida after the mine shut down. I also heard she stayed with him until his money was gone and then she disappeared. When I last heard of Calloway, he was working for some big furniture outfit in Los Angeles. He was quite clever, a handyman with tools in repairing broken furniture.

Everything shut down around this country in 1918 so my wife and I went to Salt Lake City to see if I could get a little work. On our way up in September we met the lawmen that were bringing Toab Indian home from the penitentiary. He had his narrow bed laid down on the ground and he was chained to the hind wheel of a buckboard. Well, the old feller was getting old and he couldn't stand the confinement so people got him released a few months early. However, he didn't live long; he was brokenhearted. He went to the penitentiary because he killed another Indian. He was a bad feller then.[7]

Lola Esplin had also interviewed Ivy Stratton in 1974. Stratton worked at Grand Gulch in 1909, then again in 1911 and 1912. Married and with two children, he earned $1.50 a day while working down in the mine, then later, $2 a day when working out on the range killing and dressing beef. Stratton also made runs to St. Thomas (50 miles away by trail) once a week, taking mail out and picking up supplies for camp. He'd go in on a Tuesday, start back Wednesday, camp at Willow Springs on Wednesday night, and be back at the mine on Thursday. Stratton explained that due to the great distance into town, most men who worked in the mine stayed at the site for months. They worked eight hour shifts every day of the week. When Stratton worked down in the mines initially, he stayed 187 days and put in 188 shifts. Stratton went on to say:

The women had a room in the boarding house to live. They were there for quite a long time. This was in the main big house. There is a kitchen, a dining room and Calloway's office and a room where the women lived. Where we stayed there were several tents. Maybe I am turned around but it seemed like we went south to the bunkhouse. There was nothing over by the mine but ore bins and an engine room.

Old Simon, the Indian, and his wife stayed at Tasseye [Tassi Springs in Grand Wash] as far back as 1880 ... said oldtimers there who had crossed at Pearce's Ferry ... and in 1890, the squaw and Simon were still there when they came back. They used to come up from Tasseye to the Grand Gulch [Mine] and the squaw would do our washing and scrub floors. They would come up about every two or three weeks and ... they would get enough money over three-five days and load up and buy their supplies at the mine and go back to Tasseye.[8]

In various interviews mention was made of pastimes enjoyed by those living at Grand Gulch Mine during non-working hours. Ball games and chess were played. Stratton said there were so many native turtles (desert tortoise) around at that time that they were treated as pets.

In 1913 a geologist, James Hill, described the mine when he visited:

The camp lies in a small depression and is not visible from a distance. The first view from the road shows a frame engine house, surrounded by dumps and ore houses with two long masonry buildings in the background. The shaft is equipped with a 22 horse power gasoline hoist, whose engine also operates a 10 by 10 inch air compressor capable of running three drills, and with a crosshead and bucket.[9]

According to Hill, in the summer of 1913 a Sauer gasoline truck operated between the mine and the Virgin River but this proved unsuccessful due to poor road conditions and the cost of maintaining both tires and truck.

Lumber was obtained from up on Shivwits Plateau. Some of the mine employees also worked at the saw mill in Twin Springs Canyon near Oak Grove. The mill was over twenty miles away and jack pine and red pine, some up to 3-4 feet in diameter, were harvested. The lumber cut and delivered to the mine ran $30 per thousand feet. An adobe smelter was built at the mine in 1878 but this was only mildly successful.

During early operations a road of sorts may have been made going down Pigeon Canyon south of the mine that intersected with the old Pearce Ferry road coming from St. George down Grand Wash and to the crossing at Pearce Ferry. By 1906, however, another wagon road of approximately fifty miles in length was built from Grand Gulch Mine, crossing Grand Wash, and extending to St. Thomas. This road soon became widely known as the Grand Gulch Trail. Freight teams of 6-20 horses and mules were used to transport the heavy loads across this trail, with each horse pulling about one ton of weight. It took an entire week to make a round trip from the mine to St. Thomas, then back to the mine again. Freighters charged $10 a ton to haul the ore. The ore was rail shipped from the new railhead at St. Thomas into St. George.

Returning to Hill to pinpoint the location of Grand Gulch Trail, with his description starting from St. Thomas:

The road crosses Virgin River by ford 2 miles east of St. Thomas, beyond which an ascent of 1,300 feet in 16 miles along the bottom of a narrow canyon carries it to a summit of Bitter Springs Pass over the Virgin Mountains. The road continues on the south bench of Black Canyon to a point about 2 miles from Grand Wash, which is crossed at either the Willow Spring or the Pakoon Well crossing. For about 6 miles east of the crossing the road passes over the low bench of Grand Wash to the base of the Grand Wash Cliffs, 1,250 feet high [at that point] which are ascended by a tortuous but well constructed grade, up a narrow canyon that opens to the north. The mine is about 2 miles south of the place where the road reaches the top of the first line of cliffs, but to avoid a deep canyon, a detour of 4 miles is made to reach the mine.

The torturous grade to which Hill refers may be the section going up through what is now called Grand Gulch Canyon on some maps. At times this road is still passable with a rugged four-wheel drive or heavy duty pick-up truck, but at other times, especially after heavy rains, even the most rugged vehicles cannot negotiate the wash-outs and twisted boulder piles deposited where the crude roadway formerly existed.

Harry Howell in Hafner's *100 Years on the Muddy* gave his description of the Grand Gulch Trail. Howell related that the first part started just east of St. Thomas, then wound through sand dunes until arriving at the Virgin River near the mouth of Bitter Wash. There the freighters would ford the Virgin River, then follow a narrow canyon and proceed up Bitter (or Mud) Wash, and from there go by a huge hole in the ground (probably one now referred to on topographical maps as Devil's Throat, an impressive sink hole some 180 feet deep, 200 feet across, and still present today). The road continued to Mud Springs, proceeded through the gap (now called St. Thomas Gap), down through Black Canyon to Willow Spring in Grand Wash (just south of Pakoon Springs), and from there up through Grand Gulch Canyon in the Grand Wash Cliffs to the mine.

According to Howell, the biggest worry for freight wagon drivers was right at the western end, the Virgin River crossing near St. Thomas. Sometimes the river ran deep on one side, next time it would be deep on the other, or the channel would move to center and, as the river channel changed course, it would leave soft spots and sandbars of treacherous quicksand. Often heavily loaded wagons would have to be unloaded so two or three lighter loads could be taken at a time. Other times the drivers would have to put in time along the bank for days waiting for flood waters to go down. Howell told of one man, Martie Bunker, driver of an eight-team outfit loaded with ore, who got his rig halfway across when the river rose so quickly he was soon swimming. His outfit was swept downstream and most of the horses drowned. The heavy wagon settled so deeply into quicksand that only the spring seat could be seen and it took several days to dig it out. Howell went on:

> After crossing the river, the road followed up Bitter Wash until it narrowed into a deep winding canyon. In some places it was so crooked and narrow it took a good skinner to get through. One time Jess O'Donnel, driving an eight-horse outfit, met a flood. A cloud-burst sent a wall of water six feet deep down through the canyon which caught Jess unaware. He managed to get six horses unhitched, but the other two were swept along and drowned. Jess told of the incident later with tears rolling down his cheeks as he loved "Old Rube," one of the lost horses. He said the last time he saw Rube and his mate they were straining against the tugs trying to hold the wagon until the water washed them off their feet, and team and wagon went rolling over and over

down the canyon. After the flood, parts of the outfit were found scattered for miles down the wash. Rube was an old horse, but one of the best on a freight road. He was raised in Eldorado Canyon and was first used in hauling logs from the Tehaticup Mine to the mill, on the gold roads of Arizona freighting from Searchlight to Nipton, California, and during the boom of Bullfrog, Rhyolite, and Betty. The last few years he was used on the Grand Gulch Trail. He left a record that never could be equaled by any horse of the freight roads.

At the head of Bitter Canyon was a spring of sparkling clear water which flowed down the canyon and finally sank into the gravel and disappeared. No laxative ever worked faster than one drink of this spring water. It was one of the best campgrounds along the trail, surrounded by high bluffs on all sides, affording protection in the winter and shade in the summer. Leaving the spring, the road followed a wash up a ridge, then dropped into a little valley surrounded by beautiful sandstone peaks of many colors. In the center of the valley was an out-cropping of red sandstone giving the appearance the valley was on fire. Here the freighters stored their hay and grain in big pockets made by the wind in the sandstone. The supplies were stored high above the reach of cattle that roamed the range and were used on the return trip by the freighters. Every freighter had his own store house and no one bothered it. Even today one can see the names carved or painted on the sandstone where they stored their supplies. Just to spend an evening in this beautiful valley in silent thought and watch the array of colors fade away into the shadows of night is a picture one never forgets.[10]

Howell mentioned having strange feelings about Mud Springs where a "sense of mystery" always seemed to prevail, and told of the large beautiful camp at Horse Springs, a few miles south, where Ed Syphus and Frank Burgess built a mile long rock wall (drift fence for cattle) in the 1880's, one still used by cattlemen many decades later. He also wrote of the 1905 gold discovery in Gold Butte, the high area to the south of Mud Springs (this entire area becoming known as Gold Butte on modern topo maps) and how some two hundred people or so rushed there and established a town called Gold Butte with a few stores and post office. Supplies were hauled into there from St. Thomas. However, this town was short-lived and after just a few years only Art Coleman and Bill Garrett remained.

In the *Las Vegas Review-Journal, Nevadan*, Oct. 25, 1981, Rex Jensen wrote an informative articled called "Grand Gulch Trail Was Stuff of Legend." A few quotes will be extracted:

> From 1909 until 1920, the Grand Gulch Trail was alive with six, eight, and 10 and 12-horse freight rigs. Up to 40 freighters were kept busy hauling ore from Grand Gulch, Bronzel [now Savanic Mine?], and the more recently developed mining in and around Gold Butte. The Grand Gulch mine shipped over $1 million worth of ore and was owned by the McIntyres of Salt Lake City. But the Bronzel Mine, locally owned by Harry Gentry of St. Thomas, shipped over $250,000 of ore …

Bitter Wash became the testing ground for a freighter's skills as a driver. The wash had narrow, precipitous walls, barely wide enough for a freight wagon to get through. A driver with three or four pairs of horses would be forced to maneuver a team through the twisting turns, "jumping a chain," that is, getting some of the horses on one side of the main chain to step across it and pull the wagon at an angle to the lead horses which had already turned the corner. The maneuver prevented the wagon from being pulled into the bank beside the trail.

Jensen also mentioned an encounter between the infamous Toab and freighters Harvey Frehner and Martie Bunker. The two men were loaded with ore from the Bronzel Mine and Harvey was in the lead on the trail. Before long Harvey realized he couldn't see Martie following, so set his brake and walked back. Rounding a corner, he saw Martie had developed wagon trouble and was under the wagon working. Then he saw Toab standing over Martie with a big rock, ready to hit him over the head. Harvey yelled to alert Martie and when Toab turned, Martie got away. Harvey and Martie caught up with Toab, who said he was only hungry, so reportedly the men fed him and let him go.

Some legal information on the Grand Gulch Mine is available in Roman Malach's writings, who stated that in 1876 the Grand Gulch Copper Mining Co. with houses and water improvements was noted in Mohave County tax rolls. The Grand Gulch Mining Co., consisting of 21 acres of patented land and known as Adams Mine, was sold for delinquent taxes, May 16, 1881, then redeemed by C. C. Bradley on Feb. 3, 1882 for $6.97. In 1886, Frank Jennings was the agent for the mine. In 1889, the Grand Gulch Mining Company, owners unknown, consisted of 21 acres patented mining land known as Adams Mine. 1893 tax records showed 20 patented acres, Jennings Bros., mining land known as the Adams Claim.

Malach quoted a February 3, 1906, story from the *Mohave County Miner*:

> Report has it that the Adams Lode, known as the Grand Gulch Mine in north Mohave County has been bonded to W. J. Guthrie of Butte, Montana, on account of Senator Clark's interest...[11]

The mine ran until 1918 when it was closed down as the ore seemed worked out. Individuals continued to work it on a small scale for the next twenty years, then the mine was reopened during World War II, but only for a short time. According to Malach, some of the buildings burned down in 1955 and the Grand Gulch had produced a total of over 4,500,000 lbs. of copper. *Northwest Arizona Ghost Towns*, however, notes that in 1913, an average of 120 tons of copper ore per month was shipped from Grand Gulch Mine to Salt Lake City.

Today [1990] the Grand Gulch Mine is an intriguing place to visit. The most reliable access route to the mine site is going south from St. George, through the Shivwits Plateau, and then down Upper Pigeon Canyon to the Sanup Plateau (or Grand Wash bench) area. Upon arriving, one finds a beautiful and remote setting. Remnants of stone buildings and a few wooden cabins still stand, as well as skeletal remains of vehicles and mining equipment from times long past. This is private property, however, so take or disturb nothing. Also be extremely cautious around the main shaft area as this is over 500 feet deep and has a dangerous opening with sides sloping steeply downward into the gaping hole. With this shaft being neither fenced nor closed off, it poses a very real hazard to explorers, and especially to children or animals.

A few miles south of the Grand Gulch Mine are the Savanic or Bronzel Mine and the Cunningham Mine. These are also old copper mines and both lie nestled at the top of Lower Pigeon Canyon. Lower Pigeon Canyon is rarely passable so access is usually obtained from the bench above. Both these mines were worked intermittently in the late 1800's and early 1900's, but due partly to even more difficult access, neither mine was worked to the extent of Grand Gulch. Burros had to be used to pack in equipment and gear, and then to pack the ore back out long distances to where it could be loaded on to wagons.

The Copper Mountain Mine is found by going farther east on top of the Shivwits Plateau and then down into Parashant Canyon. This mine is some one hundred miles south of St. George and about three miles north of Grand Canyon, with the mine itself resting several miles down along the side of a steep canyon. This too, was worked during the late 1800's and early 1900's but difficult access restricted production more. Again, all materials were transported in and out by burro pack animals. The burros would carry out three packs of ore each, coming out via Burro Springs and Andrus Canyon, so the ore could be stashed at Grassy Springs. At times almost 300 burros were used in this pack train. Some sources report freighters would pick up loads at Grassy Springs, go down Upper Pigeon Canyon to the Grand Gulch Mine and from there continue down the Grand Gulch Trail to St. Thomas. Another source stated that freighters at times took a longer but easier route, coming up Hidden Canyon (to the north of Grand Gulch Canyon thereby avoiding a steep incline), then to Grassy Springs to pick up the ore, and would return via Grand Gulch Mine and the old trail. This route, however, added another week to the entire freight trip. From 1913 through 1918 the Copper Mountain Mine produced 200,000 pounds of copper and $10,000 in silver. Only a few old buildings still remain at the Copper Mountain Mine today.

Ranching history of the Shivwits Plateau reveals very interesting stories. Early Mormon settlement began in earnest in the lonesome Strip country in the late 1860's, however, when the first Mormon settlers, James Whitmore and Robert McIntyre, were killed by Natives near their Pipe Springs settlement in 1866, church leaders began organizing communal cooperatives in the Strip so members would have more protection. Pipe Springs was developed into a self-sufficient fortification containing a number of families, and the cattle were run on the vast surrounding lands.

A timber mill was set up on Mt. Trumbull to provide lumber for building needs in St. George, and in 1879, one of the cooperatives hired Albert Foremaster from St. George to operate a dairy ranch at Oak Grove near Mt. Dellenbaugh on the Shivwits Plateau. This became known as the Oak Grove Ranch. It's said that the frame cabin standing at that site today, homesteaded by Murray Strutznegger, and the collapsed ruins of an older cabin just above (built by Anthony Ivins) were the first non-Native structures on the Shivwits Plateau. The Oak Grove Ranch provided dairy products for St. George residents as well as to nearby developing mines. Albert Foremaster's daughter was one of many who recalled her parents commenting about the lush grassy meadows common in the early days of the Strip before overgrazing by livestock herds changed the face of the land.

In the 1880's, Congress passed the Edmunds-Tucker Act outlawing the practice of polygamy which had been commonly accepted and practiced by many Mormon Church members. The economic aspects of the law, however, were what hit hardest since this allowed the U. S. Government to confiscate any property owned by polygamists, including properties specifically held in cooperative ventures that were not serving strictly religious functions. The Mormon Church quickly began "formally" divesting itself of outlying cooperative and economic ventures.

The Oak Grove Ranch was sold to Benjamin F. Saunders from Salt Lake City. Although not known to be Mormon, Saunders seemed sympathetic to their cause and in some ways appeared to serve as a front man for the church in this and various other purchases and dealings over the following years. Saunders hired Anthony (Tone) Ivins and John Young, both local Mormons, to manage what he called the Mohave Land and Cattle Company at Oak Grove. Several years later Saunders sold the Oak Grove Ranch to Ivins, then purchased the Pipe Springs Ranch to the east in the Strip country. In 1895, when the Mormon Church liquidated it's large ranch holdings east of Pipe Springs, Saunders sold Pipe Springs and acquired the huge ranch farther east, as well as Kaibab Ranch, which left him in control of most of the entire eastern end of the Strip Country. During this move eastward Saunders sold off remaining properties and water spring rights in the western end of the Strip, including all those on the Shivwits Plateau.

Now enters Preston Nutter, a wealthy non-Mormon cattleman who, in 1893, had just purchased a large herd of five thousand cattle in central Arizona for eight dollars per head. Recall the story (Grigg's Ferry chapter) of Nutter and his men trying to cross the huge herd at Scanlon's Ferry in Hualapai Wash, losing about half of them, then losing more when driving the herd up through Gold Butte during a bad heat spell. The remainder were driven across Grand Wash and up onto the Shivwits Plateau, where the men and herd then got caught in snow storms and had to spend the winter. However, seeing this western part of the Strip firmed up Nutter's interest in ranching prospects there.

Previous to this, water rights at the spring areas had been informally respected between Mormons (i.e. without recognition of Native American rights). It was held that the Mormon who kept the springs "cleaned and running" was considered the owner of that spring and that person usually let other Mormons use the water if supply allowed. When the previous mentioned Saunders, a non-Mormon, arrived on the scene, he had trod rather carefully and acquired water rights from locals by purchase and also by filing questionable mining claims on government lands.

Nutter, however, was of a different bent. He claimed to have traveled to Washington D. C. and purchased legal title on some of the Strip lands by having acquired land in Forest Service areas in California, then trading that for forty acre tracts surrounding springs and pockets in the Strip Country. He also claimed to have purchased "scrip" (others called it "Indian scrip") that was apparently government issued rights to water sources for Euro-American settlers with total disregard to any prior or ongoing use by Natives. Other sources say there was no evidence that Nutter had actually purchased these scrip rights and that he only claimed such.

Regardless, Nutter did purchase Saunders remaining ranch lands and grazing rights on the western part of the Strip, the Shivwits Plateau, and called his place the Parashunt Ranch. He then placed pressure on other ranchers there by claiming water rights and demanding exclusive use. He made no friends and in short order his own non-Mormon cowboys were busy trying to protect his land and livestock. Nutter found it necessary to supplement his cowboys with hired gunslingers, claiming that since he was not Mormon, no assistance was forthcoming from Mormon law enforcement in the Strip Country and he had to enforce his own. One man Nutter brought in from Texas, Ed Johnson, who had a rather notorious past, became Nutter's right-hand man. Eventually Nutter purchased smaller surrounding ranches that were slowly going under and by 1901 he had control over most of the western Strip and was running nearly twenty-five thousand head of cattle. Nutter, even though personally absent most of the time, continued to dominate and influence directions of those ranchlands for the next thirty-five years until his death in Utah in 1936.

One of Nutter's accomplishments still of interest today is a unique road he had built. Since he eventually refused to trade with St. George businessmen (or they, he), it became necessary to build a road of sorts extending west from his Strip rangelands, down through the cliffs and canyons, across Grand Wash, and over to the old town of St. Thomas. The route he selected traversed Hidden Canyon and is a delightful four-wheel drive down through gorgeous and rugged red and yellow walled canyons, however, this culminating in a cliff-balancing hairpin turn down a slick rock red vermillion butte where one is then abruptly gifted with a stunning view over Grand Wash trough to the south. This precarious part of the road soon took on the local name "Nutter's Twist."

Wallace B. Mathis was one pioneer rancher who successfully survived the Nutter onslaught. The Mathis ranch lies at the north base of Mt. Dellenbaugh. Mathis started ranching there at the turn of the century and ran cattle from Mt. Dellenbaugh to Snap Springs below Snap Point. Around 1955, his son, Reed Mathis, built the cabin standing today near the water tank by Snap Springs. In my interview with Reed Mathis, he told that Andrew Sorenson had the original lease on Snap Springs in the 1890's, but that his father, Wallace Mathis, and John Strutznegger, with the help of the elderly Paiute who was living there, Old Simon, had dug the tunnel and developed the Snap Spring water source. Reed Mathis said the old timers recalled Old Simon and his wife staying at Tassi Springs (in Grand Wash) as far back as the 1880's and during the hot summer months, the two would move up onto the plateau around Snap Springs.[12]

Besides ranching, Wallace Mathis, in partnership with John Strutznegger, drove hack (a buckboard affair) for a number of years, running a route from the Grand Gulch Mine on the lower Sanup Plateau and into St. George. It took two days to travel from the mine to town and Mathis charged five dollars each for the trip. Sometimes he would make the run once a week, bringing in miners who wanted to take a break and usually stay a month or two in town.

In 1916, the Homestead Act was passed in Congress, wherein much of the Strip area was declared public domain and opened to more new settlement. Under this act a person could apply to homestead one section of land (640 acres) and do this by "proving up" (building a living quarters and a corral) and living there for seven years. It was also permissible, at least according to pioneer settlers I spoke with, to sell one's homesteading permit before actually having lived there seven years and allow someone else to complete the proving up. Later, after World War II, homesteading was once again allowed but the acreage reduced to 160 acres or a one-quarter section. Needless to say, having access to year around water sources was of primary import for homestead sections in this arid land and declared ownership of those went fast.

About this time, Jonathan (Slim) Waring, born in New York in 1892, arrived on the scene. His widow, Mary Waring, was gracious in providing my mother and I information about Slim during an 1989 interview at her home in Flagstaff.[13]

At the age of 18, Waring, who had greatly admired the publicized western hunts and adventures of Theodore Roosevelt, headed west to Phoenix. He worked jobs around that area for several years, then did mining at the Vulture Mine near Wickenburg and ranch work at Quartzite, Arizona.

In 1916, Waring and two friends came up with a plan to make huge profits by catching and breaking wild horses up north in the remote Strip country and selling the horses to the government for use during the war. Together they purchased an outfit and headed to St. Thomas, via Searchlight and Las Vegas. They crossed the Grand Wash trough and went up onto the first plateau to Grand Gulch Mine. There they were told that a natural water trap called Hidden Lake up on the Shivwits would be a good place to trap wild horses. After arriving at Hidden Lake, setting up a temporary shelter and capturing some wild mustangs, the men decided such opportunities were not so promising. Grain needed for feeding the captured animals while breaking them was expensive and had to be brought in and railroad centers from which to ship the horses were far distant. Eventually the men split up and all left except Waring.

Slim then purchased a homestead permit and cattle from a Mr. Lamb, who was homesteading in Penns Valley and had built a small house there. Waring and another cowboy by the name of Bill Shanley, who had also come to homestead, decided to graze cattle on a peninsula of land jutting south from Green Springs toward Grand Canyon, an area that Preston Nutter had previously fenced off and used to keep his steers separate from the main herds. This peninsula of land stretched over twenty miles southwesterly, contained Blue Mountain, and extended clear to Kelly Point, one of the finest viewpoints on north rim looking down into the Grand Canyon. Waring and Shanley ran Nutter's stock out of the area and branded the mavericks (unbranded stock) and before long had built up a herd of seventy-five cattle, four horses, and one mule.

North-of-the-River Country

Nutter had little tolerance for homesteaders, not to mention this upstart, Waring. Ed Johnson, Nutter's foreman, predictably began having run-in's with Waring. Johnson built a brush fence at the northern end of the peninsula and Waring burned it down. When Johnson went hunting for Waring, Slim found it prudent to stay under cover for a time until things cooled down.

Shortly thereafter, Waring was called into service during World War I (some say Nutter had a hand in his being called). He enlisted at the Grand Gulch Mine and went on to serve in France. After returning to the United States in 1919 and briefly visiting his parents in New York, Waring once again returned to Arizona. While in Kingman, he struck up an acquaintance with Tap Duncan from the Diamond Bar Ranch on Grapevine Mesa. Duncan took Waring out to his ranch and staked him with a horse and saddle and Waring headed north down Grapevine Wash, crossed at Pearce Ferry, and returned up to the Shivwits Plateau in Strip country once again.

In Penns Valley, Waring gathered up what few of his stock remained scattered about. He purchased the homestead rights on Horse Valley from Bill Shanley who still had four years left to prove up on the place, then sold his rights on Penn Valley to a man named Welch.

At Horse Valley, Waring and a friend, Lawrence Klein, cut logs and built a large cabin, several outbuildings, and a corral, much of which still stands to this day. Green Springs was the water source for the ranch and lay several miles to the southeast at the head of Green Springs Canyon (this draining into Surprise Canyon and eventually into the Colorado River in the Grand Canyon). Because of its water source, locals often referred to this ranch as the Green Springs Ranch rather than the Horse Valley Ranch. By 1928, Waring had proven up and gotten papers on the Horse Valley Ranch. In 1936 he had Tom Wakeland and his wife stay there for four years and during that time Wakeland installed a floor in the previously floorless cabin, and also a wall partition. An eight foot wide "sundial" on the ground south of the cabin is thought to have been constructed by a young couple who stayed there for a time in 1961.

As years passed, Waring was able to obtain National Forest Service permits to operate a hunting camp in Pine Flat, just east of Horse Valley, and half interest in another, Moquitch Deer Camp. In 1929, he also purchased trail ride concessions from the north rim and down into Grand Canyon, running that during summers and the hunting camps in autumns and early winters. Before long Waring sold the trail ride concessions because there were too many problems involved. He continued, however, his much loved hunting camp operations until 1942.

In 1938, Waring met Mary Osburn, a teacher in Fredonia, and they were married in 1939. They had no children, although according to one source, Waring had had a son previously, Jack Spencer, who eventually filed on the nearby Shanley Tanks homestead. Over the years, Waring eventually purchased Spencer's rights (probably grazing right leases) on Shanley Tanks and also on a number of school sections and Santa Fe Railroad sections of land, thereby expanding his land uses extensively.

The Wildcat Ranch, located north of the above-mentioned ranches, was first a Forest Service Ranger Station. Ed Johnson filed on the area just south of the Ranger Station and proved up on it, then sold it to his boss, Preston Nutter, as soon as title was obtained. Johnson remained at Wildcat and served as ranch foreman for Nutter for some years. During this time he was involved in several gunplay incidents and eventually lost his life at Pakoon Springs in Grand Wash under highly suspect circumstances (this to be detailed in the coming Grand Wash chapter).

After Nutter's death in Utah in 1936, the Taylor Act was passed in Congress in an attempt to discourage over-grazing of public-owned rangelands on which grazing permits had been allowed, a problem sorely apparent as by then overuse had become rampant. Ranchlands were then fenced and permits were to be adjudicated according to adequate water supplies. Workers from the Civilian Conservation Corps (CCC's) were brought in and put to work. Funds and labor channeled through this organization provided many improvements on public rangelands, including hundreds of miles of fencing, building of corrals and loading chutes, cattle guards, stock trails, and the development of water projects for livestock. Most of this work and the expenses for these many projects were of benefit to the ranchers who were using public lands for grazing. Many non-ranchers complained then, and to this day, that the minimal sums charged to ranchers for grazing rights on public-owned lands were, and still remain, nowhere near sufficient reimbursement for costs to the tax-paying public regarding required maintenance and oversight by federal agencies such as Forest Service, Bureau of Land Management, and National Park Service, this to insure that the public-owned lands not become ravaged again.

Jack Wiggins from Prescott, Arizona, had purchased Wildcat Ranch from Nutter's holdings, and in 1941, Waring bought Wildcat from Wiggins. Waring had a young couple there for awhile and the house caught fire and burned down. Waring then tore down most of the buildings and in 1960 started building the large house that presently serves as headquarters for the Waring Ranch. According to Mary, the original house was south of the present home, near the big rusty tank. There had also once been some old pioneer dugouts where the present house stands. The old kitchen built by the hired hands still sits just south of the present house. Four cabins were also built there. A well was dug at Wildcat and good water was struck at an amazingly shallow twenty foot depth, the only well known to do so in the entire Shivwits area. Buster and Lola Esplin, who worked for Waring for over thirty-five years, currently reside at Wildcat Ranch.

In 1967 the Warings purchased a home in Flagstaff, moving there permanently in the mid-1970's, yet still returned to the ranch on occasion. Slim died at his home in Flagstaff in 1982 and his cremated remains were scattered over the ranch in Strip country. Later, the American Legion post in St. George made a plaque in Slims memory. Buster Esplin and his sons loaded up a big malpai (volcanic) boulder, placed it at the northeast corner near the Horse Valley cabin, and had Slim's plaque imbedded in the boulder.[14]

North-of-the-River Country

Back in the 1930's, a former partner of Waring, George Weston, purchased Penns Place (once owned by Afton Snyder and now commonly known as the Snyder Place), not far from Wildcat Ranch. One time George's wayward brother, Jack, and his even more wayward girlfriend, came to visit for a spell. Unbeknownst to George, Jack and his girlfriend started robbing sheep camps in the area after the men had been paid for shearing wool. The two then robbed a bank in Utah and were about to rob another sheep camp when the sheriff caught up with them. As the sheriff was trying to arrest the two, the girlfriend jerked away and a fight ensued, during which the sheriff shot Jack, but the pair still managed to handcuff the sheriff to a cedar tree and then left. Jack had been hit hard but the two made it to their car and the girlfriend then drove the car away. She said later that she thought Jack was dead by the time she'd crossed the bridge just south of St. George, but she continued driving and went to the Weston Ranch in Penns Valley where the family met her. They buried Jack under a tree behind the house.

Luckily the sheriff was soon discovered. He and deputies (by then accompanied by the FBI) pursued the pair, arriving at Jack Wiggins place at Wildcat Ranch. The Sheriff's posse had no way of knowing whether Jack Weston was still in the house at Penns Valley so they asked Wiggins to go with them to Penns Valley Ranch in order to inform Weston that they were surrounded and must surrender. After much persuasion the girlfriend finally surrendered. The officers dug up Jack's body to verify identity, then hung him from a tree behind the house and took his picture. The girlfriend was later sent to prison in New Mexico for a crime she had committed in that state.

On the 7.5 minute topographical map titled "Snap Canyon East," there's a "Fort Garrett (ruin)" designated at the head of Pearce Canyon. This piqued more of my curiosity. Upon traveling many rugged miles to this remote and distant point, I was surprised to find only a few remnants of rock walls remaining from what appeared to have been a simple, small, rock cabin. Reed Mathis, however, shared the story behind Fort Garrett. When Jack Wiggins owned Wildcat Ranch he used to winter cattle at the head of Pearce Canyon, on the Sanup Plateau below Snap Point. Bill Garrett, a cowboy of some renown (supposedly a cousin to Pat Garrett who finished off Billy the Kid) and Art Coleman were working cattle down there for Wiggins. The two men decided it might be good to have protection from winter storms so started building a little rock cabin with the intent of putting canvas on the top, but never actually got around to even finishing the walls. Coleman, who had worked in that area before, had previously found shelter under a rock ledge right below the rim of Pearce Canyon (a little trail goes down to the rock ledge where a few things still remain) so the men opted to use the ledge for shelter again rather than finish the cabin. Later, Garrett and Coleman left the Shivwits area and started mining over at Gold Butte. Those remnant cabin walls became jokingly known amongst locals as "Fort Garrett" and, as years passed, the spot eventually became designated as such on U.S.G.S. maps, this to be preserved forever in historical antiquity.

According to Reed Mathis, an old pioneer named Dan Sill also lived out on the Parashunt in the 1880's. He stayed alone most of the time and one canyon with Indian caves was named after him. Later, Afton Snyder also lived in that area and Penns Valley and would winter in the Indian caves in that canyon. For awhile he had a wife and kids with him but they finally left.

Mathis also took time to explain the name "Suicide Point," designated on maps as such on the peninsula of land due south of Mt. Dellenbaugh between the forks of Twin Springs and Green Springs Canyons. At one time several cowboys built a wing fence to drive wild mustangs out onto the point and trap them there. Sadly, however, when the men implemented their plan and drove the horses there, rather than stopping, most ran right off the edge of the cliff and fell to their deaths below.

Here, perhaps, more attention should turn to Bill Shanley. He was a well-liked and colorful character referred to in many interviews I had with pioneers. He seemed to have had many friends even though he was nearly always penniless and drank and partied to excess. Stories about him abound but we will pick one in particular, versions of which came from both Del Allan and Reed Mathis.

Shanley had been at a rodeo in Cedar City, Utah, and was living it up, got drunk, and started tearing up one of the saloons. He was arrested and dragged off to jail. When brought in front of the judge, the judge said, "Aren't you the Bill Shanley that was in here two years ago and I fined $5?" Shanley said, "Yup." The judge said, "Well then, I'll fine you $100 this time." Shanley, who had just won some prize money at the rodeo, reached into his pocket, pulled out $200 and handed it to the judge. The judge said, "What are you trying to do, bribe me?" Shanley responded, "No. I'm paying you right now for this AND next year's fine so you won't be able to jack up the price again!"

Today working ranches are still very much present on the Strip although few ranch houses are occupied year around, but more often the ranches are managed from more comfortable homes in Mesquite, Littlefield, or St. George. This is particularly true of those ranches located at higher elevations, ones only being more hospitable during summer months.

The problem of overgrazing as settlement increased in the Strip country was touched upon briefly. Too many cattle and horses were only part of the problem. In the early years (late 1800's) many herds of sheep were also driven into the Strip to graze on public lands after droughts hit in California. James Whitmore and Robert McIntyre were several of the first Mormons who brought sheep into this country in the 1860's. In the early and mid-1900's a number of ranchers purchased railroad sections and grazed sheep on those and on leased sections of public lands, moving the animals to higher plateaus during summer months and down into the Grand Wash trough during colder winter seasons. 1936 tax records for Mohave County showed that over fifty people were running some 70,000 head of sheep in the Strip country. In 1949, when the area experienced one of the worst snow storms, Wayne Gardner, who had some eight hundred head of sheep at the time, froze to death while trying to move them out from Hidden Rim.

Wildlife was also struggling to survive the many influences of Euro-American settlement. Ranchers often shot deer and elk on sight in order to reduce grazing competition for their cattle, horses, and sheep. And when the gun replaced the bow and arrow for the Paiutes, many of those destitute people killed more deer for food. By 1900, the deer population on the plateau had dwindled dangerously low. The Forest Service then hired hunters (paid for with taxpayers money) to destroy predators, who, no longer with enough wild game for food, were killing and eating the more easily accessible range livestock.

From 1906-1930, the following predators were killed in the Strip country with taxpayer funding: 781 mountain lions, 554 bobcats, 30 wolves, and nearly 5000 coyotes; all in order to protect cattle and sheep roaming the hills, but additionally to benefit what few deer remained. Wildlife regulations were also put into effect to give more protection to the deer populations.[15]

Deer herds recovered over the years, and then without natural predators to help keep numbers in check, the population soon began swelling at an abnormal rate. Some estimates claimed the 1930 deer herd had already reached nearly 100,000 animals. In the winter of 1924-1925, the crisis had become more than obvious; nearly 60% of the deer herd died off due to lack of food during severe winter conditions. The Forest Service tried several solutions but the quickest, easiest, and most financially appealing was to implement a program for hunters to fill the role of wild predators that were by then, for all practical purposes, nearly gone.

In 1924, permanent hunting camps were established on forest lands, with those operating them having purchased permits from the Forest Service (these camps similar to the ones operated by Waring, mentioned previously). Hunters had to stay at specific camps and could not hunt on their own or move to other camps. These deer camps were tremendously successful; so much so that deer herds again began to drop dangerously low and by the 1940's hunting camps were discontinued. From that time on, wildlife management fell under the jurisdiction of the Arizona Game and Fish Department that implemented a system of statewide permit allocations.

Still, locals noticed continued impacts on the deer herds even into the 1970's. One mentioned that when word got out about the good hunts and big deer being taken from Mt. Trumbull, so many hunters poured in that they either killed off all the deer or drove them away. Reed Mathis mentioned similar conditions on the Parashunt:

> There was one area over there between Snap and Tincanibits ... there used to be a lot of bucks there but they advertised them in one of those national sports magazines one year and I don't know how many hunters came. There were more hunters than deer, by far![16]

Another hunter who frequented the area for some thirty years, Everett Harris, from Meadview, stated in 1987:

> One year the Game and Fish Department needed money, they got greedy and issued far too many permits during one season.... There were so many hunters up there they were running into each other. Hunters were even taking

out young bucks with just buttons for antlers and the herd was cut way down, never to recover, even to this day.[17]

The U. S. Forest Service (USFS) shares jurisdiction on many of the public-owned lands in the Strip with the Bureau of Land Management (BLM). The Forest Service covers more higher elevation lands that have actual "forests" on them, and the BLM administers more of the lower elevation lands. Historically, BLM (originally, more appropriately named the U. S. Grazing Service) in the western states was created to serve ranchers needs and concerns, most often to the detriment of native plants and wildlife. On lands that both these agencies administered, overgrazing was allowed for many years. Even into the 1970's, most grazing allotments were simply based on "prior use" rather than on criteria based on what was good for the land.

"Chaining" was also allowed, a devastating technique whereby a huge anchor chain was dragged between two bulldozers with every bush and tree in the path torn up and destroyed, this to encourage the growth of grasses for livestock. Massive predator control programs were initiated and subsidized by taxpayer dollars, entailing the previous mentioned vast numbers of predatory animals being trapped, shot, poisoned, and burned; a practice still continuing on many public-owned lands in the west to this day.

In recent years, however, federal agencies have been forced to take into consideration more than the needs of ranchers, miners, or lumbermen. Other concerned groups have surfaced also wanting use of public-owned lands; such as those who bike, four-wheel drive, hike, photograph, or just sight-see and watch wildlife, not to mention others who consider the best use of the more unique public lands to simply be no consumptive use at all.

Yet the negative aspects of immigrant settlement on public lands were surely not unique here. This occurred all across the lands of America. Our pioneer ethic was one that called for conquest, domination, manipulation, and control ... of these lands, of the wildlife and plants native to these lands, and of the native peoples who live here. Our pioneer fathers and mothers suffered and fought hard during their struggle for survival and to better their lives. Yet now it seems that our determination and ingenuity may not prove to be so beneficial in the long run as we once perceived.

North-of-the-River Country

Old school building at deserted community of Mt. Trumbull

Brief pause in Whitmore Canyon, Colorado River in Grand Canyon visible beyond, 1989

My brother, Ken, improvising with tree to get Everett's truck out of wash, 1989

Ken with author's jeep in Upper Grand Gulch Canyon

Mule Team on Old Grand Gulch Trail, photo in possession of Merle Frehner, Las Vegas, NV, undated

North-of-the-River Country

Ken at Nutters Twist, March 1989

Shivwits Plateau

Grand Gulch Mine area. These photos were taken in the fall of 1988 and spring of 1989

Grand Gulch Mine area

Shivwits Plateau

Grand Gulch Mine area

Grand Gulch Mine area

Grand Gulch Mine area

Shivwits Plateau

Grand Gulch Mine area

Slim Waring, unknown date, from Maurine Bostick collection

Buster and Lola Esplin, Wildcat Ranch, 1988

Mr. and Mrs. Reed Mathis, St. George, Utah, 1989

Shivwits Plateau

Ken and author on Mt. Dellenbaugh

Slim and Mary Waring's Horse Valley Ranch, unknown date, from collection of Mary Waring

Don at Fort Garrett ruin, March 1989

Chapter Ten: Grand Wash

Due north from Grapevine Mesa, one's eye looks over the great breadth of an immense geologic depression and drainage, the Grand Wash trough. The trough stretches some forty miles in length, from Grand Wash Bay and Pearce Ferry on the south to Mt. Bangs in the Virgin Mountain range on the north, and a good ten miles in width from the Nevada border on the west to Grand Wash Cliffs on the east.

Before Lake Mead backwaters created present-day Grand Wash Bay, this southern end of Grand Wash culminated in a deep cut called Grand Wash Canyon, and there, resulting from earthen debris washed down, a rapids extended across the channel of the Colorado River. God's Pocket, just east of present Grand Wash Bay, is a cozy and interesting cove with a striking sheer red ridge on the west side, the impressive red rock uplift known as the Cockscomb, a tall ridge running nearly four miles north.

About three miles northerly of Grand Wash Bay lies historic Tassi Springs and Tassi Ranch. Varied spellings have been used for this oasis: Tasha, Tahshari, Tasseye, and Tassi. This beautiful cottonwood-covered area with fresh flowing springs was a very important seasonal camp for Native Americans, as well as for those Natives traveling the Old Ute Trail long before the coming of Euro-Americans. The springs derived their name from a Paiute woman who lived in the area for many years, one who was the great great grandmother of Mrs. LeVan Martineau, her husband being the author of *The Rocks Begin to Speak.* Martineau believed the word "Tassi" was Paiute and meant a type of barrel cactus.[1]

Tassi lived at the springs and in nearby Squaw Wash, also named for her, for decades. During the latter part of her life she lived there year around, unlike other Paiutes who usually congregated at Tassi only during winter months, then migrated up onto the cooler bench areas to the east during summer where they hunted and later gathered pinyon nuts and sap. When Tassi was older and living alone in Grand Wash during the heat of summer, she lived off plants, rodents, snakes, and lizards. Some pioneers think this woman called Tassi is the same one also known by a few ranchers by the English-given name, "Maude" and who once had a blind husband.[2] Whether this Maude actually was Tassi, and if "Old Simon" was the Paiute husband who was said to have gone blind during his latter years, remains unverified. Maude was known to have tied a rope around her blind husband's neck, get on her horse, and ride into Overton, Nevada, some thirty miles across the Virgin Mountains, leading her blind husband along behind.[3]

According to another story quoted by Belshaw, Ed Yates had mentioned coming across Tassi in a wash near the springs one time where she had nearly completed burial of her husband, the only problem being, he was still alive. Yates said he talked her out of finishing her task. From that time on, however, no one ever saw the husband with her again. No doubt it was difficult enough for the old

North-of-the-River Country

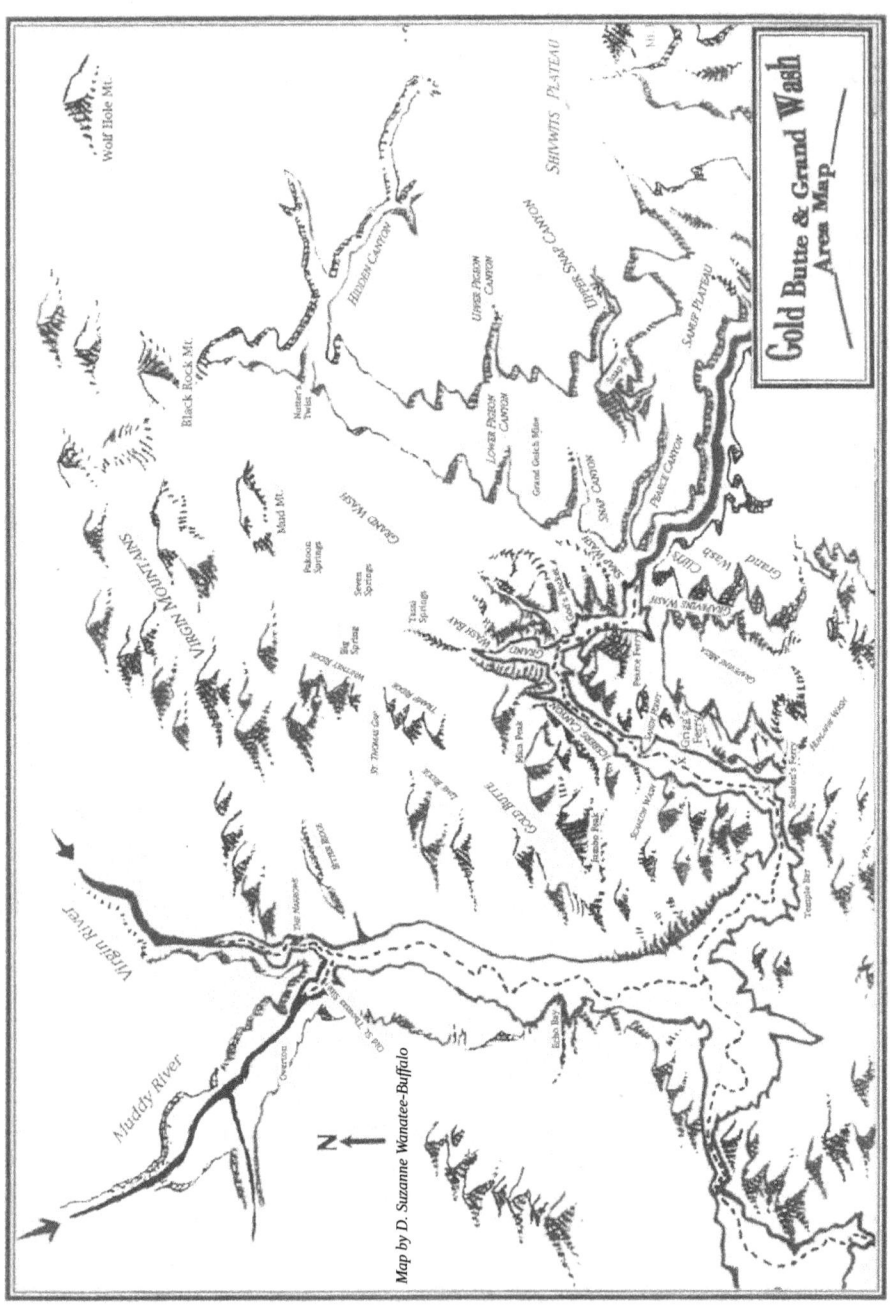

woman to survive on her own, much less provide for a blind husband. Tassi, herself, was last seen alive in the Grand Wash area in the 1930's.

We've heard stories in previous chapters of Old Simon and his wife, Tassi, who moved back and forth between Tassi Springs in Grand Wash and Snap Springs up on the bench lands. Then, too, the feared Paiute, Toab, whom many say helped kill the three men from Major Powell's expedition, also frequented Grand Wash on occasion, and in a story related previously, attempted the attack on Martie Bunker during one of his freight trips across the area.

Another Native, Queho, a renegade Indian who built up quite a fierce reputation, was also said to have hid out at times in the Grand Wash area. During research, differing stories and versions about Queho surfaced, including the claim that he was Mohave, not a Paiute, and I will relate a few versions here.

One story was that Queho went into a miners camp in the Eldorado Canyon and Cottonwood areas, just south of today's Hoover Dam, and bludgeoned the miner's head with his own pick, and is also said to have killed a woman in a tent, Maude Douglas. After the killings he took various items such as watches, guns, food, and mining tools, but rarely bothered with money.

During Belshaw's interview with the Englestead brothers, the two men told of seeing Queho amongst their sheep herds near Tassi Springs and also in the area of Pakoon Springs, about ten miles farther north. One time he came into camp while they were cooking and took a leg of lamb to eat, then left with nary a word. Homer Englestead told about one moonlit night when he saw a man on the outskirts of his sheep camp and just knew it was Queho. Pretending not to see the Indian, he slowly rounded the sheep up near camp, then went into his sheep wagon where he cleaned out everything from under the bunk and laid down underneath all night in case Queho came in to kill him. He never got a bit of sleep the entire night, but Queho never appeared. Englestead also said the Nay boys up at Whitney Ranch (on the west ridge of Grand Wash, near Billy Goat Peak) were friends with Queho and used to help hide him out when he was on the run from the law.

The September 1941 issue of *Arizona Highways* printed another story, "The Saga of Queho" by William Belknap Jr. Information from this story will be summarized here.

In 1940, two Nevada prospectors, Charles Kenyon and Art Schroeder, were working along the river mountains about ten miles below Boulder Dam (later, Hoover Dam). They spotted a cave high above on the west side of the river and climbed up to explore it. Inside, they were startled to find the nearly mummified skeleton of a man. Beside the body lay a 30-30 Winchester rifle, loaded and cocked, a twelve gauge double-barrel shotgun, a powerful bow and some steel-tipped arrows, and an old canteen. The men left and made their way to Las Vegas, Nevada, to report their finding to authorities.

In Las Vegas, Police Chief Frank Wait listened to the description of the body given by Kenyon and Schroeder. Wait remembered the tales of Queho from nearly twenty years prior and how the Indian had twenty-three brutal deaths attributed to him. In 1919, peace officers from both Arizona and Nevada had been hot on his trail, and in fact, thought they had wounded Queho when they finally lost him in the sheer canyon country near the Colorado River. Queho was never seen again after that time.

The article went on saying that a party was formed to go check on the cave and body inside. Kenyon and Schroeder led Police Chief Waite, Coroner Nelson, and National Park Rangers Schenk and Senter from Park Headquarters in Boulder City, on a strenuous hike up the mountainside to the cave. In addition to the body, in the cave they found tattered clothes, a fire-making board and drill, and a complete set of bullet molds and reloading tools. Also, a bunch of keys and watchman's badge, supposedly taken years prior from the body of a mill operator at the Gold Bug Mine whom Queho had reportedly killed. The coroner and those along determined that this weathered and dried body was, indeed, that of Queho.

A somewhat similar story was reported by Arabell Lee Hafner's book, *100 Years On the Muddy*, giving another perspective:

> Queho was also an outlaw Indian who terrorized the land along the Colorado River with his killing. He wasn't a descendant of the Paiute Tribe. Quarrels among his tribal ancestors had made his mother run into the desert with her infant, Queho. After wandering for days she adopted the Paiute Tribe. Here the boy grew up. He knew the country, had worked in the mines, was an expert boatsman, and gifted along mechanical lines. He was skilled in crossing the treacherous Colorado River, a good hunter and archer. It was in the McCullo Mountains between Searchlight and Ivanpah that he found work with a man named Woodard. He worked for some time for this man but was refused pay. He had asked many times for the money to buy food and clothes. One day Woodward returned from town intoxicated, angry words were said and the Indian picked up a stick of wood and struck Woodard on the head, the blow being fatal. Queho, realizing he would be charged with murder, fled into the mountains taking his gun and bullets. One day he came upon two prospectors, Taylor and Hansen. A Doctor Armstrong had been left in camp as cook while the two men were in the hills. They had been taken up the canyon to prospect for borax by Rhyner Hannig of St. Thomas and were to return to camp in a week. No doubt Queho had watched the men for some time and then decided to kill them and take what provisions they had.[4]

Hafner went on to tell that after Queho shot the men, he went over to the Chatecup Mine at Nelson. There he approached a bunkhouse and when the woman inside heard a noise and came to the door with a lamp in her hand, he shot her. Before long a sheriff's posse was formed out of St. Thomas and after two days they found the bodies of the men and were informed of the woman's murder. Queho was immediately suspected of the crimes. Sheriff Sam Gay, Frank Waite, and Joe Keats spent nearly two years trying to find Queho, but to no avail. Many years later, she added, after Boulder Dam had been built, a skeleton was found in a cave and it was thought to be Queho. And, this ended Hafner's version of Queho.

However, during an interview with Chic Perkins in Overton, Nevada, in the fall of 1988, Perkins stated that his father, Fay, told him the skeleton found in this cave was not Queho but that of a Paiute Indian named "Long Tom" who lived on Cottonwood Island and then later up in the caves along the river. Perkins stated that Queho died of influenza while living back amongst the Paiute people in the 1920's. Perkins also said his father told him Queho was soft-spoken and a good stone mason and he doubted that Queho committed all those murders.[5]

As early as 1861, pioneers traveling through Grand Wash had made mention of encounters with Natives camped at Tassi Springs. By 1903, settlers had begun laying claim on the water rights at this oasis and brought their livestock in for grazing and water. A short summary of what I found of Euro-American pioneer occupancy and various claims on Tassi Springs follows:

1903 = O. B. Nay and H. M. Nay recorded claim to Tassi Springs and 20 surrounding acres for mining, ranching, and running cattle (although, according to Belshaw, they never lived there).

1912 = Sam Gentry ran cattle, using the springs as a base.

1913 = Homer Englestead was there working sheep.

1917 = Ed Thomas constructed first actual building, a stone house (now where only a slab is located on bench above and behind the present rock house).

1921 = Preston Nutter's men, Henry Ferguson and Luther Swanner, were working cattle at the springs.

1922-23 = Ed Yates bought Seven Springs (north of Tassi) from Frosty McDougal, and Ed and a partner named Smith used Seven Springs and Tassi as trapping headquarters.

1924-25 = Sam Gentry sold his prior claim on Tassi to George Hartman who ran cattle he'd bought from Laura Gentry. Hartman went broke in 1925. To pay off Gentry, he gave her the deed to the water rights which she then recorded in Las Vegas.

1925-29 = Sid and Tyne Hecklethorne moved to Tassi and ran a very profitable still operation for some years until it was raided and destroyed.

1929 = Ed Yates got the claim from Laura Gentry.

1934-35 = a young unidentified couple was in residence.

1936 = Ed Yates moved to confirm his water rights before the Arizona Water Commission, after which he ran off Mr. Hecklethorne who had several thousand sheep there. Yates then brought in 100 cattle.

1938 = In Belshaw's interview with Ed Yates, Yates said he and Hecklethorne had built the stone house that now still stands ... using rocks from Thomas's original stone cabin on the higher bench.

1939 = Other locals reported that Ed and Wayne Yates (Ed's son) built the house that is there today; still others said Wayne built it by himself.

Early 1940's = Yates sold Tassi to Eldon Smith, but Smith did not keep up on the payments so it later went back to Yates.

1940's = Wayne Yates cleared a gravel airstrip on the bench south of ranch.

1973 = Dennis and James Whitmore (great great grandsons of James Whitmore who was killed at Pipe Springs in 1865) purchased Yate's rights to both Tassi and Seven Springs and have claimed such to present day.

However, the United States Government appears to have negated many of the above supposed "homestead" claims and/or water rights, as such, but did allow that various persons had possessed grazing rights. Then, Congress, by passage of the Boulder Canyon Act in 1902, authorized the withdrawal of this area of land, and it was actually withdrawn by executive order from private ownership in 1919. In October of 1936, the official boundaries of Lake Mead National Recreation Area were established, these encompassing the Tassi Springs area, thus officially bringing all this area officially back under public ownership. Recent court litigation once again established that Tassi Springs and Ranch, are, indeed, within the jurisdiction of Lake Mead National Recreation Area (LMNRA) and are public-owned.

From Michael Belshaw's interview with Homer and Earl Englestead, more stories about Tassi Springs are gleaned. While Sid and Tyne Hecklethorne resided at Tassi in the late 1920's, they had quite a moonshine operation. The Englesteads told of how the Hecklethornes would make as much as five hundred gallons in a batch and had big thousand gallon tanks where they'd store the mash. Brand new trucks would come clear out from Las Vegas, operated by fellows in fancy clothes. They'd buy the stuff by the five gallon cans, take it back to Vegas, and ship it out on the railroad. According to the Englesteads, when federal agents came in and raided Tassi, they took lots of the alcohol but for years afterward five gallon cans of the stuff could be found still hidden all around the ranch.

Belshaw's interview with Laura Gentry revealed that Hecklethornes would often take some of their moonshine over to Bill Garrett at Gold Butte (Garrett was running cattle there for Gentry) and get him so drunk that he would trade off some cattle. Hecklethornes would then bring the beef into St. Thomas and sell it. Gentry said she was sure she bought some of her own beef from them, but said, "They were awfully nice fellas."

The book, *Burro Bill and Me*, written by Edna Calkins Price in 1973, tells about the intriguing excursions she and her husband, Bill, made on foot across this remote area in the early 1930's. As they were about to enter the Strip country from the west, residents at St. Thomas warned them not to cross that country.[6] Price and her husband were told:

> That Strip ain't healthy … people live over there that dassent come out. Might be you and your burros'll end up over a cliff. Better stay out of there.

But they chose to proceed on. The following incident referred to by Price, is about the stills in the area (according to Del Allan from Las Vegas and several other locals interviewed, the "hermit" referred to herein was Ed Yates; although Belshaw thought it might have been Frosty McDougal).

> At Seven Springs we found The Hermit, a tiny gnome of a man. He staggered to the door clad only in a pair of faded jeans to welcome us with a polite flourish, ending in a hiccup. "Scuse me," he mumbled, "been tryin' out a new batch I just run off. Pretty potent this time, I guess."

Price described the Hermit leading them to his dugout storage room where he had several sacks of jerky and pointed out that some jerky was sheep, some was horse, some goat, and maybe even some burro, but said he'd swear to his dying day that he had no beef on the place; then would give a broad wink. He took some of the jerky, returned to the shack, and began whittling it into shavings for gravy. Price told him she'd always pounded the meat for gravy. The Hermit said this beef was too fresh and not hard enough yet for pounding so it had to be slivered. Price continued:

> As we finished our meal with stewed dried peaches and mulberries picked from the trees around the cabin, the Hermit collapsed. When he was able to talk, he told us that he had been kicked by a horse two days before. Had I taken a good look at his naked torso, I could not have missed the fact that two ribs were protruding awkwardly. Bill and I set to work and got the edges of the ribs together but we had no adhesive to strap them in place so we bound him in strips of canvas, making a stiff corset which gave him the look of a devilish little mummy.

While resting, the Hermit gave Price and her husband a graphic account of Seven Springs during the days of prohibition, which, it later occurred to Price, was only one year previous. The Hermit told them:

> Down at Tasi, the next water, some fellers had a still … not a measly little still … one that held a thousand gallons. Them boys was in big business. They had the Colorado guarded at Pierce's Ferry and this [Seven Springs] was the only way in. I was the lookout and I kept my horse saddled and tied right behind that big boulder up there back of the house. One day I looked down and there's a car coming down the wash. I grabbed my Winchester and raced for my horse. It was the revenuers all right and I laid right behind that rock with my rifle trained on them while they ransacked my whole place. Old Betsy kept quiet as a mouse and the minute they left, I jumped on her and galloped six miles overland to Tasi and beat them there … they had ten miles to go in deep sand. The boys (Hecklethornes) just grabbed their guns and beat

it to the river. They made it, but there wasn't much left of that still when the law got through.

Englestead relayed to Belshaw in an interview that during 1934-35, a young couple from Arizona was at the spring. He said they were very poor and didn't have anything. The girl was trying to make a quilt out of Bull Durham sacks and crocheting Arizona brands on the squares as they had an Arizona brands book there with them. Englestead said they were about starved.

Ed Yates, according to my interview with Del Allan in Las Vegas, had actually originally been "Ed Gates" from Colorado, but after running into trouble with the law there, ended up in the Grand Wash area with a slightly different last name. Many stories are told of Yates and his drinking forays which often took place in the company of Bill Garrett and/or Bill Shanley.

Allan told one story about Yates coming by the Pakoon camp pretty well stewed up and stopping to see if anyone wanted any beef. One of the men at the camp said, "Boy, yur getin awful good at skinnin' beef off old Nutter!" Yates just laughed and went on to St. Thomas where he rode right through mainstreet hollering, 'Nutter Beef, Nutter Beef!' "

According to Allan, Yates also used to put three barrels of moonshine on each of six horses and lead them out across Grand Wash and up on the Plateau to Wolf Hole. At the bar and restaurant there (probably Parker's) he would drop off one barrel, then could eat for free. He'd proceed on to St. George to one of the main hotels, put some barrels downstairs and get paid for those. Conventions were held there and if a person wanted whiskey they'd set their empty bottle outside the building and men would go back and forth from inside, filling them from Yates' barrels. Bills were settled as men left the meeting.[7]

In an interview I had with Bill Fauth of Kingman, Arizona, he told of visiting Tassi Ranch in the 1950's when Smith was said to 'have' the place. Fauth talked to a couple living there and said the man had a brass handled knife he'd found in a cave near the ranch. Fauth said the knife was very old and definitely of Spanish in origin. He surmised it might have been a relic left by Spanish explorers or one that had been traded to Natives elsewhere, then perhaps brought to Tassi. Fauth also spoke of the sunken living room in the big rock house and a buckled concrete floor in one room.[8]

During one of my visits to the Tassi Ranch in October of 1988, Jack Jones, who was there at the time, said the back part of the rock house was the oldest and the bathroom that was attached to the house had a door made of arrow weed. Arrow weed is a tall straight plant commonly occurring at the nearby springs. A deer antler served as the bathroom door handle.

Today, Tassi Springs remains a lush oasis located in the midst of sparsely vegetated brown lands. Huge old cottonwoods stand tall, green grass covers the ground, and arrow weed, willows, and creosote abound. Spring water flows along ditches and into ponds. The old rock ranch house still stands. However, many dilapidated structures are also at the site: rotting sheds, run-down camp trailers, rusted old car bodies, piles of trash. NPS recently initiated clean-up efforts at Tassi

– at one time a beautiful natural springs and campsite frequented long before Euro-Americans arrived on the scene, and one well worth preserving for future generations.

As the hawk flies, Seven Springs is located about four miles northerly of Tassi Springs and due north of Grand Wash Bay. Seven separate springs actually are actually located there, in a line along the wash. Although previously occupied for centuries by Natives, pioneers never used Seven Springs as extensively as they did Tassi, below, and Pakoon Springs, above. Frosty McDougal lived there for a time, then Ed Yates. Del Allan said Ed Yates built the dug-out that is still at the Seven Springs site. The ranch site is presently owned by Dennis and James Whitmore. From this location that's just outside the current boundaries of LMNRA, the Whitmore's oversee their current cattle grazing leases, some still retained on Lake Mead Recreation Area lands.

Pakoon Springs ... an exotic sounding name. In Barne's *Arizona Place Names*, it states Pakoon is from a Paiute word meaning water that boils up. Chic Perkins believes it to be a Paiute word meaning warm water. John Cureton Grounds book, *Trail Dust of the Southwest* tells of Vernie Grounds picking berries from the algerita bushes in Music Mountains (southern extension of the Grand Wash Cliffs) with which to make pies. He said the berries were dark blue, very sour, and grew on high sticky bushes with leaves like holly ... "the Indians used the sap from this bush for yellow paint and called it 'pacoon'."[9]

Pakoon Springs lies about twelve miles due north of Tassi Springs. Evidence of Native farm plots near the springs were readily visible when Euro-Americans first arrived. From 1900-1910 the cattle and horses of settlers grazed around the springs, with goats grazing to the north. As noted previously, by 1913, sheep ranchers from southern Utah had moved some of their herds into the Arizona Strip country and Pakoon became a favorite spring feeding ground with up to 50,000 sheep grazing there before the heat of summer settled in.

Owen Wright, in the previously mentioned BLM report, stated:

> By about 1930, people operating cattle and horses in the area became aware that these desert type ranges, once burned over, would be covered with annual weeds and grasses the following year. These areas covered with annuals were the starting places for new fires. Between 1930 and 1955 most of this area had been burned over, changing it from a beautiful desert type range to a fire-scarred annual range.

Most of these fires were not due to natural causes. Ranchers adopted the practice of burning off high desert ranges so fresh grass would sprout up quickly and be available for grazing, a practice beneficial in the short-term view, but continued annual burnings proved devastating over long periods of time, especially with such intensive grazing practices being practiced.

Here it is of interest to look at the history of Euro-American occupation of Pakoon Springs and the similarities to same at Tassi Springs farther south, although more research is needed. Information is from interviews with Reed

Mathis, Del Allan, and others, granting some did not always agree. The following is a general outline:

1900 = The Whitneys may have used the spring early on.

1920 = Jack and Maybell Welch lived there.

1929 = Luther Swanner (one of Preston Nutter's men) moved in, and married Maybell, by then a widow. (Swanner reportedly built the first house over in the west field near the tunnel in the hill; the house was backed up against the tunnel.)

1930 = Ed Johnson (Preston Nutter's foreman) lived there for some years. Johnson reportedly got Pakoon by trading a wagon).

1930's = Charley Walters, then Ozzie Herst, were occupants, and perhaps Brady Cox.

1944 = Ed and Wayne Yates became involved.

1946 = George Allan obtained it, went broke and was going to give it up for taxes when his brother, Del Allan, purchased and retained it for many years.

1981 = Del sold most of Pakoon Springs to Chuck Simmons and Don Hughes of Mesquite, Nevada. Johnny Mullineaux served as caretaker of the ranch for many years.

Del Allan also stated that the hill in the west field where Swanner built the first house might now be leveled. He said that several known acts of violence occurred at the ranch. Slats Jacobs had told Allan about one cowboy who came to his place at Balanced Rock (right next to the Whitney/Nay Ranch up on the west ridge of Grand Wash, heading toward Mesquite) and the man said he had taken a rock and beat another man's head in down by Pakoon Springs in the wash just below the ranch.

Ed Johnson, Nutter's foreman, also met his demise while living at Pakoon. He was found in a corral, hanging from one foot which was caught in the stirrup of a saddle on an unbroken horse. The other horses in the corral were all tame. By the time Johnson was discovered, the horses were so hungry they had eaten each others tails off and big chunks out of the corral posts. Needless to say, not much was left of Johnson so no one could really tell what had happened. Locals said no one would try to break a wild horse in the same corral with tame ones, and, being Nutter's foreman and having had run-in's with so many locals, it was rumored that Johnson's death was no accident.

A third incident occurred when a man named Hubbard was staying at Pakoon in about 1925. John Allan had a little place off the road some twenty miles to the northwest, up over the west ridge and on the road to Mesquite, Nevada. Some of Alan's horses came up missing and when he was in St. Thomas one day, he spotted the horses; Hubbard and another man had them. Allan told them he

Grand Wash

wanted his horses, demanded their return, and they agreed to give them back. Later, when Allan went over to Pakoon Springs to get the horses, a fight ensued and Hubbard shot and killed Allan. Allan's nephew went to pick up the body and said Allan's skull was all mashed in and both fists were broken, so there must have been a terrible battle.

An interesting adventure was mentioned in the book, *Burro Bill and Me*, which also took place at Pakoon Springs:

> In that dry brown stretch of broken ridges and gullies, Pakoon gleamed like a bright green jewel. The burros slid over the step bank of the wash and galloped to water while we followed the longer trail.

The Price's arrived on foot to find a young couple with two small children in residence (the Nays stated this was probably the R. J. White family). The family seemed to enjoy having someone camp next to them for a few days and each morning the children would come shyly to their tent bringing a gift of warm cow's milk. Edna Price (the author) delighted in the treat saying it vastly improved the jerky gravy that had become their staple three-times-a-day diet, this made simply of grease, water and flour with added dried goat meat pounded to a powder between two rocks.

Price mentioned to the rancher that they were interested in Indian ruins. The rancher said there were none close by, but then offered that there was an interesting cave up in the malapai behind the house (malapai means "bad country" in Spanish, and malapai or malpai is a term often used to describe areas of rough dark lava rock). He went on to say:

> Until eight years ago, this place was held by outlaws. The rock corrals overlooking the spring were their forts. See the gunholes in them? Nobody who came in after them ever went back. What happened, I don't know, but this cave is full of skeletons, I've heard – and not Indians, either.

Price went on with her story:

> Immediately Bill began laying plans to enter the cave. Armed with a rope, carbide lamp and snakebite serum, he and the rancher climbed the black malapai slopes while I panted along behind, determined to miss nothing. The cave entrance was merely an opening straight into the earth. Bill stripped to his shorts and wriggled his way downward. For a moment his fingers gripped the rim, then dropped from sight. It seemed a long time before we heard his voice, curiously muffled, 'Hold the rope – I'm coming up for air. This dust is terrible.'

> Once in the air, he described a gruesome cavern. 'There are two chambers ... the second is the larger. It is full of bones, some all scrambled up and some still distinct skeletons. They can't be very old because one has on a Levi waistband and one must have worn a silk dress ... the buttons are scattered around it.'

There was no way to solve this mystery and the rancher seemed glad to let well enough alone.[10]

Tantalizing information. Of course, I had to find this cave.

In the fall of 1988, Don McBee, Mignon Ruby, Clint Whitmore, and I arrived by vehicle at Pakoon Springs. I talked briefly with a man named Wilson who was at the ranch, explaining my desire to find the cave. Wilson acknowledged that there were some caves on the volcanic hill behind the ranch but said he wanted no part of them.

Arriving at the base of the hill, Clint proceeded up one side, and I, the other. Eventually he located two or three depressions amongst large volcanic boulders that more resembled sink holes than caves. Since these initially seemed the only prospects, we reconnoitered at that point.

Several openings under some of the huge boulders looked inviting so I worked my way into one by climbing down between two enormous rocks, each as large as full-sized trucks, and then slid on my back through an opening, ending up in a fair-sized room of sorts. A tiny shaft of sunlight pierced the darkness, coming from a small hole in the ceiling where I could call up to the others above. Upon further inspection, I found a long narrow slit along the floor on one side of the room, one that seemed to have unknown depth beyond. I dropped a rock into the slit and the echoes of it's tumbling went on and on. I attempted no further exploration, however, since those above had called down that they had found another more promising opening.

Returning to the top and re-joining the others, we checked out a nearby opening in the ground just big enough for a slender person to wiggle down through. This seemed more fitting to the description Price had written of her husband exploring over fifty years before. Clint, being the youngest, trimmest, and by all means the bravest, offered to go. We placed a rope around his waist and lowered him slowly through the small opening. He was gone for a time. Silence, then more silence. Nerves became a bit taut. Then his voice trailed up, "It sure is dusty down here!" A few minutes later he called that he was coming back up. After wriggling back out of the small opening and emerging covered with fine silt-like dust, Clint said he had found nothing resembling bones in the small cavern, although it looked as though a passage had at one time gone off in another direction but that the passage was now caved in.

I was disappointed that we found no bones but had the warm satisfaction from having at least found what appeared to be the location of the cave mentioned in the book.

In a later interview with Del Allan, he was able to lend more information. Del said that years ago, Wayne Yates (Ed's son) had mentioned to him that in the late 1930's or early 1940's a group of men from the sheriff's office had gone down into the caves and removed all the bones (perhaps after receiving a report from the Price's?). Allan had heard nothing further, however, about the bones after that, so whoever the bones belonged to apparently still remains a mystery ... yet another one.

Grand Wash

During our conversation, Allan also mentioned several other points of interest about the ponds at Pakoon Springs. In dredging one of the ponds in the late 1960's, they found what looked like an ancient elephant tooth. He wasn't sure where the tooth was now, but thought perhaps his son had it or had given it to a university. Another time one of the hired hands staying at Pakoon came back from a trip to Florida and brought with him a tiny alligator that he released into the ponds. Over the years, the alligator grew larger and larger and would wander from pond to pond, sometimes scaring the stuffings out of occasional visitors. Then it wasn't seen for some time, just plum disappeared. The only thing they could figure was when there were brush fires between Pakoon Springs and the Grand Wash Cliffs, BLM personnel would sometimes swoop in with the helicopter, drop a huge bucket into the ponds until filled with water, scoop it back up, then fly back and dump that on the fire. They wondered if the Florida alligator may have been mistakenly scooped up and taken aloft, never to be seen again.

In the northern part of Grand Wash lies an interesting mountain. Everett Harris, long-time resident of Meadview, once told me about a cave he'd found on this mountain. For nearly thirty years he had hunted the western part of the Strip country and knew the area well. While there in the late 1960's, he said deer tracks had led him toward a cleft high on the mountainside. He had entered and found, to his surprise, a small cave with blackened ceiling, a fire stick on the floor (drill used by Natives to start fires), and several thick branches braced across the ceiling to serve as drying racks.

Every time I would run into Everett at the store in Meadview, he would take me by arm, lead me out into the parking area, point north into the Strip country, and admonish, "You can't stop doing your explorations and research before you get over into that Strip country!" He knew I had already spent some years exploring and researching information on "our side" of the river, but he would not abide with letting me stop there.

So, in 1988, Everett and I packed our back-country vehicles, he in his old Chevy pick-up and me in my little 4 cylinder Jeep with my black wolf-dog, Keewa alongside, and we took off for the Strip country. By then, Everett was 82 years old. Since he'd just had one hip replacement and another was scheduled, he wasn't sure he could do much hiking and had come to the wise conclusion that he should also load his four-wheel ATV into the back of his pick-up. He was intent upon once again reaching that old Indian Cave and had remembered an old fire road going part way up that mountain so hoped he could drive his ATV some of the distance.

After several days camping and exploring in the Shivwits area, we approached the mountain of interest. We went as far as possible on the old fire road, then Everett unloaded his ATV and Keewa and I began walking while he bumped along beside us over rocks with his ATV, having to get off and nudge and push the ATV over wash-outs and around larger boulders. Occasionally the old trail would improve some and he would invite me to hop aboard. I would, but the day had become very hot and it didn't seem fair to leave poor old Keewa walking, so I'd grab hold of her 90 pounds and hoist her aboard, too. At first she clung tightly, trembling, as we jolted and bumped along. After a time, she and I would get off and walk, then jump back on again. Before long she got the idea and became an eager participant, leaping up behind Everett at the slightest invitation, and leaning forward with her head over his shoulder, in eager anticipation. The rest of the trip the most difficult problem was trying to get her off to walk for a time.

As we proceeded up the mountain in this slow and deliberate way, the day wore on. Many landmarks seemed unfamiliar to Everett; things had changed over thirty years. By three in the afternoon we still had not found the right area and decided to return to camp, regroup, and try another day.

The next day we rested (if you can call driving one hundred miles over bumpy gravel roads to the nearest small town for more supplies and fuel and returning to camp again late that night, "resting"). That night, around the campfire, we planned a new approach to the mountain.

Starting early the next morn we went around to the steeper side of the mountain. Again, we took the jeep and ATV as far as possible, then abandoned both in order to hike up remnants of a crude old fire trail. This seemed a shorter and more direct route up the mountain, although surely more strenuous. About half way up, Everett decided we should cut across, leaving the fire trail, and tackling the mountainside directly, thinking this would be even shorter. So off we went, scrambling over boulders, sliding on scree slopes, tottering on ridges high above the valley below, and generally just clawing our way to the top.

I found the climb very difficult and I was thirty years younger than Everett. After numerous trips, stumbles, slides, and not nearly enough rests, Keewa and I finally pulled ourselves up over a rock lip and onto a sloping bench near the top. I flopped down, not wanting to move another muscle. Keewa dropped wearily beside me. Everett was still somewhere below.

After a few minutes there was a sound of rocks crashing and boulders rolling down. Keewa jumped to her feet and rushed to peer over the edge, looking down for Everett. It took me longer, but then, too, I could see, there he was, still coming. She and I watched for a bit, unable to grasp how he could negotiate that mountainside with only a makeshift cane supporting him and his bad hips. He would pick his way along, cursing rocks or branches that obstructed his path, then push them out of the way and they would go crashing on down the mountainside. I leaned back to rest again and Keewa did the same. Soon we'd hear another ruckus and then Keewa would again leap to her feet and run to look over the edge. I just watched. First she peered down intently, then slowly her expression would relax and soon she'd turn and come back to lay down again. I knew Everett was o.k. I didn't budge an inch.

A few minutes later Everett's weathered face appeared over the edge and he growled, "What's the matter, can't you two take this mountain climbin' anymore?!!" Then off he went, trudging through junipers and pinyon for another half-mile, with Keewa and I scrambling behind, trying to keep pace with his long-legged strides.

Suddenly he stopped. He was in familiar territory. Anticipation energized us and after another ten minutes of orienting by landmarks he was sure we were close to where the cleft was located. We climbed over boulders and rounded a corner. Alas, everything looked different--- there was no cleft where one apparently used to be.

He sat on a boulder and studied the mountainside. Keewa and I waited. After a few minutes he said slowly, "It's here – I know it's here." A few more moments of silence; he seemed to be mentally zeroing on the spot. Suddenly he moved forward, disappeared around a right turn, and we heard more rocks roll as he climbed again. Then came the shout, "Here it is!!"

Keewa and I hurried to catch up. Rounding a large pile of big rocks, we saw Everett perched on a huge dark malpai boulder. The cleft that formerly had blocked the cave entrance was now gone, long ago having toppled down the mountainside. A ledge at the top of the cave entrance had also collapsed, this almost obscuring the remaining opening. Fortunately, enough of an entrance still remained that we were able to enter. The interior of the cave looked the same as Everett had previously described, even down to the drying racks still wedged into the ceiling. It was still there. Harris' Cave!

Details of the location of Harris's Cave were later turned in to Rick Malcomsen, archaeologist for the BLM St. George area office, since these lands were under that office's jurisdiction. Several historically significant Native points we found in the area, as well as descriptions of their former locations, were also turned over to Malcomsen. One point we found on the mountain was thought by several archaeologists to possibly be an ancient pinto point dating from some three thousand years past. Another larger one found later on a nearby mountain and a smaller perfectly formed arrowhead of clear and black agate were also turned in to Malcomsen.

Before leaving Grand Wash we should touch briefly upon the old Whitney Ranch located high on the western ridge of Grand Wash, in a saddle of the Virgin Mountains. This is on the gravel road that many follow when entering Grand Wash from the western or Nevada side. Big Spring is located there, with flowing waters that abound. The original homesteaders of this ranch were the Nay family. In 1910, Luke and Julia Whitney took over the ranch, had it for nearly twenty years, and every since it has been known locally as the Whitney Ranch even though the ranch returned to Nay ownership in 1930.

When approaching from Bunkerville, Nevada, and circling west of the Virgin Mountains, one eventually comes to Whitney Pockets, a striking red and buff sandstone area not far from Whitney Ranch. There, the blacktop ends. One gravel road heads east and winds up and over Whitney pass where one is greeted with a breathtaking view of the entire Grand Wash trough. Just over this pass the road splits. The road to the right passes the old Whitney Ranch, now the Nay Ranch. Trees and greenery proliferate on this lofty bench sitting high above the long broad valley below.

Luke and Julia Whitney had developed the ranch there extensively, building most of the rock work around the old buildings, putting in irrigation systems to huge orchards of fruit trees and gardens and developing fine ponds. From a collection of stories simply called *Memories*, Euzell Preston wrote:

> The Whitneys Ranch was one of the most beautiful places in that part of the country. It was nestled down in a little valley with hills on three sides and on the fourth side you looked out over the most rugged rock formation and you could see for many miles. There were hot and cold springs on the ranch and almost any kind of fruit, vegetables, berry and cold, cold water. We hiked to the top of one mountain and found trees with pinenut burrs. We filled a gunny sack and took them to the ranch and roasted them.[11]

Inez Waymire told how Luke Whitney would bring a wagon loaded with fruit and produce to town from his ranch up in the mountain ... luscious strawberries, crisp green beans, peaches, and gooseberries. Town folk loved to buy his produce to spark up their meals.

Fae Stewart also spoke of the Whitney Ranch:

> Some of the people would spend the summer at Whitney's ranch (up in the Bunkerville Mts.) where it was much cooler. There was a big (for the big kids) and a little (for we younger ones) reservoir there where we would swim. I was baptized in the big one. There were lots of rattlesnakes up there and terrible electrical storms.[12]

Others also made reference to the large number of snakes in this area, perhaps due to this having water that attracted animals (food). It was told that a rancher once had herded a whole bunch of pigs out there, some forty-five miles, from Bunkerville. The pigs had a great time eating all the snakes since the snakes could not bite through the pigs tough skin.

Over the years the original ranch was divided. Keith and Marlyn Nay now live at the ranch just off the road branching to the right (Marlyn is a sister to Dennis and Jim Whitmore who ranch at Seven Springs in Grand Wash). The road branching to the left takes one past what became a separate ranch, this once belonging to Slats Jacobs.

Whitney Pockets is located on the crest of this mountain pass and is an enchanting place. To explore amongst the Joshua Trees and magnificent slick rock red boulders there leads to unexpected surprises. Between two smooth cliff walls is a twenty foot high rock dam with concrete steps leading to the top. A smaller dam farther up was built when the area was first settled, then the CCC's came in and built the tall dam with stair steps to catch water run-off. They also built a rock water tank and some enclosures over large pocket areas in the rocks to use for shelter and equipment storage.

Whitney Pockets recently gained some rather dubious national attention. The Bureau of Land Management, under encouragement from President Reagan's administration and their "Tourism and Development Council," initiated the national "Backcountry Byways" system. This provided information to the public about scenic and interesting back roads they might want to travel since greater numbers were finding exploration of more remote places an increasingly enjoyable pastime.

The Gold Butte Loop Road (starting at Whitney Pockets, looping south into Gold Butte and circling back north again) was chosen as the first official Bureau of Land Management "Backcountry Byway" in the country and was designated as such with public ceremony in 1990. This brought adamant objections from several area ranchers who felt the area should be left alone and certainly not publicized. Yet many of these very people had also recently fought hard against "Wilderness area" designations for these same lands (wilderness designations offering far more protection to the land), fearing that their own activities might eventually be curtailed there. It seems there are definitely those who want complete and free access to public lands for themselves, yet surely do not want equal access for others.

Everett, Del Allan, and author, in Las Vegas doing route planning

Grand Wash

One of our camps, this one a luxury at the old Layton Ranch, 1988

Seven Springs area in Grand Wash, March, 1989

Grand Wash

Everett at old Rock Shelter at Seven Springs

North-of-the-River Country

Pakoon Springs pond

Pakoon Springs ranch, Nov, 1988

Grand Wash

Clint Whitmore descending into cave, Dec, 1989

Tassi Ranch site, March, 1989

Old Tassi Ranch house, March, 1986

North-of-the-River Country

Reed bathroom door at Tassi Ranch

Kitchen at Tassi

Grand Wash

Pond at Whitney Ranch

North-of-the-River Country

Whitney Pockets Area, our camp at the Red Rocks, Oct, 1988

Grand Wash

Joshua trees at Whitney Pockets

Old CCC dam in crevice at Whitney Pockets

Grand Wash

Queho, Coroner A. J. Nelson, Frank Wait, Chief of Police, Ranger Senter, NPS; NPS photo from 1940

North-of-the-River Country

Everett Harris in front of Harris's Cave in the Strip Country, 1988

Everett and author, 1988

Chapter Eleven: Gold Butte

(See map on p. 144.)

Now surrounded on three sides by the waters of Lake Mead, Gold Butte is a large peninsula of land approximately eighteen miles wide and thirty-five miles long. Before the waters rose, the Colorado ran along its eastern and southern boundaries and the Virgin River flowed down its western side from the north.

"Gold Butte" is additionally the name of a five thousand foot butte near the center of this peninsula's highest valley, and the name of a mine close to that butte, as well as the name of a historic encampment that was once in this valley, the name of the road passing through, and of a tributary wash – all situated therein. From my front porch looking northwest, an entire ridge of peaks in Gold Butte are visible, including the two tallest, Mica Peak and Jumbo Peak, each nearly six thousand feet in height.

Initial recorded mining activity from incoming Euro-Americans came when Daniel Bonelli discovered mica deposits on the east side of the range in 1873. By 1908, six tons of mica had been shipped from the area. Then, in 1905, gold was discovered in veins just south of Gold Butte (the butte, itself) bringing a sudden rush of prospectors. A small town of tents was quickly set up along with several stores and a post office, and the name Gold Butte was adopted. The town, however, did not last and most occupants had left within the year.

The exceptions were Bill Garrett and Art Coleman, the two cowboys-turned-miners previously mentioned in both the Shivwits Plateau and Grand Wash chapters. Art Coleman filed on the best gold mines in Gold Butte and dug in to stay. Bill stayed with him. Reed Mathis said the two collected a huge pile of beer cans behind their shack over the years and Bill would also go down into Grand Wash and drink with Ed Yates. Del Allan remembers seeing "Bill and Little Art" on the way to Mesquite one time. They had only one horse so Bill would walk two miles while Art rode, then they'd change places and Art would walk while Bill rode.

Harry Howell described them as an odd pair:

> Bill, a cowboy, was tall, and had seen much of the world traveling with a Wild West Show as a professional roper and rider. Art, a prospector, was little and short and only knew about ore and the workings. But a traveler going through would always find a welcome there and food to eat. It was a lonely spot with the rugged peaks and deep canyons where one could see mountain sheep looking from the high points into the valleys below. It was truly a land of dreams.[1]

In 1918 when it was finally decided to let the Hualapai people live in peace on their lands and a reservation had been set aside around Peach Springs, Arizona, one of the displaced ranchers from that area, John Nelson, moved his family over to Gold Butte. He tried to make a living ranching there but after only a few years decided it was too dry and remote. He moved his family back to Peach Springs where he became sheriff and later helped drive buckboard stage down to the Diamond Creek Hotel on the Colorado River.

Dan Marron lived at and worked the Gold Butte Ranch in the 1930's and 40's. He then sold out to a man named Taylor, a rich man from New York. When Taylor died in 1968, his wife sold the ranch to Howard Hughes – yes, the infamous Howard Hughes. Hughes hired Jim Haworth, who had frequented the Gold Butte area since 1952, to be his ranch foreman. In my interview with Haworth, he said Hughes had all of Gold Butte plus lots of land clear north; a huge spread. Haworth now lives in Moapa, Nevada, and he and his wife wrote a book about all the lesser-known holdings of Hughes that they were hoping to publish.[2] When Howard Hughes died in 1978, the Mormon Church bought the ranch and Haworth continued to work for them a short while. The Church, in turn, sold it in 1984 and Haworth said a man named Flake in Calienta, Nevada, took over the management.

Haworth shared more information. He said he once found a piece of spur up near the old road in Gold Butte and thought it was of Spanish origin. He also knew the location of one old arrastra in the area and had heard of two more. When asked if he knew anything about the grave that's marked on USGS topo maps in the Gold Butte area, he said one day in the early 1950's, Bill Garrett had found a dead man sitting up against the base of a small tree there. There was no identification on him. Garrett figured the man had come off the river, walked up the mountain that far, then died. He buried the man with only a rock on the grave. Haworth didn't recall there had ever been a town called Gold Butte, however, had heard of one called Copper City toward the north end of Lime Canyon not far from the Tramp Mine that existed in the late 1800's.

Rex Jensen wrote an article for the *Las Vegas Review-Journal* and included with this a sketch showing Copper City south of the Tramp Mine (although others disagreed as to that location):

> In 1909 a copper boom at Copper City, five miles north of Gold Butte, spurred interest in the area. In addition, the Old Tramp Mine and the Lincoln Mine, both north of Gold Butte, began producing high grade copper ores, some of it 80 percent pure. Oldtimers still speak in awe of the large rocks of pure copper taken from the Old Tramp Mine.[3]

In the winter of 1989, my husband and I did some memorable exploring of the Gold Butte area in our old Jeep. We traveled by road via Las Vegas, up toward Mesquite, NV., entered the Gold Butte area from the north, proceeded past Devil's Throat, then south up Gold Butte Wash road (the "old" Gold Butte Road). After traveling the loop through the old encampment of Gold Butte, we then headed back northerly on the Horse Spring Wash road (the "new" Gold Butte Road), and cut down through Immigrant Canyon on the even newer (not better) road to Devil's Cove on the lake. There, we met up with Richard and Greg Montgomery, longtime Meadview friends, who were waiting to join us, having arrived by boat.

Our party of four then returned to the top in search of "Treasurehawk," otherwise known as Ed Bounsall, or locally, Crazy Ed. Ed had been living on Gold Butte for nearly twenty years and had taken over most of the mines there in

Gold Butte

the high valley. I'd heard many a wild tale about Ed, especially his reputation for lack of hospitality toward strangers (shooting at them, etc.), so I simply had to meet this man.

We drove through miles of junipers in the high valley, wandered around on winding jeep trails, and finally came to a big "Absolutely NO Trespassing!!" sign. Figuring we were on the right track, I encouraged Don to push the jeep onward. We jolted on over the trail, through more cedar trees, then, rounding a corner, suddenly found ourselves approaching a number of old buildings and broken down vehicles. We stopped. We could hear machinery running, then saw several men working on a car over beyond a cabin. At the same time, they saw us. An older, shorter man turned abruptly and started at a fast pace toward us. Three younger men with him grabbed guns (one, a 44 Magnum revolver, the others, assault rifles), cocked those and followed close on the older man's heels, all coming straight for our jeep. Being the only woman (and an older one at that) in our group, I figured my chances were best, so jumped from the Jeep and headed straight for them. As we met, I thrust my hand out toward the older man and said, "Hi – are you Ed? My name is Mary McBee."

He seemed startled, a bit confused, and hesitated for a moment. His young bodyguards, in contrast, looked hostile and ominous. Then he squinted his eyes at me and said, "Do I know you?" I said, "No – I live over there on Grapevine Mesa (pointing across the lake) and I'd like to talk with you about the history of Gold Butte." He glanced apprehensively past me toward our jeep and said, "Who's back there in that jeep?" I told him they were friends from Meadview who were helping me with research on the area.

With that, Ed gave a hand signal to the young men behind him. Two lowered their guns to their sides while the third rested his on his shoulder. Ed then waved to the men in our jeep, motioning them to approach. They did, and from there on, we proceeded to join Ed for a most enjoyable tour of his unique operation at this very unique setting in that remote mountaintop basin.

Ed said his family had lived there with him in this remote area for many years and his wife had self-taught their son and daughter. Neither child had gotten any formal schooling except the daughter who spent her senior year at school in Mesquite in order to gain entrance into college after graduating. Ed showed us around his place. In addition to many kinds of complex mining equipment (most of which he had invented and made, himself), he showed us what remained of his "lab," one he said had held thousands of dollars worth of equipment before it was struck by lightning just eight months before and burned down. Ed's pride and joy, however, were small bush planes that he'd designed, built, and flown; there was one parked in nearly every outbuilding. He said he'd sold one to Ollie North at one time. Surely not what one would expect to find up here on what I'd always assumed was destitute and deserted Gold Butte country!

Ed also related some history. He said there had been a place called Copper City over by Lime Ridge at one time and he'd also heard there was an old town on top called Gold Butte that was supposed to have had five thousand people in it -- but he doubted that number. He'd been told it was set up as a tuberculosis retreat or

North-of-the-River Country

something but that it hadn't lasted long. He said in the entire twenty years he had been there, he'd only seen bighorn sheep twice, both times in the far north section of Gold Butte. He told us that Art Coleman and Bill Garrett were both buried on Gold Butte and that a man had recently put nice headstones on the graves reading, "Arthur S. Coleman, 1876-1958" and "William H. Garrett, 1880-1961."[4]

Too soon the hour was getting late so we thanked Ed and said our good-byes. It was a long way to travel back to the lakeshore camp by dark.

The next day we returned again to the top of Gold Butte and explored another road going west down Catclaw Wash to the lake, which brought us to the shore of the lake across from today's Echo Bay Resort. Later, after returning back up on top again, we started searching for the historic old road (jeep trail) down Scanlon Dugway, the road Michael Scanlon built in the 1880's to provide access from the Nevada and Utah side to his ferry down in Hualapai Wash on the Arizona side. At first we missed an almost imperceptive turn down a small wash and continued on, coming upon another mine, The Windmill. There we were met by yet another armed man. We talked briefly with him and asked directions to the turn-off going to the old Scanlon Dugway. He gave us some directions, however, after backing up the Jeep and turning around, I re-checked topo maps and realized that his information was wrong and would take us back out again (a common practice from locals in these back country areas). Ignoring his directions, we then back-tracked a bit, finally found the correct turn that was nearly hidden from view by brush overgrowth, and proceeded on another mile through a very narrow wash. Then the wash opened up and suddenly we were perched on a precipice; the steep beginning of Scanlon Dugway.

It did, indeed, appear as though this had been hand-built in the 1880's, and in fact, hadn't seemed to have had much maintenance since. We disembarked for a better look. On foot, the view of the road seemed even more ominous to me and I opted to walk a ways. Had I been alone, as was normally the case while exploring the backcountry, I definitely would have turned the jeep around and headed back, never to have experienced the thrill (and near defeat) of negotiating Scanlon Dugway by vehicle.

Richard and Greg walked on down the road. Don took over the wheel of the jeep and started down. Several hair-raising hours later we all ended up near the bottom of the dugway, and all in one piece. From there we maneuvered through narrow lop-sided one-track washes below and eventually arrived at the water's edge in Scanlon Wash, across from South Cove located on the Arizona side. By then, however, there wasn't time to attempt the trip back up the mountainside and back to camp again before dark. A quick radio call across the ten miles of lake water and land to Meadview brought an angel of mercy (Del Hassenplug) who arrived via boat to tote us back to the luxurious comforts of home for the night. As the boat pulled away from shore, I looked back at the lonely little jeep sitting there at the water's edge. The thought flashed through my mind that we might never get the poor thing out of that wash and back up the ominous mountainside once again – heaven forbid, it might become just another "historical landmark" there in Scanlon Wash for boaters to view and surmise over for decades to come.

However, with a good night's rest and the new light of morning, hope sprang anew. Back across the lake we went, with extra ropes, a pulley, and chains, just in case. We climbed back into the jeep and bounced off across the washes and up toward the mountain dugway road once again. The lower part of the dugway wasn't bad – a gently rolling area, but run-off water had cut the four foot-wide path down nearly two feet lower on one side. The next section was some better. Then, upon approaching the upper part where Scanlon had hand-dug the route through the rock hillside, I got out and walked again.

Particularly disconcerting to me was a section where a vehicle would have to tilt dangerously to the left, teetering toward the downhill side of the mountain, at the same time while negotiating a corner to the right and simultaneously bounding up over a huge slippery smooth boulder projecting from the road surface ... the boulder also tilting down toward the mountain-side. One had to get a good run at the obstacle in order to leap over, then just hope you made it; if not, the backwards slide down the mountain would not be pretty.

Don put the jeep in gear and away he went; lurching, slipping, sliding, throwing rocks. Then up the jeep bounced, jumping the awkwardly tilting boulder, and proceeded the rest of the way to the top. Relief! Good old Scanlon Dugway... never again would I try it by vehicle, but instead, would approach from the lake, shoulder my pack, and traverse up the mountainside on foot (after leaving Gold Butte, we notified the Park Service that improvements were badly needed on that section of the road if it was to be left open for travel).

Several interesting mines exist in the Scanlon Wash area, most of which we viewed during the trip. Major ones included the Joker, Lakeshore, Eureka, Union, and Jumbo.

The Lakeshore Mine, although relatively recent (1920's), was evidently the heaviest producer of gold in the wash area and production up to 1966 was estimated between $40,000 and $100,000.

In a May, 1987, interview with Horace Emery, Lake Mead pioneer and son of Pop Emery, he had told me that in the early 1940's as he was coming up the lake in his boat, someone signaled him to pull over there at Scanlon Wash:

> I went over there and these men from the Lakeshore Mine gave me a bar of gold, wanting me to take it to the bank for them. They told me not to try to get away with it because if a person does, then tried to turn it in somewhere, experts could take a sample and tell exactly where the gold came from. I marveled at that, but boy, that was a thrill to get ahold of that bar. It was about eight inches long, two inches wide, and one inch thick. I don't remember how much it weighed, but it was quite a thrill to get ahold of that bar!

Another mine, the Joker Mine, had been in existence for some time and a Meadview neighbor of ours, Jack Craig, had worked there in the mid 1950's. He stated that the mine that was currently designated by this name on modern maps was not the original Joker Mine, but had been previously called by miners, the Burro Mine. Years ago his father-in-law, Allan Nay, had worked the original Joker

North-of-the-River Country

Mine with his burros, hauling sacks of ore from diggings farther back over the hill from what is now called the Joker Mine.

Burros are, of course, still present in Scanlon Wash today, just as throughout the rest of Gold Butte and Grand Wash trough. Brought in originally to labor for prospectors, some were then turned loose to survive as best they could and although not native to the area, the burros not only survived, but fooled everyone and flourished. During the last century they've been hunted, trapped, shot, slaughtered and eaten. Ranchers disposed of them as quickly as possible so the burros would not take grass and water for cows or sheep (animals also not native to the area and probably even more destructive to fragile desert environments). Hunters also shot burros to prevent them from taking over bighorn sheep grazing areas so there would be more bighorn to shoot. Federal agencies like the national Park Service has had employees gun them down on some park lands because the burros were not native and were unnaturally eroding landscapes. Yet these same burro have, at times, also been protected by the National Park Service and BLM on other nearby bordering public-owned lands for other reasons. And the wild burros still survive. Boaters cruising the lake waters and camping its shores will often hear their loud brays of disdain echoing from far-off canyon walls.

Before leaving this "North-of-the-River" Country, we should mention a few words about the formerly designated Pahute County. It encompassed not only Gold Butte and lower Grand Wash trough, but also considerable land on the south side of the river, including Temple Bar Resort, Meadview, Grapevine Mesa, the Grand Wash Cliffs, and even part of the lower Grand Canyon.

In 1850, what we now know as Arizona was then part of the larger area called the Territory of New Mexico. President Abraham Lincoln signed a bill in 1863 separating the two, and the Territory of Arizona was created. Utah began pressuring to have the land north of Grand Canyon, with good reason, as those lands were geographically close to theirs and pioneers spreading into that area were mostly of the Mormon faith. Arizonians, however, fought to keep that northern strip of lands as they wanted the entire Grand Canyon area to remain within Arizona borders.

By 1864, four large counties had been set up in Arizona Territory; Mohave, Yuma, Pima, and Yavapai. A year later the county of Mohave was divided into two; Mohave and Pah-Ute, with the entire northern half being Pah-Ute (even including what is now Las Vegas, Nevada) – a most appropriate name since Paiutes had ranged through this northern section extensively before the influx of Euro-Americans. However, after only six months, an act of Congress transferred all of Arizona located west of the Colorado River and 114 degrees west longitude to the new state of Nevada.

Arizonians were irate, objected to the loss, and continued a fight until 1871, at which time Pah-Ute County was officially revoked and what was left was restored to Mohave County once again. In 1889, the present boundaries of Mohave County were finally resolved. Arizona became a state in 1912.

The name "Mohave" was also appropriate for at least the southern part of the county since the Mohave and Hualapai had long dominated in those lands. The word Mohave has interesting derivations. In Barnes *Arizona Place Names* the author states the word means "three mountains" in the Mojave Indian language, and that the center of their culture was amidst three distinct peaks in the Needles Mountains on the lower Colorado River. Grangers book, *X Marks the Place: Arizona's Names* says the word comes from "aha" (water) and "macave" (along or beside). Messersmith in T*he History of Mohave County to 1912* states that Mojave (Amacava) is said to mean "People along the water," or "People beside the water." He added that it has no connection, as some writers have asserted, with the "Needles" formation of the Mohave Mountains.

John Swisher, past president of the Mohahve Historical Society in southern California wrote an article in *Desert Life* regarding the name Mohave. Swisher stated that Mohahve, Mohave, Mojave, and nearly 40-some other recorded spellings were all spin-offs from the true Indian word, "Aha Macava."[5] Quoting from Swisher's article:

> In 1776, Padre Garces, the first known non-Indian to pass through the Mojave Desert, interpreted in writing what he heard as 'Jamajabs.' Kit Carson chose 'Mohave' in his 1820 records, while in 1843, General Fremont preferred 'Mohahve.'
>
> Additional early varied spellings were: Amajabas, A-mac-ha-ves, and Hah-mah-Kahvah. Having no written language, the Indian spoken word was further confused by both Spanish and English differences.
>
> From a decision made around 1900 by the United States Geographic Board, the Indian name applied to the desert and river in San Bernardino County [CA] and was spelled 'Mohave,' while the township of Kern County [CA] even back then, was officially known as 'Mohave.' Beginning in the early 1930's, a gradual change took place, largely believed due to local Mexican influence, and 'Mohave' then officially became 'Mojave.' … Even the Tribal Council of Indians, once also known as 'Amacavas,' is now using 'Mojave' in its tribes spelling.

With that, we cross over to the south side of the Colorado River.

North-of-the-River Country

Hiker viewing more petroglyph samples, 1989

Gold Butte

Hiker in Pocket Area, circled, 1989

Petroglyphs in Pocket Area of Gold Butte, Don circled toward bottom, Oct, 88

North-of-the-River Country

Don, holding discarded old Lake Mead sign found at crest of Scanlon Dugway, Spring, 1989

Heading down the Dugway

Gold Butte

Scanlon Dugway

North-of-the-River Country

Scanlon Wash

Part IV: South-of-the-River Country

Chapter Twelve: White Hills

On the south bank of the Colorado River across from Gold Butte lies Detrital Wash, named for the great amount of detritus rock that washes down through this long open valley.

W. H. Hardy, one of the first Euro-American pioneers in Mohave County, crossed the river near Fort Mohave, not far south of this area in 1864, and mentioned he found a great abundance of wildlife. In 1866, while serving as a guide for four men traveling from the Colorado River to Prescott, he gave the following account:

> The mountains were alive with game. It was common in traveling through Aztec Pass [between today's Kingman and Prescott] to see two or three hundred deer and antelope a day. A little to the north of this there were bands of elk. There were also the brown bear, the cross, the cinnamon bear, too plenty for fun. There were also the cougar, the panther, the large grey wolf and coyotes. Turkeys and quail were common.[1]

In 1879, Hardy grazed between 2000-3000 Angora goats in the Cerbat Mountains just north of Kingman. According to John Grounds, "Cerbat" means bighorn sheep in the Hualapai language. If that is correct, there must have been bighorn sheep in the Cerbats during pre-settler times. Hardy's Angora goats may have been just the first of many non-native animals brought in by settlers to occupy rangelands previously inhabited by abundant wildlife.

Soon enough, ranching on this side of the river came to show similar patterns of development and exploitation to those previously documented in the northern Strip country. Pioneers came in and took control of water sources previously used by Natives and wildlife. Most ranchers would claim from 640 acres (first Homestead Act) to 160 acres (second Homestead Act), usually placing homes and/or corrals near water sources. Ranch livestock grazed not only on the homesteaded land, but also on vast areas of bordering public-owned lands, often for minimal fees.

In 1866, only two ranches were noted in Mohave County on tax records, whereas by 1876, only ten years later, there were over thirty. One of these was Fred Nobman, listed as having improvements and sixty cattle at the Quail Springs Ranch just south of present-day Dolan Springs. No other declared ranches existed closer to our area at that time.

By 1880, R. G. Patterson, one of the earliest settlers, listed two ranches with 125 cattle on the tax rolls. One was at Mountain Springs, just west of today's community of Dolan Springs, and the other was at nearby "Doling's Springs." Patterson's cattle ranged into the White Hills and up onto our Grapevine Mesa and

South-of-the-River Country

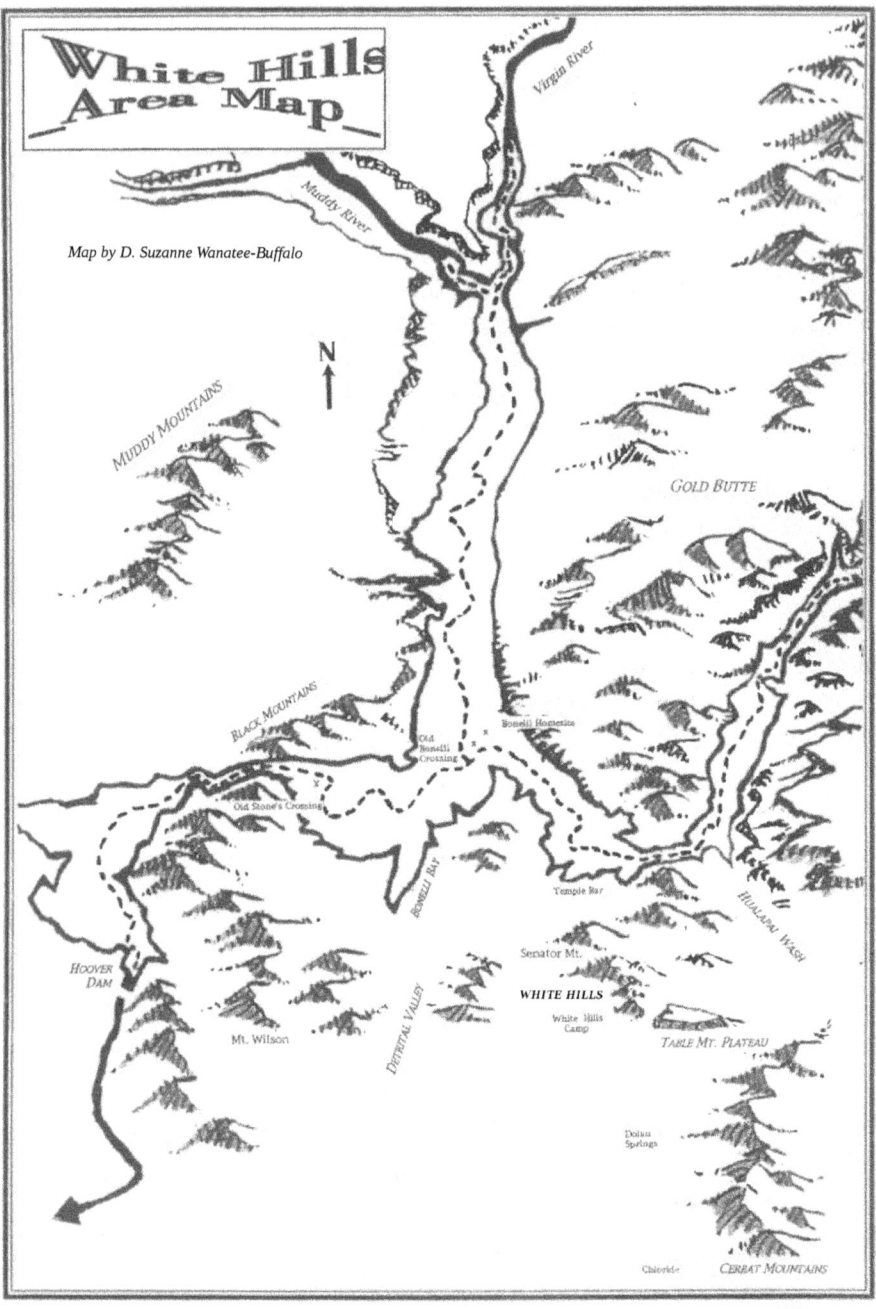

toward the river. Then, from previous discussion regarding the pony express trails, Patterson was said to have Way Stations at Mountain Springs as well as Patterson Springs on the south end of Grapevine Mesa. He was also involved in mining (as were many ranchers) which will be touched upon shortly. With this man lies the source of our present-day place names on Grapevine Mesa for Patterson Springs, Patterson Hill, Patterson Curve, and Patterson Corrals. Patterson lives on, well over a century beyond when he roamed these hills. Yet, oddly, during interviews with ranchers of other pioneer family backgrounds (including Leonard Neal), none recalled any man named Patterson.

In 1880, Wellington Starkey was listed as having a ranch with 150 cattle located some four miles from the Imus Brothers ranch which appears to have been in the Big Sandy area east of the Hualapai Mountains. By the 1890's, however, Starkey had moved and started the Grass Springs Ranch at the site of Tanakah (Grass Springs) here on Grapevine Mesa; this ranch later to be called the Diamond Bar Ranch (by Tap Duncan), then the Smith Ranch, and today, Grand Canyon Ranch.

By the late 1890's, Daniel Bonelli had also begun running cattle on the south shore from his ferry crossing at the river near the mouth of Detrital Wash. During following years he took over much of the grazing range previously used by Patterson, lands extending from his ferry crossing into Dolan Springs and throughout the north end of Hualapai Valley.

Mention of the Old Spear Ranch in the White Hills, approximately five miles northeast of the old mining town of White Hills, began appearing in about 1910, although this ranch evidently had existed for some time previous. Leonard Neal said in his interview that a family by the name of Sloan owned it in the early days.[2] The Sloans had moved here from New Mexico and brought good horses with them. At first they branded with a spear straight up and down but didn't record that since it conflicted with another brand, so they then ran their spear brand horizontally. The Sloans eventually sold out to the Duncans. Sadie Pearl Duncan stated that Charlie Duncan, Tap's son, lived there in the 1920's.

I did, however, find that two brothers by the name of Spear were active pioneers in Mohave County back in the 1870's. One, A. A. Spear, concentrated most of his efforts south along the Colorado River near Fort Mohave and could well have held rights to the "other spear brand" mentioned previously. The second, Benjamin Spear, was actively involved at Beale Spring, Mineral Park, and even the White Hills, which could have placed him at the very ranch that eventually came to be known as the Spear Ranch. Information has not yet been found, however, which would confirm whether Benjamin was actually the originator of this ranch and that spear brand.

Following Charlie Duncan's residence at the site, Leonard and Grace Neal lived on the Spear Ranch when they were first married in the early 1930's. In *Trails, Rails, and Tales*, it's stated that Leonard and Gracie Neal spent several years at the Spear Ranch while leasing it from a Mr. Thorne, and although they had a nice house there, they often located at different camps on the range. Leonard stated in his interview with me that it took them two years to gather up some thirty head of wild cattle (unbranded range cows, mostly from the Grapevine Wash area) and that this was how they got their start. By the 1950's, the Spear Ranch had been incorporated into the larger Smith/Diamond Bar Ranch. Clyde and Cecil McBee, Don McBee's parents, lived for a time at the Spear Ranch in White Hills while working for Jim Smith of the Smith/Diamond Bar Ranch.

An interesting story arose here. In the early 1970's, while Don McBee was assigned by LMNRA to serve as the first National Park Ranger actually stationed here on Grapevine Mesa, he relayed a story to me that his father, Clyde McBee, had once told him. During the 1950's, while Clyde and his wife, Cecil, were working for Jim Smith (Smith/Diamond Bar Ranch), one day while Clyde was out riding the range, he dismounted from his horse to investigate an opening in a hillside. It was a cave, and inside, Clyde found that he could stand upright and then discovered that ice covered the walls. He said it was wonderfully cool inside even though it was during the intense heat of summer.

By the time I was able to pursue more about this story, Don's father had suffered a severe stroke and could no longer provide details as to the possible location of this cave. Since Clyde and Cecil had lived at not only the main Diamond Bar Ranch site at Grass Springs, but also at various line camps on this expansive range over the years, that cave could have been anywhere between Hoover Dam on the west to the Hualapai Indian Reservation on the east, a rugged mountainous area some thirty miles wide and fifty miles long.

During the 1970's, I did contact several people who'd lived in the area for a number of years, including Boyd Tenney of the Tenney Ranch, and asked about any knowledge of this cave. No one seemed to know anything about it, but Tenney and several others suggested possibilities in the Grand Wash Cliffs area. However, Jake Friend from Dolan Springs said he'd heard something about an ice cave near Yucca Springs on the other side of Table Mountain Plateau (north of Dolan Springs, near the old Spear Ranch). It then occurred to me that Table Mountain Plateau and the entire White Hills area, including Senator Mountain, were largely composed of volcanic rocks where ice caves are often found.

After moving away from Grapevine Mesa for a time in 1975, I dropped pursuit of the Ice Cave Mystery and it wasn't until my return in 1981 and after I had begun extensive hiking and explorations of the area, that my curiosity became whetted once again. I called a man who was then foreman of the Smith Ranch, asking him about any knowledge of the ice cave, and he responded that he had "been all over the entire ranch on horseback and knew there were no such ice caves anywhere." When I asked how long he'd been in this area, he replied, "Six months."

By this time, Clyde McBee had passed away. In further conversations with his widow, however, she said that, indeed, she and her husband had been living at the old Spear place in the White Hills, not the Diamond Bar main ranch site, the day that Clyde had come home from riding and told her about finding the ice cave. This narrowed the area down immensely, and in fact, made Jack Friend's previous comment of once hearing about an ice cave near Yucca Springs and on the side of Table Mountain Plateau even more viable. The old Spear Ranch was barely three miles distant from Table Mountain Plateau, an easy one day ride, even while rounding up cattle.

Since Leonard Neal had lived at the Spear Ranch in the 1930's and mentioned having gathered wild horses, I searched him out again and asked if he knew anything about this ice cave. He said he did not, and also said there were no springs near Table Mountain Plateau called Yucca Springs and there never had been. He recalled springs at Jeff Camp, Butcher Camp (mentioning Jim Ray once had this but never lived there), Rock Spring and Rye Spring, and said these were the only ones between the Spear Ranch in the White Hills and Pearce Ferry road. Further research, however, revealed that both the 1969 Mohave County road map and an old 1871 Wheeler Expedition map clearly showed a Yucca Springs designated close to Table Mountain Plateau. Perhaps it was simply not called by that name when Neal ranched in the area.

During the spring of 1990, I was engaged in the national census effort. By then my old jeep had gained some notoriety, was considered near indestructible, and as a result, my supervisor delighted in sending me off into the most remote and desolate areas of this huge county. She said if I didn't check back in after 3-4 days they'd send someone out looking.

One morning as I was lurching along through the Joshua Tree forest, following a two-track path on the east slope of White Hills just below Table Mountain, I rounded a corner and saw a closed gate with a metal "No Trespassing" sign dangling on end from the center post. Below that sign, another wooden sign read, "Beware of Dogs." I parked the jeep, made sure my "U. S. Government Census Worker" name tag was pinned conspicuously to my shirt, unhooked the gate and pulled it open. Suddenly two very agitated little cow dogs came ripping around the base of the hill, barking, snarling, and amply displaying sets of nasty teeth. Obviously, they couldn't read my I. D. card, or, if so, cared less. I back-peddled with haste until my hand touched the front bumper of the jeep and was about to leap onto the hood when suddenly a man's voice came out of nowhere, "Rex, Ginny – that's enough! They won't bite – they're perfectly harmless," the man hollered. The dogs retreated four steps to stand glaring alongside the still ajar gate. Not for one minute did I believe him.

The man's name was Bob Cameron. Since he lived in Kingman most of the time, it turned out that counting him on my census sheet was not needed. We did, however, have a brief and most interesting visit during which the conversation turned to mention of the ice cave story. Bob pointed up at the broken dark crags visible on the edge of Table Mountain plateau and said those volcanic rocks were full of holes.[3] He also mentioned a remnant road coming in from the other side that ended fairly close to the base of the cliffs there. I told him of my intention to come back when census work was done in hopes of exploring those crags.

Regretfully, I had neither the opportunity to return nor to pursue this puzzle further. The thought has occurred that perhaps an opening may have existed some decades ago, then the entrance caved in, as often happens since these lands are always slowly on the move. It seemed as though others should have come across

South-of-the-River Country

the cave by now if it did still exist. Perhaps someone will canvas the entire Table Mountain Plateau area and come up with an answer.

Yet it was mining, not ranching, that dominated activity in this South-of-the-River Country from the 1880's into the early 1900's. Before going into mining history, however, some mining terminology might be helpful.

Mining districts were inclusive of general areas, whereas mining camps were smaller and dealt with subdivisions within districts. A lode mine is one cut into bedrock or hard rock; in contrast, a placer mine is worked from run-off sands, usually in washes. A quarry or prospect is mining done on the land's surface. Shafts go down into the earth. Headframes are timbered structures built over shaft openings, often used to operate hoists. A tunnel is a horizontal passage, at times with openings at both ends. An adit or drift is a horizontal passage with dead-ends. A shute usually describes an opening extending upward. Stopes are areas worked overhead and off from main passages, that follow ore-bearing veins for a distance and then dead-end.

Here, too, a word of caution is in order. Literally thousands of mines exist throughout the area covered in this book. Many of these mines are very old, some more than one hundred years, and unstable conditions are present in nearly all. Aged support beams shudder and give way. Ancient wooden ladders crack and shatter under weights they can no longer bear. Deep water can rest at the bottom of shafts. Rattlesnakes seek reprieve from harsh weather in mine openings and bats usually abound deep inside. People exploring these mines have been injured and killed. That said, mines are, and always will be, fascinating places.

In the Wilson Range of mountains, some 18 miles due west of Temple Bar, miners were busy poking holes everywhere by 1880, as was true throughout the county. This area was known as the "Minnesota Mining District" and it had several mines still recognized in history today.

One was the Cohenour Mine up Petroglyph Wash, west of present-day Temple Bar Resort. According to Roman Malach, retired educator and amateur historian who lived his remaining years in Kingman, a man named Porter lived at this mine for quite some time in the 1930's. The shaft of the Cohenour Mine still remains although with a dangerously funneled opening, as well as other prospect holes. Farther up another ridge lies the Old Pope Mine (not to be confused with the Pope Mine south across Highway 93, but originally operated by the same man). Time has also taken its toll on the old weakened beams providing support over this shaft.

In 1882, the *Mohave Miner* newspaper reported the following:

> One of the richest strikes yet made in Minnesota district is reported from the mine owned by Jas. Smith, Jeff Shepperd, John Mulligan, and others. Smith, while out prospecting, discovered a ledge, which for size and richness, beats everything found in that locality since the original discovery. The ledge is nearly three feet in width, over two feet of which is solid ore, running on average from 350 to 500 ounces in silver per ton. One foot of the ledge,

composed chiefly of rich chlorides, will run quite higher. The camp is not a year old yet and the development on the mine is very slight.

In a January 21, 1975 article in the *Mohave Miner*, Malach has an interesting historical tidbit from this mining district.

> We heard a tale about an Aztec turquoise mine ... old timers refer to this lost turquoise mine as having a deep shaft from which fine turquoise came. Supposedly ancient men mined the blue stone first, and in the last 100 years the white man ... also mined it.

Malach and a guide soon explored various side canyons in the area, then came upon a shaft with a waste dump containing small bits of turquoise and wondered if this was the old lost Aztec turquoise mine.

From these same mountains a large old Native American earthen pot, discovered in a wash by a visitor who graciously notified park personnel, is on display for visitors at the Temple Bar Visitor Center. Also displayed is a fine replica of an old arrastra that was found locally. Another fine reproduction of an old mining arrastra is also available for viewing in front of the Mohave Museum in Kingman, Arizona.

For those unfamiliar with arrastras, these were crude mills in which ore was crushed by having a horse, mule, or burro, drag heavy rocks around in a circle. Arrastras were first used here by the Spanish and the method was later adopted for use by miners in these rugged backcountry areas. In *Trail Dust of the Southwest*, Grounds gives a good detailed description:

> An arrastra is built by first setting a heavy cedar post where the center is to be. Then a floor is made in a circle about ten feet in diameter and a low rock wall around the outside. The floor is layered with large stones with the flattest sides for the floor surface. The crevices between the rocks are tamped with damp adobe and left an inch or more deep. The draft bar is usually an old wagon tongue with the hounds [underneath connecting parts] on the tongue base as they are on a wagon. The hounds fork the cedar post in the center of the arrastra and the draft held up by a swivel pin at the top of the cedar post which turns as the draft pole turns. Now two rocks, weighing about eighty pounds each, usually shaped like large watermelons and of granite so they would stand great wear, are brought in and centers are chiseled in several inches and a four inch wide piece of green rawhide sewed around each rock in the chiseled groove with a loop made at one place in the rawhide band to fasten a chain which anchors the rock to the draft pole. Two rocks are usually used, depending on the size of the arrastra floor and the power used to pull the rocks.

Grounds described how the ore was pounded into small pieces then strewn about on the arrastra floor, along with several pieces of quicksilver, to be worked into the crevices of the surface. Water was added, and as the mule pulled the tug rock around the course, the person tending the arrastra would have to keep the ore from bunching up and getting pushed away from the path of the tug rock. After hours of work, the ore turned into thin mud. Then the tailings were drained out through a plug, during which time more water was added to clean out the remaining muck while the mule was still pulling the tug rock. Grounds continued:

> When nothing is left but the mud in the floor cracks, the mule is unhooked to rest a shift and the clean-up job starts. All the mud is dug from the cracks along with a silvery, muddy looking substance known as amalgam. This is the quick silver mixed with free gold and silver particles which settle into the floor cracks. This mud and amalgam is put into buckets of water and completely washed out to a silvery mass which is placed into a retort and the quick silver recovered and weighed to calculate if the loss is normal. In the bottom of the retort will be the gold and silver from the ore in the form of a button.[4]

I had asked Bob Cameron if he knew how to tell if an arrastra was Spanish in origin and therefore much older, or whether it might be one made by miners who came into the area and adopted this milling technique a century or so ago. He said that in the ones built by the Spanish, the center pivot post would not be hand-hewn, but just an old stump or something and that the Spanish often used iron wedges to keep ropes secured in the hole of the drag stone, whereas more recent ones used old wood wedges.

During 1974, an NPS study was done in a drainage reaching back into the Wilson Range. Instances of vandalism were documented and photos were also taken of old engravings at Arrastra Springs that read; "Arrastra Springs GIP Dec 10, 1911" and "Harry Bauer, Feb. 17, 1911." To-date I've found no information on any Harry Bauer. Another interesting rock engraving in this same Wilson Range was noted by Malach in his Jan. 21, 1975, article in the *Kingman Daily Miner*, "Mohave's Minnesota Mining District," along with a picture of a rock engraving reading, "Feb. 18, 1893, Dick."

At Temple Bar some placer mining was done in the 1890's by a French company under the direction of a Captain Delmar (perhaps where the name of nearby "Delmar Butte" arose?). In a "Historic Resources Study" done for LMNRA in 1983, Belshaw stated regarding this area:

> Hydraulic pressure to wash gravels was obtained by the use of a water wheel between two barges which raised the water 250 feet. This may have been the operation to which J. E. Rose hauled supplies and fuel as late as 1898. A boom had been extended into the river for the purpose of capturing driftwood to fire the boiler. The erratic supply of fuel that resulted prevented continuous operation and may have been a principal reason for the failure of the effort.

The White Hills to the southeast of Temple Bar are gently rolling mountains along the east side of Detrital Valley. The hills were named for numerous silver deposits located in the area and the mining district that developed there was called the Indian Secret Mining District.

In 1892, Judge Henry Schaffer is said to have persuaded a Hualapai named Jeff to tell him the location of a mineral deposit in the White Hills that the tribe used

White Hills

for making paints. Some reports say Schaffer (also spelled Schaeffer and Shafer in various references) offered Jeff $200, others say $50, and still others say Schaffer simply gave Jeff a bottle of whiskey. Regardless, after some time Hualapai Jeff did take Schaffer to the deposit in the White Hills.

Jeff, according to John Grounds, was from Walapai Charley's bands who often ranged with the Claysprings and Peach Springs bands of Hualapais. Grounds told a story about when Jeff was a baby and his family camped along the rim of the Grand Canyon, that little Jeff had crawled away and became covered with many small black pinyon ants, ones the Hualapai called "chinapoogas." He screamed until his mother came and swept the ants off him. From then on he was called "chinapoogas" but since the settlers couldn't remember that, they simply called him Jeff.

Grounds also stated that Schaffer and a Mr. Sulliven from Gold Basin proceeded to stake out a number of claims in the White Hills area and that Schaffer later sold his claims for a few thousand dollars to John Sulliven and John Burnett (also spelled Sullivan and Barnett in other sources), who then put in a ten stamp mill.

In an article appearing in the *Arizona Republic* newspaper, March 16, 1894, there was an interview with "Hualapai Jeff," along with general information about the White Hills mining camp. Toward the end of the article it read as follows:

> Among the first men arriving at the camp was R. G. Paterson [Patterson], resident of Mohave County for 24 years. Paterson located the Prince Albert Mine, which was already a good producer in horn silver in 1893 in the amount of $75,000. The Prince Albert Mine assays ran from 400 to 1,400 ounces per ton and 2 to 8 ounces in gold. Some 25 men were working at the Prince Albert Mine at the time of the interview with Hualapai Jeff. In addition, Paterson owned several gold mining properties in Gold Basin, some 12 miles east of White Hills.

From the September, 1984, issue of *Mohave* (supplement to the *Mohave Miner* newspaper), information is given about the White Hills by Paul Taylor:

> R. T. Root was the promoter of the district. He advertised the camp as the mining center of the region. Root formed the White Hills Mining Company of which he appointed himself President. R. T. teamed up with D. H. Moffat of Colorado, who provided much of the working capital. Root lost no time in building a 12-stamp mill and excavating the first deep shafts. By 1894 his company owned the entire town site.

D. H. Moffat, it should be noted, was a financier and industrialist in Colorado, with Moffat County in northwest Colorado carrying his name (2014 information: from the Environmental Working Group website, came the following: "D H Moffat Jr. is one of 92,125 beneficiaries of a 132-year-old federal mining law that gives away precious metals, minerals, and even the title to the land itself for less than $10 an acre "... Wikipedia states that Moffat at various times held over 100 mining claims in Colorado, alone).

South-of-the-River Country

Taylor went on to write about the White Hills boom years and how the site was honeycombed with twenty-seven miles of underground tunnels. After three years, an English company bought out the White Hills Company for $1,500,000. Another stamp mill was built, water was piped in from a spring seven miles distant, and an electric light plant was set up to power the mines and town. According to Taylor, area Joshua trees and yucca palms were used as fuel for the steam hoists. However, John Grounds also mentioned that the Grounds family living at Clay Springs Ranch had obtained contracts with the White Hills mining community and provided wood from Music Mountains for fuel. No doubt both sources were used.

Taylor continued:

> The 15 mines were less than a mile from the center of town. The Prince Albert, a heavy producer, paid royalties amounting to $30,000 in an incredibly short time. The Hidden Treasure, on the discovery property, continued to pay off. And such mines as the Grand Army of the Republic, the Occident, Garfield, Bryan and the Grand Central were not far behind. But even with it's mines producing, the English corporation was unable to make its final payments and the property it had so lavishly developed was put up at the sheriff's sale. Root and Moffat bought it back and began to boost it again.

Grounds wrote that at the peak of activity in White Hills there were some 10,000 people living there, while Taylor and Malach quote 1500 as being the highest number of residents when White Hills was in its prime. In 1894, the first school opened. There was also a church, stage company, hotel, post office, and telephone service, along with twelve popular saloons. In 1897, the community was still going strong.

Roman Malach had an entertaining story in his book, *White Hills*, one that was gleaned from old materials of a Morgan Jones of Kingman. Jones had been a miner in the White Hills district in 1936:

> Jones wrote that White Hills was a mining camp, and at a certain time about thirty men were holding a wake over Jack Quinn's body prior to taking it to Kingman for burial. They all sang a few hymns, a few rowdy songs, and most anything that sounded like music. They prayed, played cards, drank whisky and told yarns all night.
>
> As morning neared, several of the men got into a fight and upset the table with the coffin, dumping Quinn's body out on the floor. No one paid any attention to it till morning when Tom Price came from the livery stable with a good team and wagon to take Quinn's body to Kingman. Most of the men were still asleep on the floor. Few of them were sober or thought they were; they put Quinn back in the coffin and nailed the lid down.

The story goes on to relate how the men put the coffin containing Quinn's body into a wagon and six of them started off, heading to Kingman for Quinn's burial ... taking along, of course, some whisky for the long drive. Down the way a piece when most of the men were asleep, knocking and kicking started coming from the coffin. The men woke with a start and were petrified. Tom Price began lashing the horses with his whip just about the time the coffin lid came flying off. The men jumped and ran, with Tom in the lead. The team also took off running but managed to stay on the road until reaching Desert Station where three men caught the team just as the man in the coffin sat up and asked, "Where am I? Where's Quinn and the rest of the men?" Turned out this body was not Quinn, but Happy Convay, who'd been put in the coffin by mistake while in a drunken stupor from the night before.

Malach continued the story:

> A few days later the boys who had gone with the coffin still stayed away from the saloon. They would not drink. Some days later, Red Flynn marched to the justice of the peace and pledged himself to drink no more whiskey. Happy took the pledge next and others followed. Tom Price was the last to pledge to leave whiskey alone.[5]

In early 1898, rich veins began playing out in the White Hills and many of the miners drifted over to Chloride, the new mining boom camp, twenty-five miles to the south. The final blow to the historic mining community came on August 5 when a heavy rainstorm in the surrounding hills caused water to pour down over the town. In an old article from the *Mohave Miner,* "Ghost of the White Hills," Taylor quotes one description:

> A shanty in its path bade good-bye to the town and started for the valley and by nine o'clock the whole town was in danger ... water came tossing down like the rapids above Niagara, the waves seeming to run four or five feet high .... a cabin in which Mr. Shallenberger was sleeping was lifted and whirled end for end. After much floundering in the water he managed to pull ashore with his blankets. The foundation was washed from under the east side of the schoolhouse and it lies tilted toward the sunrise with mud piled inside.

> In one mine, the men got out just as water filled the shaft, and at another, the men were unable to climb the 200 feet of ladders while water was running down the shaft until a trench turned the main sheet of water in a different direction and then the men escaped. Road surfaces were covered with two feet of new soil. The articled ended saying that they "might call this affair too much of a good thing, for water was selling at one dollar a barrel in White Hills and they got a million dollar bath."[6]

Another factor causing great concern in the White Hills district was an unusually large number of miners dying. According to Grounds, arsenic dust deposits from the mines were thought to cause the deaths.[7]

All these factors resulted in the eventual demise of the old White Hills camp. By 1900, the 40-stamp mill had slowed down and smaller mills were reworking the huge dumps from the mines. During it's heyday the Indian Secret Mining District had produced over $12,000,000 in silver. Today, in 1990, other than old cans and minor debris, there is little remaining of the old White Hills mining camp, however, the huge concrete water reservoir still stands near the former town

South-of-the-River Country

site, and a modern development also called White Hills is located higher in a basin just beyond.

To the north of White Hills camp is the Senator Mine and Salt Springs Mining area. Senator Mountain is a visible landmark located six miles northeast of the old White Hills Mining Camp. The tallest mountain in the White Hills and standing over five thousand feet, Senator Mountain can be seen for miles. The Senator Mine lies at the base of this mountain, a gold mine that was originally owned by John Burnett. Burnett sold it in 1892 for the amount of $14,000 to Senator Page of Los Angeles, who then sold it to a Colorado Company, yet the name "Senator" has stayed with the mine and mountain to this day. In about 1900, a 10-stamp mill called Senator Mill was installed on the Colorado River several miles below Salt Springs (near former Sulphur Springs on the banks of the river). Malach noted that the Colorado Mining Company only operated the mill for about six months and that the Salt Springs Mining Company that had its own Salt Springs Mine, also tried operating the mill but only lasted one month. It is known, however, from the previously quoted Lippincott report of October 9, 1902, that when his group passed this location while on the river, the Senator Mill was still in operation by someone at that time.

A number of smaller mines and quarries were also located in Salt Springs Wash, this wash extending all the way from Senator Mountain north to the Colorado River. There are a series of springs and seeps in the wash at this time that were once several miles south of the river, but now are located barely ¼ mile from the waters of Lake Mead. It's believed there was a mill operating right below Salt Springs at one time, but I found no documentation showing any mill in the area other than the 10-stamp mill on the shore of the river that was used first by the Senator Mine workings, and later, by Salt Springs Mine.

Lastly, we come to the modern-day community of Dolan Springs. There is uncertainty over the real derivation of the name, "Dolan Springs." Following are some references pertaining to both a Dolan and Doling.

In 1876, the Mohave County tax records show a Goodwin-Dolan ranch of 160 acres on the Sandy River (a location east of the Hualapai Mountain range, quite some distance away).

Malach related that in 1873, Colonel Sacket wrote a report about Camp Beale's Springs (on the western outskirts of Kingman):

> During my stay at the camp, three enlisted men were confined under guard for drunkenness and a notorious rough by the name of Dolan was drunk and disorderly about the traders store most of the day and evening.[8]

Malach also wrote that two men with the name of Dolan were mentioned in tax records, but it's unknown if either had anything to do with the naming of present-day Dolan Springs. A May 1883 issue of *Mohave Miner* (then from Alta, Arizona) reported that a Mickey Dolan is "in the refrigerator for disturbing the peace."

The name Dolan was featured in data about Carrington Spring and Saavedra Spring in a file in the Mohave Museum in Kingman. This information was recorded by Mamie Musser, who worked for the Works Project Administration as County Historian in the late 1930's and this seems the most viable:

> Carrington Spring: This spring near Harry Edwards Mountain was found by Mr. Carrington. He reported a "fine running spring a few miles east of Saavedra Spring," which was at the northern end of the Cerbat Range on the western slope. I have called the spring after its discoverer, Carrington Spring – Beale.' This spring was located sometime in the seventies [1870's] by a prospector named Dolan. To this day it is known as Dolan Springs. Belongs to the Bonelli Bros. who own cattle. This spring can be reached by a good valley road about seven miles from the Boulder Dam highway, one mile east from the Pierce Ferry Road and forty-four miles north from Kingman.
>
> Saavedra Spring: After one of his Mexican guides of whom Beale said, "He was absolutely worthless as a guide or anything else." Shows on Beale's map 1857-59 as a little north of lat. 114 degrees, west side of Cerbat Range, at its northern end. They were suffering for water when the guide discovered this spring. This spring is known as Antelope Spring and is on the property of John Neal. It drains northeast into Wallapai Wash. This spring is three and a half miles east from Carrington or Dolan Springs.

Antelope Springs, referred to by Musser, is situated close to the almost hidden Antelope Valley, one located several miles east of the present-day elementary school in Dolan Springs. On this little valley's southern boundary are prominently visible pinnacles best viewed from Stockton Hill Road, and near the western entrance of Antelope Valley stands the "Mitten" rock formation, this clearly visible from Pearce Ferry Road. Access is provided by a road off Pearce Ferry Road from the north, and onto Ocotillo Drive. Antelope have not frequented this area for many years (as of 1990), thus questions remain about the source of the name, however, they have recently begun ranging closer from the east and the Music Mountains so perhaps they will return.

In county assessment records, a John Doling is listed as owning a saloon in Mineral Park in 1876, this mining town being located some 14 miles southerly of present-day Dolan Springs. Recall previous reference in 1880 county tax rolls to R. G. Patterson having "two ranches, one combined with a way station which was called Mountain Springs on the road from Mineral Park to Stone Ferry [near Bonelli's Ferry]; the second was called Doling's Springs."

Mountain Springs is located just four miles northwest of the actual springs currently named Dolan Springs, and having ranches in close proximity would be logical. Since definite reference was made to this one as Dolings Springs in the 1880 tax roll, one might conclude that it was first Doling, probably named for or by John Doling who for a time had a saloon in nearby Mineral Park, then later the name was changed to Dolan out of reference to one of the other two Dolans mentioned in local history.

At any rate, the location of today's actual Dolan Springs lies just east of the present elementary school building. In the early 1900's, Bonelli ran cattle over

South-of-the-River Country

this range, land that later came under the ownership of Millers. Further development of this and other surrounding communities will be touched upon later.

The tallest mountain in the Cerbat Mountain Range along the edge and just south of the community of Dolan Springs is Mt. Tipton, reaching some 6900 feet in elevation. Mt. Tipton lies four miles south of Antelope Valley, or four miles southeast of the elementary school. This mountain was named for Lieutenant Tipton who served in Lieutenant J. C. Ives exploratory mapping expedition in 1858 and it now lies within the officially designated Bureau of Land Management "Mt. Tipton Wilderness Area."

Old mine mill operation, courtesy Mohave Museum in Kingman, Arizona

Old working arrastra, courtesy Mohave Museum in Kingman, Arizona

Chapter Thirteen: Gold Basin

Gold Basin is the mining district just south and west of our Grapevine Mesa. The White Hills define the southwest boundary of Gold Basin, Pearce Ferry road forms the southeast boundary, Hualapai Wash the northeast boundary, and the Colorado River (now Lake Mead) runs along the west and northwest. Most of the productive mines in this area were located in the northeastern portion of the district, off the Gregg's Hideout Road and not far from Pearce Ferry Road.

On several pre-1880 maps, lengthy Hualapai Valley, extending from present-day old Highway 66 and northwest to where Hualapai Wash drains into the Colorado River, was previously called Yampai Valley and Yampai Creek. The Music Mountain extension of the Grand Wash Cliffs was referred to as the Yampai Cliffs. At times this was also spelled Yampa. To preface other information that will follow, it's important to delve into this a little further.

Quoting Barnes, *Arizona Place Names*, in reference to Truxton Canyon (located at the far southeast of Hualapai Valley where Old Highway 66 leads toward Kingman):

> On October 28, 1851, Lt. Lorenzo Sitgreaves dispatched a reconnoitering party to find running water. The party returned to report finding a band of Yampais [Yavapai Indians from farther east] encamped upon the creek which today is called Truxton Wash. The guide, Antoine Leroux, learned from these Indians that the Sitgreaves party was approaching the Colorado River. On October 30, Sitgreaves named the creek the Yampai, an attempt to spell 'Yavapai.' The presence of cliffs along the eastern edge of the stream led to applying the name Yampai Cliffs to them. Today these are called the Grand Wash Cliffs [i.e. the Music Mts.]. Maps on the area are confusing for the names shift freely. GLO 1869 shows a Peacocke spring and emerging from it to empty into Red Lake [now Dry Red Lake in Hualapai Valley] is a stream called Yampa Creek.[1]

Apparently in 1851 a creek was still flowing into Dry Red Lake, or perhaps it was simply a seasonal creek as is often true in the arid southwest. Some current-day maps still label the canyon southwest of Peach Springs as Yampai Canyon, and the pass between Peach Springs and Seligman on old Highway 66 as the Yampai Divide. Barnes went on to explain other name variations and also mentioned that the Spanish expedition of Fr. Garces came through Truxton Wash in June 1775, calling that area the Arroy de San Bernabe.

From an old March 4, 1882 newspaper, the *Alta Arizona*, published for a brief time from Mineral Park, Malach quotes a story about adventurer and Mohave County pioneer, Daniel O'Leary, this occurring sometime between 1860-1882:

> Reports came in about the forming of a new mining district about 80 miles north of Mineral Park. It is called Lost Basin. The center of this district is located about five miles south of the Colorado River, near the outlet of Red Lake-Yampa Creek, as it was called on some maps. It was reported by

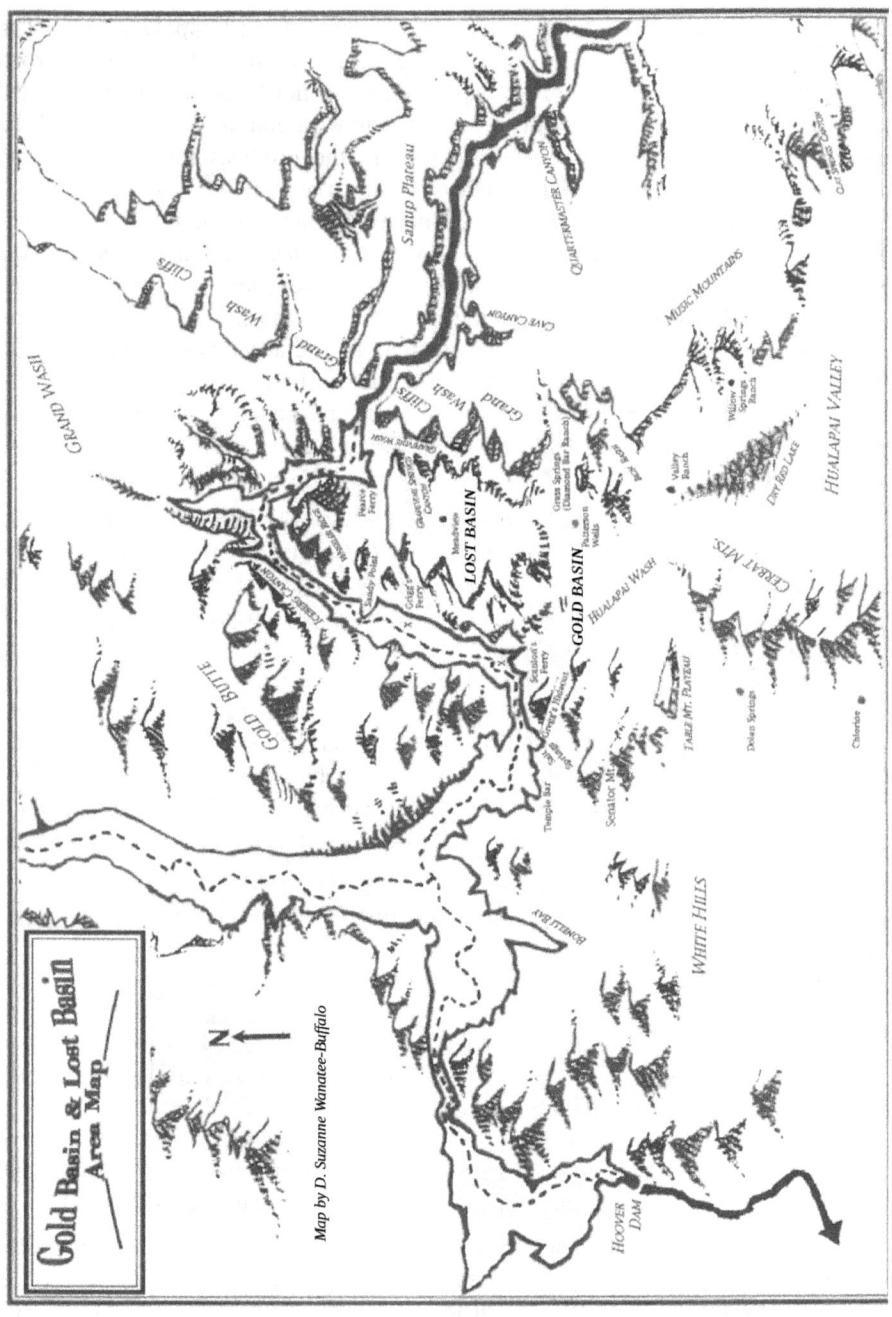

Gold Basin

reliable miners that this district was developing well and created some excitement. Gold was found in the low rolling hills along Yampa Creek by Xavier Aubrey and Pegleg Smith as early as 1857 or 1858. Pegleg Smith mined there in 1860 and gold was taken out. Dan O'Leary, the scout, with a party of miners in 1864 found gold along Yampa Creek and near the Colorado River.

This information tells us that mining had gone on as early as the 1850's by Euro-Americans in both Gold Basin and Lost Basin, and at that time, these were apparently considered one mining district before being more formally designated as separate mining districts in the 1870's.

By the 1880's, "Basin" in Hualapai Valley was a small mining camp with a processing mill. Through the years this particular site, located just off Pearce Ferry Road on the gravel road heading toward Gregg's Hideout, has been called Gold Basin, Basin, Basin Mill, O.K. Mill, Burnt Mill and Burnt Mill Ranch. Michael Scanlon, owner of the ferry that was once located at the mouth of Hualapai Wash and northwestern boundary of this mining district, established a post office called Gold Basin at this spot in 1890 and later discontinued it in 1894. For a time the mail was picked up in the White Hills. Then Eugene Chandler opened another post office at Gold Basin in 1904, calling it simply "Basin" but this was closed in 1907.

The first mill was opened at Basin in 1886 and this served to process ore from the Eldorado, O.K., Excelsior, and other mines. The mill burned down in 1892. It was rebuilt and opened again in 1902, then burned down again in 1906. Water was piped down to the mill site from Patterson Springs, seven miles to the northeast. The closest railroad station was in Hackberry, Arizona, some forty miles to the southeast, and this, according to Malach's *Cerbat Mountain Country*, was connected with Gold Basin by a stage coach line.[2]

Today one can turn off Pearce Ferry road and go a mile or so on the Greggs Hideout Road on approved road #136 on LMNRA Approved Roads maps to find the old site of Basin. A 1902 photograph of Basin taken by Barry Goldwater is featured on page 12 of the book, *Northwestern Arizona Ghost Towns* by Stanley Paher. The photo shows four buildings, a corral, water tank, and in the background part of the ten-stamp mill that was in operation. Not much is left now except foundations of the twice-burned old mill on the south side of the road and a corral with some signs of previous buildings on the north side. Several graves are kept up by the Daughters of the American Revolution Chapter out of Kingman but no one I spoke with seems to know who rests there. Pioneers interviewed stated the graves were there by 1900, so they presumed these to be burial sites of miners and their families from years prior.

During research, many names arose in association with Basin. Charlie Hand, according to his granddaughter Lillian Parsons of Kingman, lived at Gold Basin (i.e. Basin) with his family in 1891.[3] Twins were born to the Hands in 1892. Their home burned down once and all they were able to save was Grandma Hand's sewing machine. They figured that was the most important item to grab since it was the only way they had to make clothes for the children.

Charlie ran a regular freight line from Hackberry to Gold Basin and over to White Hills for several years, hauling meat and food staples as well as mining supplies. I wondered if this might be the "stage line" referred to by Malach previously. Mrs. Parsons showed me several interesting photos. One was of the Charlie Hand family and another picture had an inscription on the back which read, "To Martha Hand from Mrs. Flora Patterson, 12/25/1913." Martha was Charlie's wife. Flora Patterson may have been the wife or daughter of R. G. (Bob) Patterson, since the Patterson's were still present in this same area when Charlie first arrived. More about Charlie Hand later.

Chock and Mary Hamilton lived at Basin for a time, they being the parents of Billy Hamilton, currently of the Quail Springs Ranch just below Dolan Springs. Johnny Mullin took over Leonard Neal's lease from Al Thorne on the place at Basin in the 1930's. Mullin built at least one house and replaced the pipeline from Patterson Well down to Basin that had been removed by unknown persons. Mullin, remember, later served on the County Board of Supervisors and had proposed the name of Greggs Hideout. Johnny Mullin married the mother of Jack Walker, and Jack later ran Frenchy's Store at Lake Mead City up on Grapevine Mesa for many years.[4] Clyde and Cecil McBee, Don McBee's parents, stayed at Basin during a roundup in the late 1950's. The house they stayed in while there (perhaps the one built by Mullin) was barely standing in the 1970's and then collapsed between 1975 and 1982.

According to Schroder's *Mineral Deposits of Mohave County, Arizona*, written in 1909, the Eldorado mine, discovered in the 1870's, was one of the first to send bullion from the district. This mine is not to be confused with mines in El Dorado Canyon to the west of the Colorado River and below today's Hoover Dam.[5] This Eldorado was located approximately three miles southwest of Basin.

In *Arizona Lode Gold Mines and Mining*, information is given that by 1907 the Eldorado was owned by the Arizona-Minnesota Gold Mining Company and total production was reported as $65,000 worth of bullion. The largest amount of ore was reportedly milled at the Basin or O.K. Mill in Hualapai Valley, several miles distant.

Malach stated that the Eldorado consisted of eight unpatented claims in low hilly country.[6] Gold was found there in 1880 and was mined and milled from 1890 to 1906, producing almost 6000 tons of ore. The location was in T28N, R18W, Sec. 21 and 28. On present-day USGS maps that would put the Eldorado where the mine now called Malco is located.

Two other mines close to the Eldorado were the O.K. and Excelsior Mines. These were discovered by Patterson (yet another reference to Patterson), Rowe, and Fox, early in the 1880's (was nearby "Fox Canyon," just off to the east of what is now known as Patterson Hill on Pearce Ferry Road, possibly named after this man?).

The O.K. Mine was about one half mile south of the Eldorado. According to information from the Arizona Bureau of Mines, a Kansas City company bought the property in 1886 and built the O.K. Mill in Hualapai Valley at Basin. The mill had ten stamps and a cyanide plant was operated on water piped from a spring in the Grand Wash Cliffs. The O.K. Mine was reported to have produced $25,000 worth of gold in those early years.

The Excelsior mine was just northeast of the Eldorado, along with the Mascot. Other mines included the Never-Get-Left, owned by Henry Paully of Basin, and the Golden Rule, also discovered in the early 1880's by Robert Patterson and Saul Rowe. They hauled some of the ore to a mill at Grass Springs for treatment. Most of these mines eventually ended up under the ownership of the Arizona-Minnesota Gold Mining Company.

The old Cyclopic Mine was situated more to the southeast, several miles from the above-mentioned group. This too, was discovered by Patterson and Rowe and another miner named Glen. In the late 1890's it was leased to a Seattle company and in 1901 was sold to Robbins and Walker of Minneapolis who milled the ore using a 26 horsepower engine and a cyanide plant. Water was piped in from a spring on the west side of White Hills. In 1904, the Cyclopic Gold Mining Company of Denver purchased the mine and held it for many years. Reportedly, considerable amounts of bullion were taken from the mine but no exact figures were found. In 1923, the Gold Basin Exploration Company owned the mine and stayed in production until the early 1930's.

Placer mining was developed farther northwest in this district during the 1930's, along what is now called Elephant Wash. From a 1961 *Arizona Bureau of Mines Bulletin* we find the quote:

> The first known discovery of placer gold within this area was made in May, 1932, by W. E. Dunlop. In August of that year approximately 100 men were testing the field with dry-washers. Most of them left during the winter rainy season, but about forty were there in June, 1933. As most of these people were transients who took part of their gold elsewhere, any approximate estimate of the production is difficult to reach. Experienced, industrious workers each made $1 or more a day, but most of the operators averaged less than that amount. Drywashing here is interrupted during rainy seasons.

> During the summer of 1933, a large-scale dry-treatment plant was installed by S. C. Searles in Sec. 29, T29N, R18W. This plant, equipped with a grizzly, trommel, screens, and a battery of twelve drywashers, had a rated capacity of 20 cubic yards of gravel per hour. The U. S. Minerals Yearbook credits the Gold Basin placers, during 1834-49, with a gold production valued at $14,000.[7]

There is still mining activity in Elephant Wash today. A four-wheel drive road taking off from the Gregg's Hideout Road goes through the wash and past the present-day Owens Mine and provides interesting routes leading into the White Hills where one can then travel along the north side of Senator Mountain and the old Senator Mine. The Gold Hill Mine lies just west of Elephant Wash and more mining activity is present in this area also.

South-of-the-River Country

Here we have another unsolved mystery. Proceeding down Greggs Hideout Road and continuing on past turn-offs to Elephant Wash and the back road leading to present-day Temple Bar, one can see at some distance to the left the remnants of a small stone building. This building possibly dates back as far as 1853, and if so, would be one of the oldest Euro-American structures still standing in this entire area. It is located within the jurisdiction of Lake Mead National Recreation Area boundaries, thus, disturbing or removing anything is strictly prohibited by federal law.

How much of this old cabin is original is unknown. Work has surely been done in recent years on the floor and roof, but the basic components of the rock walls, could be very old. Inside the cabin there is a curious fresh swath of concrete laid upon an older layer, on which there is diagrammed a family tree of sorts. Evidently this was done in 1971 by persons who had reason to believe they are descendants of a man named George Brechner, someone who lived there long ago. The information, written in a circular pattern, reads as follows:

George Brechners Stone House, 1853

Children, Roy and Ruby Brechner

Lora V. Hoffman, John C. Hoffman, Born 1872 [or 92?]

Lois R. Adams, Feb. 11, 1971

Adams Family, Feb. 12, 1971

Grandchildren

Les Adams, 1926

Cora Adams, 1929

Virg Adams, 1929

Grace Adams, 1937

Great Grandchildren

Rick Adams

Steve Adams

Lyle Adams, 1957

Betty Adams, 1955

Rob Adams, 1955

C.L. A. Anaheim

It would appear the Adams family who deliberately wrote this information in concrete, evidently in February of 1971, must have had access to records that led them to believe their ancestor, George Brechner, lived there in 1853, and perhaps even built this rock cabin. If so, this could be historically significant not only for Mohave County but also for LMNRA. Yet I could not find more information about either George Brechner or the Adams family.

It can, however, be verified that the cabin was there as far back as the turn of the century. In a 1902 mining claim filed by Scanlon and Childers (Mohave County Courthouse mining records) reference was made to this very place, one they called the "stone cabin known as Scanlons Cabin."[8] Apparently by the turn of the century, Michael Scanlon either owned or lived in this cabin, or it was at least recognized to be his at that time.

Scanlon, as we know from the Grigg's Ferry chapter, was quite active and had mining claims and businesses (post office, ferry crossing, etc.) around Gold Basin as well as in Lost Basin bordering on the north, for a number of years. He also built a processing mill (Scanlon Mill) at Scanlon Springs down in Hualapai Wash near the river, this site now under the waters of Lake Mead.

Some confusion has existed over the location of Scanlon's Mill and Spring. In a study done in 1983 for LMNRA, researcher Michael Belshaw placed these both in Scanlon Wash on the Nevada shore. However, after listening to first-hand descriptions of Scanlon's Mill and Springs in Hualapai Wash as given during interviews with William Grigg's grandson, Richard Smith (see chapter on Griggs Ferry), and also seeing photos of men actually working at Scanlon's Mill and Spring (labeled as in Hualapai Wash), there's little doubt that Scanlon's Mill and Spring was located on the Arizona side, not the Nevada side of the river. Richard's cousin, Charles Grigg, also verified that Scanlon had no large mining operations (mills, etc.) on the Nevada side of the river. Leonard Neal, in our 1986 interview, stated also that Scanlon's Ferry had been below Grigg's Ferry location and that the ferry had gone in and out of Hualapai Wash. He said there was no ranch or fields or anything there, just the ferry. He also verified that a short distance up Hualapai Wash, Scanlon had a spring where a big stream of water came out of a wash drainage alongside, and that Scanlon had a mill there at one time.

In another study, information is given about a "Burt Mill" (in contrast to "Burnt Mill") site. Melvin Smith quotes from an issue of the *Washington County News* (Utah):

> In January 1909 the Burt Mill and Company of Logan, Nevada, put in a mill near Scanlon Ferry to work some of the placers. They offered laborers $2.00 per day to work on the mill, which at that time, even with room and board, was not too attractive.[9]

Belshaw may have drawn erroneous conclusions based on this information since he placed Scanlon's Ferry on the Nevada side, and as a result, in his later NPS study, also placed "Burt Millsite" directly on the banks of the Colorado River on the Nevada shore. To date, I've been unable to verify the location of any such a mill on the Nevada side. Richard Smith and his cousin, Charles Grigg, agreed.

South-of-the-River Country

Perhaps this "Burt Mill" was not on the river's edge at all, but farther up the wash on the Nevada side, or, references being made were actually to Scanlons Mill in Hualapai Wash and to the old Burnt Mill located even farther up in Hualapai Wash on our Arizona side.

To the far south end of Gold Basin stood Butchers Camp, a site right along Pearce Ferry Road. This was a small mining camp in the early 1900's, located four miles southwest of the old Eldorado Mine. A windmill near there is marked on some maps as Butchers Windmill but very little remains of the actual camp today. Bob Cameron said he didn't know why the place was called Butchers Camp but had heard that some folks living there once had sold the east corral to a man named Archibald and this is why the corral nearby is still called the Archibald Corral. Access to this area is made by turning west off Pearce Ferry road at the Archibald Corral, about two and one-half miles south of the intersection of Stockton Hill Road and Pearce Ferry Road. The people who gave their names to these two landmarks seem at least temporarily lost in history.

Gold Basin

Charlie Hand Family, courtesy Lillian Ridenour Parsons, no date

Our camp on gravel bar, lower end of Hualapai Rapids, Sept., 1924, Householder Collection

Scanlon Wash, setting up for getting gold out of ore, Richard Smith collection

Stream Arrastra at O.K. City, Courtesy Grounds Collection, Mohave Museum, no date

Gold Basin

Hualapai Wash area, 1990

George Brechners Stone House, March 1988

Ron and Sharon checking old crumbling timbers over shaft opening

Chapter Fourteen: Lost Basin

Herein lies Home. Meadview sits nearly dead center of what was called the Lost Basin Mining District, perched high atop Grapevine Mesa. This basin district was so-named for its secluded and remote location in this South-of-the-River Country, and for having a special mystique uniquely its own. Hualapai Wash (i.e. Hualapai Valley) forms the south and southwest boundary of this area, the Colorado River (Lake Mead) lies north and northwest, and the Grand Wash Cliffs loom above on the east. To the north, residents on Grapevine Mesa enjoy far distant horizons into Nevada and Utah.

There is an intriguing story about the origins of mining in Lost Basin. In an old 1885 article from the *Mohave Miner* (then published in Mineral Park) information reads as follows:

The Lost Basin: New Discoveries of Old Workings

In the Lost Basin district many and strange discoveries have been made during the past three or four weeks which prove conclusively that in years gone by mining was conducted on a large scale in this portion, the gold region, of Mohave County. How many men were engaged in the undertaking will probably never be known as it is evident from the recent discoveries that many of them met their death from the hands of Indians while prosecuting their search for gold, and of those who escaped, if any, nothing has ever been heard.

There are many of our readers who have heard of the 'Lost Shaft' in the Lost Basin district, and probably some of them have visited it. It lies about six miles northwest of Patterson's wells, and many a hardy prospector has come across it in the last five years and probably speculated on the fate of those who had the temerity to sink it. There is a tradition among the miners here that the work was done by a party of Mormons on their way to Utah, some of whom took the gold fever and left the main party to prosecute their search for gold, and most likely forfeited their lives in so doing. As the old main-traveled road [Grapevine Wash] runs within a few miles of the place, this story is probably correct. A few weeks ago, we are told a lady visited Fred Nobmann's house at Hackberry siding, and stated that many years ago her husband, now dead, was in this portion of Arizona, engaged in mining, but was driven out by the Indians and many of his companions killed. He had given her a good description of the locality and told her if, as then appeared very unlikely, she should ever visit Arizona, to make some inquiries about the mines.

From her description of the locality, Mr. Nobmann, who is an old prospector in this county and knows the whole country, readily recognized the neighborhood of the Lost Shaft. Her inquiries, and what little information she was able to impart concerning the richness of her husband's discoveries,

South-of-the-River Country

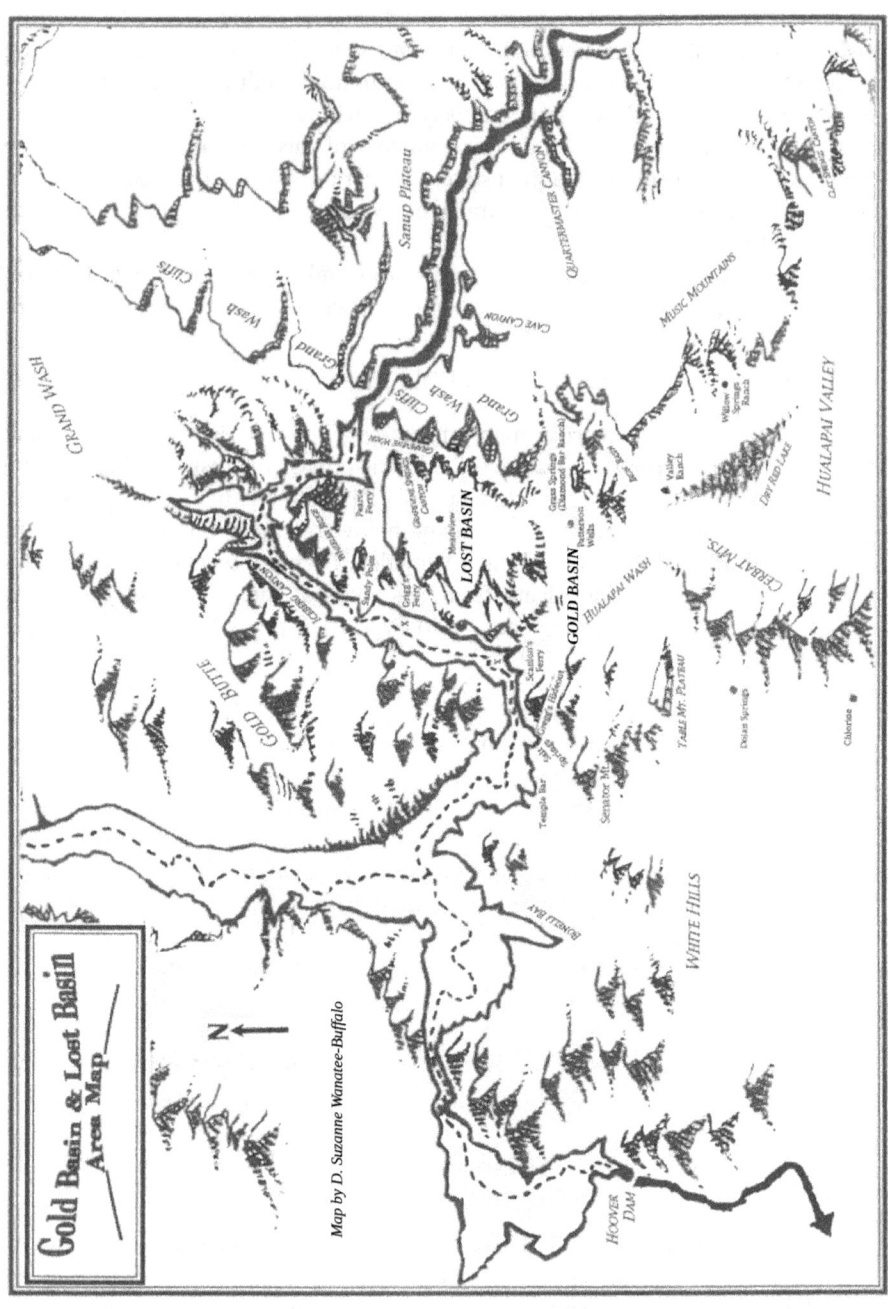

Lost Basin

induced Mr. Nobmann to make another visit to the Lost Shaft. Taking with him John Tillman, one of the oldest settlers in this county, and who is an experienced gold miner, and another man whose name our informant had forgotten, Mr. Nobmann left Hackberry about three weeks ago, and immediately upon his arrival at the shaft, commenced the work of cleaning it out. It was filled almost to the top with debris, brush, cactus, etc., and swarmed with rats, which is probably the main reason that many prospectors who have visited it have never made a closer examination of the mine. At the depth of about eighteen feet, the opening of a tunnel was found and it was at once decided to explore this tunnel before going deeper in the shaft. After cleaning out the tunnel for a distance of forty feet or more and finding it filled with brush and cactus, which had evidently been packed in by innumerable colonies of rats, it was decided to burn it out, as being the quickest way to clean it, besides making it interesting for the rats. This was accordingly done, and the party waited patiently for it to burn out.

After waiting two days, with no signs of the fire burning out, they concluded to fill in the time by thoroughly prospecting the ground in the vicinity. The shaft lies on one side of a small butte or mound, and in a few hours Mr. Tillman, who was prospecting on the opposite side of the mound, found a small crevice or aperture, which bore traces of having been made by the hand of man instead of nature. After cleaning it out and enlarging it, he found that it was evidently the mouth of an old tunnel. It being also filled with brush, he set fire to it, and an hour or two afterwards an immense sheet of flame, with clouds of smoke and dust, burst forth from the opening with a roaring noise like that from a furnace. The rest of the party were attracted to the spot by the noise and at once arrived at the conclusion that the tunnel extended through the hill, a distance of between three and four hundred feet, and was the same tunnel which they had found in the shaft, and that they were in a fair way to make an important discovery. When our informant left the spot, the fire had been burning in the long tunnel for four days with no signs of its dying out. If it should turn out that the tunnel has been timbered, the fire will no doubt work much injury and probably result in its caving in, but from the character of the walls it was supposed that no timbering had been done.

While waiting for the fire to burn out the party continued prospecting and were rewarded by finding an immense pile of rocks, some of which were still standing in walls, being evidently the remains of a stone cabin, or more likely from the size of the ground plan, a fortification of some considerable extent. Behind the remains of one of these walls a human skull was found, tending to prove the nature and purpose of the building. Continuing their search the party found evidences of placer mining in many of the gulches running down towards the Colorado, and extending over a stretch of country some fifteen miles in width, lying between Steen's Ferry and the point where the Wallapai wash runs into the river. When our informant left the scene of those interesting discoveries the party were still prosecuting their search, and we, in common with many others, await with considerable interest the results. One thing is certain, from the numerous traces of old work found in many different portions of our mining districts, that Mohave County was once peopled by a generation of miners of whom we know nothing, and of whom nothing remains but a few scattered bones, and the evidence of their work.[1]

Fascinating. And keep in mind this was written back in 1885, when few miners of Euro-American origins were known to have really been mining in this area, and yet the workings and remnants of these particular mines were by then already deemed "old." This, and other bits of information yet to come, lead me to believe the Spanish had, indeed, once worked mines in this area. Let's take some time here to focus upon a few details in this interesting article.

Having myself extensively hiked these particular canyons and drainages on foot over a number of years, I've tried to piece together my own explorations of these mines and historical data gathered, in order to try pinpointing the location of what was a century earlier called this "Lost Shaft."

The statement "six miles northwest of Patterson's wells" would put the location somewhat near the drainage where the present day Bluebird Mine is located. However, the informant who came to town that day was no doubt giving an estimate of distance. While exploring the canyon of the Bluebird Mine and the mine tunnel, itself, (not a shaft) it became apparent that this mine did not fit the description given, nor seemingly ever could have, nor were there remnant rock walls of any significant size in that or other drainages close by. So although the "northwest" direction was probably accurate, one could probably give or take a few miles.

Then, the quote "tradition among the miners here that work was done by a party of Mormons on their way to Utah..." can be questioned. As covered in the Pearce Ferry chapter, we know the old Mormon road was through Grapevine Wash some six miles east, and most Mormon parties who crossed at Pearce Ferry were either heading north to the St. George area, south to Mesa, AZ., or into northeastern Arizona to Hopi and Navajo reservation lands, and none of these documented trips mentioned taking time to divert anywhere into surrounding lands here in Lost Basin for mining purposes. According to diaries of the few Mormon parties that actually traveled this route, the groups stayed together and moved right along toward specific destinations elsewhere, this for settlement and for proselytizing. Moreover, the Mormons that traveled the old Mormon trail through Grapevine Wash had done so only a decade or two previous, so knowledge of any mining by those persons should still have been fresh in memories of both mining and Mormon communities in 1885 when this article was written.

Fred Nobmann (also known as Nodmann, Nodman, depending upon source) did, indeed, know this area. In 1876, recall, he had Quail Springs Ranch just south of present-day Dolan Springs and prospected extensively, even though he apparently lived in Hackberry nearly ten years later when this article was written.

Lost Basin

Toward the end of the article, mention is made that evidence of placer mining had been found in a fifteen mile stretch of gulches running down toward the Colorado River between "Steen's Ferry" and the point where "Wallapai wash runs into the river." Reference to Steen's Ferry is curious. In all the research I've done, there's no mention of a Steen's Ferry ever existing on the river in this area. There was, however, Stone's Ferry about fifteen miles to the west and Stone's Ferry was said to be operating around the time this article was written. A Robert Steen was serving as sheriff of Mohave County the year this article was written, but it seems most likely the reference to Steen's Ferry was probably meant to be Stone's Ferry. From this premise, the approximate "fifteen miles in width, lying between Steen's Ferry and the point where the Wallapai wash runs into the river" might have been appropriate as there was placer mining going on throughout those hills and washes at that time, this mostly in the bordering Gold Basin mining area.

There are several other interesting theories to consider that might aid in pinpointing the location of the Lost Shaft. One, that it was actually several miles farther north than described, where several potential sites actually do exist. Another, that those who "mined there earlier" were either soldiers from the La Paz and Fort Mohave areas who had mined at various points along the Colorado River in the 1860's, or, that they were explorers and trappers from even earlier times. Recall Xavier Aubrey and Pegleg Smith were reported mining gold in "low rolling hills along Yampa Creek" as early as 1857, and that Dan O'Leary led a party of miners in 1864, who found gold along "Yampa Creek" (i.e. Hualapai Creek) and near the Colorado River. There is also the interesting prospect that George Brechner of "George Brechner's Stone House" in Hualapai Wash may well have been mining in the area as far back as 1853.

Yet another intriguing possibility remains, one I strongly suspect; that the Spanish were mining through this very area an entire century or more previous to those above. Certainly there are recorded instances of their presence in Mohave County and other parts of Arizona at that time. It would only seem probable that in their unending search for minerals, they might follow along the Colorado River up to the entrance of Grand Canyon. There were indications of their presence in this area; part of a Spanish spur and old arrastras on Gold Butte right across the river, a piece of Spanish bridle bit in Meriwittica Canyon (story yet to come), the knife with the Spanish handle from Tassi Ranch, documented records of slave trading by the Spanish across nearby Pearce Ferry, and even an older type arrastra that was originally located in Hualapai Wash right near the river's edge. And, there is a unique and puzzling trail, also to be discussed shortly.

When traveling the top of Grapevine Mesa along road #142 (gravel four-wheel drive trail approved for travel within LMNRA, these maps available from LMNRA), #142 eventually drops off the western edge of the mesa and winds down through a narrow canyon. After about a mile, there's a narrow post along the road designating the entrance boundary to LMNRA. Here you are passing onto "common lands." These are our lands, owned by you and me, administered by the National Park Service for our benefit and for those yet to come. Change nothing, leave nothing, take only photos. Observe, absorb, appreciate.

South-of-the-River Country

Not far from the boundary marker, an intersecting drainage comes in from the right. The Old Ford Mine is located up that drainage, so-named because there, for some thirty years, rested the remains of an old Model A Ford. At this drainage intersection are some very interesting rock structure ruins. The small rock cabin on the left was crudely made, with a rough fireplace and window openings containing bits of wood framing. In contrast, the two rock structures on the right were built with special craftsmanship and have very thick, precisely cut rock walls. No wood fragments at all remain in the structures of these, which would lead one to think they are older than the one on the left. Alongside these rock ruins on the right side is a huge tumble of rocks that does not appear to be debris washed down from the drainage above. Could this possibly have been the "barricade rock wall at one time" like the one mentioned? And, might this just be the place where Nodmann and his men found the human skull behind the remnant rock walls?

Proceeding on down the main drainage of road #142, and alongside the road, bits and pieces of cable are at times visible. Warren Mallory of Meadview, area manager of Apache Oro Mining Company in Lost Basin during recent years, said a cable was originally used to transport ore from the Ford Mine down to the rock ruins, but during later years the main part of the cable had been moved to the Harmon Mine that was located over the ridge on the right.[2]

Mallory related several stories about a contemporary miner, Woody Harmon. He said Woody had mined around here for many years, arriving in the 1950's. One day when he and Woody were looking around in a mine, Woody broke off a rock sample, it punctured one of his veins badly and blood squirted everywhere. Woody grabbed one of his cigarettes, chewed up the tobacco, then put wet tobacco on the cut and the cigarette paper on top and it stopped the bleeding immediately. He said Woody just kept right on working. The particular opening Harmon was working in at the time became known locally as the Blood Mine, one located just over the ridge from the road here being traveled on.

Continuing on down the road, the canyon opens up and to the left on the last hillside, an outcropping of quartz is readily visible. At the base of the outcropping is an opening to a tunnel. This is the old Golden Gate Mine, an extremely interesting mine and the one I believe has the best potential of being the "Lost Shaft" previously mentioned.

The Golden Gate has two lengthy adits or tunnels, one being some 500 feet in depth, it has two downward shafts, and also excellent examples of stopes and shutes. The main tunnel is also safer than most old mines, consisting of solid hard rock walls, so little timber shoring was required, plus fresh air circulates freely throughout the main part.

Near the end of the main tunnel, heavy framing is perched over a shaft going eighty feet down, with an old ladder still in place there, however, one no longer safe to negotiate. Of particular interest are the huge old rough-hewn timbers that provide support and framing over that shaft. A brief perusal by one archeologist led him to believe that from the type of wood, notching, and wooden pins used in places, these supports were well over 100 years old. At the very end of the main tunnel is a heavy wooden shute coming down from above. Behind that shute is another ladder that shinnies steeply upward alongside for some 60-80 feet, to an opening at the top (this accessible from outside and on top the hill, from where it would be considered a shaft). This upward passage behind the shute was marginally safe until someone attempted an illegal mining operation there in the fall of 1990 and in so doing, caused extensive damage to the ladder and top exit. Now old support beams near the top are broken making exit difficult, rocks are loose along the upward passage, ladder rungs are broken and entire sections are no longer attached firmly to walls or supports. As a result, the only relatively safe way to explore this mine now is to limit access just to the main tunnel on the main level, the opening of which is located near the base of the hillside where most visitors park their vehicles near the front entrance to the mine.

Outside, one can follow a path going up to quarries (surface digs) along the quartz vein on the hillside and to the shaft opening at the top of the shute. Around the right side of the hill are more tunnels burrowed into the hillside, along with an additional shaft or two, none of particular interest and all quite unsafe. There are also, however, some interesting older trash dumps in front of the main tunnel of the Golden Gate. According to two different archeologists who accompanied me there, Don Simonis, and also George Teague, one dump dates to the 1930's and 1950's but the other is much older.

This is a fascinating and beautiful old mine and one well worth a visit. Perhaps one day NPS will have necessary funding to showcase the Golden Gate as an excellent example of historic lode mining in the area and provide periodic informational tours for those interested.

Is the Golden Gate the famed "Lost Shaft"? Possibly. Descriptions of the physical workings fit quite well, although much work has been done at the mine since the date of the old article so various parts would have been changed. But in walking every other drainage from Grapevine Mesa and down to the lake, from the mouth of Grand Canyon and extending to the landing at Temple Bar to the west, these particular rock ruins and this old mine best fit the descriptions related in the article.

Mallory also offered that he had heard rumors passed down from generations of miners in this area telling of how three mines had initially been worked by the Spanish before the first wave of Euro-Americans arrived; the Bluebird Mine, the Scanlon-Childers Mine (recently known as the Empire-Manhattan) and this, the Golden Gate. Again, giving yet more validation that the Spanish had once worked here long before.

According to Roman Malach, recorded historical information on the Golden Gate is as follows:

> Hard rock mining was opened mostly in quartz, rich in wire gold. Golden Gate mine was considered the largest ledge in Lost Basin. It was situated close to a wash near the Colorado River. John Kreiner located it in the 1880's and the outcroppings were plainly visible from a long distance. Kreiner sold his original claim for $1,000 because it was 'too big for him to handle.'

South-of-the-River Country

In 1881 on the Mohave County tax rolls, Golden Gate Mill and Mining Co. listed a five acre mill site on the Colorado River at the place called Gaun Spring. There were one frame building, one adobe building, a complete 10-stamp quartz mill and a boarding house. J. T. Luthey was mine superintendent.[3]

This is somewhat confusing, and then there were also the following bits of information extracted from the *Mohave Miner*:

May 27, 1886 ... J. F. Luthy came in from Lost Basin, via Mineral Park, last Sunday. Mr. Luthy informs us that the work of developing the Golden Gate Mine is progressing satisfactorily and that it is showing up well. After patronizing our merchants quite liberally he took his departure for the Basin Monday. The Lost Basin Mill has closed down. No fault has been attributed to the mine, but the mill has not done the work guaranteed by the firm from whom it was purchased. It is probable that everything will be settled up in a satisfactory manner and a new stamp mill erected. The mill which so far has been used is a Huntington crusher with capacity of 10-14 tons a day, but the trial proved it would not crush over 2 tons per 24 hrs.

June 27, 1886 ... The connection between the 300-foot long tunnel and the 150-foot shaft in the Golden Gate Mine at Lost Basin was made last week. The men are now running a crosscut.

Aug. 1, 1886 ... W. H. Gann of Lost Basin was in town last Wednesday on his way to Hackberry ...

May 14, 1887 ... Beecher and Company's 10-mule team leaves Kingman today for the Lost Basin with 8000 pounds of lime and other supplies for the Golden Gate Mine and Mill Company.

"Guan Spring" on the Colorado River mentioned in this reference, must have been in Hualapai Wash, the most direct downhill route to any spring or to the river from the Golden Gate Mine. This may have been the same spring and mill-site used later by Scanlon and called Scanlon's Spring. But why was it referred to as Gaun? I found no other reference to this name; however, there was the reference in the Aug 1, 1886, excerpt to a W. H. Gann of Lost Basin. And there is also a Gann Spring shown on modern-day maps in Gold Butte across the river, some ten miles distant from Hualapai Bay. Could it be that the Gaun Spring mentioned in Malach's historical information was really a spring named after Gann and a printing error of one letter has caused confusion?

Another item in Malach's information from county records has thrown some researchers off in reference to our Golden Gate Mine. From his book, *Mohave County Mines*, Malach wrote:

The Golden Gate Mine consisted of 3 unpatented claims in the Chemeheuvis [Mohave] Mountains three miles west of the Mohawk mine. The mine was in the foothills on the western side of the mountains about five miles east of the

Colorado River. In 1939 the mine had a 40 foot deep shaft, at the bottom of which a crosscut had been driven for 50 feet. The mine was discovered in 1934 and the ore averaged $35.00 in gold per ton.[4]

This other Golden Gate Mine was, in reality, in the Mohave Mountains, farther south and near today's Lake Havasu City. Much confusion between the two mines occurred through the years with the result being a downplaying of the true significance of the Golden Gate Mine in Lost Basin, which, in reality is far older, far more extensive, and of much greater historical importance.

Shortly after leaving the Golden Gate Mine, one reaches a branch in the road. The left branch (continuation of approved road #142) wanders over the foothills, then down into Hualapai Wash where a right turn takes one on down the wash (usually four-wheel drive still required) some seven more miles to the shore of the lake. Or, by proceeding straight when reaching the wash, it leads on over to the Gregg's Hideout Road.

However, back to the 'y' in the road immediately after Golden Gate Mine; there one will find that another approved road, #144, veers off to the right, curves around and up a ridge where one soon comes upon another fine old rock cabin ruins not ten feet off to the right. This one is also fascinating; it, too, being exceptionally crafted with thick precisely-cut stone and a chimney expertly done with thick carved blocks of stone. Don Simonis estimated cans in one dump outside the cabin dated to the late 1800's. Whether it was occupied even earlier remains in question.

Continuing past this cabin ruins and up the drainage the road becomes more difficult, eventually coming to a dead-end at the old Scanlon-Childers Mine (now Empire-Manhattan). This mine consists of several tunnels 30-50 feet deep, surface scrapings and quarries. Schroder wrote that Mike Scanlon of Basin and Cy Childers of Kingman owned this and several other gold properties, and mentions in regard to this mine:

> Considerable ore was removed and occasionally treated in arrastras or milled, but the ground on the whole is little more than prospected. This is probably due to lack of water. The nearest water supply is Colorado River at Scanlon Ferry, 8 miles to the north, whence water is now hauled at a cost of $2 a barrel.[5]

The Arizona Bureau of Mines reported that in 1915 the Lost Basin Mining Company took over the Scanlon-Childers prospect. Several early river expeditions also made mention of an old arrastra present in Hualapai Wash down near the river (now under the waters of Lake Mead).

One will also notice curious paths and ledges near the Empire-Manhattan Mine. There is one particularly intriguing pathway just over the ridge from this mine to the south. To access this area by vehicle, go back toward the rock cabin ruin and make a sharp left on a small branch road that goes up a parallel side drainage and dead-ends. Located there is a rock-lined pathway that wanders up and around the hillside. Walk up that path and look closer. This path averages 3-5 feet in width, is pleasantly level, and makes for easy walking. Rocks and boulders reinforce the outer edge, sometimes twelve feet in height where the path crosses ravines and wash-outs. The path is too narrow for a wagon, yet wider than needed for a foot trail, and its intricate construction required far more work than was necessary for just a temporary walking path leading from one dig to another.

It might be this trail was made for pack burros to haul ore down to the river below. Warren Mallory said miners had dubbed this path the "Spanish Trail" but no one really knew when it was built or by whom. Most miners working in remote areas did not use time and precious energy to build such an extensive trail for burros. Yet there is the possibility that miners who had slave labor could afford such a luxury, and the Spanish, did, indeed, have slave labor. Recall that they were trading for Paiute slaves across Pearce Ferry, not ten miles distant, long before pioneer miners and settlers had arrived, and the Spanish looked for gold and silver everywhere. So, we have another possible tie to earlier Spanish presence, and yet another unsolved mystery.

Other mines located along this western side of the mesa include the Harmon Mine, the Troy, and the Clipper, while many others remain unnamed and unclaimed since they now lie within LMNRA boundaries and most leases have expired. Many are also filled with debris and packrats nests, so they rest smugly, holding keys to secrets only they will probably ever know.

In the canyons on the south end of Grapevine Mesa lie the Bluebird and Golden Mile mines. The Bluebird may also be very old. The narrow twisting road up to the entrance makes for interesting travel. The tunnel, itself, might be the longest of tunnels in Lost Basin, close to 700 feet. It doesn't have intriguing chutes and shafts or fresh air flow as the Golden Gate, neither are the sides solid rock so these did require some timbering for support. Tiny stalactites have formed along one wall where seepage occurs. At the far end of the tunnel, pieces of old track are still imbedded in the floor where ore carts once rumbled to and fro.

The Golden Mile, some distance from Bluebird, appears to be quite recent in origin, and in fact, I found no recorded information about this mine. This is accessed via Gregg's Hideout Road, then one takes a jeep trail off to the right that's usually in reasonably good shape until entering a narrows about ¼ mile from the mine, itself; one that sits in a small higher basin. At that narrows, one usually has to jump up a few short dryfalls with the vehicle to continue, so high clearance is essential. Two dumps at the former living area of the Golden Mile show signs of occupation during the 1930's and 50's. Five old buildings were standing when I first visited this mine site in 1974, however, by 1990, only three remained upright. The main tunnels, shafts, and quarries are farther along the little jeep path and over a saddle. The trail dead-ends at the mining area, itself, so one must then return past the buildings and again exit from the little high basin, once more negotiating the dryfall area on the return trip.

According to Barnes, Michael Scanlon started a post office in Lost Basin in 1882, before doing so in Gold Basin. But where? In Lost Basin, possibly at a very small old rock cabin still standing just south of approved road #142 on top of Grapevine Mesa. No one seems to know who built this small cabin or when. Or, perhaps his post office was at the Way Station that apparently existed at Patterson

Wells, one of the few former structures known to have been here during that time frame. Quoting Mamie Musser once again:

> Patterson Well is on the summit between Duncans Ranch and Wallapai Wash, six miles from Duncan's and seven miles from Wallapai Wash. In the early days of the Pony Express there was a station at Patterson Well consisting of saloon, post office, and Pony Express station. Here the riders changed horses. The end of this route being Pierce's Ferry where the express was exchanged and the rider returned to Patterson Well. The Pony Express riders went from there to the Railroad which was building from the East. Also, to Prescott. Three of the old riders were Hank Lefler, Fred Brawn and Lee Raught.

Since Michael Scanlon evidently came first to Lost Basin upon arriving in Mohave County, this may also be the appropriate place to run his obituary from the *Mohave Miner*, Feb. 3, 1912:

Death of M. Scanlon

M. Scanlon, one of the old timers of this county, died at Chloride sometime during Tuesday night, being found dead in bed the following morning. His death was from natural causes and apparently the end came without a struggle.

Deceased came to this county in 1883 or 1884 and settled in Lost Basin district of this county, where he engaged in mining and established a ferry on the Colorado River. This ferry he maintained for many years, but after the White Hills was discovered he removed to that place, having disposed of the ferry business to Mr. Grigg. He was married to Mrs. Agnes Merrill in the year 1900, and together they lived happily in the great silver camp. Several years ago Mr. and Mrs. Scanlon removed to Yavapai County where they were interested in a recovery plant at the McCabe Mine, later removing to Los Angeles.

Among the old timers that knew him well Mr. Scanlon had many fast friends and many of these attended his funeral in a body. Mrs. Scanlon was called from Los Angeles, arriving here Thursday night.

The funeral was held yesterday afternoon from Elks Opera House under the auspices of the Elks Lodge, of which deceased had been a member. The officers of the lodge conducted the beautiful funeral service of the order and Judge Carl Krook delivered the eulogy. The remains were followed to the grave by a large body of people.

Michael Scanlon was at one time a Supervisor of the County, the Chairman of the board during 1894 and 1898. He was the owner of valuable property in the Lost Basin district and had a sale on when death claimed him. He leaves his widow to mourn his loss.

South-of-the-River Country

When the Lost Basin mines were worked in the early 1800's, much of the ore was first treated in local arrastras, as were some also from Gold Basin, then transported and treated at a quartz mill at Grass Springs (later, Grass Springs Ranch/Diamond Bar/Smith/Grand Canyon Ranch). According to Mamie Musser's 1930's information, she had mentioned that in the early days a mill was built at Grass Springs by Grounds, Morey, and Paul Brown.

Here are some further excerpts taken from the *Alta Arizona* newspaper, May 1883:

> W. R. Jones from Grass Springs called on us this week. The Grass Springs Concentrator is running right along giving entire satisfactions. About 20 tons of ore is being put into one, and about 8 tons is crushed in 12 hrs. The Miners are all highly elated over the success of the mill.

> W. F. Grounds has gone to Grass Springs and will ship a load of concentrations.

> W. Grounds and R. G. Patterson have returned from Grass Springs. They report the concentrator panning.

In June, 1883:

> Mr. E. L. Morey came in yesterday from Grass Springs and we gathered the following items: Bob Patterson has 10 men employed at the El Dorado mine, taking out ore. Three teams are hauling ore from this mine to the concentrator at Grass Springs. Plenty of water has recently been found, and it was brought to the mill by pipe, to run it day and night. A full set of hands are employed at the mill. Mr. Morey will in a few days put in copper plates and amalgamate for the free gold, and then concentrate after amalgamation for the base metals.

> About the 15th the mill will commence running night and day. The mill has a capacity of about 14 tons per 24 hours. Very rich ore is being brought to the mill, by pack trains and wagons, from Lost Basin. Enough ore has been worked to prove conclusively that the mill is a complete success.

Located on top of Grapevine Mesa are two more mines, these of more recent workings. One is the Climax Mine located nearly on the western rim of the mesa and the south slope of Tut Peak (high point on this part of the western rim and designated on USGS maps). The other, close by, is the King Tut.

In the 1930's, George Musser owned the Climax Mine and with the help of a friend, worked hard to dig the shaft. According to a newspaper article, "Climax Mine Still Worked in Lost Basin near Lake Mead," by Malach (*Mohave Miner*, February 28, 1974), Musser and his partner first started the shaft by using a windlass for lifting waste and it took the men several months to get just 30 feet deep. After installing a Fairbanks-Morse hoist, work progressed faster until they reached 105 feet. At the 60 foot level they found a stringer of gold and followed it a short distance. Ore from the mine assayed at $400 and over a ton of good ore was taken to a smelter in Clarkdale.

Included in the article were interesting entries from the daily diary of a man who worked at the Climax Mine in March of 1939. No mention is made in the article as to whether this diary was written by Musser or a partner. Only partial excerpts will be quoted here:

March 1 ... Here it is the first of March, and we have not struck the ore as we have planned all along. Had panning of gold out of two drill holes today for the first time below the 75 foot level. Hoisted one bucket of waste. Baked bread tonight. Clear and slightly warm all day. Put in 5 ½ holes today. Will be working on Byron's boat the rest of the week [Byron Duncan was Tap Duncan's son over at Diamond Bar Ranch].

March 2 ... Made our trip to the lake this morning only to find no one on deck to explain the work to us in fixing Byron's boat. Came on home and finished our round and blasted. Had one missed hole, so decided to wait till morning before going back in the hole. Max washed his clothes, while I greased the truck all around for our trip to town Monday morning. Slightly cloudy and warm all day.

March 3 ... Hoisted 16 buckets of waste. Shot the missed hole off. It threw rocks out of the collar of the shaft at 80 feet. Clear and warm 'til noon, then turned off cool and cloudy.

March 4 ... Woke up and found a white world staring us in the face. Over an inch of snow fell during the night, and then cleared off before daylight. Max gadded this afternoon, while I framed timbers. I gadded awhile this morning. Hoisted ten buckets of waste.

March 5 ... Worked up til noon. Max gadding and I framing timbers to go in the 60 foot level... Made the trip to Bann's for information about our future jobs with them. Clear and warm." [I wondered if this reference to "Bann's" may have been mistakenly deciphered from hand-written notes in the diary and should have been "Gann's" since the previous newspaper article had mentioned a "W. H. Gann of Lost Basin]

The writer, whoever he was, and Max traveled to Kingman on March 9, running out of gas just before reaching "Coyote Hole Pass" (today referred to as Coyote Pass) west of Kingman, and a Dick Rucker gave them fuel to get home. They spent the night in town and Max returned to camp the next morning where he got caught in a snow storm. The writer stayed in Kingman to attend his cousin's funeral, then rode back out to Lost Basin with Mrs. Byron Duncan and their oldest girl.

March 12 ... We made a trip to the lake to help Byron put the engine in his boat. Late this afternoon Emery [probably Pop Emery, information on him to follow in the Lake Mead chapter] took us out on a fishing trip where Byron caught a five pound bass that he gave us. Came back by Byron's place to help load a piano on a truck. Had supper with them. Clear and warm.

South-of-the-River Country

Over the next week the writer made another trip to Pearce Ferry to work on Byron's boat, during which he observed Tap Duncan working cattle near there and also mentioned lots of people and cars being at the landing.

> March 20 ... Made a few odds and ends here at the mine for the boat, then went back to install it. Made a trip to Emery's Falls [now called Columbine Falls] up in the canyon. Had a small bass for our lunch. Returned by dark. Had supper with Willis Evans at the CCC Camp before returning to camp. Cloudy and warm [recall that Evans and his CCC crew had discovered Rampart Cave while working in the lower canyon].

> March 21 ... Ending winter and beginning of spring. Put in a set of timbers this morning and mucked out 14 buckets of waste late this evening. Powe [Rowe?] came over from the Cyclopic mine to hire us to work for him, only to turn him down for reason of staying with our work and the promise of jobs with Stoddards. Byron came late for a few minutes, bringing some mail for me. First thunder and showers this year.

> March 22 ... Put in four holes and blasted by 10:30. Sharpened all the steel by noon. Hoisted 11 buckets of waste. Made two pumpkin pies this noon. Thunder storms were raging all around camp all day.

> March 27 ... Hoisted 31 buckets of muck putting the shaft at 90 foot depth. Made a trip to Byron's this morning to send letters in by them to mail. Raining off and on all day in the country. Baked four loaves of bread at noon.

.... Thus, we have first-hand insights into daily activity of one miner in Lost Basin, 1939.

Tom Godwin, science fiction writer who later lived in Dolan Springs, worked the Climax Mine during later years and lived in a shack previously located alongside approved road #142 where he also had a unique old wooden travel trailer. A cousin of Musser's by the name of Putman was working the Climax Mine in 1974 and later Clyde Hart took it over. Now it is owned by Apache Oro, also known as American Heavy Minerals. Today the shack is gone and only the axle of the wooden travel trailer remains. Trash lies scattered about. The head frame and most of the mine equipment is gone. Little is still present at the mine, itself, except the shaft and quarries. Tom Godwin had requested that upon his demise his ashes be left in the area and his wish was granted.

The King Tut Mine is located several miles south of the Climax Mine. Interest was spawned here when it was said that Mrs. Duncan (from nearby Diamond Bar Ranch) picked up a nugget in a wash near the area in about 1930. According to Bill Fauth of Kingman who worked at the King Tut in 1934 or 35, this was Mrs. Charles Duncan (Charles was Tap's son).[6] While roaming around during a break from driving chuck wagon, she had picked up a rock that later proved to assay out at $900 (in those days, gold was $35 an ounce). However, Mamie Musser's report from the late 1930's differs, and she credits Mrs. Tap Duncan with finding a piece

Lost Basin

of quartz heavy with gold while riding the range, stating she and her husband then searched farther for a ledge in the area but none could be found.

At any rate, before long Tap Duncan of the Diamond Bar Ranch (formerly Grass Springs Ranch) told W. E. Dunlop, a geologist and prospector, of the find and made an offer to him to prospect for the source. Dunlop started prospecting out from the Diamond Bar Ranch and eventually found placer gold to the west in the King Tut area. Promoters became interested and development of a big placer mine operation soon followed. It's said that Tap Duncan named this mine the King Tut. Sadie Pearl Duncan stated that the Duncans and Neals were in some kind of partnership on the King Tut Mine originally, then Tap traded the Valley Ranch for Neal's share in the mine so he then came to control full ownership of the King Tut.[7]

By 1936 a large adobe main building had been erected at the mine, along with another big wooden structure. Jimmie Ray (Taps grandson) and Sadie Pearl Duncan both recalled seeing workers tents surrounding the main buildings.[8] Jimmie Ray said he and Sam Oldfield made all the adobe bricks for the main building, working from a location about one-quarter mile east of Diamond Bar Ranch. They worked an area near a small spring where the soil was of clay consistency. While making the adobe bricks, Ray got fifty cents a day for "punching a burro" around the arrastra.

Sadie Pearl said a talented young Mexican man named Dick Noley made a wonderful fireplace in the big adobe building and that a beautifully carved and finished wooden bar was put in. She thought the bar was later moved to the American Legion Hall in Kingman. Porter Munson was manager and main promoter of the King Tut placer mine. In 1935, Munson had a mining engineer draw a sketch of the projected placer mining operation. This drawing, shown in the book, *Trails, Rails, and Tales,* was mainly used for promotional purposes, although about half the equipment shown in the drawing was actually installed and used in the operation of the mine for a time. A water line was put in from Iron Basin up behind the Diamond Bar Ranch and extended over to the King Tut.

Bill Fauth of Kingman (interview with author, June of 1986), was about 16 years old when he worked at the King Tut for six weeks one summer. He said the main adobe building was a huge mess hall with a real pretty fireplace and that great food was served. While he was there, most of the men stayed in board shacks behind the main building. Fauth was told he would be paid 50 cents an hour which was really good pay in those days so he worked very hard. They put him on the "grizzly," a big screen made out of railroad tracks about 4-6 inches apart. The larger rocks coming down the conveyor belt to the crusher would get stopped by the grizzly and then Bill had to break them with a big hammer. There was a diesel power plant at the camp and it generated about 200 kw of electricity. Fauth also remembered newly painted gasoline-powered Ford dump trucks, along with a big shovel outfit that worked the washes.

Mary Grace Joy, wife of Ben Joy, the field superintendent at the mine, talked about the King Tut in *Trails, Rails, and Tales.*[9] She spoke of how there seemed problems from the very beginning but that unscrupulous promoters finally led to the demise of the King Tut operation. Munson and other promoters would often come out to camp to pick up the gold. It was later learned that rather than deposit the gold to cover the men's wages, they used it to promote more money and then divert investments to their own use. In the end, Joy, and a man named Harper there at the mine, refused to turn more gold over to them until the workers received their pay. The sheriff became involved and some weeks later, according to Joy, the "big bosses" finally came out with the necessary money to pay off the men who were still there waiting for wages. The camp was then closed down. The management left much of the equipment, just dropped payments, and over the years the mine was stripped of remaining valuable machinery.

Fauth, however, was not among those fortunate who got paid. He said he never received a dime for his six weeks work on the grizzly, but only "lots of sore muscles and sweat" for all his effort during the bristling heat of that summer.

Lost Basin was the site of another interesting memory relayed by Fauth. In 1932, before the King Tut had become a big operation, Fauth often had come out to Lost Basin with friends to dry wash for gold when they couldn't find work elsewhere. One time he and an uncle were dry washing in an area between where the King Tut was later developed and the western edge of the rim. It took them ten days to get a 30-30 rifle shell full of gold (about an ounce) which was $28 worth. At night when they made camp, he would look out across Grapevine Mesa and see almost 100 campfires; people were scattered all over out on the mesa working with dry washers, just trying to get an ounce of gold.

Tom Godwin, previously mentioned author from Dolan Springs, also spent some time working the King Tut. In an interview by Julia Moser in the *Joshua Journal*, April, 1977, Godwin reported finding a quarter pound nugget at the King Tut.

From an *Arizona Bureau of Mines Bulletin #168*, 1961, comes the statement "during 1934-42 a gold production valued at $25,510 was credited to the Lost Basin placer area."

Yet death did not come to the King Tut. Interest was again revived, as documented by a March 1944 article in the *Mohave Miner*. The title of the article was "New Playground Area for County is Receiving Post War Consideration" along with the subtitle, "Million-dollar Recreational Project to be Located at King Tut Guest Ranch near Grand Canyon, Lake Mead." A photograph showed part of the big adobe building and called it the King Tut Ranch House. No author was credited for this interesting article that expressed high post-war hopes and plans for the area:

> The opening of new playground areas, which are expected to fill an important role in the everyday life of the civilian in peace time, is now among the necessary issues taken into consideration by people with foresight and sufficient capital to bring their dreams to a reality. Just such a recreational spot in Mohave County, the vast potentialities of which are still untapped, is M. B. Dudley's King Tut guest ranch project which got its start some years

Lost Basin

ago and was shaping up for permanent development when the all-out-for-war production loomed on the horizon and halted procedure.

It is Dudley's aim, he explains, to establish at King Tut an extensive western guest ranch that will have modern comforts and facilities comparable to any up-to-the-minute hostelry in the country, combined with the natural grandeur of the desert setting at that particular spot, plus the attractions of Boulder Dam and Lake Mead.

The King Tut ranch consists of 6,000 acres of desert and mountain land which includes a large portion of the country's world famous Joshua Tree forest. It is located near the western end of the Grand Canyon and the eastern end of Lake Mead. It skirts the edge of the recreational area around the lake which has been set aside by the government. It is only a few miles from Pierce's ferry where an excellent camp has been established and docking facilities for power boats and yachts are said to be perfect. The Pierce's ferry paved road, which branches from the main Kingman-Boulder dam highway about 34 miles north of Kingman, goes within one mile of the 11-room adobe bungalow which will serve as the nucleus for the new units to be built later.

Situated on top of the low rolling Joshua tree covered hills of Grapevine mountain [Grapevine Mesa], this typically rambling ranch house is modernized in every phase. Water has been brought through a four-inch pipe from Iron Springs in the mountains eleven miles away, to a storage tank nearby, which affords sufficient pressure for modern plumbing and everyday water usage besides being ample in supply for the swimming pool, gardens and lawns that are envisioned in the plans for the future. Up to the time of Pearl Harbor, this host house had already become the headquarters for Lake Mead fisherman and seasonal hunters of deer and small game which abound in the near vicinity. It will afford its own stables and rodeo grounds, Dudley states, and already the corrals are supplied with running water. The King Tut property is also said to be located in the center of one of the largest grazing sections in the west and the famous Diamond Bar ranch owned by Tap Duncan, lies not many miles away.

This pleasant oasis, as one writer has called it, was originally taken up as a placer gold project and considerable free gold was taken from the gravel in the area then known as the King Tut placers. Nuggets weighing as much as an ounce are said to have been found by the miners during the time the property was being operated.

In the days when gas and tires were plentiful, many stories were published praising the beauties of the drive from Kingman to Pierce's ferry which, to those who have made the trip, is a scenic holiday of the first order. The distant wind-carved mountain outlines, veiled in ever-changing desert lights, the numerous species of cacti, the shiny-leafed creosote bush and fantastic Joshua

South-of-the-River Country

Trees draw comments of awe from strangers and are a never-ending source of surprise to the old-timer. In the early spring, when the desert blooms, a counterpart for every heard-of flower can be found in the mosaic that carpets the undulating landscape on either side of the road and reaches to the far lava slopes of the foothills.

Besides the western atmosphere which will be created at the King Tut ranch for its guests, there is very fine bass fishing to be enjoyed in Lake Mead. The camp at Pierce's ferry, 16 miles away, where the government has expended a large sum of money for improvements, will be the starting point for many fishing jaunts and day's outings in motor boats. Grand Canyon tourists from the resort across the Colorado river will find the King Tut a convenient place for stop-overs.

Lake Mead, which has reached a length of approximately 125 miles, can be navigated by power boat from Pierce's ferry up into the Grand Canyon for 25 miles. This trip is said to be one of the most scenic tours made possible by the great Boulder Dam....

In reading this article, keep in mind that when one is told that a ranch "consists of 6000 acres," this generally means that the ranch owner has leased grazing rights on many acres of public-owned lands, not that the rancher owns all that land, himself (many did not want ownership of vast areas and the obligation to pay taxes on same). I have, however, found no other information or mention of Dudley's King Tut Guest Ranch from that time forth.

Today, from Pearce Ferry Road, one can see large tailing piles just to the west in the area of Lake Mead City, these left from the King Tut Mine workings. At the King Tut site, itself, a few ruins of some old buildings are still standing, as well as remnant sections of adobe walls, flooring, foundations, water tank, concrete footings for the conveyor belts and crusher, and the water tank above the mine. The water line still stretches to Hillside Spring in Iron Basin but is in bad need of repair. At various times some mining activity is still present at the King Tut today, and a watchman is often present. (2014... sadly, now as one makes the turn on Pearce Ferry Road above Patterson Hill, a massive ugly gravel pit greets one right alongside this well-traveled road, one where many Joshua's were destroyed and removed, this on private property that the owner leased for gravel mining ... a crying shame, since many gravel sources are readily available down in Grapevine Wash, close by, where no Joshua Trees would have been damaged).

Located in the southeast of Lost Basin and Grapevine Mesa is what today is known as the Grand Canyon Ranch, the one originally homesteaded on the historically important site of Grass or Tanakah Springs, with the first ranch settled on that site by Wellington Starkey who called it the Grass Springs Ranch. As covered previously, this site was a very special place for the Hualapai's before the arrival of Euro-Americans. The fine flowing spring with lush vegetation was called Tanakah. It was also the Hualapai "crying grounds."[10] Here, for centuries past, they held many ceremonial rites in honor of their dead, as well as for other purposes, and it was long considered to be a sacred place. It was also reported by some to be the site of the last Ghost Dance by Natives in this southwest area. To this day, the Hualapai are still trying to regain ownership of the springs and site that they have long called Tanakah.

Recall that Joseph Hamblin made reference to Grass Springs during his trips from St. George, Utah, when he crossed at Pearce Ferry and brought several Mormon parties up Grapevine Wash. There were also many references to this particular spring in the 1883 mining notations. Grass Springs was not only an excellent water source for many centuries, but was also crucially located at the summit of Grapevine Wash and at the first break in the southern part of Grand Wash Cliffs where one section of the old Indian trail wound on up through a side canyon called Grapevine Canyon (now the route the Hualapai Tribe uses to bring the public to their Grand Canyon West development), eventually coming out on top the plateau. From Grass Springs, one could also access Iron Basin and Iron Springs to the south, or, more commonly, go over the crest to Patterson Springs and on down to Hualapai Valley.

In Grounds, *Trail Dust of the Southwest*, the author shows a picture of Bill Ridenour's mill that was located at Grass Springs. The Mohave Museum of History and Arts in Kingman has another booklet displaying this same photo, with accompanying information reading "Quartz Mill at Grass Springs ... destroyed by Indians during the Ghost Dance in 1887." Ridenour and Grounds were mining partners in 1883 when this mill was built at Grass Springs. The old photo shows several men standing on and near the stamp mill, a fenced field in the background, along with a small house.

And what of this "Ghost Dance" that was held at Grass Springs? In the early 1880's, a Paiute named Wavoka (local settlers called him Jack Wilson) had a vision of Jesus, the man killed by his own people so long ago. Wavoka's vision told him that Jesus would return as a Native American, that the intruders would disappear, and Indians would then have their lands restored to them once again. However, for this to happen, they must pray extensively and dance for days on end. Natives across the country, devastated by the over-whelming invasion of Euro-Americans, began following the way of Wavoka and Ghost Dances were held by many tribes. The last one held in the southwest was said by some to be this gathering at our nearby Grass Springs in 1887. According to Grounds,[11] an estimated six or seven hundred Indians came to Grass Springs and danced for three days (another source stated a week), during which they destroyed the mill. Then a troop of African-Americans were sent to disband the Indians and herd them over to Hackberry, ending the Ghost Dance and ceasing any further Indian occupation of Grass Springs.

Euler and Dobyns stated in their book that five hundred people danced at Grass Springs; then later, the tribe had two more Ghost Dances below Koara Springs in the central Cerbat Mountains. Eventually, however, when nothing positive resulted except increased apprehension amongst neighboring settlers, enthusiasm for the Ghost Dance waned.[12] Another source, Chester Cheel, said the sudden illness and death of Wavoka, himself, led to the demise of the Ghost Dance religion.[13]

Wellington Starkey was the first Euro-American rancher recorded as living at Grass Springs during the 1890's (one source stated the name was Walter, but this was found erroneous). Starkey had come into Mohave County, as did many other cowboys, accompanying cattle drives from Texas in the mid-1870's.[14] By 1890, Starkey showed up on the County Tax rolls as having several hundred cattle at Grass Springs Ranch. According to Mamie Musser's historical information, the Starkey's put in alfalfa, fruit orchards, and a garden at Grass Springs. A few sources have referred to it as the Iron Springs Ranch, although Iron Springs was actually south of the ranch and higher up in Iron Basin.

Starkey was married and had a family. Leonard Neal stated that Starkey was a fine carpenter and had built the house down at the Valley Ranch, which Neal later dismantled, moved, and rebuilt over at his place at Cane Springs where Neal raised his family. Starkey, however, was prone to drinking bouts. During one stage of depression he shot and killed himself while in the small rock house at Grass Springs Ranch, portions of the walls still standing at the old ranch site today (1990). Starkey's widow sold the ranch to Tap Duncan in around 1910.[15]

George Taplin Duncan, known as Tap Duncan, was a flamboyant person of some renown. He and his wife, Ollie, had left Texas and moved to Idaho where he worked for a big outfit for several years before coming to Mohave County. It's said Tap killed a man in Texas, then while in Idaho, got into a fight and killed another one there. A man named Glancy in Kingman used to say, "Tap had shot a lot of people, but he said they all needed it."[16]

In 1898, Tap and Ollie had moved their family south by wagon from Idaho, crossed at Bonelli's ferry, and bought a ranch at Knight Creek, east of today's Kingman. A decade later they purchased the Grass Springs/Starkey Ranch and gave it the name Diamond Bar. In time, they also purchased the Spear Ranch in White Hills, the Fielding place (later known as Lincoln Ranch, then the Willow Springs Ranch) in the Music Mountains, and the Clay Springs Ranch, also in the Musics (later owned by the Grounds), thereby consolidating a very large area of springs and grazing leases. In fact, the Diamond Bar eventually became one of the largest ranches in the southwest, with cattle grazing over some 1,450,000 acres of mostly leased public lands. Of the children born to the family, there were two sons, Charles and Byron, and two daughters, Tappie and Laura. Tappie later married Jim Ray, and in an interview, their oldest son, Jimmie Ray, provided interesting stories that will follow. Jimmie Ray spent every summer at the Diamond Bar from 1927 to 1940 and also returned there after World War II for a short time.

Tap Duncan liked to travel to Hollywood, made acquaintances there, and often invited these friends to his ranch. The author Will James at times frequented the Diamond Bar. Andy Devine attended Jim Ray and Tappie Duncan's wedding at the ranch (Andy Devine had been raised in nearby Kingman). Jimmie Ray said his granddad, Tap, "didn't like his dad, so Grandad took it out on Andy that day," but did not go on to explain that comment further. Louis L'Amour, the prolific and well-known popular western writer, mentioned that he once met and visited with Tap Duncan but regretted not having time to question Duncan more so he could draw upon Tap's stories as sources for his frontier novels.[17]

Here is one story told by Sadie Pearl Duncan, who was married to Don Duncan, Tap's grandson:

> Tap Duncan bought a fancy Cadillac convertible. One day he brought Will [James] out in it and he parked the car by the fence near the house. Mother always had some goats around the ranch that lived in the hills. While Tap and Will were in the house exchanging stories, the goats came down and got up on top the convertible, jumped up and down, and their little sharp hooves just tore everything apart.

Tappie is also quoted several times in Trails, Rails, and Tales. She told of when they had to burn down the wonderful orchard at the ranch because so many snakes came in to enjoy the cool shade, and how the mountain sheep, coyotes, and mountain lions would often come right up near the ranch. She said there were many deer but the Duncan's didn't hunt the deer because they preferred eating beef.

During our interview, Jimmie Ray offered the following memories about the ranch:

> The Indians used that spring there, and they called it the "crying grounds." They came there to mourn their dead, but they wouldn't camp right by the springs, they'd camp over on the hill.

> Many years before, there used to be a quartz mill right there where the remains of the blacksmith shop now stands -- that's the one the Indians destroyed during their Ghost Dance. During prohibition some used to make booze in the two story tin barn that sat over the rock foundation [now only the tall rock foundation stands].

> Lots of the orchard was there before Tap and Ollie came – some of those were 50 years old when I remember in the 1930's. Big old trees. Years later, after we left the ranch, some relative of Dale Smiths lived there and the woman was allergic to cotton off the trees so they cut down lots of the huge ones.

> That dirt dam below Meadview [in Grapevine Wash not far from Lucky 7 corral] we called "Cramp Springs," because my mother got cramps there real bad. Forest Moses and I built the first dam there in 1946. It was so cold we'd sleep with stocking caps on and there was frost inside the tent.

When I asked Jimmie about the big roasting pits located not far from that spring, he said, yes, they'd seen those, but none of them knew what the structures were. He also mentioned that the windmill and corral (locally called the "Lucky 7 corral," apparently because it's located in Section Seven) were not put in until the 1950's, so, until then, Cramp Springs was the main water source located between

South-of-the-River Country

Grapevine Springs and the main ranch at Grass Springs. Jimmie's stories continued:

> Forest Moses and I prospected all over that country looking for uranium. On top of the cliffs, north from New Water Springs, we once found a place we called Sheep Spring and it had lots of petroglyphs around it.
>
> In 1939, Granddad had 1000 head of Mexican steers shipped in to pasture on the range, some went over toward Willow Beach. One day he told my cousin and a guy named Ed Murphy to go over there and get them. Granddad packed up something for them to eat, which they rolled up with their bedrolls, then threw them on the packhorse and took off. The next day when they got down there and took everything off the packhorse, they found all they had to eat was a case of canned sauerkraut.
>
> Another time Granddad sent Ed and Penie Duncan down into Grapevine Wash to work there. When you go down into Grapevine, there's something about that canyon that scares horses and you can't get them to stay in it overnight, even if they're hobbled. Sure enough, the next morning, the boys horses were gone. They were left with all their camp outfit there and no way to haul it back out, so they walked on down to Pearce Ferry and caught a ride with a fisherman, back up to the ranch. Then Penie and I went back down to gather steers and pick up the camp outfit. We only had one extra saddle horse each and no pack horse, so we roped three steers, put pack saddles on them, tied the two beds and camp equipment on, and turned the steers loose. I never saw anything like it. Those steers went crazy and they scattered stuff for five miles going back up that canyon.
>
> Once when we were gathering steers, Granddad hired an old guy that used to be sheriff over at Yavapai Co., a guy by the name of Johnny Munds. Granddad hired him because he had a pick-up and we needed someone who could use one for a chuck wagon.
>
> Old Johnny was the sorriest cook there ever was. If you had fried eggs for breakfast and didn't eat all of them, there'd be fried eggs in the stew that night. Everything went into the stews. We were camped up there where Meadview is right now and Johnny had made some raisin and rice pudding about four days before and it just got all hard – you couldn't even eat it. We figured we'd have it in the stews for days til it was gone, so when I had the pan, I kind of chiseled around the outside of the hard pudding, then hung the handle of the pan out over the chuck box. Then I had my brother chase me by there and I 'accidently' hooked it with my hand and jerked it off onto the ground so we'd get rid of it. Otherwise, we'd still be eating it.
>
> Another time we were camped out on the mesa, right about where Meadview is now. We'd camped there to work cattle back down towards Greggs Ferry. One morning we put a roast in the Dutch Oven over the coals and just cracked

the lid a little, hoping it wouldn't spoil. That night we came in after dark and ate the roast. The next morning when it was light we looked in the Dutch Oven and the thing was filled with maggots.

Ray stated he built the concrete trough at Grapevine Springs Canyon, the one above the first pond. But he said the big pump and pipes at the springs had been put in later, in the early 1950's, by Smith, to pump water up on the mesa to the dirt cattle tank near the airstrip.

After serving in World War II, Jimmie Ray returned to Diamond Bar. His grandmother gave him a small house (one-room line shack) located at the King Tut Mine, and a guy who worked for the Bureau of Reclamation gave him an old trailer. Ray moved both up into Iron Basin, set them side by side, and for a total of $12, had his own small place (this to be designated the "Ray Place" on many maps thereafter). However, he didn't stay for more than about six months, and upon returning in 1982, found someone had stolen both the wood cook stove and pot-bellied stove from the cabin. Both living units are now badly deteriorated and collapsing, however, the site itself remains pleasant, being situated on the edge of a picturesque wash and seep with large apricot trees close by.

In the 1940's, Byron Duncan, Tap's younger son, also built a place in nearby Hackberry Springs Wash, this visible from the Diamond Bar Road and off to the south, just before one reaches Diamond Bar Ranch. No verification could be found, however, that he actually lived there for more than a few months at a time.

Brief mention was made of Tap Duncan in the *Mohave Miner* column, "recalling yesteryear" of November 7, 1914: "G. T. Duncan, the big cattleman of the Grass Springs section, was a visitor to Kingman a few days ago."

Tap, however, was not immune to ill fortune. His high living ways came to an end when he lost money during the Depression and was forced to sell many of the ranch holdings. A May 19, 1939, letter in BLM files showed notification to G. T. Duncan that the $23.65 grazing fees, his cost for running cattle on vast areas of public lands for the first half of 1939, had not yet been received.[18] On November 18, 1944, Duncan was killed when hit by a car in Kingman near the railroad crossing and Fourth Street. The Diamond Bar Ranch was sold in 1950.

Notes in BLM files in Kingman show the following record of ownership for the Diamond Bar Ranch, with their historical sketch starting only in the late 1940's.[19]

1. J. M. Ray and Tap Duncan Ray (Jimmie's parents)

2. Harry and Rose Handlery

3. Handlery Hotels, Inc.

4. J. M. and Dale Smith

5. Ownership transferred to Dale Smith in 1961

Handlery was from California and did not keep the ranch long, selling it to Jim Smith from southern Arizona in the early 1950's. Smith, according to Sadie Pearl Duncan, was a State Senator who also made an unsuccessful bid for Governor of

South-of-the-River Country

Arizona. From the time Jim Smith bought the ranch it was designated the Smith Ranch, however, the older name of Diamond Bar Ranch continues to be used by many locals. Since purchase by the Smiths, the ranch house at Diamond Bar was only occupied intermittently by ranch foremen and ranch hands. Clyde and Cecil McBee lived there for a time during the 1950's while working for Jim Smith.

BLM records on the Diamond Bar Ranch yielded data prepared by Elno Roundy, Natural Resource Specialist, in November of 1973. AUM= Animal Unit Month and designates the amount of forage required to feed a cow and her calf, or a horse, or five sheep or goats for one month. CYL= Cows Year Long. Some revealing information of particular interest I have underscored in the following:[20]

> Prior to 1973, base property qualifications had never been established. Range surveys were accomplished in the late 1930's and early 1940's, but other than range-type maps, there is no information regarding these surveys in the District files. <u>Consequently, in 1973, the District Manager established base property qualifications on the basis of the last ten years historical use.</u> This was in accordance with the Advisory Board Resolution dated January 22, 1973. <u>Historical use on the Federal Range for this allotment average 729 AUM's</u>, or at 75% Federal Range, the equivalent of 81 CYL's year long for the allotment. <u>The allottee did file a timely protest at the protest meeting</u>, the Advisory Board recommended that the District Manager attempt to satisfy the protest administratively. <u>Through subsequent negotiation, the allottee agreed to a base property qualification on the Federal Range of 3780 AUM's.</u> The base property qualifications were for the perennial portion of the allotment which is 63% Federal Range. The allottee further agreed to a classification of Ephemeral Range on the Ephemeral portion of the allotment which is 100% Federal Range, and is separated from the perennial portion by fencing and natural barrier.

This illustrates how liberally grazing leases on public lands were often determined in the area, even up into recent years. The number of animals allowed to graze on public lands were not decided by any scientifically determined conditions or actual carrying capacities of the land, but, instead, set according to "previous years historical use." And even then, if protest was made by the rancher, subsequent adjustments were made to appease that rancher and allow for even heavier grazing impacts.

Anyone seeking an in-depth overview of the many problems inherent in our western system of cattle grazing on public lands should read *Sacred Cows at the Public Trough* by Denzel and Nancy Ferguson. The book abounds with eye-opening facts and figures rarely placed before the public eye, and also pinpointed some problems that specifically occurred in this Mohave County area.[21]

In regard to wild burro presence in South-of-the-River Country, these burros were not native to the area (just as range cows were not), but instead, were descendants of burros that had been brought in, used, then turned loose by miners. The burros subsequently flourished in this arid land. Today the burros thrive in the Temple Bar area and from there west to Hoover Dam. They are also present on the

Hualapai Reservation east of the Grand Wash Cliffs in Spencer Canyon. At one time they could be found throughout Gold Basin and Lost Basin but most of those were shot by ranchers in the 1940's and 1950's to decrease grazing competition for their cattle. None are known to exist here today [1990]. Only time will tell whether peripheral populations will eventually spread and thrive in our area again.

Patterson Springs and Patterson Well lie several miles west of the Diamond Bar Ranch. From Mamie Musser's story it's known that a pony express Way Station was located at Patterson Springs in the 1880's. Out of an old *Notice of Mining Location* book in the court house in Kingman is drawn information from a mining claim filed in the area by George Eaton in 1902, this located "seven miles from O.K. Mill and about one mile from what is known as Patterson's house." Both Jimmie Ray and Sadie Pearl Duncan recalled being told there had been a house at Patterson Well at one time. Ray said, in addition, there used to be some old rock house remains about one-half mile east of the corrals, up by the spring, and that there was a ranch house at Patterson Well that had burned to the ground before he was born. Sadie Pearl said Charlie Duncan once lived there, but after the place burned down, it was just used as a watering place for Tap Duncan's cattle from then on. Leonard Neal remembered lots of wild horses being around Patterson Well at one time. In 1936, L. B. Thorn and John Mullin had the grazing lease on Patterson corral and well (around the same time they were involved at Burnt Mill down in Gold Basin, some six miles to the southwest).

The Patterson Corral still stands to this day. The spring a mile or so east of the corral, has been capped off and water is piped down to the cattle tanks. Warren Mallory was told that somewhere near Patterson Wells were remnants of two old arrastras, but neither he, I, nor several others have found any sign of those.

There were two ranches just south over the ridge and beyond Iron Basin (on the Hualapai Valley side of the Musics), south of the Diamond Bar Ranch. The first was called the Fielding Ranch (later part of the Diamond Bar), then , after Boyd Tenney, former State Senator, lived there it was called the Tenney Ranch. Then it became known as the Lincoln Ranch, and finally Willow Springs Ranch. This ranch site can be seen and accessed from the Hackberry or Antares Point Road, about eight miles in from Pearce Ferry Road. The ranch rests in a small valley several miles off Hackberry road and up against the base of the cliffs, near Willow Springs (also known as Granite Springs, this named for the huge bald-domed rock face on the uppermost part of the cliffs and plainly visible from Hualapai Valley below). The road passes near the ranch and continues on up the edge of the Music Mountains, proceeds past Cedar Springs, on through beautiful pine-tree covered Hells Canyon Springs and Basin, then, on top, meets the Buck and Doe road on the Hualapai Reservation.

The other ranch in that area of Hualapai Valley is called the Valley Ranch. No buildings remain at the site presently, however, the corral is still standing and foundation ruins still exist. The location of this site is about four miles off Pearce Ferry road on Hackberry road. The corral is readily visible along the north side of Hackberry (Antares) Road, and close by is the former location of the ranch house. This is where the home stood that Wellington Starkey had built, the one Leonard

South-of-the-River Country

Neal later dismantled and took to Cane Springs, some ten miles south in the Cerbat Range at the eastern base of the pinnacles.

In 1925, the Valley Ranch was used during the filming of a Buster Keaton movie called *Go West*.[22] For interested movie buffs, it's said copies of this movie are available from Grapevine Video in Phoenix, Arizona. Water for the Valley Ranch was, according to Neal, piped down from Granite Springs. Historically the name Granite Springs seems to have been used at different times for both the Valley Ranch Springs (on BLM maps) and for Willow Springs Ranch in the next valley over. Jimmie Ray said water was piped down to the Valley Ranch from the saddle just above, a small basin called Banana Valley, but he didn't know why the valley was called this. The only clue I found was that Banana Yucca thrive in this little valley and perhaps that was the name's source.

Garnet Mountain provides the backdrop for both these ranches. This mountain forms the entire southwest corner of Iron Basin, the very spot where the Grand Wash Cliffs turns southeasterly and then becomes known as the Music Mountain Range. Garnet Mountain was named for an old Garnet Mine that sits high on the edge of the mountain, a site possessing a fine view out over Hualapai Valley, Dry Red Lake, the White Hills, and the Cerbat Mountain Range. Garnet Mountains twin-sister peak, Iron Mountain, forms the northern boundary of Iron Basin. Iron Mountain, with numerous iron deposits, provides an impressive backdrop for Lake Mead City, ten miles south of Meadview on Grapevine Mesa.

Last, but surely not least, we will dwell upon Grapevine Springs, a very special and unique place in Lost Basin, both historically and today, and this is what we will cover in closing our Lost Basin chapter.

Grapevine Springs is a beautiful hidden oasis huddling deep within Grapevine Springs Canyon, a sheer-walled gash cutting through the eastern edge of Grapevine Mesa and reaching down into the large expansive drainage, Grapevine Wash, located on this south side of the river and along the base of Grand Wash Cliffs.

We already covered many of the interesting stories about early stop-overs at this ancient and crucially important water source and resting place, as humans negotiated around the western end of Grand Canyon; the Natives, the Spanish slave-traders, Mormons, frontiersmen, trappers, explorers, miners, ranchers. First historical notations and maps from the 1850's called this particular spring, Dinbah or Dinboah, a Native name whose meaning is apparently long lost, although it must have been either Hualapai or Paiute in derivation.

In BLM files the following water rights were recorded on Grapevine Springs:[23]

> December 1912: William Smith [Bill Smith, stepson of William Grigg from Grigg's Ferry]

> March 1933: William Smith and Irene Smith sold for $10 their Grapevine Springs water rights to Richard T. Robinson.

> 1937 and 1939: Lease to J. M. Ray and Claude Hall.

Lost Basin

July 1941: J. M. Ray. Grapevine Springs water rights.

1949: John Frederick McPherson requested hearing reference denial of grazing privileges in community with J. M. Ray and Ollie Duncan.

Leonard Neal said he had rounded up wild horses and cattle around Grapevine Springs in the 1930's, although, when references are made to wild horses or wild cattle, it should be kept in mind that ranchers had been operating in this area for some forty years prior, and as a result, many "wild" stock (although not all) were unbranded animals originating from previous ranch stock.

Located at Grapevine Springs there is a most interesting cliff face with old inscriptions. I called it the Signature Wall. When entering the side canyon of Grapevine Springs Canyon from the large drainage of Grapevine Wash below, and upon approaching the first narrowing cliffs, look across the stream to the rock face on the other side. Just below an overhang a black signature is visible, "J. Judd May 7, 1883." While climbing up along the ledge in an attempt to get a close-up photo of this historic signature (later to be tied in with historical occurrences at crossings, this in the Pearce Ferry chapter), I was delighted to find numerous other old signatures and dates not nearly so obvious. Although Judd's was the oldest, others ranged from 1901-1950. Names I recorded from the wall on April 22, 1986, starting from the east end, read as follows: (The notation, [?], designates letters or numbers I was unable to accurately decipher.)

Loren Rucker 1901

WAK [?]

J. Judd May 7, 1883

Roy Richter

Charles S. Holford CCC573, Boulder City Nev., Nov. 28, 1941 born in 1920

Wm L. Cook CCC 2536 [?], Boulder City, Nv.

Roy Richter, Reno, Nev.

W. Grounds

Lon Wells A D 1905

Deed 3H

B. T. Duncan July 13, 1911

S. F. Walters

J. Leonard Neal 1935

Linda [?]

Wm L. Cook, CCC Co. 2536, Boulder City, Nev. Feb. 2, 1941

Ralph Cameron DIUSBR 11-16-41

M. E. Butler [?] 11/16/41

Sam Devlin

Kevin 1944

Jimmie Ray 1950

[others unreadable]

R [or K?] Harding June 22, 1938

Charlie Hand of Hackberry, Ariz., Sept. 14, 19[?]1

Charlie Hand Hackberry, Ariz. Feb. 25, 1901

The Ruckers are an old family in the Kingman area but I do not know whether the Loren mentioned here was related. J. Judd was already discussed in the Pearce Ferry chapter; chances are good this was the brother of Judd from St. George who loaned Harrison Pearce money in the early 1880's to repair his ferry. Several names were obviously CCC crew members. W. Grounds, we'll meet again in the next section on Music Mountains. I came across Lon Wells name in an old Kingman paper while doing research: "Lon Wells and his wife coming down from the mine in Hualapai Mountains for supplies" around this same time period, but what he was doing over here, who knows. S. F. Walters was involved in mining adventures with Grounds and his signature has been found in far remote places. J. Leonard Neal, is, of course, Leonard Neal who was a pioneer rancher in the area and was interviewed. And Charlie Hand was the grandfather of Lillian Parsons (Lillian's other grandfather was William Ridenour, whom we'll get to know more about shortly, and was also one of the men in the photo standing by the old quartz mill at Grass Springs before it was destroyed by Indians). Charlie Hand, recall, lived at Burnt Mill in Gold Basin with his family and ran a freight and mail route to Hackberry and White Hills.

Signature Wall is a historical treasure at truly historic Grapevine Springs.
With that, we leave Lost Basin.

Lost Basin

Joshua Tree at historic overlook on west rim of Grapevine Mesa in Meadview looking westerly over Gregg Basin, 1988

View from west rim of Grapevine Mesa, looking into Greggs Basin and toward Sandy Point and Iceberg Canyon, 2010

South-of-the-River Country

My wolf-dog, Keewa, on west rim of Grapevine Mesa, Virgin Canyon in background, 1990

Dry Washing at Lost Basin, Courtesy Mohave Museum, no date

Lost Basin

Mining in Lost Basin, Richard Smith Collection, no date

Elephant Arch, with person inside circled, May 1989

Looking down on Elephant Arch from above, located just over rim from historic overlook on Grapevine Mesa, and a tad southerly, 1987. Ron Seeba named this formation.

Don in front of Empire Mine, April 1988

Bob and Beryl at Rock Cabin ruin below Empire Mine, July, 1989

Lost Basin

Troy Mine, April 1989

247

Clint Whitmore alongside 'Old Spanish Trail' near Empire Mine, Nov, 1988

Lost Basin

Main entrance to Golden Gate Mine, 1988

South-of-the-River Country

My brother, Ken, looking down from opening above, Golden Gate

Ron in main tunnel of Golden Gate

Arnella coming under rear chute of Golden Gate

My brother, Ed, beside some of the huge timber framing above the downward shaft in Golden Gate

Ladder going up alongside the shute in back of Golden Gate Mine

Lost Basin

Golden Mile Mine area, March, 1989

Small rock cabin on top Grapevine Mesa near Climax Mine, 1987

South-of-the-River Country

King Tut Mine area on top Grapevine Mesa

Foundations of old main building at King Tut Mine area

Bunkhouse at King Tut Mine area, no date

Arnella looking into Copper Glance shaft

Don McBee descending Humdinger dryfall just off South Cove Road, 1984

My daughter, Suzanne, and Larry ascending Marbled Falls, another beautiful dryfall area between Grapevine Mesa rim and Hualapai Wash, 1986

"Wellington Starkey Family... was born in San Luis Obispo, CA... came to AZ in 1875." Starkey is the man who first established "Grass Springs Ranch," this later to become the Diamond Bar Ranch (Tap Duncan), then the Smith Ranch, and now, Grand Canyon Ranch tourist resort.

Lost Basin

"Quartz mill at Grass Springs. Destroyed by Indians during Ghost Dance in 1887. Elev. 4220," Courtesy Mohave Museum in Kingman, AZ. This is the historic Grass Springs (Tahnakah Springs) located at the crest of Grapevine Wash that has long been sacred to Natives. The same photo is in John Grounds book and is identified as "Bill Ridenours Mill – Bud Grounds on left."

Tap Duncan, courtesy Mohave Museum in Kingman, AZ

Diamond Bar Ranch house, 1988. The old rock cabin on the left is reportedly where Starkey killed himself.

Lost Basin

Foundation walls of old barn at Diamond Bar, 1988

Lincoln Ranch House, April, 1987

South-of-the-River Country

Old Valley Ranch site in Hualapai Valley, July, 1986

Upper Pond and falls at Grapevine Springs, 1989, Cecilia Brand and Susan Pettijohn in photo

Lower Pond and falls at Grapevine Springs in the 1980's, photo by Dave Gensley

Dave Gensley and Don Simonis at 'Signature Wall' in Grapevine Springs Canyon, May 1986

Dave Gensley's son beside old diesel water pump that was at Grapevine Springs until it disappeared about 1982-83. Photo by Dave Gensley

"J. Judd, May 7, 1883," the oldest inscription at Signature Wall

Lost Basin

Thomas Judd at his store in St. George, May, 1986

'Frog' in Grapevine Wash, 1988

Greg Montgomery in side canyon of Grapevine Wash, November, 1989

Corral at Lucky Seven, looking north toward Pearce Ferry, Feb, 1987

Lost Basin

View down Grapevine Wash, north toward Pearce Ferry, 1989

Chapter Fifteen: Music Mountains

The Music Mountains are actually the southeastern extension of the Grand Wash Cliffs. This mountain range parallels Hualapai Valley and extends over thirty miles from old Highway 66 near Hackberry and northerly to Pearce Ferry Road.

There are different versions about the naming of this range. According to Barnes, the Musics were named by Lieutenant Joseph Ives when he first saw the mountains during an expedition in 1854 and thought the exposed strata on one peak looked like a musical staff. Barnes added that when Captain George Wheeler came along later, he mistook a peak ten miles to the west for Music Mountain and mismarked it as such on his map.[1] Ivo Lucchitta, geologist with the U. S. Geological Survey in Flagstaff, wrote that Cherokee Point, farther to the east and as seen from the Truxton Canyon area, was the original Music Mountain designated on the 1858 Ives survey maps.[2]

Another version of the naming is from Grounds who informed readers that the mountains were named after a mining engineer from San Francisco by the name of Jim Music.[3] Grounds stated that Music helped Bud Grounds search for ore during the 1870's, using the "Musics" to designate this range of mountains when filling out mining claims. Other sources say Jim Music was simply an old miner who dabbled around with claims in this mountain range.

A thirty-five mile long gravel road, Antares Point Road, also known as Hackberry Road, extends along the base of the Musics. Antares Point lies at the intersection of this road and old Highway 66. Granger gives the following information in *Arizona's Names*: "It is not known why this company railroad section house was named for the brightest star in the constellation, Scorpio. No town remains there." While the Grounds book states, "In a short time a carload of barbed wire was unloaded at Anterrez, a siding and section camp about eight miles west of Hackberry" (time period referenced around 1911).[4] In interviews, several pioneer families noted that homes had been set up every six miles along the railroad tracks, one for each section of land, that railroad section hands and their families had lived in those homes, and many section houses or camps were named after the families who lived there. The possibility exists that the family living at this place might have been named "Antares" or "Anterrez." Herb Voight of Kingman suggested Antarrez may have been named after Anterri's Tower, the name of a conical outcrop of rock not far from that location that Voight had seen referenced on several early maps.

The Music Mountain rim extends about thirty miles in length. Almost mid-center, Clay Springs Canyon cuts down from the rim, offering an interesting access route from the top to the valley below. Just to the southeast of this canyon, a sheer escarpment towers over the valley floor and on the northwest edge of that ridge are two distinct points that protrude upward. Ivo Lucchitta stated this landmark of limestone pillars was called "Two Tooth" by Native Americans who used it as a reference point to estimate distances and travel times for many miles around.[5] I have personally viewed Two Tooth from peaks in the Hualapai

South-of-the-River Country

Mountains, from high ridge roads in the Cerbats, and from the north while standing on the south rim of western Grand Canyon. It's not hard to believe this was widely used as a landmark reference.

Due north from Two Tooth lies Meriwhitica Canyon, the place long of great import to the Hualapai people. A deep gash into the earth, this canyon heads northerly toward Grand Canyon. About two miles into Meriwhitica is located Indian Gardens, an area of lush vegetation watered by a year-around fast-flowing spring. Above the spring and on a steep cliff wall nearby, is the location of the sacred cave mentioned previously. At the opening of the cave, ruins of old masonry walls still stand. There, Euro-Americans left their mark also, as I recorded the following names carved into the cave wall: John Tillman (Tillman was mentioned in the Fred Nobman story about the Lost Mine in Lost Basin), E. Farner, 2-7-79, Wm. Ridenour 79 (this would be 1879), and Mahoney.

In the late 1980's, I was one of several hikers given permission to go down through Meriwhitica Canyon with permits in hand. One of the other hikers, Craig Freisner, of the County Attorney's office in Kingman, discovered en route what appeared to be a decorative piece of an old Spanish horse bit, this half-protruding from the soil. Two others in our party, Don Simonis, BLM Archeologist, and Richard Leibold, a local sculptor who had worked with metals for many years, both thought the engraved plate on the bit was very intricate, that the metal itself seemed of high quality, and that the design could well have been Spanish. I took pictures of the bit, then Craig disappeared to return the bit to its original resting place. There are stories that the Spanish came to these canyons in search of gold. Perhaps someday we'll know if this bit really was Spanish. If so, here could be more possible evidence that the Spanish actually were in this exact area, probably several hundred years before the next wave of Euro-Americans arrived.

The Hualapai people carry by far the deepest and history of this Music Mountain area, however, since we previously covered the tribe's history in some depth in Chapter Three, I will only reference special aspects of their history in this chapter, mainly ones related to local settlers or other affairs.

In the 1860 census of Mohave County, not one settlement of Euro-Americans was noted, although the military post of Fort Mohave did exist along the Colorado River. Charley Spencer and Dan O'Leary were two army scouts serving in the area at this time, both to later become legends of sorts in their own right.[6,7]

Charley Spencer served as a guide for the Wheeler Expedition in 1870, and while on one trip in the Flagstaff area, some Natives brought him samples of fine silver ore. At first he could not convince them to tell the source of the ore, but at a later date was able to get a description of the location, this being on a south bluff of the Colorado River just below the junction with the Little Colorado River northeast of Flagstaff. Spencer and Dan O'Leary went to the location and brought out rich samples of silver ore that they took to Prescott where the ore samples assayed at over $3,300 to the ton. On another occasion, Spencer found silver in Havasu Canyon, also known as Havasupai Canyon (home of the present-day Supai people), northwest of Flagstaff.

South-of-the-River Country

For a time, Spencer was employed at Camp Willow Grove (a site just east of today's Interstate 40 and Highway 93 interchange east of Kingman) as a packer for $100 a month. O'Leary and Spencer had done a variety of jobs. In the army they had served as guides for mapping expeditions, were trackers, and also mail carriers. Between jobs, they did a great deal of prospecting and mining, and each also dabbled in some ranching.

Before many years passed and due mainly to his advantageous association with the Hualapai and his marriage to a Hualapai woman named Antelope, Charley Spencer had worked up quite a ranching empire. He ran cattle on Hualapai lands and eventually moved into their sacred Meriwhitica Canyon where he built several rock cabins. He had garden crops near the lush springs. Spencer Canyon, the larger canyon into which Meriwhitica drains, was named after Charley. After residing in Meriwhitica for some years, Spencer then moved his place of residence out on top the mesa to Milkweed Springs, allowing him easier access to the outside world.

Charley spurred on efforts to have lands set aside for the Hualapai, mainly, of course, so his own cattle empire would be protected. By 1883, the boundaries of the Hualapai Reservation were designated. However, not only Charley, but also a number of other settlers continued ranching and mining on those lands as well as run businesses in the Hualapai community center of the reservation, Peach Springs.

John Grounds, in *Trail Dust of the Southwest*, related a story about Charley Spencer and Charles Cohen, one we will summarize here.[8] In 1886, Spencer had met a Jewish man named Charles Cohen (variously spelled Cohan and Cohn), and asked Cohen to provide him with funds in return for half-shares of profit from stock that he sold off each fall. Cohen agreed, but it wasn't long before Spencer began finding ways to finagle Cohen out of his shares. Then one day Spencer wrote Cohen asking him to come via train and stop at Truxton Canyon where they could meet for a talk. Spencer and his small boy, Sammy, took a horse and wagon to Truxton and waited for the train to arrive. Spencer drank whiskey, whetted his knife, and seemed to those few persons present to be agitated.

When Cohen arrived, Spencer immediately took him aboard the wagon and headed off to Milkweed Ranch. En route, Spencer became increasingly irascible and began shoving and pushing Cohen until a full scale fight broke out. Both men fell from the wagon and the horse ran away with little Sammy aboard. Spencer lost his knife in the fracas and a long fist-to-fist battle ensued. In the end, Cohen delivered a fatal stab to Spencer's neck with his penknife. After Cohen recovered, he found Sammy and took him back to the Crozier Ranch at Truxton Canyon and sought medical help.

Folks found it difficult to believe that the little Jewish man had finished off cantankerous and aggressive Charley Spencer. In surveying evidence at the scene of the struggle, however, it was determined that Cohen had killed Spencer in self-defense so no charges were brought.

John Grounds, in his writings, went on to tie-in Mr. Kemp, a neighbor of Charley Spencer, to a proposed plot where Kemp was supposed to kill Cohen so

Spencer could then bring in Kemp as a partner. After hearing of this, Bud Grounds is said to have run Kemp out of the country. (The spring where Kemp lived is still called Kemp Water even though it was later leased by Billy Grounds Jr., then Ben Joy, and recently, Frank Hunt). Bud Grounds and Sam Crozier then bought Spencer's cattle and Grounds was able to obtain a lease in the western part of the newly-designated Hualapai Reservation lands.

West of Spencer Canyon, also running north into the Grand Canyon, lays Quartermaster Canyon, with Quartermaster Viewpoint perched high on top, a gorgeous overlook on the south rim of western Grand Canyon. According to Barnes, a Hualapai known as Quartermaster and his family used to live near the springs in this canyon.[9] In Casebiers work, *Camp Beale's Springs and the Hualapai Indians*, quartermasters were said to be army personnel who submitted monthly reports on the status of persons and articles. The Hualapai known as Quartermaster had served with the army for a time although it was thought he served as a scout, not a quartermaster. Several recent stories also told by locals in our area rumored that Quartermaster Canyon received its name because soldiers stood on the rim and sent mirror signals to far distant points. I found no evidence to support this last assertion. A heliograph system (mirror signals) was used by the Army for a time in Arizona, but much farther south, not on the south rim of Grand Canyon.[10]

Regardless, signs of long-term Native occupation are still in evidence near the springs in Quartermaster Canyon. An old miner's camp near the springs also validates that Euro-Americans were present for a time. Mention of the Hualapai man named Quartermaster was made in a story told by John Riggs and quoted by Malach.[11] Riggs told how an old "Wallapai called Quartermaster" had brought to Mineral Park some quality pieces of turquoise and showed them to a man named Sherman. Quartermaster took the man to the source of this turquoise deposit on Ithaca Peak (in the Cerbat Range), where Sherman then staked claims on that turquoise mine.

William F. (Bud) Grounds Sr., Sam Crozier, the Cureton brothers, and William (Bill) Ridenour were prominent among cattlemen and miners who arrived in this area of Mohave County in the 1870's. Ridenour and Crozier had located and started the big Hackberry Silver Mine near present-day Hackberry. They had also prospected on the south rim of the Grand Canyon and located another find they called the Ridenour Mine, down in a beautiful red rock area on a lower bench north of Prospect Valley (later within the Hualapai Reservation). Crozier, Ridenour, and Grounds all became active in various businesses and county politics through the years, thereby having direct influence with early directions of this young county.[12][13]

The Grounds family originally located one of their ranches in Clay Springs Canyon in the Music Mountains, on the southeastern edge of our focus area in this chapter. John Cureton Grounds book, *Trail Dust of the Southwest*, gives an extensive overview of the Grounds family history. This work is very interesting and certainly of important historical merit. I did, however, question two things mentioned in this work. One story appears to have been mistakenly placed at

South-of-the-River Country

Gregg's Ferry when, from all appearances (to myself, as well as Grigg descendants), it should have been at Bonelli's Ferry, and also, the authors story of incidents surrounding the murder of the Hualapai Chief, Wauba Yuma, contradict several historical documentations from other sources.

I will summarize some of the information from Grounds work here:

In 1873, William F. (Bud) Grounds and the Cureton brothers came to Mohave County bringing a herd of cattle from Texas. They located first in the Truxton Canyon area (named earlier by Lieutenant Beale, whose wife's maiden name was Truxton) and ran cattle there. In 1880, they sold the Truxton Springs Ranch to Sam Crozier. Crozier built up the ranch considerably over following years and this historic ranch is still a beautiful place to this day. A son, Ila Grounds, was born in 1878 to Bud Grounds and his wife, Mellisa (sister of the Cureton brothers) at the Truxton Springs Ranch and this was reported to be the first Euro-American male child birth recorded in Mohave County. In 1879 they had a daughter, Julia, and she was the first Euro-American female whose birth was recorded in the county. In 1880, while the family lived in Mineral Park in the Cerbats, a second son, William F. Grounds Jr. (later to be known as Bill or Billy) was born.

Bud Grounds both ranched and mined. He built a small house and corral in Claysprings Canyon (just under Two Tooth on the Music Mountain ridge) and ran cattle. By 1880, several men had started developing the Music Mountain Mining District several miles below the ranch and Grounds joined them. Joe Prisk, Dave Southwick, and Bill Hatch were working with arrastras and shipping ore to mills since no water was available at the location. The Ellen Jane was the most productive mine and Malach stated in *Mohave County,* that in the year 1892, it produced 165 tons of ore averaging from $32-$42 per ton.[14] However, in another book of Malach's, *Cerbat Mountain Country,* he states that Ellen Jane ore ran $10-$12 in gold per ton. Grounds bought into the mines and then ran a water line from Clay Springs down to the mine camp. A mill was built, the remnants of which can be seen today right alongside Hackberry road, close to one of the cattle guards. Later, Grounds sold his shares to the Gold Mining Company of Washington D. C. and this company installed another larger mill closer to the base of the hill. The Ellen Jane had a main shaft 200 feet deep, 1500 feet of underground workings, and hit some 20 feet of water. Other mines in the district included the Lucky Cuss, the Southwick, and the Rosebud.

Mining has continued in this district by various owners up to the present day. Contemporaries involved in recent development of mining there include Leonard Neal (rancher from Kingman who leased grazing rights close by) and Mohave County Supervisor, Bill Roper.[15] There are presently many old tunnels in this area, almost all of which are now unstable and unsafe to enter.

A reference is made to Bud Grounds and the mining district, this from the October 20, 1895, *Mohave Miner* (recall that Charlie Hand, mentioned in this excerpt, previously appeared in the Gold Basin chapter and also that his and W. F. Grounds signatures are written at the Signature Wall down by Grapevine Springs in Lost Basin):

W. F. Grounds started up his 4 stamp mill at Music Mountain for a trial run yesterday, and expects to make regular shipments of bullion shortly. Chs. Hand had the contract to haul 200 tons of ore from the mines to Clay Springs, and sufficient ore is now being taken out to keep the mill constantly employed.

Grounds described another unusual event. He told that during the fall of 1887, Bud and his family were moving into the newly built home at Clay Springs when they felt deep rumblings from the valley below. They saw the canyon fill with dust, and boulders began rolling down the steep canyon walls. After things quieted down, Bud went out into the valley to get several horses and saw a deep fissure that had split the ground. The fissure ran length-ways down the valley for nearly fifteen miles and at places was very deep. I wonder if this was the most recent quake of noticeable intensity in that valley or whether there have been more since, but it is common knowledge that fissures do exist along the floor of Dry Red Lake. This should be given important consideration for present or future underground development of wells and storage areas in the Dry Red Lake area.

Another very interesting story was recounted by Grounds, here paraphrased:

In the spring of 1888, Bud's partner, Jack Cole, was helping at Clay Springs Ranch. He and Bud went into Meriwhitica Canyon (the Hualapai's sacred canyon) and planted a garden at the springs there. They threw piles of ocotillo around the garden to keep out horses belonging to visiting bands of Indians. They were confident, however, that the Indians would not disturb the garden since "Spencer had taught them about leaving the garden alone." Every two weeks Cole would go back into the canyon to pick ripe produce and bring it back out to the ranch. Come fall, Bud and Cole and two young boys went into the canyon, along with a pack string of animals, in order to bring out remaining produce for drying and pickling. At the garden they picked the ripe produce and threw anything that was overripe into a pile over beyond the ocotillo fence. After several days a long caravan of Indians came down into the canyon and two approached the men to ask if they could have the produce that had been thrown away, to which the men readily agreed.

That night wailing and loud chants were heard from the Indian camp nearby and a bright fire burned the entire night. In the morning, two horses were led away with what appeared to be bodies wrapped in blankets. Women led the horses up a steep incline along the canyon wall to ledges and shortly thereafter, smoke could be seen curling from there and up into the sky. Then other horses with blanketed bundles were taken up to the ledges and more fires burned. The next night even more mourning was heard and the following day more trips were made to the high ledges. Finally, over twenty smokes were counted, rising dizzily from the high canyon walls. Cole, Grounds, and the boys were not sure what happened but began to worry that the Indians were stricken by smallpox, so they packed up and left. It wasn't until later they discovered the real reason: the Indians who had eaten the discarded produce had sickened and died.

South-of-the-River Country

The Indians, suspecting someone had put coyote medicine (poisons ranchers commonly place on dead carcasses or bait in order to kill many species of predators) in the vegetables, sent a runner to Peach Springs to have samples of the food examined. Weeks later, when an analysis was returned, it was found the Indians died from eating wilted ripe cucumbers. They were told that when the ripe fruit became wilted, it contained prussic acid, a poison far more deadly than strychnine, and that was what caused the deaths.

In 1904, Bud Grounds received some $3000 from the government for cattle he had reported as being destroyed by the Indians thirty years prior, and for which he'd been trying to collect compensation ever since. In 1906, he found buyers for his group of mines in the Music Mountain mine district.

By then, son, Billy, had grown up and married Vernie Crozier, youngest daughter of Sam Crozier. For a time they lived at the Milkweed Ranch on the ridge up in the Musics (Charley Spencer's old place). From Malach's *Early Ranching in Mohave County*, a short story written by Vernie is quoted:[16]

> Having your first baby alone, fifty miles from a doctor, is a frightening experience, but a memorable one. It was on the afternoon of March 5, 1908, that we realized our first baby was about to be born, a month ahead of schedule. Here we were at Milkweed Ranch, fifty miles from Kingman, with about six inches of snow on the ground. It was real cold and there was no way of getting out except by horseback.
>
> Naturally we were panic stricken, two young people, with their first to be born child, and no one to turn to for help. After calming ourselves down, we realized that the only thing to be done was for Will [Billy, her husband] to go for help. So about 9 p.m., he saddled his colt which had been ridden only a few times, and started out for the Crozier ranch, where we knew my sister was. It was truly a black night. I can't imagine what Will's feelings were, leaving me so sick, with no one near. He started to ride, but turned around and came back after thinking of the big fire he had built in the fireplace to keep me warm, for he thought of sparks flying out and setting the house on fire. He stayed for a while, then realized we had to have help, so he went on his way again.
>
> It was a fearful night for me. However, at 2 A.M., my little son made his appearance. It was a fortunate thing for me that I had been with my sister when her baby was born, so I knew a little about what to do. After I had done all I could, I went to sleep, waking up only when Will came into the house around 5 A. M. He was rather surprised, but delighted, and the next thing I knew he was walking the floor with the child, although I think the baby was sound asleep. About 9 A. M., Dr. Tilton arrived with my sister and her husband, and everything was fine.

By 1909, Billy decided to build a new two-story home down in Clay Springs Canyon (this canyon named for the pale blue clay carrying water through the soil) below the Milkweed Ranch. Years before, his father had built a small house and stone corral there, and Billy chose a spot a half-mile above the old house. In 1911, another son was born to Billie and Vernie Grounds, this boy named Howard. In that same year, Billy incorporated the Clay Springs Cattle Company and the ranch was branding several thousand calves each year.

However, the family only stayed at the Clay Springs Ranch for five more years. Their fifteen-year grazing lease on the Hualapai lands expired and more and more pressure was being applied to the Interior Department to cease issuing grazing leases to Euro-Americans on Native lands. Eventually, it's said the Interior Department bought out those who lived on or grazed their livestock within reservation boundaries.

Billy sold his ranch and used the profits to purchase a ranch allotment in northwest Colorado. He moved his family there, where they ranched for nearly twenty more years, but when hard times hit during the depression they, like so many, lost nearly everything and returned to Arizona once more. Billy went to work for the State as a cattle inspector, while his son, Howard, worked as a bronc buster for Preston Nutter up in the Arizona Strip. Nutter was highly respected in this South-of-the-River Country and was perceived as being a big successful cattleman farther north. However, as Nutter had expanded up in the Strip Country and taken over many water sources, he had inevitably made many lifelong enemies amongst former Euro-American settlers (mostly Mormons) up in the Strip area in the process.

Eventually the Grounds saved enough money to start buying more ranch land and grazing rights in this area once again and the family purchased the Peacock Mountain Ranch just east of Kingman. They again obtained the Truxton Springs Ranch, keeping that until the 1950's when Billy sold that ranch for the last time. Billy went into real estate in Kingman, while Howard and his wife, Betty (formerly of the Clack family) ran the Peacock Mountain Ranch. Years later, Howard and Betty moved to Kingman after retiring, and their son, Hubby, took over the ranch where he and his family live today.

During modern times, some descendants of these various pioneer ranch families, especially the Grounds and Neals, profited from growing economic trends by capitalizing on demand for land from the newer immigrants flowing into the area, doing sales and subdividing of their various properties and also making profitable land trades with public land agencies.

To regress into the earlier history once again, in 1884 the railroad had reached Peach Springs and a small town had developed there around the railroad station. Jacob Cohenour, from Illinois, was a bridge carpenter for the railroad and after completion of the track on down to Needles, California, he returned to settle at Peach Springs. He and his family had a store there and also ranched near Pine Springs in the Music Mountains, thus the source of the names for Cohenour spring and Cohenour Canyon. Many suspect that another spring and mine designated "Kohinoor" on present-day maps was simply a variation of his names spelling.

Just west of the town of Peach Springs, a turn-off designates entrance to the Buck and Doe road. This road was built by the Civilian Conservation Corps (CCC's) during the late 1930's, providing better access up to and along the top of

South-of-the-River Country

the Music Mountains and over to the west end of the Hualapai Reservation lands. It reached the south rim of western Grand Canyon at Quartermaster Viewpoint and joined the road coming up through the Grand Wash Cliffs from the west.

The CCC was created during the Great Depression in the 1930's in order to assist with providing food, shelter, and clothing to unemployed workers and their families. Its main purpose was to teach unskilled and unemployed people a trade, provide paid employment while they learned, and also to assist in conserving our nations natural resources. Most of the beautiful old rock cabins and shelters in Hualapai Mountain Park, the county park in the Hualapai Mountains east of Kingman, were built by the CCC's, as well as numerous other constructive projects throughout the area.

It's surprising to learn that as far back as 1884, the Farlee Hotel, also known as the Diamond Creek Hotel, had already begun catering to Grand Canyon visitors. At that time there was not yet an access route for travelers to viewpoints on the south rim of Grand Canyon, and since the railroad stopped at Peach Springs, J. H. Farlee, being an enterprising sort, started taking tourists down Peach Springs Canyon on a 23-mile winding, narrow, path to Diamond Creek, and then ¼ mile farther to where the canyon emptied into the Grand Canyon, to the banks of the Colorado River.[17]

In 1886, Mohave County tax records showed J. H. Farlee of Peach Springs listed with the following assets: a lot on Main Street with improvements consisting of a building, lodging house, blacksmith shop, house at Grand Canyon known as Farlee Hotel, furniture, 5 horses, 2 mules, 5 wagons. 4 sets of harnesses, 2 saddles and blacksmith tools, all valued at $1,155.[18]

Malach uncovered an interesting story written by Mary Wager Fisher, published in the July, 1893, issue of *Outing* magazine, telling of her memorable trip down to the Farlee Hotel.[19] She and two other family members had disembarked from the train at Peach Springs and inquired about Farlee's tour into the canyon. They then found Farlee, who agreed to take them on the trip for ten dollars each. He told them it was twenty-three miles down and they could stay as long as they liked, during which time he would serve as guide and host. He said he had a small but comfortable house in the canyon where they could have meals at seventy-five cents each. The partial story as told by Mary Fisher:

> … As we walked back toward the station we passed an enclosed lot which had sufficient wire stretched about it to keep two small horses from wandering away. This went by the name of 'corral' and Farlee was just entering it, as he had to catch 'Pop and Rowdy' and hitch up. When asked about the vehicle advertised, Farlee answered that the coach had not yet arrived, but he hoped some day to have it draw up at the station just as pictured in the railway folder. In the meantime, the actual vehicle was a rickety-looking buckboard, which was not inviting for a trip to the canyon. Farlee reassured us and inspired confidence in his ability to extricate the team from any difficulty into which they might fall by the way.

Farlee proved to be an ideal companion for such a trip, chatty, social, and direct. He talked to Pop and Rowdy as if they were intellectual beings; but if they misbehaved and failed to make the right wriggles when worming themselves among the rocks and boulders, he would screech at them equal to the scream of an engine whistle. The buckboard was without cover, the sky was cloudless, the sun blazed down in full splendor, and, after the first few miles of comparatively level, dusty road, it was impossible to hold a sunshade, as both hands were required to keep one's body from being bounced off the buckboard. "Oh, this air, Madam!" chimed in Farlee. "I should have been a dead man if it hadn't been for this Arizona air. I came here now three years gone, given up as good as dead … lungs bleeding and generally banged up anyway. You see I have been in the war, in Libby Prison … a hell, you know. I've a rifle bullet now in one leg, the lightning struck my gun once when I was on picket and cut the muscles of them two fingers so I can't lift them, but you can see how that I am well and hearty a feller." Then followed his experiences in the canyon. He had climbed the highest peaks. He told us the names of flowers, the trees, and the stones.

Peach Springs Station itself was 3,960 feet above the sea-level and the ridge we were on when a mile from the station, was still two hundred feet higher. From that point to the Colorado River the descent was 3,960 feet. After crossing the ridge the road lay through Peach Springs Canyon, and, when four miles from the station, we came to Peach Springs, about which were wonderful to see, a few peach trees in full bloom, kept alive by the moisture from the spring … an oasis in this almost rainless region. Some good soul had planted the trees there and they gave the name to the spring.

As we proceeded down the canyon, the way increased in roughness. Gradually, the way became hedged in on both sides by gigantic walls of rock. Still nothing so grand and wonderful as we expected; and we arrive at noon, after a jolting of three and a half hours, at the 'Grand Canyon Hotel', a crude little house, roughly boarded, but clean and comfortable, with a 'lounge' and rocking chairs, as Farlee had said. Where the 'hotel' stood seemed to be the only building spot in the canyon, which here formed a junction with the Diamond Creek and Colorado River Canyons. It is unquestionably the most unique hotel in the country. But we were too tired and too hungry to more than glance at the sights about us.

Fisher continued the story telling about going on down to the Colorado River, and also of Farlee leading them up through Diamond Creek Canyon until they were closed in by perpendicular cliffs from 2,500 to 3,000 feet high, a place with plants and vines growing from every crevice. He told them Diamond Creek was named for the prominent landmark, Diamond Peak, that towered high above and looked very much like a diamond gem rising up to reach the sky. She continued:

…When we returned to the open space whence we started, the sun was low and we sat down on a boulder to review the mighty scene at sunset. The

South-of-the-River Country

> longer we looked at the cliffs, the walls, the vast rock exposure, the more they grew in magnitude. But the whole scene was one of appalling desolation.
>
> Six hours it took Pop and Rowdy to pull us up out of the canyon ... for ten miles out, the walls on either side ranged in height from 2,200 feet to 4,280 feet. When about four miles from the hotel, we were opposite the Sphinx, outlining the top of the wall on the left, at a height of 6,000 feet.
>
> Young Fisher noticed a hole near the top of the right wall. Farlee explained that at one time, with an exploring party, he had been let down from the cliff above by means of a rope tied about his body, to investigate the hole. A Fisher guest asked how far it was from the top, and how large was the entrance. Farlee answered that they dropped him 320 feet and the hole entrance was approximately 60 feet high. The cliff projected so far in front of the cave that Farlee was unable to swing himself into it, and the cave remained unexplored.
>
> After nine o'clock we were sensitive to a considerable degree of cold, but not a particle of dew fell, and there was no dampness in the air. Pop and Rowdy pulled steadily on, with occasional halts, until the long and wonderful ride came to an end.

So ends a descriptive and entertaining old story by Mary Wager Fisher. Those tours operated into the canyon from 1884 until 1889. Soon however, a more popular access route to the south rim overlook into the canyon was developed, after which commercial trips into Peach Springs Canyon never operated again.

During 1985, I corresponded with famed western author, Louis L'Amour, and in one letter he wrote:

> I used to get off the train at Peach Springs and catch a ride with some Indian friend and hike the canyons opening into the Grand Canyon from that area. I spent some time in the Strip, too, rounding up wild horses. We had an idea of rough breaking them and selling to rodeos. We did, but barely made our expenses. We also had fun. I was less than twenty years old then, and a lot of rough stuff was fun.

This was the first time I had heard any mention that L'Amour might also have been involved in rounding up wild horses in the Strip country years before. I wondered if he may have already begun building upon stories he'd heard once from Tap Duncan.

Today, the road down Peach Springs Canyon is remarkably unique and usually accessible, although four-wheel drive is often needed for the last several miles nearing the river. During rainy seasons, however, the road does occasionally wash out at the lower end. A permit must be purchased at the tribal office in Peach Springs in order to enter and travel upon Hualapai Reservation lands, and inquiries can be made there as to current conditions of this scenic roadway. It is the only access route in the entire length of the Grand Canyon where one can drive a vehicle completely down to the shore of the Colorado River.

Music Mountains

B.W. Brown at mill in Music Mountains, Grounds Collection, Mohave Museum, no date

South-of-the-River Country

Farlee Hotel at Diamond Creek in Peach Springs Canyon, built in 1884, probably destroyed in 1914 to use in study on dam site camp. Householder collection at Mohave Museum

Diamond Creek where it enters the Colorado River in Grand Canyon (via Peach Springs Canyon), 1991

Charley Spencer, courtesy Mohave Museum, Kingman, AZ

South-of-the-River Country

Old Spanish bit found by Craig Friesner in Meriwhitica Canyon, April, 1987

Dave Gensley resting beside remnants of old rock cabin at Indian Gardens in Meriwhitica Canyon, 1987

Music Mountains

"Road" leading off canyon edge in Hualapai lands, to second plateau where old Ridenour Mine is located, 1989

South-of-the-River Country

Intriguing ancient old wall sketch at area of Ridenour Mine

Music Mountains

Bob Arnold views another of the puzzling sketches at area of Ridenour Mine, 1989

South-of-the-River Country

Road going "up" from Ridenour mine

Bob and Beryl Arnold and Cecilia Brand enjoy lunch by the hearthside fire at ruins near old Ridenour mine, 1989

Author's small tent on the south rim. Vulcans Throne, the large volcanic mountain in the background, is across on the north rim of Grand Canyon

View westerly into Grand Canyon from the old Quartermaster Viewpoint, 1987

Lake Mead, showing approximate lake levels during the 1980's. Map by D. Suzanne Wanatee-Buffalo

Part V: The Leviathan

Chapter Sixteen: Lake Mead

Historically, the 1400 mile-long Colorado River extended from the Rocky Mountains in Colorado and emptied south into the ocean in Mexico. Today, it still drains over ten percent of the total land mass of the lower forty-eight states. Major flooding along the lower portion of the river has always occurred as a result of spring run-off from higher elevations. Native Americans simply lived with such seasonal fluctuations, pulling back from flood plains when high water occurred, then returning to plant crops in the damp soils as the river receded. Euro-American settlers were not so accepting. We've long had pride in our ingenuity and inventiveness, our ability to control and manipulate nature ... advantageous at times, but now we are finding, not so great in the long view.

By 1901, Euro-Americans had constructed major canals extending from the Colorado River and stretching into expansive Imperial Valley in California – a valley actually lower in elevation than the Colorado River. With constant irrigation, Imperial Valley flourished with produce. Then, in 1905, the unruly Colorado again flexed its mighty muscles, poured violently over canal banks, destroyed homes, towns, fields and gardens, and flooded the entire valley for nearly two years. After the Colorado returned to its main channel once again, the land-trapped 300 square-mile body of water named the Salton Sea remained in the valley, a potent reminder of the power of this mighty river.

Congress had decided something must be done to harness the Colorado, that a dam beyond all dams must be built. The Bureau of Reclamation was established in 1902, along with the Boulder Canyon Act. Some seventy possible dam sites were studied (several studies detailed in preceding Chapters 5-8) and the locations decided upon in our immediate area were eventually narrowed down to two within close range of each other; Black Canyon and Boulder Canyon. By 1924, it was concluded that Black Canyon was the best site.

Herbert Hoover was Secretary of Commerce during the early planning stages for this immense dam project. He had helped create the Colorado River Compact in 1922, one that tried to work out near-equitable water allotments amongst the six states directly affected by use of Colorado River waters, and then obtained signatory approval from those, as well as one pressured from Mexico.

The Boulder Canyon Project Act was passed in 1928 (oddly named such, even though the dam was actually going to be built in Black Canyon, not Boulder Canyon) while Coolidge was President, providing $175 million dollars to cover the complete cost, all of which was to be paid back with three percent interest over the next fifty years. Two years later, after Herbert Hoover became president, Congress voted to officially call the giant structure Hoover Dam, this to

The Leviathan

acknowledge all of Hoover's earlier efforts in pulling together this project so it could finally materialize.

Contracts were let on the dam project in 1931 and actual work began that same year, although the first concrete was not poured until June of 1933. By February of 1935, after some ninety-six lives had been lost during this immense project, tunnels temporarily diverting water around the dam were closed and water began backing up into the canyons and valleys above.

By that time, the unique year-round recreational opportunities that would also become available by the transformation of this area of desert and canyons into a huge desert lake, had become quite apparent. The Bureau of Reclamation asked assistance from the Department of Interior, and in October of 1936, the National Park Service and Bureau of Reclamation joined in a partnership to administer the expansive area, this resulting in the proclamation of Boulder Dam Recreation Area. Over thirty years later, President Lyndon Johnson established the Lake Mead National Recreation Area which would additionally incorporate then yet-to-fill Lake Mohave below the dam, upon completion of still another structure, Davis Dam, farther downstream.

Lake Mead was named after Elwood Mead who served as commissioner for the Bureau of Reclamation during most of the dam construction during years previous. Although initial boundaries had been laid out earlier, in 1974, the perimeters of Lake Mead Recreation Area were again modified by National Park Service when the boundaries of Grand Canyon National Park, just to the east, were extended and moved down to include the western entrance of Grand Canyon. This then took the entire Lower Granite Gorge of Grand Canyon away from previous Lake Mead NRA jurisdiction. In addition, part of the Shivwits Plateau, which at one time had been Grand Canyon National Monument, also became part of Grand Canyon National Park.

It's very interesting to look closely at a number of events that occurred as Lake Mead was filling and to see how this effected change locally.

Charles Cannon of Kingman, stated that in 1929, at five years of age, he had stayed with his father who was then operating the ferry at Pearce Ferry. His father's family were the Alzers, and he said one of his uncles beached the ferry while there. During this time there were only a few ranchers wanting to cross the river and those crossings were rare.[1]

The first route of extensive use through the Grapevine Mesa area, was, as covered previously, the well-known prehistoric/historic Old Ute Trail coming south up Grapevine Wash, parallel to our mesa. This route had been used widely by Native Americans, then the Spanish, then in the late 1800's by more explorers , again by the Mormons for their wagon route around the western end of Grand Canyon, then by ranchers, surveying parties, and fisherman and miners.

The "Old Grigg's Road" still visible that came up from Grigg's Ranch and Ferry on the western edge of Grapevine Mesa, the one topping out right near the mesa rim overlook at Meadview, was first built around 1905 by William Grigg and later improved by his two stepsons, Tom and Bill Smith. Michael Scanlon was never involved in the building of this road; his road work was done over on the Nevada side, on what is now called Scanlon Dugway.

The exact date of the "original Pearce Ferry Road" that was graded from the north part of our mesa and down to Pearce Ferry landing on the lake is uncertain. A section of this old road section is still visible as one drives the "new paved road" from the mesa and toward the lake. About four miles north of Meadview and just past the turn-off to the airport strip, as one begins the descent down through the cut, look down and to the west, and the old "original road" is still plainly visible. This was neither the "Old Mormon Trail" nor was it a "section of the Old Honeymoon Trail that Mormons once used to travel to St. George in order to marry at the Temple" as some realtors have promoted (I did, however, find numerous historical references to the Old Mormon Honeymoon Trail that crossed the river at Lee's Ferry, around the far eastern end of Grand Canyon, but not here). This old gravel road is reported to have actually been put in by the Mohave Country Board of Supervisors when Lake Mead was filling in order to serve as an access road so fisherman and boaters could more easily reach Pearce Ferry landing. Original Meadview residents, Elmer Duffield and Jess Ladd, both said that this gravel road was there in the early 1930's when they began coming out here to fish.[2,3] While some of the presently existing paved section of "New" Pearce Ferry Road on top the mesa uses a similar route as the original graveled part, it does not when going through that cut. Some eight miles south of the town of Meadview and on Grapevine Mesa, another section of the old original graveled portion of Pearce Ferry Road runs right close to the old King Tut mine. A colored photograph taken from this portion of the old road graces the May, 1962, cover of *Arizona Highways* magazine.

New sections and improvements were made on Pearce Ferry Road while the CCC camps were present in the early 1940's. Then later, in 1965 and 1966, more improvements were made when road crews built the new hard-surfaced road to provide yet another lake access at this northeast end of Lake Mead, this being the present-day route down to South Cove boat landing.

In 1936, when the National Park Service became involved with administration of the Recreation Area, the lake was already well on its way and filling. Sadly, no funds were available for hiring professionals to investigate many prehistoric sites present along the shorelines, most of which were quickly being lost under the rising waters, so interested parties did their best to check out what they could.

CCC crews were already at work in the Pearce Ferry area, removing and burning mile after mile of driftwood that rising waters had lifted afloat and now were clogging the waterways. These crews were also called on to assist with work at archeological sites, even though few of the men had any training. As mentioned earlier, Willis Evans, the crew foreman of the group working out of Pearce Ferry, had previously been involved with an archeological dig in Gypsum Cave near Las Vegas, Nevada, so he was at least familiar with fundamental techniques.

Park Service files in Boulder City contained a report written by Evans in 1936 as he and his crew worked on a cave in the western end of the canyon while water was fast approaching. The report reveals vividly how little time the crews had, and

The Leviathan

sadly, what an immense amount of valuable archeological information was lost beneath the rising waters. One section written about the Helldiver Cave, located about ten miles east of Pearce Ferry, reads:[4]

> June 8, Monday. Started work in Helldiver Cave which is located about one mile east of the Helldiver Rapids and about 15 feet above the present river level. This cave was probably formed from an undercut made by the river which was later covered over by a deposit of travertine. The cave is approximately 25 feet long, 15 feet deep, and about 12 feet high. Evidence of only one entrance was found. The material collected from the ash dump beyond the entrance of the cave is as follows:
>
> 1. Broken pottery some of which is painted red, red and black, and black and grey.
>
> 2. Broken spear points, darts, knives, and scrapers.
>
> 3. Beads made of olivella shells. It is of interest to point out that the genus olivella is a marine gastropod limited on the Pacific Coast to waters south of San Francisco and that trading must have been carried on extensively in order to bring these shells into this area.
>
> 4. Fragments of animal bones.
>
> June 9, Tuesday. Continued work in Helldiver Cave. Discovered the following materials in the ash dump. This ash dump is approximately 10 feet in diameter and from 1 to 2 feet deep.
>
> 1. Broken dart points and scrapers.
>
> 2. Broken pottery
>
> 3. Fragments of animal bones.
>
> Party ... 16 men.
>
> June 10, Wednesday. Continued work in Helldiver Cave and started excavating the interior of the cave. The material found is as follows:
>
> 1. Scrapers and dart points
>
> 2. Broken sherds some of which are corrugated
>
> 3. Work sticks and broken gourds.
>
> 4. Several pieces of hemp rope.
>
> 5. Evidence of a rock wall which divided the cave into two rooms. The roof of this cave is covered with a thick layer of soot signifying that many fires had been built within the cave.

Party ... 12 men.

June 11, Thursday. Continued work in Helldiver Cave and discovered the following objects which were new in the collection obtained from this cave.

1. Drill Points

2. Large rope made of Yucca fiber

3. One foreshaft

Party ... 17 men

June 12, Friday. Continued the work on Helldiver Cave and discovered the following objects which were new in the collection obtained from this cave.

1. Corn cobs

2. Hand Hammers

3. Small cooking rocks

4. Yucca chews

5. Pigment for yellow paint

Party ... 18 men

June 13, Saturday. Stayed in camp and conducted regular Saturday camp routine.

June 14, Sunday. Stayed in camp and reviewed notes and sorted material.

June 15, Monday. Continued the work in Helldiver Cave and found only one object which was new to the collection. This object was a dice about three inches long and contained three stripes on one side.

Party ... 17 men.

June 16, Tuesday. Continued work in Helldiver Cave. As the river is rising rapidly and is at present only a few inches below the floor of the cave further work will not be possible. For that reason a brief resume will be presented. As new evidence has been accumulating this resume may not exactly conform with the notes previously presented.

Helldiver Cave is located ten miles east of Pierces Ferry in the wall of the river canyon at an elevation of approximately 1000 feet [placing the location much lower than present water levels now in 1990]. Its origin is due to an overhanging wall of travertine at a place where the river had made an undercut. Evidence was present indicating that Pueblo Culture 2 was the last to inhabit the cave. Below the two foot level of the floor, Basket Maker,

The Leviathan

perhaps Culture 2 or 3, was found. In the first level of the cave, broken pottery, black and grey, red and black, corrugated and plain was quite abundant. In addition, sandals made of mescal fiber, mescal chews, Pueblo arrow points, scrapers, string, metates and manos, work sticks, arrow cane, corn cobs, olivella shells, and limonite and hematite used for paint were found. Below the two foot level, crude scrapers, crude spear points, bone awls, Indian hemp strings, arrow cane, Indian dice, buckskin thongs were present indicating Basket Maker Culture. Unfortunately the rising of the river prevented further work. A map has been made of the cave and all the material found allocated. In addition, the items discovered have been carefully labeled and will be stored in a systematic manner for future use.

Party ... 12 men.

Other excavations were done on sites closer to the mouth of the Canyon until these, too, went under water. The Muav Caves on the south side of the river were excavated even though these were above high water level. Various items were found, including two ancient human skeletons, an adult and child, under the main fire pit. It was presumed they had either fallen into the fire, or were cremated and buried there, and perhaps later fire pits were built over the same spot. At deeper levels, scattered signs of giant sloth (bones and dung) were also found, although nothing compared to the treasure of quantities in nearby Rampart Cave located higher up on a nearby canyon wall (delved into previously in Chapter One), nor were these sloth remnants in association with the signs of human occupation.

Evans referred several times to the "spike" camp at Pearce's Ferry and also to the "stub" camp, both of which were CCC camps, although distinctions between the two were not made. He and Edward Schenk occasionally went off scouting for other ancient Native American sites. Schenk, a geologist, was also interested in archeological sites and was in charge of other CCC groups. Evans and several men took time to work on Iron Springs not far from the camp, at times cleaning it out, since this was the main source of their drinking water. This spring must have also gone under water, as I've seen no references to an Iron Springs at Pearce Ferry since that time. The CCC camp loaded up and moved out in September of 1936.

During the spring months from 1935 through 1938, the huge man-made lake continually rose due to maximum run-off from the mountains, at times coming up nearly an inch every hour. In 1938, Russell Grater had become Junior Naturalist for Lake Mead NRA. Grater's primary responsibility was to study wildlife at LMNRA, and with the backfilling of this large lake area, he had a unique opportunity to observe various species and the effects upon them.[5] By this time, what had previously been hills near the river were now little islands surrounded by water and blocked off from the mainland. Trapped on these islands was a good cross-section of the wildlife from nearly every native species in the area. Grater said it was strange to see rattlesnakes, wood rats, ground squirrels, mice, lizards, rabbits, tortoise and coyotes, all sitting together on one island. During that time he obtained collections of many small animals, although had to be very careful as the rattlesnakes were really buzzing on the islands. The animals were all, understandably, stressed. I asked if it wasn't difficult seeing all those stranded animals and inquired as to whether there had been any effort made to save or transplant them. He said it was impossible to remove so many off the islands, although the snakes probably eventually swam to land. Russell later wrote and published a book resulting from his studies, *Snakes, Lizards, and Turtles of the Lake Mead Region.*

Grater's recollections of Pearce Ferry were that the CCC fly camp was located right down on the landing where people camp today, but he didn't recall any camp up on the bluff north of the landing. He knew the CCC's took boats out on the lake to clean driftwood off the water and said Iceberg Canyon was the most dangerous for boats because many of the floating logs were submerged just beneath the surface. He also remembered Pop Emery being at Pearce Ferry with his boat.

Recounting an experience he had in Quartermaster Canyon, Grater said he went there one time to check out the bighorn sheep situation and camped overnight. Upon waking in the morning, he found himself completely encircled by little wild burros, and whenever he moved they'd bray, making a terrible racket. Then finally they ran off. He said the burros were typical of the small old Mexican burro, not big ones like most others around the lake. "You could sit on them and drag your feet on the ground." He added that not far from the spring he saw signs of an old miners camp so figured the miner must have brought the small burros in there somehow and then left them stranded in this canyon.

Grater related another interesting story:

> One time Ed Schenk and I got a boat and outfitted the thing to go up into the Canyon for a few days. I was going to look for bighorn sheep and he wanted to check on the geology. We also didn't know too much about what the water was like. I had sampling devices to sample the 'ph' on the water here and there.
>
> One hot day we went up into the Canyon and got to Columbine Falls. I decided to take a sample and lowered this can device down to get cool water. As I put the device down in the water, it stopped. We couldn't figure it out so tried again about ten feet farther out and the same thing happened. So then we spent the whole day running a transit right across the lake at that point with this sampling devise. It was the same way all the way across.
>
> When we returned to Boulder City, Ed wrote a report to Park Service that a big delta was forming there and predicted that in the short time of 2-3 years, Pearce Ferry might be blocked off. And here the Park Service was getting ready to lease out concessions and have a big set-up there. Tour boats were already running out of Hemenway Harbor and coming up. Schenk proved to be right, but sooner than even he thought, as the entire Pearce Bay silted in within a few short months. And that ended the whole show.

The Leviathan

> That was when I got a lot of aerial pictures. You could see that whole delta from the air. Where it was forming and how wide, the whole bit. Then later when the lake went down, you had a canyon within a canyon, of course, with steeply cut mud banks all along the sides.
>
> The reason why I began taking samples to begin with, was because we were finding fish out in the lake going belly up. They'd wiggle a little bit and then they'd die. I couldn't find anything wrong with them except their gill arches looked a little red. Then I remembered a Dr. Ruby from Tennessee Valley Authority and wrote him to see if they'd seen fish like that in their newly made lakes. He replied that they sure had. Dr. Ruby explained that when the water is rising and covering all the vegetation, it feeds an enormous food chain in there in relatively still water. The fish would feed in those areas of plenty for weeks and months. They then would swim farther out and hit the fresh water current coming downstream and it would be of entirely different gas content then the other. They couldn't handle the fast adjustment so would turn belly up and die.
>
> That's why the native river fishes (squawfish, bonytail, and sucker) got into big trouble when the lake came up. They couldn't adapt to living in that clear water and they couldn't lay eggs and raise their young in clear water. Even the beaver were having difficulty trying to survive. They were drowned out of their homes with nowhere to go. Game and Fish had to take a bunch of them out of there.

Another interesting aspect Grater brought up was that, early on, an old mining camp was located in Peach Springs Canyon, not far from the river. He and a friend hiked in there and found remains of the camp close to where the old Farlee Hotel had also later stood. From his past readings, he was quite sure this mining camp had been active at the time Powell came down on his first memorable river expedition through the canyon. Grater figured if Powell and his group had only stopped there on the south side of the river rather than farther down at Separation Canyon, the men who chose to leave would have found the mining camp only a mile away and would have survived.

Grater continued:

> The lower Grand Canyon was such an attraction to me because so little was known about the wildlife there. One time I did a report on the lake and canyon and estimated there to be some 300 bighorn sheep in this region. A Fish and Wildlife guy from the Overton area said there absolutely weren't that many sheep, so their department hired Utah State to do a biological survey. They found that in the Muddy Mountain country alone, there were over 300 sheep!
>
> Another time they gave me a list of 70 species of birds for the area. I went out and counted over 100 in just one week and ended up with over 200 species shortly thereafter.

There was one place I thought Park Service really missed the boat. The Bat Cave [up in the lower Grand Canyon] had been occupied for centuries and perhaps thousands of years, by bats, many of which had died over the years and fallen down into the guano. They should have had an excavation done to find out what kinds of bats had lived there long ago. Being a biologist, I felt that was more important than just getting the guano out for fertilizer. It would also have told us a whole lot about insect life, plant life, and everything else for centuries prior.

Nestled in the western end of Grand Canyon, some fifteen miles upriver from Pearce Ferry, is the opening to this cave, one called simply, the "Bat Cave." The opening is nearly 800 feet above the river on the north wall of the canyon. I will summarize historical information about this cave as drawn from four different articles written over a thirty-two year period. The first is Russell Grater's article, "Black Gold," that appeared in the June 1951 issue of *Arizona Highways*; second, Robert Greenawalt's article, "Guano Tramway in Granite Gorge," appearing in the January 1959 issue of *Desert Magazine*; third, author unknown of an article printed in the April, 1973, Mohave feature issue of the *Mohave Miner* newspaper in Kingman; fourth, another article printed in the December, 1983, issue of Mohave feature of the *Mohave Miner*, this story told by Bill Freiday Sr. and to Herb Voight of Kingman.

The cave was originally discovered by Harold Carpenter in the late 1930's. He had come to Boulder City, Nevada, quickly fallen under the magic spell of the Mojave Desert, and had taken a job working at the boat docks on newly forming Lake Mead. He worked on a sailing boat called the Loki and one day while boating in the lower canyon, spotted a rather unimpressive slit some 800 feet high in the north wall. He decided to explore this cave and three days and many improvised ropes and ladders later, succeeded. Inside he found a high, long, narrow cave, some 700 feet in length, with what appeared to be massive deposits of bat droppings on the floor. Interest soon grew over this discovery as it had become known that bat guano was an extremely rich fertilizer.

For a larger perspective here; back in the early 1800's, the scientist, Alexander von Humboldt, had researched fertilizer potentials of bird guano (manure) in Peru. He soon determined that bird guano was a rich nitrate source. This became popular knowledge and bird guano quickly became desired in Europe where long-practiced farming methods and limited land resources had badly depleted available soils of needed nutrients. By the mid-1800's, large-scale mining had begun of bird guano on islands off Peru and Chili, eventually initiating a war between Spain and a Peruvian-Chili alliance for rights to this guano. During the late 1800's over 100,000 indentured Chinese immigrants were imported to do this mining work. Eventually it was determined that bat guano, however, was even richer in nitrates than bird guano, but also more difficult to find and mine. In addition, although of little concern back then, bat colonies proved highly vulnerable to disturbances within their caves.

The Leviathan

Walter Swartz of Boulder City started a project to take guano out of the Grand Canyon Bat Cave by hand, digging and sacking it, then bringing the guano down from the cave and loading it on to barges. One author said Murl Emery (Pop Emery's son) and a brother of Kingman's Beal Masterson, were involved in the early effort to remove the guano by barge.

During this time a camp was built on the shore of the river at the location. This shoreline was actually a ridge that had been the rim of an inner gorge before the waters of Lake Mead filled and backed that far into the Canyon. Frame cabins were built on this terrace and a small diesel power plant was brought up the canyon by barge for supplying electrical needs. A wooden cableway was built up to the cave entrance and a gasoline motor provided power to pull a wooden deck up and down the cableway. The guano was bagged and sent down to be loaded on the barges below. Each sack weighed some 50 pounds. How much could be loaded at once depended on the size of the barge and depth of the water downstream. The loads usually consisted of about 35 tons of sacked guano and those were taken to the boat harbor many miles distant near Boulder City, then loaded into trucks for the remainder of the journey. However, one barge sank and almost 60 tons of guano were lost, which was devastating to this operation.

A few years later the property was sold to the King-Finn Fertilizer Company and they tried several methods of removal, including flying the guano out in small planes. George Steinke and Buzzy Wescott of Kingman made numerous trips for the company. They dismantled a D-2 Cat and flew the pieces into the location, put it back together, and scraped out a 1100 foot landing strip on a sand bar about one-quarter mile upstream from the cave. Then spring floods arrived and washed out the sandbar and airstrip.

By 1957, a whole new fascinating story began unfurling about the Bat Cave. The U. S. Guano Corporation, a subsidiary of New Pacific Coal and Oils out of Toronto, Canada, purchased the mine and invested heavily, expecting to extract some $10,000,000 worth of bat guano. Engineers decided the only reliable means of taking the guano from the cave would be a giant tramway installed across the entire canyon. The cable would extend from the mouth of the cave on the north wall of the canyon, located some 800 feet above water, to the top of the canyon rim on the south side, a good 8300 feet in distance across. This was a mind-boggling feat at that time and many thought it could not be done at all. The horizontal main span with no support would cross a width of some 7500 feet while rising 2500 feet in height. Compare this to San Francisco's Golden Gate Bridge with a main span of some 4200 feet and no elevation change at all.

The U. S. Guano Corporation let out bids for the work and contracted with Consolidated Western Steel, a construction division of United States Steel Company. Their bid to build the entire tram operation, $439,000, was not the cheapest, however, the clincher was their offer to successfully complete the project no matter how far the cost exceeded that figure (something they soon came to regret).

Simply installing the anchors in the unstable cave walls was problematic. Blasting powder could not be used for fear of weakening the walls even further.

All footings had to be drilled 27 feet deep with regular jack-hammers, and rocks broken apart with expanding studs. Then it took nearly a year to simply build the main terminal up on top the south rim, the terminal located on Hualapai Reservation lands. Footings for that huge structure were 12 feet square and 18 feet deep. Footings for the next tower, on a ledge 1000 feet below, could not be blasted because of overhanging ledges, so these were also all cut by drilling and expansion, with slabs of rock removed piece by piece.

Down on the river, another small airstrip was put in along a mud bank. Buzzy Westcott was once again called into service and proceeded to make hundreds of flights bringing in the entire 35 tons of structural steel needed for work near the mine, itself. However, due to the short length of the runway, Westcott could only bring in ten foot lengths at a time with loads not over 1000 pounds.

Huge cables were needed for the tram. The gut cable would cross the canyon and remain in place to support the tram. The pull cable had to be a long continuous length of 20,000 feet and 1 ¼ inches in diameter. This cable would cross the canyon twice, in a revolving fashion, to carry the tram, soon to be known as the "Bat Car," back and forth. The car, itself, was a large aluminum cargo bucket with a 3500 pound capacity (2500 pounds of bat guano and six men). It was soon determined, however, that no continuous cable of the 20,000 foot length could be obtained, so two 10,000 foot cables were ordered and these joined together with a 60 foot splice. When finished, the cable weighed nearly 300 tons.

A one-eighth inch cable was first strung across the canyon by helicopter. With this cable, the men used a power winch to pull a three-eighths inch cable across, and then used that to string a three-quarter inch cable. After that the three-quarter inch cable was used to string the 1 ¼ inch gut cable. But alas, when tightening the gut cable, the man operating the main winch forgot to "set the keeper," the ratchet began to slip, and when he applied the brake all the teeth were ripped from the ratchet and the cable plunged deep into the canyon. Since damage had no doubt been done to the cable when it hit the ground and removing it from the canyon was also deemed too risky, another cable was ordered.

The new cable was finally successfully installed and in May of 1957, the tram started operations. The Bat Car would start from the tower on the south rim, drop 500 feet in elevation and 1100 feet in distance to the top of the first tower on the ledge below, then take off on a long 9,890 foot trip across the canyon. The one-way trip across the great gaping space took nearly ten minutes.

An amazing video of this tram operation is available for viewing at the Mohave Museum in Kingman. This VHS tape was transferred from an old movie (at one time shown during news feature short films at Saturday Matinees) that had been made while the tram was in operation and Bill Freiday of Kingman was in charge of operations. Freiday is actually shown astride the pulley on the cable, while below him, the hinged trolley with men in the Bat Car slowly sways to and fro, and the film rolls on showing Freiday riding atop this cable during the entire trip across the canyon in order to visibly check the condition of the cable as it passes beneath him.

The Leviathan

Everything went along fine during these mining operations for several months until Freiday noticed the splice was stretching. A cable expert brought in from Switzerland determined that the original splice had not been done correctly. A Swiss crew was then brought in and a new splice made. Operations resumed, but only a month later shut down again because neither was the new splice holding. The company then decided that only one unbroken 20,000 foot cable would work effectively. So, cable number two was dropped into the canyon.

By this time U. S. Steel had begun to regret its commitment to the project, even though it was receiving lots of publicity over the whole affair. The company then went ahead and special ordered a continuous 20,000 foot steel cable which was finally brought in and successfully installed. Once again, everything seemed to be running along smoothly. By now U. S. Steel figured it had spent over one million dollars on the tramway project. They were delighted that mechanical problems were finally over.

Yet trouble still loomed. After a few more months of operation, Freiday noticed that the nitrogen content of the guano was decreasing. He moved the vacuum pipe to other parts of the cave to mix in richer nitrate guano, but eventually the same thing happened in each area. Further analysis was done and the bitter truth soon became apparent; deposits in the cave were not nearly as extensive as first thought. The cave actually contained only about 1000 tons of bat guano, in contrast to the 100,000 tons previously estimated. Mining operations at the Bat Cave ceased.

Columbia Pictures decided to use the Bat Cave tram while making a movie in Mohave County in 1959. The film, *Edge of Eternity*, starred Cornell Wilde, Jack Elam, Edgar Buchanan, and Mickey Shaugnessy, along with Bill Freiday. Freiday took his crew to the location and started up the motors, but the tram only moved about 150 feet. In checking the cable with binoculars, it appeared the main operating cable had been broken near the counterbalance tower on the other side of the river. They went ahead and filmed a scene showing Freiday riding the tram while looking for a supposed murder victim below, but while shooting the film, the tram was actually only moving across the first 100 feet of cable, not on across the canyon. Further investigation revealed that just prior to the movie shoot, a fighter plane out of Nellis Air Force Base in Las Vegas, Nevada, had come into base missing three feet from one of its wing tips. The pilot, it was learned, had been hot-dogging (flying very low) in the Canyon and the wing tip of his plane had clipped the cable.

After filming was completed, the U. S. Guano Corporation wanted to avoid the possibility of future accidents and liability so made the decision to drop the last main cable into the canyon. Currently there are some 1000 tons of cable weight lying in the bottom of the canyon in this area.

I've included photos from both 1975 and 1985 when Don and I made visits to the Bat Tower and Bat Car on the south rim. At that time, nothing else existed there. Quartermaster Viewpoint, on a short trail to the east, was still wonderfully peaceful and quiet with not a human soul in sight, and there one could enjoy a spectacular viewpoint overlooking a sheer drop into the western part of Grand Canyon. By the early 1990's, however, although the main operating tower still sat poised on the south rim, the Hualapai Tribe had begun plans for a big tourism development in that beautifully isolated area, one to be called Grand Canyon West. They built a restaurant in the lower section of the old tower, and plans were in the works for far more. On that date on the north side of the river, the windsock post remained where the landing strip once existed. The other tower below the entrance to the cave on the north side was still intact and bits of debris were scattered about on the shore.

From the river just below where the Bat Cave is located, a foot trail still winds around and up a ridge to the west, then backtracks east to the tower. From that ledge, an 80' steel ladder was at one time still in place to provide straight-up access to the cave entrance. When I first climbed that ladder in 1973, I found only one small loose bolt remaining in place at the top, this barely securing the entire ladder to the rock cliff wall. In the early 1980's, administrators of Grand Canyon National Park decided to remove the ladder since it was a hazard to visitors and proved too much a liability.

In May 1987, I had the very good fortune to find and interview Horace Emery. Horace, age 77 at the time, was the youngest son of a legend on the Colorado River, Pop Emery.[6] Horace, himself, spent many years on the river from 1929 until the early 1970's. He worked for the Bureau of Reclamation and covered the river from Grand Canyon down to Yuma on the border of Mexico. He said, during the early days, his dad, Emery, and oldest brother, Clyde, had worked for awhile in the mines around Chloride. In those days, however, they didn't allow two related people to work in the same mine so Clyde always called his Dad, "Steve," and when anyone asked if they were related, they'd say, "Nope ... we just happened to run into each other." Horace went on to relate the following:

> Later, my brother, Murl, had a store in what was called Ragtown, during construction of the dam, down on the river above Black Canyon. Cashman had a ferry just below Murl's store. Cashman's ferry ran just above the dam and was operated by a family named Schwartz. Some people thought that was the ferry Murl operated, but it wasn't. There was a boat dock there and they were going to put in gambling and have boat trips down the lake. That was started by Lacey in Las Vegas and he's the one that built the Miss Vegas boat. It was bigger than the Mud Hen [the one Horace operated] but was also a tunnel stern boat. When they went bankrupt, Murl got the boat and that's what we used to haul men up and down the river at the start of the construction of the dam.
>
> Murl and I had 'Emery's Landing' at Boulder Wash near Boulder City, and in the early 1940's we ran tours across the lake and up into the Canyon. Murl had four tour boats; the Hualapai, Mohave, Paiute, and Navaho, which were all red and known as the Red Boat Tours. Cashman had tour boats also, but his were painted white and called Cashman's Tours.

The Leviathan

The Paiute, a 45 passenger boat, was patterned after the 'water taxis' at Long Beach, California, with a Liberty engine. It was built by a fellow who shipped it up to the lake. Murl had hired a fellow down there who used to run rum-running boats. They had Liberties in them and he knew those engines from one end to the other. I can't remember when they brought the Paiute up there and put it in the lake. We got in, started it up, put it in gear, and went right up on the bank. They'd put a left-hand propeller in rather than a right-hand one, and we had to send back to Los Angeles for the right one.

Dad was from Missouri and came out here in about 1900. He did some mining, then by 1918, he was running the old motor car ferry across the Colorado River between Searchlight and Chloride. At that time [before the Hoover Dam/bridge was built] it was 14 miles from Searchlight, Nevada, to the river, and about 26 miles from Chloride to the river. Otherwise, to cross the river, you had to go clear down to Topock to get across, so people [from Nevada or California] would come down here, take the ferry, and go up to Kingman. There were big alfalfa fields on the Arizona side just below Searchlight and they had two 16" pumps and big 60 horsepower Bessemer engines, single cylinder, and Dad ran those, pumping water to the alfalfa fields, then ran the ferry in-between.

Around 1923, Dad was running a stamp mill for a mining company not far out of Searchlight. Some years later Murl said, 'You know, I wonder if that old stamp mill is still there?' So he and I hiked for many miles to get up in there and sure enough, it was still there, half buried in gravel. Murl said, 'By golly, that's not bad ... I'm going to go back and get the cat and scrape a road in here, get that old stamp mill and move it to Nelson.' And he did.

Murl set the stamp mill up at Nelson and ran it with an old 12 horse Fairbanks-Morris horizontal engine. People would come down to see the old stamp mill and he'd crank it up, put some ore in it, stamp it out, get it real fine, then pan it and get colors of gold. But he'd take this pan and slip it underneath when they weren't watching. Then the next bunch would come down and he'd reach down and get the pan out and go through the same process. Nine times out of ten he'd get just a little more gold, yet it was always the same gold in the pan. Then, one day he reached in there to get the pan and boy, drew his hand back in a hurry ... there was a rattlesnake curled right up in the middle of that pan.

Murl used to love going out and starting up that engine and the old stamp mill. I'll bet you don't know where that old stamp mill is now. It's in Disney World in Florida! That outfit bought it and moved it back there, but didn't take the engine because in the early days they ran all this equipment by steam, steam boilers and steam engines, and I understand they have it all set up with a steam engine there now. If I ever get back there, I'd sure like to see it.

Dad came up here to Pearce Ferry in about 1933 and was here until around 1940 or 41. He worked for the Bureau of Reclamation. They had these big evaporation pans that floated out on the lake and would go out and fill the pans and measure to see how much evaporated and they also measured rainfall. That's what Dad did in-between. We brought the old ferry up here and set it up at Pearce Ferry but no cars ever went across because the road on the other side [north shore across from Pearce Ferry] in the Strip was always washed out. There was no through traffic, just a cattleman once in awhile. So finally Dad converted the old ferry into a houseboat.

Dad's real name was Eliphalet Horace Emery. It was from the Bible and Dad was far from religious. He'd never let anyone call him that so just used his initials, E. H. Emery, but everyone just called him Pop. My name was Edmund Horace Emery and because our initials were the same, the Bureau of Reclamation kept getting our checks mixed up and about every other month I'd have to drive clear to Hualapai Bay or Pearce Ferry, find Dad, and switch checks with him. Finally I had my name changed to Horace Edmund Emery to avoid so much confusion.

I used to run the old Mud Hen down around the construction site at the dam. We carried passengers and came up the lake. It was a tunnel stern boat, where they had a tunnel that goes back and the propeller was above the bottom of the boat.

While interviewing Horace, I reached into a folder I'd brought along and pulled out some copies of old 8 x 10 photographs I had found in files at NPS headquarters in Boulder City, ones that I had suspected were of boats at Pearce Ferry, yet there was no identifying information. I showed one to Horace and he quickly identified not only the old ferry after his father had converted it to a houseboat, but also the Mud Hen alongside, both anchored in what he said was the bay of Grapevine Wash there at Pearce Ferry (this was also, the same photo I had once seen in the June, 1973, issue of the Mohave section of the *Mohave Miner* newspaper, p. 13, where it was misidentified as "Temple Bar Consolidated Mining Co. used these floats to test gravel banks for gold," in one of Roman Malach's series of articles entitled, "Some Interesting Old Towns Now Covered by Waters of Lake Mead"). Horace said he had no doubt whatsoever this was the Mud Hen which he had driven up and down the lake many times, and was also very sure it was the old ferry/houseboat alongside.

I then showed him another photo, this one of a man leaning against the post of what appeared to be a building situated on a dock. Horace immediately responded; "Hey, that's Dad! Where in the world did you find that?" I told him the original photo was in Park Service files at headquarters in Boulder City but there was no information with the picture and no one seemed to know the identity of this man. He said, "Yes, that's Dad – Pop Emery! He's standing right beside the building he had on the dock there at Pearce Ferry." Horace couldn't get over what a good picture it was of his father and I was delighted to finally get a positive identification that this was of the 'real Pop Emery.' Horace then continued:

> Dad lived down there at Pearce Ferry. Part of the time he lived in an old trailer at the landing and sometimes in a little house floating on an old barge. He also had a building on a dock rigged up there. He sold bait and supplies from the building and had fishing boats he'd rent out.
>
> One time Dad left his Model A Ford sitting in the wash there at Pearce Ferry. A cloudburst came down and buried it in sand, so I had to come from Boulder City, dig it out, load it on a truck, take it down to Las Vegas to where I was living, and clean it all up so he could use it again.

While Horace looked at another old picture, I asked if this, a different larger boat, was a tour boat. He explained, "No, this light-colored boat isn't a tour boat – all the tour boats had names on them. This might have been the big Los Angeles Water Department boat. They had a nice cruiser on the lake.

Then Horace explained another picture where some boats were tied up to the dock/house at Pearce Ferry:

> Years ago a party made a trip down through the Grand Canyon and they pulled in there at Pearce Ferry to get supplies before going on down the lake to Boulder. That was their boats – see how the hatches and everything are enclosed so they wouldn't sink?"

He then asked if I had run into any information about the steamboat that sank over by where Bonelli's Ferry used to be. I told him that I hadn't. He went on:

> One time in about 1890, they brought a steamboat over land and assembled it there at Bonelli's Ferry and were going to go down to Yuma. Well, they sank it in Boulder Canyon on its maiden voyage. See, you'd be going down the river and there would be an eddy running backwards to the river. They hit one of those eddies and it turned the boat around real quick because of the side wheelers -- you can't operate one wheel at a time, and they couldn't control the boat. It hit a big boulder in Boulder Canyon and sank, so we used to call that rock there in the river, Steamboat Rock.
>
> I remember the CCC camp there at Bonelli's. It was fairly close to the river up on a little plateau so they wouldn't get any flood waters. And in the early days, around 1933 or so, when we would come up the river we could still see the walls of the old Bonelli House standing. It was a big adobe house, had eight rooms or more in it. They'd put canvas in as dividers between the rooms and then painted the canvas, and each room had a fireplace.
>
> We also went by the site of the old Grigg's Ranch one time, but there were no ranch buildings still remaining. People had taken the lumber and everything. The springs were still there that fed the big ponds. It was a beautiful place.

Dad moved down to Hualapai Wash toward the later part of his stay there. They wanted the evaporation pans measured there, too, and he'd go out and check those every day. Fred Gibson, who was manager of a chemical company in Boulder City had the Lakeshore Mining Company across in Scanlon Wash on the other side of the river. They were getting a fair amount of gold from there [recall the story I related previous that Horace had told of men from the mining company calling him to shore and having him take a gold bar back to Boulder City for them]. They'd have supplies brought down to Dad, then he'd take them over across to the Lakeshore Mining Company. This was when the lake was much higher.

The airstrip road up on top Grapevine Mesa [north of Meadview] above Pearce Ferry landing was built by the CCC's and was to be used for Grand Canyon Air Tours. Emery Falls, the waterfalls up in the mouth of the Canyon, was named after Dad. Everyone called it Emery Falls in those days, but when Park Service came in and took over they changed the name to Columbine Falls. They said nothing in this country could be named after a living person.

Dad died in about 1960, down at Nelson's Landing on the river and below the dam. There was an old graveyard back up on a little bank about two miles from the lake. That's where Dad wanted to be buried, but the Bureau of Reclamation was going to have to move the graves since Lake Mohave was filling and water levels rising, so Dad was buried at Nelson.

As the interview with Horace came to an end, I showed him an old mining claim slip, a small paper previously removed from a tobacco can (then the policy regarding old expired claims inside NPS boundaries), one that I had found on a ridge running back from Hualapai Wash. It was dated in the 1930's and was signed, "E. H. Emery." Horace verified that this was, indeed, his father's handwriting. This slip of paper is presently on display at the Meadview Ranger Station.

I found some summary information about the old Pearce Ferry landing in a National Park Service hand-out, *Lake Mead National Recreation Area: Area History and Information*:

> The area became popular during the Grand Canyon-Boulder Dam tours in the 1940's. A concession maintained a floating dock, supply depot, dining room, and had elaborate plans for improvements. The tour boats left Hemenway, stopped at Pearce Ferry, continued to Rampart Cave, and then on 12 miles into the Grand Canyon. The tour cost $101. With the filling of Lake Mead, a delta formed at Pearce Ferry. This silting in, followed by the lowering of the lake level after 1941, forced the concession to be abandoned.

The previous interview with Bill Fauth had unearthed further details.[7] Fauth told of how, during his youth, he and a group of boys had gone up to Pearce Ferry in 1937. He said there was a small wooden building and dock at the landing at Pearce Ferry where one could buy gas and they paid a man by the name of Emery

The Leviathan

to take them up to Columbine Falls and leave them there for eight days, paying him $8 for the ride. He thought this was Murl Emery, however, not Pop. The group hiked and fished the entire time they were up there. One, Bob Winsett, climbed up above Columbine Falls and found pottery in a cave. Fauth said Winsett later worked for Jacques Cousteau, the famous underwater explorer, and lived in Hawaii.

In an excerpt from the old historical information of Mamie Musser, we also find reference to Pearce Ferry landing in what appears to be the late 1930's. Again, here we see mention of Murl at the landing, not Pop, which either means people were confusing father with son, or, that Murl may have stayed at the landing at various times, perhaps in his father's absence:

> The traffic that once passed over the river at this point [Bonelli's] now is carried to Pearce Ferry, where a wharf and boat landing is being built. A Mr. Murl Emery has the concession for boating at this point. An airplane landing field is being built where passengers can combine the boat trip with the air.[8]

In 1986, when I interviewed local Meadview resident, Jess Ladd, he spoke of having come up to fish in this area years before moving up to the new Meadview development. Jess spoke of an old man with a long beard who was down at Pearce Ferry between 1935-1940, and said this man was on contract with the City of Los Angeles and did seismograph readings at Pearce Ferry as the lake filled. Jess related, "There was a two-room white pre-fab house or cabin in front of the cave shelter in the hillside, about where the covered canopy or picnic patio is now. The house was removed later when the project was over. The old man said he'd been 'on the river' for more than 50 years."[9]

Jess also mentioned that during the late 1930's and early 1940's, he had lunch with CCC boys at Pearce Ferry several times. He said they had about fifty tents and a big one for a mess hall. Jess recalled their camp being located up on a ridge … as one was going down to Pearce Ferry landing, there was a road to the left, leading up on to that mesa. Remains of that camp area, along with rock-lined walkways and tent circles, are still visible there today. I've wondered, however, if the CCC camps at the Pearce Ferry area may have been at different places at different times, since reported locations of these by first-hand eye witnesses seemed to vary somewhat.

I had been told by someone that there had also been a CCC camp up on top Grapevine Mesa, just off the east side of Pearce Ferry road not far from where the road branches to go to the airstrip. I had seen concrete foundations and old dumps in this area and asked Jess about this location. He thought there had been a smaller camp up there for awhile, perhaps where supplies were delivered and left. Jess continued:

> In the bay just beyond and left of Pearce Ferry Bay there was a big floatation rig, maybe 30' by 30'. It had lots of equipment on it for seismograph readings. The airstrip up on the mesa was built in the early 1930's and I think the engineer who worked on the Bridge Canyon Dam Project [a potential dam site farther up in Grand Canyon, a project eventually defeated by

environmentalists] had something to do with directing CCC work on the airstrip.

Jess also mentioned that when the water was really low down at Pearce Ferry in the 1960's (while Lake Powell was filling at the other end of Grand Canyon) that he and his wife, Fae, had walked clear out on the mudflats at Pearce Ferry to the river – almost three miles. They saw potholes that had fish dying in them and when they finally reached the river, they could almost throw a rock across.

Sadie Pearl Duncan mentioned an Emery being at Pearce Ferry during her interview:[10]

> When we lived at King Tut, in the evening a lot of times we'd drive down to Pearce's Ferry. There was a ferry boat there and a man named Emery was running it. His house was on pontoons.
>
> Then when my husband went down to work at Pearce's Ferry in early 1937, people were building some sort of recreational facilities, like a hotel or motel. We just had a little bitty tent house up in Grapevine Wash, a ways from the water. I was only there about a month but he'd been working for them longer than that – they were building quite a lot of extensive buildings. Pop Emery was gone. He'd moved.
>
> The last trip I made was up the river and I imagine it was Emery Falls that I saw. It was spring, and all that moisture, the snow and everything, you can't imagine how beautiful that country was. I'd heard about the beautiful flowers that were down from Emery Falls, and, in the boat you couldn't go much further as the debris was beginning to back up with the lake so we turned around and went back. But I got to see Emery Falls. And where I was living in this little cabin, this little tent house in the mouth of Grapevine, the purple sage was in bloom. It was so beautiful that year.

Elton Hart from Meadview recalled going to Pearce Ferry with 45 of his classmates on senior skip day in 1937.[11] He said there was a nice dock there, that they had all gone up to Emery Falls in one boat, and that another cabana was then at Pearce Ferry and it was on skids. Then Elton told of another incident that happened in about 1946. He was out fishing near the mouth of the canyon when he saw a man waving his arms frantically on the north shore of the river. Elton took his boat over there and talked with the man. The fellow hadn't eaten for three days, his shoes were worn out, and he was sort of crazy. Apparently he was from the mine operation at Bat Cave and the fan belt had broken on the barge they were using to haul guano out from the Bat Mine and he had walked out. Elton also mentioned seeing someone down at Pearce Ferry who had a shanty on pontoons and was selling cigarettes, lures, pop, etc. I'm not sure who this person was as Horace had said that his father, Pop Emery, had left Pearce Ferry by 1941.

Several times between 1986 and 1989, I interviewed Elmer Duffield, another original resident of the Meadview community. He told about first coming to his area when prospecting and fishing in 1931. He had also worked on a civil service

The Leviathan

job at the prospective Bridge Canyon Dam site up in the Canyon during 1941 and 42 when studies were being done to survey possibilities of a big dam in Grand Canyon just below where Peach Springs Canyon empties into the Colorado at Diamond Creek; this site being called the Bridge Canyon Dam site. Elmer said they built three barges at Pearce Ferry and had a camp up at the Bridge Canyon site for several years, during which time they drilled at three different places, testing for footing strengths. Elmer remembers boats called the Navaho and Apache carrying passengers, and "big shots" around, but he thought those were National Park Service boats.

The Bridge Canyon Dam, however, was never built. After the national environmental group, Sierra Club, at that time led by David Brower, mounted a nationwide campaign to stop construction of any dams at all within the walls of Grand Canyon, and when they were eventually able to show that public opinion was strongly in their favor, the Bridge Canyon Dam plans were finally shelved. There have been several other times during ensuing years when various Hualapai Tribal members, as well as one Arizona State Representative, tried to revive interest in the old Bridge Canyon Dam effort, but to no avail.

Elmer also recalled the small concrete buildings up on the mesa at Pearce Ferry that were used with seismograph equipment, and said at one time there was a light-colored house at Pearce Ferry when he was there, and the rock cave in the hillside was used for storage of blasting materials. He said the CCC camp consisted of old army tents shaped like teepees, and added that there were many desert tortoise and gila monsters in the area then, although these are a rare sight today.

Elmer said he knew Pop Emery, and remembered going up to the Bat Cave with Pop in the early 1940's. In the cave at that time there was a telephone pole with boards off to the sides and they had walked on one of those. Pop stepped off one of the boards and sank up to his knees in bat guano, and he had enough of that.[12]

According to Herb Voight of Kingman, at one time in the early 1930's a Harvey House actually had a restaurant at Pearce Ferry, just north of the landing. He said he'd once seen a picture of the building on the landing and heard they had brought in a French chef, had the best food in the world, and planned to fly people in for a nice stay and give them a two-day outing on Lake Mead. I had found previous reports of plans for such a restaurant and tourist destination, but this was the first mention I'd heard that the concession may have actually existed, at least for a short time.

In a July, 1986, interview, Joe Ricca of Kingman also mentioned the concessions being in operation at Pearce Ferry:[13]

> I worked as a ticket agent at the South Rim of the Grand Canyon for Fred Harvey Company in about 1936. Then the company put in some cabins and a mess hall at Pearce Ferry and they had tours. Mr. and Mrs. Phil Pogette operated the outfit for the company. It was on the right side as you go down to the water.

This could be the restaurant also referred to by Sadie Pearl Duncan, as being the one her husband helped build. And, it may have been the white building Jess Ladd mentioned that was "removed after the project was over." Recall, too, Russell Grater having told of his discovery of the huge delta forming in Pearce Bay, after which plans for "big operations" at Pearce Ferry were abandoned. Regardless, any restaurant that may have been there was apparently not in existence for long.

Several interesting old articles on Lake Mead, Pearce Ferry, and the Lower Grand Canyon were featured in 1941 issues of *Arizona Highways*. Included is a photograph of Pearce Ferry showing a white house visible sitting on the dock, one that Pop Emery used for a number of years, and also small bath houses newly built in the background, situated on the landing itself.

Regarding the origin of Pearce Ferry airstrip that's located up on top and at the north end of Grapevine Mesa, there are differing stories. Some say it was built by the CCC's to bring in supplies for their camps. Others said it was either built by the CCC's for the forthcoming Fred Harvey Resort down on the Pearce Ferry landing, or, for supplying the Bridge Canyon Dam crew working up in the Canyon. Still others said it was built so planes could fly in and out during barge operations at the Bat Cave mining venture. Lastly, others have said Air Force planes were parked there during World War II, where they would have a "fast take-off" in order to fly out and defend Hoover Dam if the need arose.

It has also been rumored that the old water pipes going up alongside the cliff wall from Grapevine Springs (in Grapevine Springs Canyon and up to the top of Grapevine Mesa) had been placed there by the CCC's in order to supply water for their camps on top, near the airstrip. However, Jim Ray refuted this stating that he, himself, built the concrete water tank down at the springs, and that Smith later had the water pipes and line put in, in order to run water up to the dirt water cattle tank up on the mesa. This dirt tank is now designated on some USGS maps as "Ray Tank" and is located not far from the airstrip.

Further information was uncovered about the two small concrete structures still standing up on the mesa just north of Pearce Ferry landing. In a 1982 study done for NPS by Nick Scrattish titled, *Historic Sites Within Lake Mead National Recreation Area Deemed Ineligible for National Register Nomination*, the following information is given about the old seismic station at Pearce Ferry:

> This site is located at the eastern edge of the Iceberg Canyon, Arizona-Nevada fifteen minute quadrangle. The site's approximate center is one-half mile due north of the Pearce Ferry Boat Anchorage ... Specifications and drawing for the buildings were issued by the Department of Interiors' BOR in February of 1940.
>
> Pearce Ferry Seismic Station began operating in December 1940 and was abandoned during 1943. The Overton, Nevada, Seismic Station also began operating in December 1940. These stations were preceded in 1937 by an installation in the basement of the BOR's District Headquarters building in Boulder City, Nevada. Use of the Pearce Ferry Station was short-lived

because of exigencies caused by World War II. The Pearce Ferry Station was not reopened. I recommend against nominating it to the NRHP because:

1. It was far less important than the Boulder City Station, which monitored induced earthquake activity as the result of the filling of Lake Mead, and,

2. Because of the short duration of its operation.

As lake waters deepened, NPS also took bids for concessions on other lake access points, and before long resorts sprang to life at Overton and Echo Bay, both located on the Overton Arm of Lake Mead. Temple Bar, on the Arizona side, which for years had been simply a landing for fishing boats, also blossomed with full-blown resort facilities. Temple Bar had the unique distinction of being the "last to offer services" at this end of the lake for boaters making the long trip farther up to the end of the lake and especially for those going on into the lower Granite Gorge of Grand Canyon.

In 1943, George Olcott prepared a report for LMNRA, writing that during a 30-year period several proposals had come about to create a surfaced highway that would run north from Highway 93 in Arizona and cross this western end of Grand Canyon, this in an effort to shorten travel distance to Utah. Herb Voight in Kingman also provided information about this project.[14]

One plan originated in the 40's when it was thought the Bridge Canyon Dam project would be completed, and that the dam would, itself, provide a bridge across the Lower Granite Gorge of Grand Canyon. In this case, a road would have been built from Peach Springs northerly to tie in with the proposed dam, then cross the river/canyon, from there access the Esplanade (lower bench on north side of the canyon) via a side canyon, travel through Twin Canyon to the rim west of Mount Dellenbaugh, and from there, proceed on to St. George. Needless to say, numerous construction problems would have been encountered. Olcott also pointed out that the highway distance from Phoenix to Salt Lake City via the Bridge Canyon Dam, would only have been about 60 miles less than the existing route from Phoenix to Salt Lake City via Lee's Ferry around the eastern end of Grand Canyon. However, when the Bridge Canyon Dam project went down in defeat, plans for such a road were quickly dropped.

Another plan, one given brief consideration by NPS, was less ambitious. This entailed improving the Pearce Ferry road to Pearce Bay, having a ferry once again operate to provide a river crossing for vehicles, then make a better road going north up Grand Wash via Hidden Canyon, Toroweap Valley, and on to St. George (basically once again following the ancient Old Ute Trail on the north side). This plan, too, was dropped. Trying to maintain a daily ferry operation (not to mention 24 hr. service) at Pearce would have been costly and difficult, and modern-day travelers wouldn't have appreciated delays while waiting for the Ferry on busy days. And, no small factor, maintaining a road up the long natural drainage of Grand Wash on the other side during rainy seasons would have been a costly and never-ending challenge.

Lake Mead

The prospect of a new Recreation Area also sparked the interest of land developers who foresaw financial opportunities loom, and some began developing and promoting outlying communities with access to the new lake.

Dolan Springs, as a "new desert community," got its start even before the lake was filled. The following information is from Florence White in Dolan Springs:[15]

> In the Dolan Springs area, land was subdivided down by Highway 93 back in 1929, but the recession stopped sales. Then, in the late 1930's, the CCC's put in a two inch water line extending from the 'springs' of Dolan Springs, over to the present area where the business district is now located. Bonelli's had that land from way back, then the Millers. In 1958, Bill Parker bought the development project from the Millers, formed Lake Mohave Ranchos, and started subdividing from the business district on south. Tom and I came in 1959 and worked with Parker, then bought Parker out in 1969. We got our first post office in the late 1960's. The U. S. Postal Service wouldn't allow business names for post offices [as in "Lake Mohave Ranchos"], so a vote was taken and the name Dolan Springs resulted.

The community of Meadview, up here in Grapevine Mesa and 40 miles north of Dolan Springs, had its beginnings in the late 1950's and early 60's. This development was laid out adjoining LMNRA boundaries on top of Grapevine Mesa, some ten miles from the lake, itself. The beautiful view of Lake Mead from the west rim of the mesa ridge provided the name origin.

Original developers of Meadview were informed by federal government representatives that LMNRA intended to preserve this far upper end of the lake as a backcountry experience for boaters, thus, no rim view lots should be marketed and sold as that would cause "visual intrusions" for boaters on the lake. However, rim view lots were advertised and sold despite this advisement. A decade or so later, Congress reluctantly allocated taxpayer money (i.e. your money and mine) to then buy back rim view lots that had been sold by developers anyway. By then, lot prices had escalated and hard feelings were expressed by owners who had built on those lots and whose homes then had to be removed. This was an attempt by the National Park Service to retain an enriching experience for everyone on this end of the lake; boaters, campers, and fishermen on the waters below, as well visitors viewing from rim overlooks above. Inevitably, however, there will always be those who work to defeat good intentions for the many in order to serve private interests for a wealthy few.

Everett Harris, long-time resident of Meadview, reminisced about the communities early beginnings:[16]

> In the late 1950's, developers Frank Glindmeier and Paul Mullane began activity on Grapevine Mesa under the name of Revcor, an engineering company. In the early 1960's they did little up here at Meadview but concentrated instead on developing and selling their properties in Riviera, down near Bullhead City on the river. After they sold all their land there, they came back up to concentrate on developing Meadview, in the late sixties, I believe. I came here in 1967 and was hired to build the trailer park and many

The Leviathan

of the roads. The old marina/store was on the rim then. Hal Brown managed the whole area for Revcor at that time, including the development of Golden Horseshoes over in the White Hills. We put some water pipes into the terrace section in 1967. Generators were still in use to supply electricity up until the early 1970's.

Jess Ladd had some even earlier memories of Meadview:[17]

Jerry Wakefield was in charge of the area early on. He was the first salesman for Frank and Paul. The only water here was down at the Lucky Seven Corral and windmill in Grapevine Wash and anyone wanting water had to go down there and get it. Jerry ran the store on the rim. He had horses and hounds and hunted lots. He'd take parties out from Las Vegas and hunt mountain lions. As recent as 1970, the local rancher here, Smith, brought in a government trapper [paid for with your tax money and mine] and in one winter, it's said, the trapper took out 22 mountain lions.

Elmer Duffield, also referenced previously, moved into Meadview permanently in October of 1960. He offered the following information in one of our interviews:

The house I built [now just the kitchen/dining unit] was the first actual 'house' in Meadview, in that it wasn't a mobile home. I had my own brick maker so while digging the septic tank, took that soil and made my first bricks. The septic tank had two brick rooms, one lined with tar, the other not, and with no leach line at first, not til much later. I built the second larger part of the house a few years later, then the garage in 1989. Most of the rocks in the chimney and elsewhere came from this area. Some were from Pearce Ferry where the CCC camp was, up on the mesa there. A few were from the Sedona area, but not many. I used a lot of driftwood from the lake while building this house.[18]

Lake Mead City, another land development area, sits near the crest of Grapevine Mesa just to the south of Meadview and some 1000 feet higher. This community was also started in the late 1950's and is located within and bordering the most dense part of Grapevine Mesa's unique and striking Joshua Tree Forest.

Lake Mead

E.C. LaRue at Pierce (sic) Ferry, Sept., 22, 1924, Householder Collection

LaRue Camp at Pierce (sic) Ferry, Sept, 22, 1924, Householder Collection

The Leviathan

Pop Emery at dock at Pearce Ferry, NPS photo, LMNRA, undated, perhaps in late 1930's

Lake Mead

Horace Emery at Pearce Ferry, 1987

Looking east at Pearce Ferry, Oct 1935, NPS photo, LMNRA

The Leviathan

Pearce Ferry boat landing in Grapevine Wash showing barge and houseboat and passenger boat, July 1936. NPS photo, LMNRA. (Horace Emery identified this as the Mudhen that he operated, and his dad's barge/houseboat).

One of two small concrete buildings on mesa at Pearce Ferry, 1988

Upper or main camp at Bridge Canyon damsite, south side of river. Historic photo belonging to Elmer Duffield of Meadview, 1941 or 1942

The Leviathan

Diamond drill barge at Bridge Canyon, 1941, Elmer Duffield Collection

Elmer Duffield aboard the Navaho, 1941, Elmer Duffield Collection

Emery Falls, NPS photo, 1930's (soon to become Columbine Falls)

Lake Mead

Don in NPS boat, Columbine Falls in 1988

Dovey Cornelius and author descending from Travertine Cave, 1986. Photo by Fran Wilson

Lake Mead

Don Simonis and author in Travertine Cave, March, 1987, photo by Fred Wilson

The Leviathan

Iceberg Canyon, showing "Flat Iron" rock slabs forming wall, 1989

Lake Mead

Don standing under tower at south rim of Grand Canyon on Hualapai land, the tower that once took cable to and from Bat Cave, 1975

The Leviathan

Bat Tower framework on south rim

Lake Mead

Don by Bat Tower on south rim, 1985

The Leviathan

Bat Car at the Bat Tower, 1985

Lake Mead

Barge in lower canyon, hauling guano. NPS files, LMNRA, 1948

Worker operating cable. NPS files, LMNRA, 1948

The Leviathan

Workers cabin on shore below Bat Cave. NPS, 1948

View from within entrance of Bat Cave, NPS photo by Belknap, no date

Lake Mead

Receiving tower on north wall below Bat Cave entrance, 1988

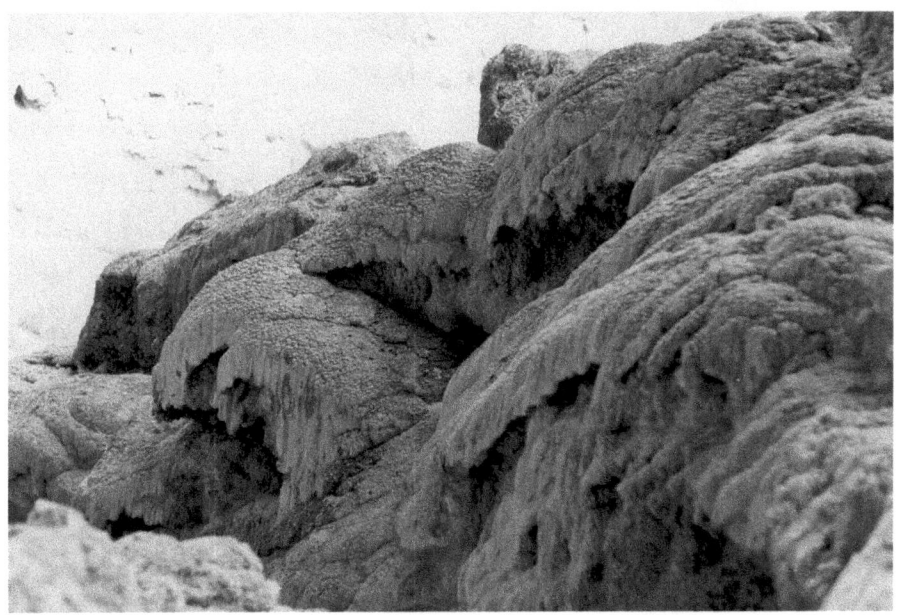

Huge travertine deposits at river's edge entrance to Quartermaster Canyon, March, 1988

The Leviathan

Greg Montgomery checking old irrigation ditches with travertine deposits on edges, Quartermaster Canyon, March, 1988

View from top of Wheeler Ridge, looking north at Cockscomb ridge and Gods Pocket and into Grand Wash, Jan. 1990

Lake Mead

View from airstrip overlook on Grapevine Mesa; morning sunrise over Snap Point, 1987

Looking through Elephant Arch and into Gregg Basin on Lake Mead, 1986

Lake Mead

End of rainbow at mouth of Grand Canyon, view from my front porch, May, 1987

The Leviathan

Other end of rainbow over Meadview, view out my back door, May, 1987

Part VI: Splendor on the Mesa

Chapter Seventeen: The Joshua Tree Forest

Grapevine Mesa is host to a very special gift; imbedded in the ancient layers of this landscape is an extraordinary Joshua Tree Forest. Distinct, strangely impressive; it has been determined by a number of researchers to be the most outstanding stand of Joshua Trees in existence. This Forest has exceptional density of growth, it has individual Joshua Trees measured as the largest known, and the Forest contains some of the oldest Joshua Trees to still be living. It truly is a rare gem on the land.

Joshua Trees are the "indicator species" of the great Mojave Desert, not prevalent in either of the other two expansive deserts in the west: the Sonoran Desert in southern and western Arizona, or the Great Basin Desert that covers most of Nevada and Utah and spills into bordering states. The Mojave Desert covers much of southern California and extends into southern Nevada, the Arizona Strip country north of the Colorado River, and down through our Grapevine Mesa, Hualapai Valley, and the Dolan Springs areas. The best species of Joshua Trees are found right here, focused with greatest intensity on the crest of Grapevine Mesa.

Joshua Trees do exist elsewhere. There is the Joshua Tree National Monument in California, as well as Anza-Borrego State Park, and another area, the Joshua Forest Parkway along Highway 93 northwest of Phoenix. Some sparse stands are reportedly still present and scattered in the Mediterranean area. None of these, however, can challenge the quality and impressiveness of the Joshua Tree Forest on Grapevine Mesa.

Why, then, has this Forest been so little known for so long? Perhaps more importantly, why has it not been given more protection? For one, Grapevine Mesa is at "the end of the road," a 40-mile long dead-end road. Then there is popular Grand Canyon National Park to our east, long a common destination for sightseers. Las Vegas, the party-place of the nation, is just to the west. We are somewhat in "no-man's land" in a vast middle (which I've always found highly desirable).

In addition to the remoteness of its location, protection of this forest has long been a problem due to land ownership issues. As touched upon briefly before, the railroad corporations in our nation were originally given, for free (i.e. corporate welfare), every other section of land (640 acres each) in much of our entire western landscape, this to provide incentives so the corporations would expand their rail lines. This was a humungous "give away," not to mention, these gifted sections were often not located anywhere near where railroad tracks were ever planned to go, and still don't. The railroad corporations then sold off many sections to land developers, making 100% profit, so those sections of lands soon

Splendor on the Mesa

became privately-owned. One such area lays here on Grapevine Mesa, long a checkerboard of land ownership, this being the main factor that has created major hurdles for both agencies having jurisdiction over public-owned lands in our area, the National Park Service and Bureau of Land Management, and in their continued attempts to provide protective status for this most unique Forest.

Regarding the historical human significance of the Joshua Forest, although many details were provided in previous chapters, I will reiterate just a short summary here. The Old Ute Trail came down from the north and crossed the Colorado River in the area of what we now call Pearce's Ferry (i.e. the Old Ute Crossing), with both ancient and historic tribes using this as their main route around the western end of Grand Canyon, this route then continuing south up Grapevine Wash, with use of Grapevine Springs, Grass Springs, and other springs in the area, while the Natives hunted, camped, and harvested in the land of this Joshua Tree Forest. The Spanish explorers (and perhaps Spanish miners) are on record as having used this same route, often for the despicable goal of slave-trading Indian children with the Utes in Utah. Then the Mormon wagon trains came through, as well as ranchers with their livestock. Euro-American miners used the route and dug for minerals almost everywhere in the area. And government survey crews from Kingman traveled the Joshua Forest and through Grapevine Wash when launching on the river at Pearce Ferry. Then came the 'tourist' component of the King Tut Ranch in the midst of the Forest. After that fisherman, river runners, and photographers have been amazed at the forest as they have traveled through and continued on to the lake for recreation. Grapevine Wash, Grass Springs, and the Joshua Tree Forest, and have long been both main thoroughfares and unique natural attractions in this area.

Mining and ranching were about the only industries that actually took hold in this remote part of northwest Arizona, including here in our Joshua Forest. Mining, in particular, was, and continues to be, very destructive to the land and many great trees on the west side of Pearce Ferry Road have been damaged and removed due to mining ("mining" includes gravel pits, these classified as placer mining). Fortunately, no big mineral deposits were actually found east of Pearce Ferry Road where the heart of the Forest is located. However, land developers also came, individual lots were quickly developed, and far more Joshua Trees were destroyed than should have been during construction of both roads and homes. Then, in the 1990's, the Hualapai Tribe came up with the plan to run a much wider hard-surfaced road through the heart of the forest, this to provide tour bus access up to their new development on the south rim, Grand Canyon West, which took out even more of the great old trees. Then concerned citizens on the mesa began pushing, once again, for more protection for the Great Old Forest.

During previous decades, various protection efforts were attempted. In 1967, the National Park Service designated an area involved in the Forest as the "Joshua Tree Forest National Natural Landmark." Then in the early 1990's, the Bureau of Land Management gave this an "Area of Critical Environmental Concern" designation, which included the previous NNL along with an additional larger area and gave special management to the protection of resources within those

The Joshua Tree Forest

boundaries. However, local citizens also were aware this still left the Forest with fragile and inadequate protection. Again, the checkerboard land ownership in the area has caused huge jurisdictional issues.

In September, 1979, Michael Kliemann, Resource Specialist for the Bureau of Land Management office in Kingman, Arizona, completed an in-depth study of this Joshua Tree Forest, one entitled, *A Review of the Natural Values of the Hualapai Valley Joshua Tree Forest: An Examination of the Appropriateness of Current Protective Measures at the Site; and Various Recommendations Aimed at Improving Protection of the Resource.* Although this is titled the "Hualapai Valley Joshua Tree Forest," it refers to and includes the most impressive part of the forest extending northerly onto Grapevine Mesa. Due to the importance of Kliemann's excellent report, I will include a number of excerpts here:[1]

> In April of 1930, the public lands within a four township area on Grapevine Mesa were included within a National Monument Withdrawal under executive order. These withdrawn lands contained the best Joshua Tree stands known. The problems of 'checkerboard' land ownership; privately-owned sections interspersed with government-owned lands, effectively foreclosed opportunities to bring the National Monument into reality in a period when National Park Service (NPS) acquisition funds were low.
>
> Since that time the area was again considered for various other protective designations, but none of these initiatives resulted in the acquisition of the extensive private in-holdings, thus the area remained without any official designation until 1967. In April of 1967, after another evaluation by the National Park Service initiated in 1966, certain sections of land containing the very best Joshua Tree Forest were declared a National Natural Landmark. The landmark site in 1979 still has no officially set boundaries and thus remains non-registered due to the complicated mix of land ownership.
>
> In 1968 the NPS again studied the area for possible National Monument status and various boundary proposal alternatives were made. To date, there has been no such National Monument established. The biennial status reports made of the landmark site by NPS, including the 1979 report made by Heritage Conservation and Recreation Service, stressed the need for definitive action aimed at 'blocking up' federal ownership of the forest and pointed to the attrition of natural values of the site.
>
> In April of 1970, the BLM held a public hearing on the classification of certain public lands (23, 239) in the north Hualapai Valley (within an area of Joshua Tree concentration) for retention of the same 'for multiple use management' purposes or for eventual disposal to private ownership. At that time, there arose great public support for the retention option, with many of the public and local governing bodies supporting various state park and/or national monument proposals for the 3,000-5,000 acres comprising the most outstanding areas of Joshua Tree Forest.

Splendor on the Mesa

As a result of the public support for the retention of these areas and because of the inherent values of the interesting region, the BLM did classify these lands for retention for multiple use purposes.

Most recently, as part of its ongoing Natural History Resource Management program, the BLM was directed by Congress to conduct an inventory of the Hualapai Valley National Natural Landmark and surrounding lands to study the appropriateness of the existing boundary and to 'initiate preplanning for interim protection of values which qualify for inclusion in the Landmark System.' The following report addresses these directives ...

... Quite probably, much visitation within the area of the study is incidental to the prime focus of visitor interest: Lake Mead National Recreation Area, lying to the north and west of the 'forest.' Access to several popular boat put-in sites is by way of Pierce Ferry Road, which passes through the prime portion of this Joshua Tree Forest.

The Joshua Forest does have local and regional recognition. Area Chambers of Commerce as well as other local groups have, from time to time, pressed for the preservation of the Joshua Forest in a protective classification such as a National Monument.

The area is popular with landscape and nature photographers, especially when the Joshuas are in bloom. Though easily accessible, the rather isolated location of this 'forest' decreases the visitation potential ...

... Residential use, throughout this region and within the area covered by the study, is almost all associated with the existence of the remote subdivisions developed there during the last two decades. The Lake Mead Land and Water Company has three sections of land within the study area which contain active subdivisions in varying stages of settlement. These developments have attracted mostly retired couples. Most of the homesteads built to date are very near, the owners having apparently left standing most of the Joshuas in their respective lots.

The commendable stewardship evidenced by most owners in these developments contrasts greatly with the wide, invaryingly straight roads pushed through the forest by the land company. No attempt has apparently been made to eliminate the windrows of bulldozed Joshua trees pushed to the side of these roads during their construction.

The residents are very protective of the Joshua Forest and many voiced hope to this author that the forest be given protection. None of the area residents questioned were aware of the twelve and one-half year old National Natural Landmark designation on lands adjacent to their own. When asked their opinion concerning possible active government protection of the adjacent lands, several decried governmental 'landgrab' and the possible expropriation of their homesites.

Kliemann's study discussed the ineffectiveness of the present National Natural Landmark status and recommended the area either be designated a Research Natural Area, or an Area of Critical Environmental Concern, both of which would grant slightly more protection. He also suggested giving plaques of recognition to private land owners who agreed to maintain the status-quo of the lands involved. He then commented, "Timely protection for the Hualapai Valley Joshua Tree Forest is imperative. Conservation of the resource and perpetuation of its many extraordinary values can best be effected through the alternatives discussed (RNA or ACEC)."

During the 1980's, under orders from Congress, BLM again reviewed its administered lands in order to pick out unique and picturesque areas with consideration of appropriateness that these be set aside as Wilderness Areas. The term "Wilderness Area," however, was actually misleading for much of the public since in nearly all such areas, cattle, horses, and sheep would continue to graze, hunting and trapping would continue, as well as horseback riding and hiking. Much mining that had already been taking place on those lands would often also be grandfathered in. Old trails would remain, however, new road building would not be allowed, thus future vehicular travel minimized. "Wilderness Area," therefore, did not represent "true wilderness," as many environmentalists would have preferred, but instead, simply put restrictions on new road construction, new mining, and motorized travel in those places from such designation forward. So although "wilderness area" designations frightened many locals in western states and eventually led to the creation of a so-called "wise use" movement to fight such action, to many others the very same designation was considered diluted and incredibly inadequate. Thus, "Wilderness Area" designation became, at best, simply a compromise for many.

That said, then during the late 1980's, several local citizens and state environmental groups requested that an area encompassing the face of the Grand Wash Cliffs and visible foothills down to the eastern edge of Grapevine Wash, and also sections near Lake Mead City containing dense growths of Joshua Trees, be placed under Wilderness designation by BLM. This plan had been carefully drawn to still retain the historic route allowing vehicular travel within the entire length of Grapevine Wash (in contrast to rumors spread to the contrary by opposition), as well as along Diamond Bar Road and up to the Reservation and viewpoint at Ramparts Overlook.

In a BLM booklet I had located and previously made public about areas to be considered "Wilderness" in Mohave County, one reason the BLM gave for NOT recommending such designation for our Grand Wash Cliffs, themselves, was said to be "due to a possible open-pit mineral mine projected there for the future." This area of possible mining interest was described to be "located in the foothills at the base of the cliffs and extend up the face to the top" (with map locations showing the general area known to locals as the "dryfall", readily visible from Meadview).

Splendor on the Mesa

When queried further about this potential mine site, Bob Harrison, Mining Specialist at that time for BLM in Kingman, stated flatly to both myself and others present, that there "was no mineral potential" in the Grand Wash Cliffs and that the information on the mine was just "thrown in" to that booklet (for what reason, he never explained, although presumably to justify not recommending the Cliffs as a wilderness area). Other Kingman area BLM employees also dismissed any concern over this issue, perhaps influenced by Harrison's assertion.

From research done for this book, however, I found three different historic sources[2,3,4] designating that mineral deposits did exist in that area of the Grand Wash Cliffs and on top the plateau and all of those sources were readily available to Bob Harrison as the Mining Specialist at BLM, particularly the Schroder book referenced that had served as the "bible" for Mohave County miners for decades. I copied and relayed this information from Schroders book to Harrison at the BLM office in Kingman but received no response; then, of course, soon learned that Bob Harrison had left BLM and was freelancing as a consultant for mining companies in the area.

However, since the request for wilderness designation of the Grand Wash Cliffs and Joshua Trees was just one of many that was submitted to Congress for consideration, this area was not considered as critical enough to be chosen when final decisions were made, so was passed over yet again. In Mohave County, Mt. Tipton, in the Cerbat Mountain Range to the south, was given Wilderness designation, along with Waubayuma Peak in the Southern Hualapai Mountains.

In 1990, BLM took another look at the Joshua Forest, itself, and issued a report, *Hualapai Valley National Natural Landmark* (available at Kingman area BLM office). Since the Joshua Forest had not been given wilderness protection, other options were again considered.

In this report the negative effects of over-grazing were noted, especially around the corrals and water sources, and recommendations were made to not allow an increase of stock levels for grazing, with consideration even given to a possible decrease of livestock permit numbers. It was also noted that commercial plant collecting or harvesting permits should become totally prohibited, as, unbelievably, BLM had actually been allowing harvesting of limited Joshua Trees as well as other plants in the area.

Further important statements to note from this BLM report:

> The scenery quality of the Grapevine Mesa/Grand Wash Cliffs area is considered to be of Class A caliber by the BLM which rated these and other areas as part of the Unit Resource Analysis for the Cerbat Planning Unit. Indeed, the strikingly unconventional, yet severely simple forms of the Joshua Forest, coupled with the massively layered backdrop of the Grand Wash Cliffs, are an unusual coupling of landscape elements. Tightly and repetitiously organized, the stiff and pointed leaves of the Yucca Brevifolia contrast with the curved sweep of its upturned branches. Red, maroon, dark brown, and buff, the colorful regularly occurring layers of the Grand Canyon series outcrop with nearly horizontal regularity in the nearby Grand Wash

The Joshua Tree Forest

Cliffs. From overlooks on Pierce Ferry Road (T29N, R17W, Sec. 26 and 35) the view across the forest to the cliffs beyond is presently impacted but minimally, man caused visual intrusions are few....

... The Joshua Forest at the south end of Grapevine Mesa (Hualapai Valley) is important as widespread, knowledgeable opinion and present landmark status point to this resource's 'more-than-local' significance. The inherent natural qualities of the locale as discussed previously, and the uncommon and striking combination of natural elements, all point to the importance of the site.

Another aspect of the areas importance is the wide spectrum of age classes represented within the forest here. Natural regeneration is vigorous throughout the forest. Most other notable Mohavian concentrations of this species have not been generally observed to equal this locale's vigorous regeneration. Most other stands are seemingly in a static or declining condition. Perhaps it would be important to know the particulars of this difference in natural regeneration between various Joshua stands otherwise similarly situated.

In conclusion, this particular report recommends once again that either Research Natural Area (RNA) or Area of Critical Environmental Concern (ACEC) designation be granted to the area. Presently (1990) it is unknown whether the Kingman BLM office has taken any action on these more recent recommendations from within their own department. The NPS also again expressed sincere interest in the Joshua Forest, but lack of acquisition funds still did not allow significant action from that agency.

BLM did recently incorporate another new project previously mentioned in the Gold Butte chapter, this called the "Backcountry Byway" program, one initiated during the Reagan administration and tied into an effort to increase tourism. Every state was asked to identify roads other than well-traveled highways that would be interesting for people to travel. In the southwest, this often meant country gravel roads and sometimes even remote four-wheel drive roads.

In Mohave County, the ridge road going south along the top of Hualapai Mountains was under consideration as a Backcountry Byway; also, the Alamo Road south of the Hualapai Mountains, as well as old route 66 going through Oatman. The fourth prospect was the Diamond Bar Ranch Road branching off Pearce Ferry Road that travels through some of the most dense and picturesque areas of the Joshua Tree Forest here on Grapevine Mesa, passes on through the old Grass Springs Ranch/Diamond Bar Ranch/Smith Ranch home site, then winds through Grapevine Canyon to eventually reach the top of the plateau. There the road splits, with one branch going to the Hualapai Reservation to the east (toward the newly proposed Grand Canyon West development) and the other, at times barely a jeep trail, winds around to the northwest and eventually (if one doesn't take a wrong turn toward the cliff's edge too soon) comes to the very top-most edge of the Grand Wash Cliffs at Ramparts Overlook where one can park right on

Splendor on the Mesa

the overlook, itself (a special treat for elderly or handicapped who cannot hike). Having a picnic, or better, spending the night in that spot, is truly something for memories. For reasons unknown, however, neither was this road chosen as a scenic Backcountry Byway.

One early morning I was up at the Ramparts overlook, exploring leisurely around to see if I could locate a viable route for hiking down off the cliffs some fine day, and back to Meadview. I finally found a take-off spot that looked good, although anyone who has hiked the area knows that what might appear to be a good route from far above, can quickly become blocked by unforeseeable dryfalls or cliff walls farther down. The one that appeared viable here was on the far side of the high butte situated along the rim just north of the Ramparts Overlook parking area. I began exploring the downward route and eventually, to my surprise, found an amazingly easy 'stair step' route that seemed to go all the way down the cliffs. I kept going, and before long, arrived down in Grapevine Wash. From there I strolled on by the Lucky Seven Corral, up onto the mesa to Meadview, and, in short order, through my front door in time for noon lunch. The only difficulty being, when Don returned home after dark from a long day of rescuing boaters on the lake, we then had to make the lengthy drive back up on top the cliffs to the overlook to retrieve the abandoned Jeep. We arrived on the rim again around midnight and found the jeep resting quietly there, happily overlooking its vast and grand fiefdom far below.

That dramatic and awe-inspiring overlook, Rampart, was named after the barren peak just to the south of the parking area. The peak, a U.S. Geological Service triangulation station, was used extensively during surveys over decades past and has a bench mark imbedded on its highest point. The marker reads "Ramparts," and is designated as such on most USGS topographical maps, this term meaning a high point or overlook from which to protect or defend. The spectacular view from this point encompasses not only all of Grapevine Mesa below, but the entire sprawling expanse of eastern Lake Mead, west clear beyond Las Vegas, Nevada, as well as the southern arm of the Virgin Mountain Range in Nevada, and far north into Arizona Strip country.

Katherine Rhode, Chief Interpreter for LMNRA for years, wrote of the Mojave Desert in the March/April 1991 issue of *Nevada* magazine. To quote a few of her eloquent passages:

> Contrasts ... this is the Mojave Desert. In a world that is busy, hectic, polluted, and growing smaller, the Mojave Desert gives the feeling of timelessness, clarity, solitude, and space...

> ... The Mojave is a land of solitude. It is not difficult to find a space in the desert where for miles there is not another soul. The wind whistles through the creosote. A lizard scoots across the sand, leaving tiny tracks. A cactus wren sings, unseen in her fortress of cactus spines. This is solitude. This is the magic of the Mojave again, because you are alone, but not lonely. The Mojave is timeless.

The Joshua Tree Forest

Traveling through Joshua Forest, 1989

Splendor on the Mesa

Author, standing under one of the large Joshua Trees, photo by Sharon Baur, 2011

The Joshua Tree Forest

Joshua Tree fruit, 1990

Joshua Tree in bloom

Chapter Eighteen: Public Lands

(1990 … with a few update notations from 2014)

Today, public-owned lands comprise vast areas of the western landscape. Historically, these had been left in government ownership because they were considered by settlers to be "worthless" with little ranching potential, and no one wanted to actually purchase or own these vast areas and have to pay taxes on them. Yet many ranchers, miners, and foresters still wanted to be able to use and cheaply "lease" these lands and especially the resources upon them. Consequently, there has long been great tension regarding how these lands should and can be used. By far the majority of Public Land areas in the west remain under the jurisdiction of the Bureau of Land Management and the National Forest Service, these departments under the Department of Agriculture, and most of these lands are classified as "multiple use." Most National Park Service lands (this agency administered under the Department of the Interior), on the other hand, allow some multiple-use, although not nearly to the extent as BLM or NFS lands. Since multiple-use is by far the most commonly implemented administrative policies on public lands of the west, some explanations follow that will illustrate what can and cannot be done on most of those lands as of 1990.

Ranchers have long leased federal public lands for minimal fees and allowed livestock to range over immense areas. Meanwhile, as private individuals, if you purchase a lot, even on privately-owned land in a developed community such as Meadview or Dolan Springs, in order to keep the rancher's cattle off your property, you must pay to fence your own lot. If a rancher's cow walks in front of your car on a dark night on Pearce Ferry Road (no fencing on 'open-range'), you will not only have to pay for your own car/injuries, but also pay the rancher for his cow. If a range bull attacks you when you're out hiking on public lands and you have to shoot the animal in self-defense, you must pay the rancher for the loss of that animal. Antiquated open-range laws relieve ranchers of responsibility for damages their cattle cause to you, your children, your car, your pets, or your property, not to mention, damage to the very public lands themselves.

"Multiple-use" category allows hunting on many of these lands, some hunts being controlled with the sale of permits by Game and Fish Departments, although many predators (long considered worthless "varmints") can be hunted and killed in many places with no regulation or seasons at all. Trapping is also allowed. Trappers obtain permits and then hide deadly traps almost anywhere during the November to March trapping season. These traps take lives indiscriminately and trapping regulations established by respective state Game and Fish Departments (that receive income from trappers) are ridiculously lax on public lands. Hidden traps are usually baited with lures, either foods, urine scents, or other strong odors, that attract dogs, cats, birds, and any other domestic or wild animal that happens along. A person cannot themselves safely walk, nor take the family dog out for a stroll, or even the grandchildren, and go safely up a wash or out to harvest a permitted Christmas tree, without danger. Should a person or a pet inadvertently step into a trap (as has happened numerous times), not only can injury occur, but the Arizona Game and Fish Department has actually threatened to press charges against such persons, claiming they were at fault for having "disturbed" the hidden traps. Hidden booby traps lurk everywhere, and sadly, even on Lake Mead Recreation Area lands where one would least expect to find them. Yet, unbelievably, trapping on public lands remains perfectly legal.

Even worse, if cattlemen, sheepmen or agribusinessmen suspect that coyotes, wolves, bears, or mountain lions might be killing unsupervised livestock ranging somewhere out in those hills on public-owned lands, they can call in Animal Damage Control (now in 2014, euphemistically called "Wildlife Services") also long known as "government trappers," at any time of the year and have them kill predators in the area with traps, poisons, fires in dens, shooting, or by whatever means possible. Government trappers are allowed to function in total disregard of time period requirements for checking traps, of birthing or nursing seasons of wild creatures, or any of the already inadequate State Game and Fish regulations that exist regarding trapping. This takes place on many BLM and Forest Service public-owned lands year around and also on many Recreation Area public lands. And the services of these "government trappers" are paid for by you and me ... OUR tax dollars are used to pay for killing OUR wildlife on OUR public-owned lands.

To quote some figures from "The Killing Fields" by Zoe Loftus-Farren, featured in the Spring 2014 issue of *Earth Island Journal*:

> In 2012 alone, this agency and its contractors killed 300,000 red-winged blackbirds, 76,000 coyotes, 567 black bears, 396 cougars, among thousands of other animals .... During the past five years, Wildlife Services had killed an estimated 1.5 million animals annually, including coyotes, foxes, wolves, prairie dogs, river otters, and grey wolves, to name just a few. Some of those animals are endangered and threatened species. Roughly 52,000 'non-target animals' have been killed during the past ten years.

Fortunately, now in 2014, there is growing recognition by many that state wildlife management agencies need a major overhaul, as also does the USDA Wildlife Services which was originally set up to serve the interests of ranchers and agribusiness and has operated pretty much without regulation or transparency for over one hundred years.

"Multiple-use" allows mining, lots of mining, practically anywhere and everywhere. The out-dated and antiquated old "1872 Mining Law" is still in effect, kept so by mining corporations and lobbyists. This law literally ties the hands of BLM and Forest Service employees so even if desired, they are usually unable to properly regulate and limit destruction caused by most mining on our public lands. On Recreation Area lands administered by NPS, however, more discretion for staff is allowed and some districts have been closed to mining, others kept open only to prospecting by individuals. Thankfully, only a few mining operations are still allowed within LMNRA boundaries.

"Multiple-use" allows extensive harvesting of trees in our National Forests by privately-owned/corporate-owned lumber companies. Never mind that unbelievable quantities of harvested trees from our public lands end up in Japan and other far-away countries. And, permits have long been sold by BLM for the harvesting of cactus of all kinds from our area, at times even including Joshua Trees.

"Multiple-use" allows vehicles not only on the incredibly vast network of already-existing back roads (most put in decades ago for the benefit of mining, forestry, and ranching industries), but, in addition, on many BLM and Forest Service lands, access is often even allowed in the majority of washes and open country. Such vehicles range from pickup trucks to dune buggies, four-wheel drive jeeps to all-terrain vehicles, and motorcycles to mountain bikes. These are capable of going almost anywhere off established roads and often do, destroying sensitive desert soils and wildlife habitat in the process. More restrictions do exist on this regard on NPS Recreation Area lands where no off-road travel is allowed and only certain back roads are designated for excursions.

And as present-day human populations have increased and moved west, "multiple-use" has also come to mean; picnickers, day hikers, back packers, explorers, bird watchers, photographers and more. It means fisherman, boaters, water skiers, jet skiers, scuba divers, swimmers, and nearly any other imaginable water use. It means more water needs for land developments, more irrigation needs for corporate farmers, and more energy needs for fast growing metropolises.

Historically, the mining, ranching and forestry industries totally dominated public land use policies across the western states. Even today, many back country travelers exploring remote areas of public lands are often made to feel as though they are somehow trespassing when approached by a rancher or miner. Some confrontations are outright antagonistic while others are more subtle, often masked in the form of neighborly interest, yet nearly always one is placed in a position of feeling obligated to explain who they are and why they are there on those public-owned lands.

Yet things are changing dramatically. More people with many more diverse interests are discovering the intermountain and desert west. Recreational activities have increased immensely, along with money spent on those activities, and in our society, money talks. It talks not only to local communities and businesses, but also to state and federal agencies, and certainly to politicians. Recreational users have come to realize that they, also, have weight to throw around and have come to demand a larger share of the "user" pie.

As a result, more conflicts are now occurring between all of these many varied groups who want use of the public lands. Federal land agencies are having to adopt entirely different perspectives than in the past, often trying to balance on a tightrope in order to serve the needs of everyone as best possible, not an enviable situation. No matter what action is taken, few of the many varied user-groups are happy, and certainly not those who have begun to feel their previously powerful hold over public land uses slipping away.

Splendor on the Mesa

National Parks, however, control smaller and more isolated public land areas and are managed with a different mandate, yet with their own share of inherent problems. "Multiple-use" is not the guiding principle on those lands, but rather there are dual goals, ones sometimes in direct conflict. One is to insure the preservation of natural resources within (including wildlife, as well as lands and waters), and the other, to also provide means for visitors to see and experience many of those resources. Overwhelming visitor populations have impacted some parks adversely, as have growing numbers of scenic planes, recreational boats, every make and kind of vehicle, and these have at times had devastating effects upon our parks and the ability of park personnel to provide a fine "Park Experience" for visitors.

Our perceptions of the public lands have surely begun to alter with the passage of time. In addition, the health of the natural environment has increasingly become a vital concern for many, this followed by an increasing awareness of the need to protect the remaining lands that still lay within the public domain. Inevitably, the public lands will certainly become the most valued lands of all.

While compiling this "deep map," this in-depth look at what has existed here over the long passage of time, one cannot help but have increasing concern for what the future might hold for this entire precious landscape.

Epiloque: 2014

Here it is, almost 25 years from the time I finished the initial research work for this manuscript and how so many things have changed. A big one is that while doing the original work, I had no access to the internet. Today one can do internet searches and find video tours on topics such as exploring Arizona's mines, comparing past and present Lake Mead water levels, taking visual tours of Grand Canyon and river running through the canyon. The armchair traveler has an amazing variety of low-impact ways to explore and research today, which could actually be a good thing for the health of this land.

Another huge factor, Lake Mead levels have dropped drastically since I explored this area during the 1980's. Lower water and re-emerging and dangerous rapids below the mouth of the canyon have greatly restricted boating access into the spectacular Lower Granite Gorge of Grand Canyon, this closing off one of the huge attractions for both residents and visitors at the upper end of Lake Mead. Pearce Ferry landing no longer has water and a road has been built across the mud flats so River Runners exiting the canyon can rig out there. Everything on the lake and river looks very different now. It's been interesting to see that some old sites previously underwater in the 1980's and that I'd read about extensively, are now beginning to re-appear. This lowering of Lake Mead, of course, carries huge implications for the sprawling megalopolis's downstream that depend on the Colorado River for water; Las Vegas and Phoenix, even some for Los Angeles. As for me, I've found it oddly comforting to see the Colorado River returning at least somewhat to its former ancient self.

I would like to mention two contemporary mapping errors that have recently begun showing up on several maps of this area, both involving critical historical sites, so worthy of note. The first is on the 2008 version of the "Approved Backcountry Roads" hand-out created by park personnel at Lake Mead National Recreation Area. On the specific map section showing Grapevine Mesa and upper Lake Mead, the entire drainage of the lengthy and historically important Grapevine Wash that parallels Grapevine Mesa and lies between there and the Grand Wash Cliffs, has been misnamed on this map as "Grapevine Canyon." In all the historical references and maps I ever found, this large drainage was always called Grapevine Wash, never Grapevine Canyon. The smaller side canyon from which Grapevine Springs flows and enters the larger Grapevine Wash, has always been called Grapevine Springs Canyon. The only reference I've seen in this area to simply a "Grapevine Canyon," is the side canyon followed by the Diamond Bar Road from Grass Springs and up to the Hualapai Indian Reservation on top the Grand Wash Cliffs. Perhaps due to the error on this LMNRA Backcountry Approved Roads Map, the 2010 version of the Benchmark Company published "Arizona Road and Recreation Atlas" that's widely marketed, also now shows this error. Once made, map errors are difficult to get corrected.

The second error is on the large 2002 version of the Bureau of Land Management map available at the BLM office in Kingman, this featuring the north half of Kingman Area District. On this map the name of the important old historic site of Tinaka/Grass Springs has been moved south, with the "Tanaka Springs" name attached to a completely different springs up in Iron Basin. Perhaps this other significant error occurred because there is a benchmark high on Iron Mountain called "Tinaka" and this was shown on some older maps as surveyors placed them at benchmarks on high points, often naming them after significant sites nearby. All previous references I found, both historical and in maps, have Tinaka or Grass Springs right where Wellington Starkey first established Grass Springs Ranch, later to become the Diamond Bar/Smith Ranch and what is now known as Grand Canyon Ranch, a contemporary tourist development.

Certainly there have been many changes in land use policies during the last twenty-five years. Arizona voters passed a referendum to forbid trapping on public-owned lands, a big "thumbs up" to the voters ... not to the Arizona Game and Fish Department that fought this effort every inch of the way for years. New attitudes and efforts are also evolving within BLM about multiple-use issues, especially regarding better preservation of the designated critical areas under their management. And as noted in the 'Public Lands' section, recently there has been growing recognition by many that state wildlife management agencies need a major overhaul, as also does the USDA Wildlife Services which was originally set up to serve the interests of ranchers and agribusiness and has operated pretty much without regulation or transparency for over one hundred years. Let's hope that gets done soon.

In the mid-1990's, a powerful flash flood charged down Grapevine Springs Canyon from Grapevine Mesa and changed much of the exceptional beauty in this canyon. The flood took out at least one of the huge ponds along with many water lilies, reeds, and altered other aspects. Parts of the Signature Wall crumbled down, although many signatures can still be found if one climbs up close to the remaining sections of the wall. The Park Service has also fenced off the entrance to this canyon in order to keep ATVs and livestock out, providing a walk-through to allow hikers to enter, with native deer and bighorn and other wildlife still accessing the springs and creek from along the ledges. The path entering is now often overgrown and a bit difficult since cattle are no longer clearing away the underbrush and debris, however, it is for the best in the long run. The canyon will surely re-vitalize itself in time, just as it always has.

Park Service now has installed another fence extending across the larger historic Grapevine Wash, this barrier just below the side entrance to Grapevine Springs Canyon, also providing only a walk-through gate. This was reportedly necessary as local ATVs were running through the wash drainage and down to the lake, but were also being recklessly driven up on benches and other areas where off-roading was neither desirable nor legal. Because of the thoughtless and careless actions of those ATV'ers, now no one can drive down to the lake on that old historic thoroughfare.

LMNRA has also found it necessary, mainly for liability purposes, to close most of the mine entrances in the area, both shafts and tunnels, and to remove old

Epilogue: 2014

partially-standing buildings from such sites. More windows to adventure closed. Sadly, the ladder leading up to the Bat Cave entrance in Grand Canyon also had to be removed. Inevitable, I suppose. The more popular our public lands become, the more Public Land Agencies get sued. This, all while funding sources for public agencies have been continually cut.

Elmer Duffield's "pioneer home" that he built by hand, sitting alongside Pearce Ferry Road and across from the lake overlook in Meadview, was taken over by NPS personnel after Elmer's death (as per previous buy-out agreement) and this was made into the South Cove Ranger Station ... although during recent years, few people ever find it open or find any park personnel accessible there for visitors, nor with any local phone number posted to contact. Apparently long gone are the days when the locally-assigned National Park Ranger was readily accessible not only by both office and home phone, but also at his front door, 24/7, as when we served there in the 70's and 80's. Those days certainly no longer exist.

Park Service administrators have been debating, due to deterioration of one part of the Duffield home and other factors, if they should simply tear down Elmer's old place and put up a new office. Several of the Grand Canyon and Lake Mead NPS boats and vehicles are now parked in and near new storage buildings at the site.

The Hualapai Tribe has succeeded in having development projects for "Grand Canyon West" built and fully operating on the south rim of Grand Canyon at the site of the old Bat Cave Tower, as well as on nearby Quartermaster Viewpoint. They bring in helicopter tours that buzz crazily down into western Grand Canyon, whiz over boaters on the river, land down in Quartermaster Canyon, itself, as well as on sand bars on the river, and activity goes on constantly at buildings and tourist settings up on the rim. I visited there once when development was in its initial stages and was sickened at the contrast between this and the beautiful solitude and quiet that had reigned there previous. I have never gone back again.

Lastly, but certainly not least, a few years ago, interest again surfaced in renewed efforts to try yet again to secure better protection for the exquisite Joshua Tree Forest on the mesa. Partly this re-birthed because of the Hualapai Tribe's desire to widen and hard-surface a better road through the forest so tour buses from Las Vegas could bring numerous busloads of visitors up to their new tourist development on the south rim above. Impacts from this road widening and the additional traffic were definitely bad for the Forest. Yet, BLM, to their credit, had also been quietly working to trade a few sections of land in the Lake Mead City area in order to consolidate more of the boundary around the Forest and make that ACEC more viable. Residents have also grown more concerned about new ATV trails showing up, these winding through the trees.

A number of locals have joined together and formed "Friends of Joshua Tree Forest" (joshuatreeforest.org) and members of this group are devoting a great deal of time and effort into bringing awareness to both locals and the visiting public about the uniqueness and great value of this Forest, and of the BLM designation of the "Area of Critical Environmental Concern" that has been given this site.

Splendor on the Mesa

Their goal is to continue with these efforts and keep pushing for better protections for the Joshua Tree Forest in the future. Another big "Thumbs up!"

I left the mesa in 1990. However, for me, Grapevine Mesa has been, and will always remain, my "Magic Mesa of the Great Southwest."

> ... *There Was a Time Before Life ....Then, today, the earth took in her first mighty gasp and breathed out sea creatures of delicate simplicity. Reptiles walked for hours. Mammals followed by minutes. And Man... still locked inside his first second ... remains less than one heartbeat old."* (by D. Suzanne Wanatee-Buffalo)

Endnotes

For more details on authors and works noted, refer to further information in Bibliography section following.

Chapter One: Remote Beginnings

1. Huyghe, Patrick, *Columbus Was Last*, 1992, Chapter One, "First Americans"; Wells, Spencer, *Pandora's Seed: The Unforeseen Cost of Civilization*, 2010, p. 15, 103; Loewen, James, *Lies My Teacher Told Me*, 1996.

2. Grounds, John Cureton, *Trail Dust of the Southwest*, 1977, p. 157.

Chapter Two: The Paiute

1. Inter-tribal Council of Nevada, *Nuwuvi: A Southern Paiute History*, 1976.

2. Snow, William, "Utah Indians and Spanish Slave Trade," *Utah Historical Quarterly*, Vol. 2, #3, July, 1929, P. 69.

3. Jones, Daniel, *Forty Years Among the Indians*, Bookcraft, Salt Lake City, p. 47.

4. Palmer, William, "Indian Slavery on the Old Spanish Trail," manuscript, as drawn from the Leroy and Ann Hafen article regarding the Old Spanish Trail in Historical Series, The Far West and The Rockies 1820-1875, Vol. 1, 1954, p. 263, 281.

5. Fairley, Helen, and Altschul, Jeffrey, *Man, Models, and Management; An Overview of the Arizona Strip*, p.160, 1989.

6. Larsen, Gustive, *Journal of the Iron County Mission*, as quoted in *Nuwuvi*, p. 60.

7. "History of Brigham Young," manuscript, May 13, 1851, as quoted in *Nuwuvi*, p. 66.

8. Ibid., p. 67

9. Ibid., p. 67, 68

10. Stoffle, Richard, and Evans, Michael, *Kaibab Paiute History, the Early Years*, 1978, p. 21.

Endnotes

Chapter Three: The Hualapai

1. Euler, Robert C., *Walapai Culture-History*, 1958, p. 176, 178, 238

2. *Trails, Rails, and Tales*, Kingman Centennial Committee, 1981, p. 196

3. Ibid., p. 196

4. Euler, Robert, *The Walapai People*, 1976, p. 60, 61

5. *Trails, Rails, and Tales*, p. 198.

6. Malach, Roman, *Peach Springs*, 1975, p. 45.

7. Ibid., p. 19.

8. Ibid., p. 46.

9. *Trails, Rails, and Tales*, 1981, p. 201.

10. Purcell, Roy, *Long Journey from Wikame*, 1988, Las Vegas, NV.

Chapter Four: Trade Routes and Inroads

1. Casebier, Dennis, *Camp Beale's Springs and the Hualapai Indians*, 1980, and *The Mohave Road and Other Desert Trails* 1870's map.

2. Schroeder, Albert, *The Archeological Excavations at Willow Beach*, AZ., 1950, paper on file at LMNRA Headquarters, Boulder City, NV.

3. Smith, Melvin, *The Colorado River: It's History in the Lower Canyon Area*, PHD dissertation for University of Utah, 1972, p. 15, 16, 45-51, 103-114, 121, 122.

Chapter Five: Pearce's Ferry

1. Smith, Melvin, *The Colorado River: It's History in the Lower Canyon Area*, PHD Dissertation for University of Utah, 1972. Smith did excellent research on stories of various historic Mormon activities and river crossings in the Pearce Ferry area, and in this chapter I relied heavily on information from his fine work and quoted some stories he related. Additionally, some information was also drawn from the *Historic Resources Study* done for NPS in 1980, by Belshaw, Michael, and Peplow Jr., Ed, this on file at LMNRA Headquarters, Boulder City.

2. Sadovich, Maryellen, "Brother Pearce Ferried Mormons into Arizona," *Las Vegas Review-Journal*; Nevadan section, Sept. 14, 1986, p. 12 cc.

Endnotes

Chapter Six: Grigg's Ferry

1. Smith, Richard, several interviews with author, Chloride, AZ., 1987, and Charles Grigg, interview with author, Kingman, AZ., 1987.

2. Smith, Melvin, p. 410.

Chapter Seven: Bonelli's Ferry

1. Barnes, Will, *Arizona Place Names*, p. 203, 224, 1960.

2. Smith, Melvin, p. 113, footnote p. 54.

3. Ibid., p. 105.

4. Musser, Mamie, Notes from Amy Neal Collection, Mohave Museum, Kingman, AZ.

5. Thompson, Albert, "Those Early Days," *Sedona Westerners*, p. 61, 104.

6. Barnes, Will, *Arizona Place Names*, 1960, p. 203, 224.

Chapter Eight: Lower Granite Gorge

1. Kelley, Charles, "The Mysterious D. Julien," *Utah Historical Quarterly*, Vol. 6, #3, as quoted in *Mohave Museum Newsletter*, Vol. 248 and 249.

2. White, James, as quoted in *Mohave Museum Newsletter*, Vol. 250.

3. Powell, Major John Wesley, *The Exploration of the Colorado River and It's Canyons*, 1961, p. 284.

4. Smith, Melvin, p. 382.

5. Ibid., p. 15.

6. Ibid., p. 383.

7. Grounds, John Cureton, *Trail Dust of the Southwest*, 1977, p. 218.

8. Cox, Nellie Iverson, *Footprints on the Arizona Strip*, 1973, p. 84.

9. Ibid., 99-102.

10. Goudy, Karin, "Letter from Kingman – Nov. 1886," *Kingman Journal*, Nov. 1986.

11. *Grand Canyon National Park: A Photographic and Comprehensive Guide*, p. 68, 1977.

12. Cox, Nellie Iverson, *Footprints on the Arizona Strip*, 1973, p. 99-102.

Endnotes

13. *Grand Canyon National Park: A Photographic and Comprehensive Guide*, p. 84, 1977.

Chapter Nine: Shivwits Plateau

1. *Grand Canyon National Park: A Photographic and Comprehensive Guide*, p. 47, 1977.

2. Hafen, Lyman, "Three Who Dared," *Arizona Highways*, Sept. 1991, p. 13.

3. Belshaw, Michael, *Historic Resources Study*, p. 75-76, 163, 245.

4. Marston, Dock, "Separation Marks", 1972, p. 19.

5. *Arizona Highways*, April, 1986.

6. Butchart, Harvey, *Grand Canyon Treks II*, p. 33-34, and author's interview and correspondence with Butchart in 1985.

7. Esplin, Lola, her interview with Othole Milne, June, 1974.

8. Ibid., her interview with Ivy Stratton, May, 1974.

9. Fairley, Helen, et el, *Man, Models, and Management*, p. 208.

10. Howell as quoted in Hafner, Arabell Lee, *100 Years on the Muddy*, 1967, p. 132-139.

11. Malach, Roman, *Mohave County*, p. 127.

12. Mathis, Reed, interview with author, May, 1989, St. George, Utah.

13. Waring, Mary, interview with author, Feb., 1989, Flagstaff, Arizona.

14. Esplin, Buster and Lola, interview with author, 1988, Wildcat Ranch in Arizona Strip.

15. *Grand Canyon National Park: A Photographic and Comprehensive Guide*, p. 90, 1977.

16. Reed and others quoted in Cox, Mellie Iverson, *Footprints on the Arizona Strip*, 1973, p. 105-106.

17. Harris, Everett, interview with author, 1986, 1987, 1991, in Meadview and during explorations in the Arizona Strip back country.

Endnotes

Chapter Ten: Grand Wash

1. Martineau, LeVan, conversation with author after his presentation at Mohave Community College, March 25, 1987, Kingman, AZ.

2. Nay, Keith and Marlyn, interview with author, Oct., 1987, Nay Ranch.

3. Belshaw, Michael, *Historic Resources Study*, 1983, p. 163-165.

4. Hafner, Arabell Lee, *One Hundred Years on the Muddy*, 1967, p. 19.

5. Perkins, Chic, interview with author, 1988, Overton, NV.

6. Price, Edna Calkins, *Burro Bill and Me*, 1931, p. 94-95.

7. Allan, Del, interview with author, Jan., 1989, Las Vegas, NV.

8. Fauth, Bill, interview with author, June, 1986, Kingman, AZ.

9. Grounds, John Cureton, p. 214.

10. Price, Edna Caulkins, p. 92.

11. *Memories*, unpublished stories in possession of Nays, quoting Preston, p. 4.

12. Ibid., quoting Stewart, p. 36.

Chapter Eleven: Gold Butte

1. Hafner, Arabell Lee, *One Hundred Years on the Muddy*, 1967, quoting Howell, p. 136.

2. Haworth, Jim, interview with author, Moapa, NV, Dec., 1989.

3. Jensen, Rex, "Grand Gulch Trail Was Stuff of Legend," *Las Vegas Review-Journal*, Oct. 25, 1981, p. 6 J.

4. Bounsall, Ed, interview with author, Dec., 1989, Gold Butte.

5. Swisher, John, "The Magic of a Name," *Desert Life Magazine*, Aug. 1987, p.13.

Chapter Twelve: White Hills

1. Malach, Roman, *Mohave County*, p. 59.

2. Neal, Leonard, interview with author, July 1, 1986, Kingman, AZ.

3. Cameron, Bob, interview with author, May, 1990, White Hills, AZ.

4. Grounds, John Cureton, p. 144.

Endnotes

    5. Malach, Roman, *White Hills*, p. 51-55.

    6. Taylor, Paul, "Ghost of the White Hills," *Mohave*, Sept. 1984, p. 8.

    7. Grounds, John Cureton, p. 161.

    8. Malach, Roman, *Mohave County Place Names*, p. 22.

Chapter Thirteen: Gold Basin

    1. Barnes, Will, *Arizona Place Names*, 1960, p. 224-225.

    2. Malach, *Cerbat Mountain Country*, p. 35.

    3. Parsons, Lillian, interview with author, May 1988, Kingman, AZ.

    4. Walker, Jack, interview with author, Sept. 1986.

    5. Schroder, F. C., *Mineral Deposits of Mohave County, Arizona*, 1909, p. 118-120.

    6. Malach, Roman, *Mohave County Mines*, p. 53.

    7. *Gold Placers and Placering in Arizona*, 1961, Arizona Bureau of Mines, Bulletin 169.

    8. *Notice of Mining Location*, Book T, p. 98, Mohave County Courthouse.

    9. Smith, Melvin, p. 410.

    10. Belshaw, Michael, *Historic Resources Study*, 1983, map on p. 126.

Chapter Fourteen: Lost Basin

    1. "The Lost Basin," *Mohave Miner*, March 22, 1885.

    2. Mallory, Warren, interview with author, July, 1988, Meadview.

    3. Malach, Roman, *Mohave County*, p. 108.

    4. Ibid., *Mohave County Mines*, p. 43.

    5. Schroder, F. C., p. 150.

    6. Fauth, Bill, interview with author, June, 1986, Kingman, AZ.

    7. Duncan, Sadie Pearl, interview with author, April, 1986, Kingman, AZ.

    8. Ray, Jimmie, interview with author, March, 1986, Cornville, AZ.

    9. *Trails, Rails, and Tales*, p. 32.

    10. Ray, Jimmie, Interview with author, March, 1986, Cornville, AZ.

    11. Grounds, John Cureton, p. 149-153.

Endnotes

12. Euler and Dobyns, *The Walapai People*, 1976, p. 68-70.

13. Cheel, Chester, "The Ghost Dance," *Nevada Magazine*, 1978, p. 14-15.

14. *Mohave Ranching*, Brochure #7, Messersmith, 1987, Mohave Museum, Kingman, AZ.

15. Neal, Leonard, interview with author, July 1, 1986, Kingman, AZ.

16. Duncan, Sadie Pearl, interview with author, April, 1986, Kingman, AZ.

17. "Louis L'Amour," *Mohave* supplement, Dick Waters, April, 1976, p. 9.

18. BLM correspondence to G. T. Duncan, May 19, 1939, Kingman BLM office.

19. BLM files on Diamond Bar Ranch allotment, Kingman office.

20. Memorandum: Diamond Bar Ranch allotment, Roundy, Nov. 20, 1973, BLM, Kingman office.

21. Ferguson, Denzel and Nancy, *Sacred Cows at the Public Trough*, 1983, p. 195-202.

22. Adamson, Joe, correspondence to Mohave Museum, Oct. 9, 1988, forwarded to author.

23. BLM file on Diamond Bar Ranch, BLM office, Kingman, AZ.

Chapter Fifteen: Music Mountains

1. Barnes, Will, p. 217.

2. Lucchitta, Ivo, and Young, Richard, *Geology of Central and Northern Arizona*, 1986, p. 164.

3. Grounds, John Cureton, p. 111-112.

4. Ibid., p. 199.

5. Lucchitta, Ivo, p. 166.

6. Barnes, Will, p. 223-224.

7. Malach, Roman, *Daniel O'Leary*, p. 13, *Early Ranching in Mohave County*, p. 33.

8. Grounds, John Cureton, p. 136-140.

9. Barnes, Will, p. 220.

10. Goodman, Burt, "Heliograph Network Helped Army Pursue Indians," *Mohave Daily Miner*, Nov. 6, 1989, p. 8.

11. Malach, Roman, *Mohave County*, p. 124.

Endnotes

12. Parsons, Lillian, granddaughter of Wm. Ridenour and Charley Hand, interview with author, May, 1988, Kingman, AZ.

13. Grounds, Howard and Betty, interview with author, July, 1986, Kingman, AZ.

14. Malach, Roman, *Mohave County*, p. 121.

15. Gray, Jo, "There Was Once Gold in Them Thar Hills – and Canadian Firm Plans to Extract It," *Mohave Daily Miner*, Dec. 15, 1985, p. B1.

16. Malach, Roman, *Early Ranching in Mohave County*, p. 30.

17. *Grand Canyon National Park: Photographic and Comprehensive Guide*, 1977, p. 53.

18. Malach, Roman, *Peach Springs*, p. 9.

19. Ibid., "Peach Springs on Diamond Creek in 1893," *Kingman Daily Miner*, March 26, 1975, p. 10.

Chapter Sixteen: Lake Mead

1. Cannon, Charles, telephone interview with author, 1987.

2. Duffield, Elmer, interviews with author, Feb., 1986, July, 1989, Meadview.

3. Ladd, Jess, interview with author, July, 1986, Lake Mead City, AZ.

4. Evans, Willis, "Work Progress Report for the Archeological Project at Pierce's Ferry from June 1 – June 15, 1936," on file at LMNRA Headquarters in Boulder City, NV.

5. Grater, Russell, interview with author, Sept. 1986, Boulder City, NV.

6. Emery, Horace, interview with author, May, 1987, Meadview, and Pearce Ferry landing.

7. Fauth, Bill, interview with author, June, 1986, Kingman, AZ.

8. Musser, Mamie, "From the Past," *Mohave Museum Newsletter*, 1988.

9. Ladd, Jess, interview with author, July, 1986, Lake Mead City, AZ.

10. Duncan, Sadie Pearl, interview with author, April, 1986, Kingman, AZ.

11. Hart, Elton, interview with author, June, 1986, Meadview.

12. Duffield, Elmer, interviews with author, Feb., 1986, July 1989, Meadview.

13. Ricca, Joe, interview with author, July, 1986, Kingman, AZ.

Endnotes

14. Olcott, George, "Survey of the Recreational Resources of the Colorado River Basin," 1943, p. 13, on file at LMNRA in Boulder City, NV.; and, Voight, Herb, interview with author in 1987, Kingman, AZ.

15. White, Florence, interview with author, 1987, Dolan Springs, AZ.

16. Harris, Everett, interview with author, 1991, Meadview.

17. Ladd, Jess, interview with author, July, 1986, Lake Mead City, AZ.

18. Duffield, Elmer, interview with author, Feb., 1986, and July, 1989, Meadview.

Chapter Seventeen: The Joshua Tree Forest

1. Kliemann, Mike, *Review of the Natural Values of the Hualapai Valley Joshua Tree Forest,* his excellent study done for the Bureau of Land Management in 1979 and on file at BLM regional office in Kingman, AZ.

2. Schroder, F. C. , *Mineral Deposits of Mohave County, Arizona,* unknown publisher, 1909, Historic Books Collection at Mohave Museum, Kingman, AZ.

3. Malach, Roman, "Gold Was Found in Grand Canyon," *Meadview Monitor,* 1973, p. 23.

4. Wenrich, Karen, "Finding Breccia Pipes in Northern Arizona," *Mohave Miner,* Mohave special, Dec., 1983, p. 6.

Bibliography

Ambler, J. Richard, *The Anasazi*, Museum of Northern Arizona, 1977.

Arizona Lode Gold Mines and Mining, Arizona Bureau of Mines, 1961.

"Arizona Strip: The Splendid Isolation," *Plateau Magazine*, Vol. 57, No. 2, 1985.

Baldwin, Gordon C., *Archeological Survey of Whitmore Wash and Shivwits Plateau*, Northern Arizona, 1942, paper on file at LMNRA, Boulder City, NV.

Barnes, Will C., *Arizona Place Names*, University of Arizona Press, Tucson, 1960.

Barnes, F. A., *Canyon Country Prehistoric Art*, Wasatch Publishers, Inc., Salt Lake City, 1982.

Barnett, Franklin, *Dictionary of Prehistoric Indian Artifacts of the American Southwest*, Northland Press, Flagstaff, 1973.

Beal, Merril, *Grand Canyon, The Story Behind the Scenery*, K. C. Publications, Las Vegas, NV., 1983.

Belknap, William Jr., "The Saga of Queho," *Arizona Highways*, Sept. 1941, p. 28.

Belshaw, Michael and Peplow Jr., Ed, "Historic Resources Study," on file at LMNRA in Boulder City, NV. 1980.

Belshaw, Michael, "Mines and Mining Districts in LMNRA," on file at LMNRA, Boulder City, NV., 1979.

Belshaw, Michael, "Historic Resource Study," on file at LMNRA, 1983.

Bezy, John, *A Guide to the Desert Geology of Lake Mead NRA*, Southwest Parks and Monuments, Globe, 1978.

Brooks, Richard, et el, *An Archeological Survey of Proposed Development Areas in the Lake Mead National Recreation Area, Nevada and Arizona, and a Preliminary Archeological Inventory of High Use Recreational Areas Within the Lake Mead Boundaries*, University of Nevada, Las Vegas, 1974.

Brooks, Richard and Sheilagh, "Review of Archeological research in the Lake Mead Recreational Area" on file at LMNRA in Boulder City, NV, 1977.

Butchart, Harvey, *Grand Canyon Treks II*, La Siesta Press, Glendale, CA. 1975.

Butchart, Harvey, *Grand Canyon Treks III*, La Siesta Press, Glendale, CA. 1984.

Casebier, Dennis, *Camp Beale's Springs and the Hualapai Indians*, Tales of the Mohave Road Publishing Co., Norco, CA., 1980, and "The Mojave Road and Other Desert Trails," 1890's map.

Cheel, Chester, W., "The Ghost Dance," *Nevada Magazine*, 1978, p. 14-15.

Bibliography

Collier, Michael, *An Introduction to Grand Canyon Geology*, Grand Canyon Natural History Association, 1980.

Cox, Nellie Iverson, *Footprints on the Arizona Strip*, Horizon Publishing, Bountiful, UT, 1973.

Crampton, Gregory, *Land of Living Rock*, Knopf, NY, 1972.

"Cultural Resources Management Program: An Addendum to the Resources Management Plan," on file at LMNRA, Boulder City, NV, 1985.

"Death of M. Scanlon," obituary from *Mohave County Miner*, Feb. 3, 1912.

Elmer, Carlos, *Mohave County, Arizona*, self-published, Scottsdale, 1974.

"Environmental Assessment: Management Options for Exxon Uranium Leases," in LMNRA files, Boulder City, NV, 1977.

Ervin, Richard, "Lake Mead Developed Area Surveys," LMNRA, Western Archeological Center, Tucson, 1986.

Everett, Walter, *Directory of Southern Nevada Place Names*, self-published, 1963.

Euler, Robert, *Walapai Culture-History*, PHD dissertation, University of New Mexico, 1958.

Euler, Robert, and Dobyns, Henry, *The Walapai People*, Indian Tribal Series, Phoenix, AZ, 1976.

Evans, Douglas; Maxon, James; Gale, Richard; "Reconnaissance of the Shivwits Plateau," LMNRA, Western Archeological Center, Tucson, 1969.

Evans, Willis, "Work Progress Report for the Archeological Project at Pierce's Ferry from June 1 to June 15, 1936," LMNRA, Report #2058, Boulder City, NV.

Fairchild, Mahlon Dickerson, "Pioneer Reminiscences to the Colorado River, 1862-1863," 1904 paper at Mohave Museum, Kingman, AZ.

Fairley, Helen, and Altschul, Jeffrey, "Man, Models, and Management: An Overview of the Archeology of the Arizona Strip and the Management of Its Cultural Resources," U. S. Forest Service, U. S. Bureau of Land Management, Flagstaff, 1989.

Ferguson, Denzel and Nancy, *Sacred Cows At The Public Trough*, Maverick Publications, Bend, OR, 1983.

Fish, Frank L., *Buried Treasure and Lost Mines*, Amador Trading Post Publishing, Amador, CA, 1961.

Franklin, Robert J. and Bunte, Pamela, *The Paiute*, Chelsea House Publications, NY, 1990.

Bibliography

Geerlings, Paul, *Down the Grand Staircase*, Grand Canyon Publishing, Salt Lake City, 1978.

"Geology Notes on Colorado River and Lake Mead from Mile 235 to mile 280," unknown author/date, on file at LMNRA, Boulder City, NV.

Gold Placers and Placering in Arizona, Arizona Bureau of Mines, Bulletin, 168, 1961.

Goodman, Burt, "Heliograph Network Helped Army Pursue Indians," *Mohave Daily Miner*, Nov. 6, 1989, p. 8.

Goudy, Karin, "Hyde Mystery Still Haunts Colorado River," *Las Vegas Review-Journal, Nevadan*, Oct. 5, 1986, p. 6 cc.

Grand Canyon National Park, Photographic and Comprehensive Guide, National Parkways, by Hoffman, John, World-Wide Research Publishing Company, Casper, WY, 1977.

Granger, Byrd, *X Marks The Spot*, Falconer Publishing, Tucson, AZ, 1983.

Grater, Russell, "Black Gold," *Arizona Highways*, June, 1951.

Grater, Russell, "Last Stand of the Ground Sloth," *Arizona Highways*, July, 1958.

Grater, Russell, *Snakes, Lizards, and Turtles of the Lake Mead Region*, Southwest Parks and Monuments, Globe, AZ, 1981.

Gray, Jo, "In 1936 One Could Buy a Good Cow for $45," *Mohave Daily Miner*, Sept 24, 1986, p. 6.

Gray, Jo, "There Once Was Gold in Them Thar Hills – and Canadian Firm Plans to Extract It," *Mohave Daily Miner*, Dec. 15, 1985, p. B1.

Grayson, Donald, "Death by Natural Causes," *Natural History*, May, 1987, p. 8.

Greenawalt, Robert, "Guano Tramway in Granite Gorge," *Desert Magazine*, Jan. 1958.

Grounds, John Cureton, *Trail Dust of the Southwest*, self-published, Marysville, UT, 1977.

Hafen, Leroy and Ann, "Old Spanish Trail: Santa Fe to Los Angeles," *The Far West and The Rockies*, Historical Series, 1820-1875, Vol. 1, 1954, p. 263 and 281, Arthur Clark Co., Glendale, CA.

Hafen, Lyman, "The Deadly Lure of Separation Canyon," *Arizona Highways*, Sept., 1991, p. 12.

Hafner, Arabell Lee, *One Hundred Years on the Muddy*, Springville, UT, 1967.

Hamblin, W. Kenneth, and Rigby, J. Keith, *Guidebook to the Colorado River: Part I*, Brigham Young University, Provo, UT, 1968.

Bibliography

Hamblin, W. Kenneth, and Rigby, J. Keith, *Guidebook to the Colorado River: Part II*, Brigham Young University, Provo, UT, 1969.

Hall, Sharlot, *Sharlot Hall on the Arizona Strip*, Northland Publishing, Flagstaff, 1975.

Harrington, Mark, "Paiute Cave," *Archeological Explorations in Southern Nevada*, p. 1, Southwest Museum, Los Angeles, 1930.

Heizer, Robert and Baumhoff, Martin, *Prehistoric Rock Art of Nevada and Eastern California*, University of California, Berkley, 1962.

Henderson, Randall, "Mescal Roast," *Desert Magazine*, August, 1951, p. 8.

Hughes, J. Donald, *In the House of Stone and Light*, Grand Canyon Natural History Association, 1978.

Hughes, J. Donald, *The Story of Man at Grand Canyon*, University of Denver, 1967.

Huyghe, Patrick, *Columbus Was Last*, Hyperion, NY, 1992.

Iliff, Flora Gregg, *People of the Blue Water*, University of Arizona Press, Tucson, 1954.

"Jacob Neff Cohenour, Pioneer Passes Away," obituary, *Mohave County Miner*, Feb. 28, 1920.

Janetski, Joel, and Hall, Michael, "An Archeological and Geological Assessment of Antelope Cave, Mohave County, Northwestern Arizona," Brigham Young University, Provo, UT, 1983.

Jensen, Rex, "Grand Gulch Trail Was Stuff of Legend," *Las Vegas Review-Journal*, Oct. 25, 1981, p. 6J.

Kliemann, Michael, "Review of the Natural Values of the Hualapai Valley Joshua Tree Forest: an examination of the appropriateness of current protective measures at the site and various recommendations aimed at improving protection of the resource," 1979 study for Bureau of Land Management agency, on file at BLM Regional Office, Kingman, AZ.

"Lake Mead National Recreation Area," NPS area history and information pamphlet, revised April, 1985, on file at LMNRA, Boulder City, NV.

LaRue, E. C., "Colorado River Dam Site Investigation, Lower Grand Canyon to Needles, September-October 1924", papers and excellent historic photographs on file at the Mohave Museum in Kingman, AZ.

Laudermilk, Jerry, "Cave of the Giant Sloths," *Desert Magazine*, Nov. 1942, p. 24.

Lauritzen, Jonreed, "Arizona Strip, the Lonesome Country," *Arizona Highways*, June, 1951.

Bibliography

Lavender, David, *Colorado River Country*, E. P. Dutton, NY, 1982.

Lavender, David, *Pipe Spring and the Arizona Strip*, Zion Natural History Association, Springdale, UT, 1984.

Lawler, Florine, "Exploring Nevada's Gypsum Cavern," LMNRA files, source/date unknown.

Lewis, Georgia, "Born to Wander," *Las Vegas Review-Journal, Nevadan*, May 26, 1974.

Lewis, Georgia, "Star Pony Express and its Boy Riders," *Las Vegas Review-Journal, Nevadan*, Aug. 30, 1970.

Lewis, J. Volney and Chappell, Walter, "Discovery and Exploration of Rampart Cave in the Lower Grand Canyon, AZ," 1936 paper on file at LMNRA in Boulder City.

Lippincott, J. B. "Reconnaissance of the Colorado River above Needles, CA.," 1902 paper in possession of Dave Huntsinger, Chloride, AZ.

Lister, Robert and Florence, *Those Who Came Before*, Southwest Parks and Monument Association, Tucson, AZ, 1983.

Loewen, James, *Lies My Teacher Told Me*, New Press, NY, 1995.

"Lost Basin," Mohave Miner, March 22, 1885.

Loving, Nancy J., *Along the Rim: A Road Guide to the South Rim of Grand Canyon*, Grand Canyon Natural History Association, 1981.

Lucchitta, Ivo, and Young, Richard, *Geology of Central and Northern Arizona*, field trip guidebook of the Geological Society of America, Rocky Mountain Section meeting, Flagstaff, AZ, 1986.

Malach, Roman, *The Arizona Strip in Mohave County*, Arizona Bicentennial Commission, 1975. Malach was a former educator who moved to Kingman, Arizona, during his retirement, enjoyed writing and history, and did extensive historical research in the county. He published a number of articles as well as a series of small books, the publishing of those paid for by the regional Bureau of Land Management office in Kingman and Mohave County Board of Supervisors. Malach passed away in Kingman in 1985.

Ibid., *Cerbat Mountain Country: Early Mining Camps*, Arizona Bicentennial Commission, 1975.

Ibid., "Climax Mine Still Worked," *Mohave Miner*, Feb. 28, 1974.

Ibid., *Early Ranching in Mohave County*, Mohave County Board of Supervisors, 1978.

Ibid., "Gold Was Found in Grand Canyon," *Meadview Monitor*, 1973, p. 23.

Bibliography

Ibid., *Home on the Range: Civilian Conservation Corps in Kingman Area*, Bureau of Land Management, Kingman office, 1984.

Ibid., *Hualapai Mountains*, Arizona Bicentennial Commission, 1975.

Ibid., *Kingman, Arizona*, Arizona Bicentennial Commission, 1974.

Ibid., *Lost Mines*, County Board of Supervisors, 1978.

Ibid., *Mohave County Mines*, Mohave County Board of Supervisors, 1977.

Ibid., *Mohave County Northland*, Mohave County Board of Supervisors, 1979.

Ibid., *Mohave County Pioneer, Daniel O'Leary*, Mohave County Board of Supervisors, 1982.

Ibid., *Mohave County Place Names*, Arizona Bicentennial Commission, 1976.

Ibid., *Mohave County: Sketches of Early Days*, Arizona Bicentennial Commission, 1974.

Ibid., "Mohave's Minnesota Mining District," *Kingman Daily Miner*, Jan. 21, 1975, p. 6.

Ibid., *Peach Springs in Mohave County*, Arizona Bicentennial Commission, 1975.

Ibid., "Peach Springs on Diamond Creek in 1893," *Kingman Daily Miner*, Mar. 26, 1975, p. 10.

Ibid., "Rampart Cave Repository of Fossils," *Kingman Daily Miner*, July 30, 1975, p. 10.

Ibid., "Some Interesting Old Towns Now Covered by Waters of Lake Mead," *Mohave Miner*, Mohave section, June, 1973, p. 19.

Ibid., "White Hills," Arizona Bicentennial Commission, 1976.

Mallory, Warren, M. "Summary of Gold, Silver, Copper, Molybdenum Deposits of Lost Basin, Mohave County, Arizona," paper for Apache Oro Company, 1966. Mallory was area manager of the Apache Oro Mining Company in Lost Basin for a number of years.

Marston, Dock, "Separation Marks," paper in possession of Mack Miller, Temple Bar, Arizona, 1972.

Martin, Paul, "Death of American Ground Sloths," *Science*, Vol. 186, p. 638.

Martin, Paul, "Sloth Droppings," *Natural History*, Aug. 1975, p. 74.

Martin, Paul, "Clovisia the Beautiful," *Natural History*, Oct. 1987, p. 10.

Martineau, LeVan, *The Rocks Begin to Speak*, KC Publications, Las Vegas, NV., 1973.

Bibliography

Matthews, John Joseph, "Paleozic Stratigraphy and Structural Geology of the Wheeler Ridge, Northwestern Mohave County, Arizona," 1976 Dissertation, NAU, Flagstaff, AZ.

Maxon, James, C., *Indians of Lake Mead Country*, Southwest Parks and Monument Association, Globe, AZ., 1971.

Maxon, James C., *Lake Mead-Hoover Dam, the Story Behind the Scenery*, KC Publications, Las Vegas, NV., 1980.

McClellan, Carole, and Phillips, David, Jr, "Archeological Survey North of Lake Mead, Arizona: Wahl-Yee and Mobil Mineral Leases Final Report," Western Archeological Center, Tucson, 1978.

McClellan, Carole, and Phillips, David, Jr., and Belshaw, Mike, "Archeology of Lake Mead National Recreation Area," LMNRA files, Boulder City, NV. 1980.

McClintock, James H., *Mormon Settlement in Arizona*, University of Arizona, Tucson, AZ, 1921.

"Memories," collection of unpublished stories in possession of Keith and Marlyn Nay, 1988: Waymire, Inez Gibson, p. 14-15, Preston, Euzell, p. 4, Fae, Stewart, p. 36.

Messersmith, Dan, *The History of Mohave County to 1912*, Mohave Museum, Kingman, AZ, 1991.

Michener, James, "Where Did the Animals Go?" *Readers Digest*, June, 1976.

Mitchell, Roger, *Grand Canyon Jeep Trails: North Rim*, La Siesta Press, Glendale, CA, 1983.

Moser, Julia, "Ranchos Home of Famous Science Fiction Writer," *Joshua Journal*, Dolan Springs, AZ., April, 1977, p. 4.

Musser, Mamie Jones, "From the Past," (late 1930's) *Mohave Museum Newsletter*, 1988, Kingman, AZ.

Musser, Mamie Jones, "Notes from Amy Neal Collection" on file at Mohave Museum, Kingman, AZ. Musser was W.P.A. (Work Progress Administration) Historian for Mohave County in the late 1930's.

"New Playground Area for County is Receiving Post War Consideration," no author noted, *Mohave Miner*, March, 1944.

"Notice of Mining Location," Recorders Office, Book T, Mohave County Courthouse, Kingman, AZ, p. 98.

Nuwuvi: A Southern Paiute History, Inter-tribal Council of Nevada, University of Utah Press, 1976.

Bibliography

Olcott, George, W., "Survey of the Recreational Resources of the Colorado River Basin; Report on Further Study of the Bridge Canyon Reservoir Region," 1943 paper, p. 13, on file at LMNRA Headquarters, Boulder City, NV.

Paher, Stanley W., *Northwestern Arizona Ghost Towns*, Nevada Publishing, Las Vegas, 1970.

Parker, John, "Arizona Badmen," *Desert Magazine*, July, 1982, p. 18-19.

Perkins, George, "Trail of a Renegade Pahute," *Desert Magazine*, Nov. 1939.

Powell, John Wesley, *The Exploration of the Colorado River*, University of Chicago Press, 1957.

Powell, John Wesley, *The Exploration of the Colorado River and Its Canyons*, Dover, N.Y., 1961.

Price, Edna Calkins, *Burro Bill and Me*, Strawberry Valley Press, Idylwild, CA., 1931.

Price, L. Greer, *Grand Canyon: The Story Behind the Scenery*, KC Publications, Las Vegas, NV, 1991.

Purcell, Roy, *Long Journey from Wikame*, Creative Adventures, Las Vegas, NV, 1988.

Purcell, Roy, *Mohave Epic: The Footprints in Time*, Mohave County Historical Society, Kingman, AZ., 1992.

"Reflections: 100 Years: Truxton County," The Truxton Valentine Bicentennial Committee, 1976.

Rhode, Katherine, "Magic of the Mohave," *Nevada Magazine*, March/April, 1991.

Ruppert, David E. "Lake Mead National Recreation Area: An Ethnographic Overview," NPS Western Archeological Center, Tucson, 1976.

Sadovich, Maryellen, "Brother Pearce Ferried Mormons into Arizona," *Las Vegas Review-Journal, Nevadan*, Sept., 14, 1986, p. 12 cc.

Sanita, Frances, "The Hualapai," *Arizona Highways*, Sept., 1941, p. 30.

Schenk, Edward T., "Notes on the Occurrence of a Lava Flow in Lower Grand Canyon,", 1937 paper on file at Lake Mead NRA, Boulder City, NV.

Schmidt, Keith, "The Grounds Family Knows What Beefs All About," *Destination Kingman*, March, 1986, p. 9.

Schroeder, Albert H., "Archeological Excavations at Willow Beach, Arizona," 1950 paper on file at LMNRA, Boulder City, NV.

Schroder, F. C., *Mineral Deposits of Mohave County, Arizona*, 1909, unknown publisher, Historic Books Collection, Mohave Museum, Kingman, Arizona.

Bibliography

Scrattish, Nick, "Historic Sites Within Lake Mead National Recreation Area Deemed Ineligible for National Register Nomination," 1982 paper on file at LMNRA, Boulder City, NV.

Shutler, Richard and Mary, "Archeological Survey in Southern Nevada," Nevada State Museum, Carson City, NV., 1962.

Smith, Melvin T., "The Colorado River: It's History in the Lower Canyon Area," PHD dissertation, University of Utah, Salt Lake City, 1972.

Stano, Mary, "Dan's Ferry," *Las Vegas Review-Journal, Nevadan*, Feb. 26, 1989.

Stevens, Larry, *The Colorado River in Grand Canyon: A Guide*, Red Lake Books, Flagstaff, AZ., 1983.

Stokes, Wm. Lee, *Scenes of the Plateau Lands and How They Came to Be*, Starstone Publishing, Salt Lake City, UT, 1969.

Stoffle, Richard and Evans, Michael J., *Kaibab Paiute History: The Early Years*, Kaibab Paiute Tribe, Fredonia, Arizona, 1978.

"Stories from the Land," *Plateau Magazine*, vol. 53, No. 2, Museum of Northern Arizona, Flagstaff, 1981.

Sturtevant, William C., editor, *Handbook of North American Indians*, Vol. 9, 10, 11, Smithsonian Institute, 1986.

Swisher, John, "The Magic of a Name," *Desert Life Magazine*, Aug. 1987, p. 13.

Taylor, Paul, "Ghost of the White Hills," *Mohave Miner*, Mohave, Sept. 1984, p. 8.

Thompson, Albert, and Willard, Ron, "Those Early Days," *Sedona Westerners*, p. 61, 104.

Trails, Rails, and Tales, Kingman Centennial Committee, Kingman, AZ., 1981.

"The Treasure That Wasn't There," *Mohave Miner*, Mohave, no author, Kingman, AZ., April, 1983.

Voight, Herb, "Mining Bat Guano in the Canyon," *Mohave Miner*, Mohave, Kingman, AZ., Dec., 1983.

Walker, Henry P., and Bufkin, Don, *Historical Atlas of Arizona*, University of Oklahoma, Norman, 1986.

Wallis, Orthello, "Preliminary Observations of Cave in Columbine Canyon, Arizona, Lake Mead National Recreation Area," 1954 paper on files at LMNRA Headquarters, Boulder City, NV.

Wallace, Robert, *The Grand Canyon*, The American Wilderness/Time-Life Book Series, NY, 1972.

Bibliography

Wampler, Joseph, *Havasu, A Canyon Home*, self-published, Berkeley, CA, 1981.

Waters, Dick, "Louis L'Amour," *Mohave Miner*, Mohave, April, 1976, p. 9, Kingman, AZ.

"Welcome to Lake Mead Country," *Arizona Highways*, May, 1983.

Wells, Spencer, *Pandora's Seed: The Unforeseen Cost of Civilization*, 2010.

Wenrich, Karen, "Finding Breccia Pipes in Northern Arizona," *Mohave Miner*, Mohave, Dec. 1983, p. 6, Kingman, AZ.

Wilson, Robert W., "Preliminary Report on the Fauna of Rampart Cave, Arizona," 1939 paper on file at LMNRA Headquarters, Boulder City, NV.

Wormington, H. M., *Prehistoric Indians of the Southwest*, Denver Museum of Natural History, 1964.

Wright, Marlene, "Conserving the Natural Resources of the Arizona Strip," 1950's research paper in BLM files at St. George, Utah.

Wright, Owen B., "Background and History of the Arizona Strip District," paper in BLM files at St. George, Utah.

Whitney, Stephen, *A Field Guide to the Grand Canyon*, William Morrow and Co., N.Y., 1982.

Author

Of Norse/Scottish descent, born and raised in the upper rural Midwest, Mary has always had deep empathy for the Earth and its many species. She has also possessed irrepressible curiosity and the need to understand larger patterns while incorporating long-term historical views.

At the age of thirty, Mary and her two amalgate Native American children migrated to the west and southwest, a land of mountains, desert, and canyons where Mary had always longed to be. During the 1970's while in Colorado, she became deeply involved with the survival of wolves and other large predators in the wild, animals at that time fast disappearing from vast western landscapes. While living near Lake Mead and western Grand Canyon with her National Park Service Ranger husband, Don McBee, during the early 1970's and again throughout the 1980's, Mary spent years hiking, four-wheel exploring, and intensely researching this remote and fascinating high desert country, all of which resulted in this inclusive work.

The author left the Long Shadow lands in 1990 and since has shared time between her native Heartland in Iowa, family, and continued roaming of her beloved Southwest. Mary can be reached at mmcb444@gmail.com.

Index

Allan, Del, 127, 149-152, 154, 160, 173
Basin Mill, 203, 220
Bat Cave, 307, 308, 310, 311, 317 - 319, 335, 340, 341, 365
Baur, Sharon, vii, 356
Belknap, William Jr., 145, 340, 377
Black Canyon, 37, 42, 58, 59, 80, 97, 116, 117, 299, 311
Bonelli (Daniel, Ferry), v, 47, 57, 79, 80-83, 85-88, 173, 187, 197, 232, 280, 314, 316, 321, 369
Boulder Canyon, 58, 59, 83, 93, 148, 299, 314
Boulder City, vii, 5, 146, 239, 240, 301, 305, 307, 308, 311, 313-315, 319, 320, 368, 374, 375, 377-381, 383-386
Boulder Dam, 2, 53, 106, 145, 146, 197, 229, 230, 299, 300, 315$
Bounsall, Ed (Crazy Ed, Treasurehawk), 174, 371
Brechner, George, 206, 207, 211, 217
Bridge Canyon Dam, 100, 316, 318-320, 327, 328
Buffalo, Johnathan, viii
Burnt Mill, 51, 203, 207, 208, 220, 237, 240
Butchart, Harvey, 113, 370, 377
CCC, 6, 125, 158, 170, 226, 239, 240, 283, 284, 301, 304, 305, 314-319, 321, 322
Cerbat Mountains. 185, 231
Chloride (cloride), 51, 52, 54, 55, 56, 57, 59, 60, 66, 80, 81, 191, 195, 223, 311, 312, 369, 381
Clay Springs and Ranch, 23, 63, 194, 232, 280, 281
Clay Springs Canyon , 23, 275, 279, 282, 283
Coleman, Art, 118, 126, 173, 176
Columbine Falls, 6, 226, 305, 315, 316, 330, 331
Conger, Leonard, 81
Cox, Nellie Iverson, 96, 105
Craig, Arnella, Jack, 177, 252, 257
Crozier, 27, 278, 279, 282
Cureton, 279, 280
Dellenbaugh, 111, 113,
Detrital Wash, 79, 185, 187
Diamond Bar Ranch, 42-45, 124, 187, 188, 225-227, 229, 235-237, 260, 262, 353, 373
Diamond Bar Road, 235, 351, 363
Diamond Creek, 91, 93, 104-106, 174, 284, 285, 288, 318, 374,
Dinbah Springs (and see Grapevine Springs), 41, 44, 238
Dolan Springs, 60, 81, 85, 185, 187, 188, 196-198, 204, 216, 226, 228, 321, 347, 359, 375, 383
Dry Red Lake, 4, 23, 201, 238, 281

389

Duffield, Elmer, 301, 317, 322, 327-329, 365, 374, 375
Duncan, 42, 43, 45, 63,187, 223, 225-227, 232, 233, 235, 237, 239, 317, 319, 372-374
Duncan, George Taplin, 42, 124, 187, 225-227, 229, 232, 233, 235, 237, 260, 262, 286, 373
Dutton, Clarence Edward, 94
Emery Falls, 315, 317, 330
Emery, Horace, 12, 177, 311, 313, 325, 326
Emery, Murl, 308, 316
Emery, Pop, 177, 225, 305, 308, 311, 313, 314, 317-319, 324
Englestead, 145, 147, 148, 150
Esplin, Buster and Lola, 114, 115, 125, 140, 370
Evans, Willis, 6, 12, 226, 301
Farlee Hotel, 284, 288, 306
Farlee, J. H., 284, 285, 286
Fauth, Bill, 150, 226, 227, 315
Fisher, Mary Wager, 284, 285, 286
Freiday, Bill, 307, 309, 310
Galloway, Nathaniel, 83, 95
Garnet Mountain, 238
Garrett, Bill, 118, 126, 148, 150, 173, 174, 176
Gensley, Dave, vii, 11, 266-268, 290
Gentry, Laura, 147, 148
Ghost Dance, 32, 231-233, 261, 373, 377
Glindmeier, Pearl, 39
Godwin, Tom, 226
Gold Basin, v, 51, 65, 193, 201, 203-205, 207, 208, 217, 222, 224, 237, 240, 280
Gold Butte, v, 51, 52, 60, 118, 121, 126, 148, 159, 173-178, 181, 185, 217, 220, 353, 371
Golden Gate Mine, 218-221, 249, 254
Grand Canyon West, 29, 231, 311, 348, 353, 365
Grand Canyon Ranch (formerly, Grand Canyon West Ranch), 3, 41, 187, 224, 230, 260, 364
Grand Gulch Mine, 42, 113-116, 118-120, 122-124, 135-139
Grand Gulch Trail, 116-120, 133, 371, 380
Grand Wash, 2, 15, 36, 39, 41, 42, 44, 46, 47, 52, 93, 94, 100, 101, 109, 112, 115-117, 119, 121-123, 125, 127, 143, 145, 147, 150-152, 155, 157, 158, 162, 172, 173, 178, 320, 342
Grand Wash Cliffs, xiii, 2-5, 23, 41, 45, 94, 109, 112, 116, 143, 151, 155, 188, 201, 205, 213, 231, 237, 238, 275, 351-353, 363
Grapevine Canyon 41, 231, 353, 363
Grapevine Mesa, xiii, xiv, 5, 8, 23, 32, 51, 53, 109, 124, 143, 175, 178, 185, 187, 188, 201, 204, 213, 217, 219, 222, 224, 228-230, 238, 241, 242, 244, 255, 256, 259, 300, 301, 315, 316, 319, 321, 322, 343, 347, 348, 349, 352- 354, 363, 364, 366

Grapevine Springs, xiv, 3, 41, 42, 44, 47, 234, 238-240, 265-268, 280, 319, 348, 363

Grapevine Springs Canyon, xiv, 235, 238, 239, 319, 363, 364

Grapevine Wash, 3, 11, 41, 44, 50, 93, 94, 98, 100, 124, 188, 213, 216, 230, 231, 233, 234, 238, 239, 261, 270, 271, 273, 300, 313, 317, 322, 326, 348, 351, 354, 363, 364

Grass Springs (and see Tahnaka Springs, Tinaka Springs, Tanaka Springs), 3, 23, 32, 41, 44, 45, 93, 187, 188, 205, 224, 227, 230-232, 234, 235, 240, 260, 261, 321, 348, 353, 363, 364

Grass Springs Ranch, 3, 23, 41, 187, 224, 227, 230, 232, 260, 364

Grater, Russell, 304, 307, 319, 374, 379

Greely, Horace, Lewis, 41

Gregg (and see Grigg), 51, 53, 54, 58, 59, 61, 68, 74, 270, 280, 369, 380

Gregg Basin, 51-53, 54, 241, 344

Gregg's Hideout, 53, 92, 201, 203-206, 221, 222

Grigg's Ferry (and see Greggs Ferry), 51-54, 56, 59, 60, 68, 70, 79, 95, 96, 102, 103, 106, 121, 207, 234, 238, 280, 369

Grigg (Gregg), William, Bessie, 52, 53, 56, 58, 59, 207, 223, 238, 300

Griggs Ranch, 52, 53, 59, 60, 65, 66, 67, 69, 300, 314

Griggs Road, 53, 59, 75, 76, 77, 300

Grounds, 151, 210, 224, 232, 279, 280, 283, 287, 374, 384

Grounds, John Cureton, 4, 5, 96, 151, 181, 191-195, 231, 261, 275, 278-281, 367, 369, 371-373, 379

Grounds (William, Billy, Bud), 27, 63, 96, 224, 231, 239, 240, 261, 275, 279, 280, 282, 283

Gypsum Cave, 5, 6, 301, 381

Hackberry (Town, Springs, Road, Mine), 45, 56, 58, 82, 203, 204, 213, 215, 216, 220, 231, 235, 237, 240, 275, 279, 280

Hamblin, Joseph, 20, 21, 39, 41, 45, 80, 231

Hamblin, Kenneth, 379, 380

Hand, Charlie, 203, 204, 209, 240, 280

Harris, Everett, vii, 128, 131, 155-157, 160, 163, 172, 174, 321, 370, 375

Harris's Cave, 157, 172, 174

Havasupai, 17, 41, 277

Hecklethorne, 147-149

Helldiver Cave, 301-303

Hidden Lake (Springs, Rim, Canyon), 44, 120, 122, 123, 127, 320

Homestead Act, 123, 185

Hoover Dam, 58, 59, 83, 97, 145, 188, 204, 236, 299, 312, 319, 383

Hualapai Jeff, 193

Hualapai Mountains, 187, 240, 284, 352, 353, 382

Hualapai Reservation(Walapai), 26, 28, 29, 41, 237, 278, 279, 284, 286, 309, 353

Hualapai Tribe (Walapai), 2, 3, 23, 25-27, 29, 30, 56, 193, 231, 311, 348, 365, 368, 373, 378

Hualapai Valley, 4, 44, 45, 82, 85, 187, 201, 203-205, 213, 231, 237, 238, 264, 275, 347, 349-353, 375, 380
Hualapai Wash (Dam) (Walapai Wash), 51, 52, 54, 56-58, 60, 65, 73, 92, 121, 176, 201, 203, 207, 208, 211, 213, 217, 220, 221, 259, 315
Huntsinger, Dave, 54, 381
Hyde, Glen and Bessie, 103-105, 107, 379
Ice Cave, 188, 189
Iceberg Canyon, 92, 93, 102, 241, 305, 319, 334
Iron Basin, 44, 45, 227, 230-232, 235, 237, 238, 364
Iron Mountain, 238, 364
Iron Springs, 45, 229, 231, 232, 304
Joy, Ben, 227, 279
Joy, Mary Grace, 227
Judd, J., 47, 239, 240, 268
Judd, Thomas, 47, 269
Julien, D., 89, 369
Kaibab Plateau, 109
Kaibab Ranch, 121
Kaibab Tribe (Reservation), 22, 367, 385
Keifer, Jim, vii
King Tut Mine, 226, 227, 230, 235, 256, 301
Kingman, vii, 21, 24, 28, 29, 42, 45, 48, 51, 52, 55, 57, 60, 77, 80, 81, 85-87, 97-100, 102, 104, 106, 107, 124, 150, 185, 189, 190-192, 194, 196, 197, 199, 201, 203, 220, 221, 225-227, 229, 231, 232, 235, 237, 240, 261, 262, 275, 277, 278, 280, 282-284, 289, 300, 307, 308, 309, 312, 318, 320, 348, 349, 352, 353, 363, 364, 368, 369, 371-378, 380-386
Kliemann, Mike, 349, 351, 375, 380
Kolb, Ellsworth, 103
Kolb, Emery, 59, 95, 103, 104
L'Amour, Louis, 232, 286, 373, 386
Ladd, Jess, 301, 316, 319, 322
Lake Mead, v, xiii, 1-3, 6, 8, 35, 48, 51-53, 59, 60, 65, 85, 89, 91, 92, 106, 143, 173, 177, 182, 196, 201, 207, 213, 221, 224, 225, 228-230, 299-301, 305, 307, 308, 313, 315, 318, 319-321, 344, 354, 363, 365, 374, 377-379, 382, 383, 386, 387
Lake Mead Land and Water Company, 350
Lake Mead National Recreation Area (LMNRA), vii, 8, 54, 89, 148, 151, 188, 192, 203, 206, 207, 217, 222, 300, 304, 315, 319, 320, 321, 324-326, 339, 350, 354, 360, 363-365, 368, 374, 375, 377, 378-381, 383-386
Lake Mead City, 204, 230, 238, 322, 351, 365, 374, 375
Lake Mohave, 2, 35, 300, 315, 321
Lake Powell, 317
Land of Long Shadows, vii, xi, xii, xiv, 15, 23
LaRue, E.C., 48, 49, 97, 103, 323, 380
Lee, John D., 43

Lee's Ferry, 35, 39, 43, 89, 95, 103, 301, 320
Lincoln Ranch, 232, 237, 263
Lippincott, 54, 56, 59, 80, 103, 196, 381
Lost Basin, v, 51, 65, 201, 203, 207, 213, 216, 218- 220, 222-226, 228, 230, 237, 238, 240, 242, 243, 277, 280, 372, 381, 382
Lost Basin Mill, 220, 221
Lost Basin Mining District, 213, 223
Lost Shaft, 213, 215-219, 277
Lower Granite Gorge, v, xiii, 6, 11, 29, 89, 300, 320, 363, 369
Lucchitta, Ivo, 275, 373, 381
Lucky Seven Corral, 322, 354
Malach, Roman, 21, 119, 190, 194, 219, 313, 368, 370-375, 381
Mallory, Warren, 218, 222, 237, 372, 382
Martin, Paul, Dr., 7, 8, 13, 382
Martineau, LeVan, 3, 4, 143, 371, 380, 382
Mathis, Reed, 122, 123, 126-128, 140, 151, 152, 173, 370
Mathis, Wallace, 122
Maude, 143, 145
McBee, Clyde and Cecil, 188, 204, 236
McBee, Don, vii, 8, 89, 142, 154, 175-177, 181, 182, 188, 204, 245, 258, 310, 331, 335, 337, 354, 387
McDougal, Frosty, 147, 149, 151
Meadview, vii, viii, xiii, xiv, 39, 53, 61, 71, 76, 128, 155, 174-178, 213, 218, 233, 234, 238, 241, 300, 301, 315-317, 321, 322, 327, 346, 351, 354, 359, 365, 370, 372, 374, 375, 381
Meriwhitica Canyon, 23, 24, 33, 277, 278, 281, 290
Meskwaki (Fox) Tribe, viii, 89
Messersmith, Dan, 21, 51, 80, 179, 373, 383
Michener, James, 7, 13, 383
Milkweed Springs, 41, 278
Mineral Park, 42, 52, 81, 82, 187, 197, 201, 213, 220, 279, 280
Minnesota Mining District, 190, 192, 382
Moccasin Springs, 21, 22, 112
Mohave County, 21, 25, 26, 51, 53, 80, 84, 96, 97, 119, 127, 178, 185, 187, 189, 193, 196, 201, 204, 207, 213, 216, 217, 220, 223, 228, 232, 236, 277, 279, 280, 282, 284, 301, 310, 351-353, 370-375, 380-384
Mohave Desert (Mountains), 35, 220, 221, 384
Mohave (Mojave) (Tribe, Valley, Fort), 2, 17, 24, 35-37, 93, 145, 178, 179, 185, 187, 217, 277, 311
Mohave Miner (Mohave Daily Miner, Mohave County Miner), 119, 190, 191, 193, 195, 196, 213, 220, 223, 224, 228, 235, 280, 307, 313, 372-375, 378-386
Mohave Museum, vii, 48, 77, 87, 88, 107, 191, 196, 199, 210, 231, 242, 261, 262, 287-289, 309, 369, 373-375, 378, 380, 383, 384
Mohave Trail (Road), 3, 368, 377
Montgomery, Gregg, Richard, vii, 11, 174, 271, 342

Mouse, 82-85, 95
Mt. Dellenbaugh, 111-113, 120, 122, 127, 141, 320
Mt. Tipton, 198, 352
Mt. Trumbull, 80, 105, 111, 120, 128, 130
Muav Caves, 12, 304
Muddy Mountains, 84
Mullin, Johnny, 53, 204
Music Mountains, v, 4, 23, 151, 194, 197, 232, 237, 240, 275, 279, 283, 284, 287, 373
Musser, George and Mamie Jones, 197, 223-226, 232, 237, 316, 369, 374, 383
Nay, 145, 147, 152, 153, 157, 158, 177, 371, 383
Neal, 96, 187, 189, 197, 204, 207, 227, 232, 237-240, 280, 283, 369, 371, 373, 383
Nobmann, Fred, 213, 215, 216
Nutter, 52, 97, 121-125, 134, 147, 150, 152, 283
O.K. Mill, 203-205, 237
Old Simon, 112, 115,122, 143, 145
Old Ute Crossing(Old Ute Trail, Old Ute Trail), 2, 3, 18, 35, 36, 39, 41, 46, 51, 94, 143, 300, 320, 348
Old Ute Ford (Ute Ford), 35, 39
Overton (Overton Arm), 1, 3, 35, 52, 84, 85, 92, 143, 147, 306, 319, 320, 371
Pahute, 82, 84, 178, 384
Paiute, v, xiv, 2, 3, 6, 15-22, 35, 46, 82, 83, 84, 92, 109, 111-113, 122, 128, 143, 145-147, 151, 178, 222, 231, 238, 311, 312, 367, 378, 380, 383, 385
Pakoon Springs, 52, 93, 117, 125, 145, 151-155, 164
Parson, Lillian Ridenour, 203, 209, 240, 374
Patterson, Robert (Bob), 85, 185, 187, 193, 197, 204, 205, 224, 230, 237
Patterson Corrals, 45, 187, 237
Patterson Springs (Well), 45, 63, 187, 203, 204, 213, 216, 222, 223, 231, 237
Pattie, James Ohio, 36, 90, 112
Peach Springs, 25, 26, 29, 37, 41, 104, 173, 193, 201, 278, 282-286, 320, 368, 374, 382
Peach Springs Canyon, 93, 104, 285, 286, 288, 306, 318
Pearce Canyon, Wash, 41, 42, 44, 126, 143
Pearce (Pierce) Ferry, v, 6, 35, 36, 39, 41, 42, 44-51, 91, 93-98, 100, 101, 103, 113, 115, 116, 124, 149, 216, 217, 222, 223, 226, 229, 230, 231, 234, 239, 240, 272, 273, 300-305, 307, 313-320, 322-326, 348, 350, 353, 363, 368, 374, 378
Pearce Ferry Road, 50, 53, 93, 116, 189, 197, 201, 203, 204, 208, 230, 237, 275, 301, 348, 353, 359, 365
Pearce (Pierce), Harrison, 43, 44, 46-49, 240, 368, 384
Perkins, Chic, 85, 147, 151, 371
Perkins, Ute, 81, 82
Perkins, George, 82, 83, 84, 384
Peters, Shannon, 96
Pierce (see Pearce)

Pigeon Canyon (Wash, Springs), 41, 42, 44, 46, 113, 114, 116, 119, 120
Pipe Springs, 112, 120, 121, 148
Pony Express, 80, 81, 187, 223, 237, 381
Powell, John Wesley, 21, 91, 92, 111, 112, 145, 306, 369, 384
Price, Edna Calkins,153, 154, 371, 384
Public lands, v, 58, 125, 127, 129, 159, 232, 235, 236, 349, 359-362, 364-365
Purcell, Roy, 29, 30, 368, 384
Quartermaster Canyon, 29, 279, 305, 341, 342, 365
Quartermaster Viewpoint, 279, 284, 297, 310, 365
Queho, 145-147, 171, 377
Rampart Cave, 6-8, 12, 13, 226, 304, 315, 381, 382, 386
Rampart Overlook, 351, 353, 354
Ray, Jimmie, 189, 227, 232
Red Lake (Dry), 4, 23, 201, 238, 281
Ricca, Joe, 318, 374
Ridenour, William, 231, 240, 261, 277, 279, 291-295, 374
Rioville, 47, 48, 57, 58, 80, 81, 82, 85
Roasting pits, 2, 4, 5, 11, 233
Roper, Bill, 280
Ruby, Mignon, 154
Santa Fe Trail, 90, 94
Sanip, 16
Sanup (Sanip) Plateau, 42, 109, 113, 119, 122, 126,
Scanlon Dugway, 51, 176, 177, 182, 183, 301
Scanlon Ferry, 51, 52, 56, 59, 121, 207, 221
Scanlon, Michael, 51, 52, 59, 176, 177, 203, 207, 219-223, 300
Scanlon Mill, 51, 65, 207, 208
Scanlon Springs, 51, 52, 73, 75, 207, 220
Scanlon Wash, 51, 52, 176-178, 184, 207, 210
Seeba, Ron, vii, 212, 244, 251
Selinsky, Chris, Ray, vii
Senator Mountain, 188, 196, 205
Separation Canyon, 91, 92, 106, 112, 113, 306, 379
Seven Springs, 147-149, 151, 158, 162, 163
Shanley, Bill, 123, 124, 127, 150
Shivwits Band of Paiute, 3, 22, 109
Shivwits Plateau, v, 15, 22, 80, 109, 111, 112, 116, 119-126, 155, 173, 300, 370, 377, 378
Sierra Club, 318
Signature Wall, 42, 47, 239, 267, 268, 280, 364
Simonis, Don, vii, 34, 219, 221, 267, 277, 333
Smith, Jedediah, 35, 36, 93
Smith, Jim (Dale, Smith Ranch), 3, 23, 26, 41, 187, 188, 224, 233, 235, 236, 260, 319, 322, 353, 364
Smith, Jim (cowboy surveyor), 26

Smith, Melvin, 37, 39, 42, 48, 52, 207, 368, 369, 372, 385
Smith, Thomas (Pegleg), 36, 52, 90, 203, 217
Smith, Richard (Griggs Ferry), 51, 53, 59-61, 66, 77, 96, 207, 210, 243, 369
Smith, Tom, Bill (Griggs Ferry), 52, 53, 59, 60, 67-69, 70, 77, 238, 300
Snap Canyon, (Wash, Springs), 41, 42, 44, 46, 112, 122, 126, 128, 145
Snap Point, 109, 113, 122, 126, 128, 343
South Cove (Landing, Ranger Station), 51, 92, 93, 96, 258, 301, 365
Spear Ranch, 187-189, 232
Spencer Canyon (Creek), 23, 34, 36, 104, 237, 278, 279
Spencer, Charley, 26, 27, 277-279, 281, 282, 289
St. George, Utah, xiii, 22, 35, 39, 42- 48, 52, 57, 79, 80, 93, 105, 111, 113, 114, 116, 119-122, 125-127, 140, 150, 157, 216, 231, 240, 269, 301, 320, 370, 386
St. Thomas, (Town, Gap), 47, 52, 57, 79, 80-82, 84, 85, 113, 115-118, 120, 122, 123, 146, 148, 149, 150, 152
Stanton, Robert Brewster, 52, 91, 94, 95
Starkey, Wellington, 187, 230, 232, 237, 260, 262, 364
Stoltenow-Baur, Sharon, vii, 212, 356
Stone's Ferry, 79, 217
Table Mountain Plateau, 188-190
Tanaka Springs (Tahnakah Springs, Tinaka Springs, Grass Springs), 3, 23, 32, 41, 44, 45, 93, 187, 188, 205, 224, 227, 230-232, 234, 235, 240, 260, 261, 321, 348, 353, 363, 364
Tassi (Tasseye), 115, 116, 143, 145
Tassi Ranch, 44, 143, 150, 165, 166, 217
Tassi Springs (Tashari Springs), 44-47, 97, 112, 115, 116, 122, 143, 145, 147, 148, 150, 151, 165, 166, 217
Teague, George, 219
Temple Bar, 35, 57, 58, 79, 80, 85, 88, 91, 178, 190-192, 206, 219, 236, 313, 320, 382
Tenney Ranch, 188, 237
Thomas, Mary Abigail Pearce, 47
Tinaka Springs (see Tanaka Springs, Grass Springs)
Toab, 92, 112, 113, 115, 119, 145,
Treasurehawk (Crazy Ed, Ed Bounsall), 174
Truxton Canyon (Springs, Wash), 27, 93, 201, 275, 278, 280, 283, 384
Twin Springs Canyon, 116
Two Tooth, 275, 277, 280
U.S. Guano Corporation, 308, 310
Ute Crossing (see Old Ute Crossing)
Ute Ford (see Old Ute Ford)
Valentine, 26, 93, 384
Valley of Fire, 84, 85
Virgin Basin, 79
Virgin Canyon , 54, 93, 102, 103, 242
Virgin Mountains (Peak), xiii, 15, 111, 116, 143, 157, 354

Virgin River, 18, 35, 47, 52, 79, 80, 82, 83, 85, 92, 93, 116, 117, 173
Voight, Herb, 275, 307, 318, 320, 375, 385
Walapai, Walpai, (see Hualapai)
Walapai Wash (see Hualapai Wash)
Wanatee-Buffalo, D. Suzanne, vii, viii, x, xii, 40, 110, 144, 186, 202, 214, 259, 276, 366
Wanatee, David, viii
Waring, Slim, Mary, 60, 123-126, 128, 139, 141, 370
Wavoka, 231, 232
Westcott, Buzzy, 309
Wheeler Ridge, 39, 93, 94, 342, 383, 342
Wheeler, Lt. George, 3, 93, 94, 189, 275, 277
White Hills, v, 55, 56, 81, 82, 84, 185-189, 192-196, 201, 203-205, 223, 232, 238, 240, 322, 371, 372, 382, 385
White, James, 90, 91
White, Tom, Florence, 321, 375
Whitmore Canyon, 130
Whitmore, Clint, 154, 165, 248
Whitmore, Dennis and James, 151, 158
Whitmore, Dr. James, 112, 120, 127, 148, 151
Whitmore Wash, 105, 377
Whitney Pockets, 111, 157-159, 168-170
Whitney Ranch, 145, 157, 158, 167
Wildcat Ranch, 114, 125, 126, 140, 370
Willow Beach, 3, 35, 81, 234, 368, 384
Willow Springs (Ranch), 44-46, 115, 232, 237, 238
Wilson Range, 190, 192
Yampa Creek, 201, 203, 217
Yates, Ed, Wayne, 143, 147-152, 154, 171
Yavapai Creek (Valley, County), 178, 201, 223, 234
Yavapai Tribe, 201
Yucca Springs, 188, 189
Ziniel, Ron, vii

www.ingramcontent.com/pod-product-compliance
Lightning Source LLC
Chambersburg PA
CBHW071645090426
42738CB00009B/1429